Legacy:

An Ancestral Journey
Through American History

Scott MacDonald

Other Books by Scott MacDonald

Education Without Debt: Giving Back and Paying It Forward (2021)

Think Like a Dog: How Dogs Teach Us to Be Happy in Life and Successful at Work (2019)

Saving Investa: How an ex-factory worker helped save one of Australia's iconic companies (2016)

Behold the righteous live long in the earth,
And in old age resign their breath;
They and their offspring here are blest;
When done in life they go to rest. *

---

* From the tombstone of ancestors John and Mercy Breed in Wequetequock Burial Ground in Stonington, Connecticut. Erected in 1772, the year of Mercy's death, by six of their children.

This is a publication of Del Mar Publishing, LLC, San Diego CA

ISBN 979-8-9858162-0-4 (hardback)
ISBN 979-8-9858162-1-1 (paperback)
ISBN 979-8-9858162-2-8 (ebook)

Library of Congress Control Number: 2022905379

Front cover art: *The Mayflower in Plymouth Harbor* by William Formby Halsall 1882, at Pilgrim Hall Museum, Plymouth, Massachusetts, USA. Accessed through *Library of Congress,* https://www.loc.gov/pictures/item/2016817166/.

Book design by MCD Advertising.

Printed by IngramSpark© in the United States of America.

To my family.

To my son Andrew, his wife Davida,
and my grandchildren Claire, James, and Elise.

To my son Ross and his wife, Kaylen.

To my mother, Bernice Corson MacDonald (1910–2000),
and my father, Walter Bingham MacDonald (1905–1954).

To my siblings: Judith Anderson (1935–2015)
and her husband Bob Anderson (1934–1991),
Walter "Bing" MacDonald (1937–2015) and his wife Molly Sullivan,

Margot Welch and her husband Norman Welch.

And to my ancestors who came before and live within me.

Thank you.

Contents

Life in a Basic Early Settlement or Frontier Structure
Photo by Nils Schlebusch

Figure 1: Immigrants bound for America — 1800s

Preface:

The Story of Immigrants

My research on my ancestry began in earnest more than ten years ago. At first, I had little information about my past relatives; my father died as a young man, and my mother left only a dictation about her memories growing up. The process of tracing my lineage was a long process with many dead ends, wrong turns, and misinformation. There are almost certainly some mistakes hidden among the many names and connections presented in the following pages. I turned to professional genealogists when I encountered an issue that exceeded my ability or available time, in particular Susan Wilkinson, who helped me considerably.

As the book took shape, I realized the story of my family is in many respects the story of America. My relatives were among the first Pilgrims in New England, and many followed and helped establish the early communities there. Other relatives were active participants in the founding and development of the Virginia Colony. And some of my ancestors were Native Americans whose families' presence pre-dated the Europeans. When new territories opened to settlers, my relatives packed their wagons and moved to Ohio, North Carolina and other territories with their families despite the treacherous journey. And when the country went to war, my ancestors took up their guns and marched off to battle.

I also realized my family's history is largely the story of immigrants. Today's Americans are the product of immigrants who braved the dangerous journey across the seas, cleared the wilderness, fought battles, and worked hard under the most challenging circumstances to build this country. Those less adventurous stayed home.

Today's Americans are also descendants of Native Americans who survived death, disease, and exile and slaves forcibly brought here against their will but who found ways to survive incredible hardships. This immigrant spirit, the will to survive, and determination to succeed despite major obstacles contributed significantly to what has made the United States of America a great country and established the basis for its future growth and prosperity.

Most early immigrants to America including many of my ancestors came from England. They came for a variety of reasons: some sought economic opportunity or religious freedom, and some were fleeing dire political and economic conditions in England at the time. They brought with them the English language, culture, and legal process. They also brought an energy and determination that enabled them to overcome the hardships of the new world and set a foundation of courage and perseverance. According to historian and author, James Evans, "such a decision to relocate without any likely return, to undertake a long voyage, with all the uncertainty that accompanied it regarding a subsequent new life, did require gumption, did require a certain energy, did require a certain lively, youthful disposition. Those it marked out were, as was said, among the country's more 'vivid people.'" [1]

Between 1717 and 1776, about 250,000 Scotch-Irish immigrants, including ancestor James Cunningham and his brothers, came to America from Ulster and Northern Ireland.[2] Many sought religious freedom from royal attempts to impose Church of England rules. Others sought economic opportunity compared to restrictions at home.

Before the American Revolution, about eighty-five thousand Germans, many from the Palatinate region, emigrated to America.[3] They fled constant wars, economic deprivation, and despotic rulers. In the 1800s, another eight million Germans came to America.[4] Germans like ancestor Peter Bloom fought bravely against the British to help America achieve its independence, and his brother, Issac, gave his life to the cause of independence.

Scottish emigration to the American colonies accelerated after the Jacobite revolution failed and the English initiated severe reprisals against Scottish highlander villages following the Battle of Culloden in 1745. These immigrants likely included Jared McDonald, the Immigrant who started the MacDonald family presence in America. There were about one hundred thousand Scots (not including Scotch-Irish) in the American colonies by 1776.[5]

Even tiny Wales contributed its share of immigrants beginning in the 1600s. These immigrants were typically seeking religious freedom, especially the Quakers, and generally moved to the "Welch Tract" established by William Penn outside Philadelphia. They lived there with fellow immigrants sharing language and culture, but their descendants often moved away to Virginia, Ohio, and parts distant, integrating into the greater American population. Welsh ancestors include John Griffith and his wife Jane Owen and Owen Wynne with his wife Grace Williams. In 2008, there were about three million people living in Wales compared to two million people of Welsh descent living in America.[6]

Later in America's history, more immigrants came searching for economic opportunity, religious freedom, and a better life for their children. About one million Irish fled the potato famine for America between 1845 and 1852.[7]

Between 1880 and 1914, about four million Italians emigrated to the United States.[8] Most were in search of better economic opportunities for their families.

After the Vietnam war, the United States sponsored 125,000 Vietnamese immigrants. A second, bigger wave of refugees occurred in the late 1970s and encompassed about 280,000 "boat people." Today, there are about two million people of Vietnamese origin living in the United States.[9]

There has always been Cuban emigration to the United States, but after Fidel Castro took power, emigration from Cuba accelerated greatly. In the six decades before

Castro, about one hundred thousand Cuban immigrants came to the United States. Today, the Census reports about 2.3 million residents are of Cuban origin.[10]

Mexican emigrants have long come to the United States. In 1900, there were an estimated five hundred thousand people of Mexican descent living mostly in the Southwest. Before 1836, Texas was part of Mexico, and before the 1840s California and adjacent southwestern states were also ruled by Mexico. After the end of the Mexican-American War (1848), Americans and Mexicans flowed fairly freely across the border until the 1920s when the United States placed more controls on border crossing and formed the Border Patrol. Beginning in the 1950s Mexican emigration increased, and today there are probably twelve million Mexican immigrants living in the United States.[11]

Jews immigrated to America beginning in the mid 1600s, first to New Amsterdam which later became New York City. They continued to emigrate from Europe, especially Germany, due to persecution, discrimination, and legal restrictions. By the start of World War I (1914), about 250,000 German Jews had immigrated.[12] Between 1880 and 1924, over two million Jews (including my ex-wife's grandparents) came to America from Russia, Austria-Hungary, Romania and nearby areas. In the 1930s and 1940s Jews came fleeing Nazi Germany. Jewish immigrants typically first settled in East Coast cities, and their descendants frequently moved to other areas over time. Current estimates of the number of Jews in America vary, but there are likely around seven million.[13]

The American economy has always depended on immigration, but in recent years, the critical technology industry has been largely driven by immigrants to the United States. Sixty percent of the top twenty-five technology companies have a first or second generation immigrant founder.[14] The majority of new start-up companies with over $1 billion capitalization have an immigrant founder.[15] Many of the major tech firms have an immigrant founder and/or CEO, including Google, Oracle, eBay, Yahoo!, WeWork, PayPal, Microsoft, Uber, etc.[16] Without immigrants, the United States would not be the global leader and economic powerhouse it is today.

The vaccine development and distribution for the COVID-19 pandemic was largely driven by immigrants and foreign citizens. Pfizer's CEO, Albert Bourla, is a Greek immigrant, and Moderna's CEO, Stéphane Bancel, is a French immigrant. Johnson & Johnson's leader of pharmaceuticals, Joaquin Duato, is a Spanish immigrant and the company's chief scientific officer is Paul Stoffels, an immigrant from Belgium. Moncef Slaoui, who oversaw America's Operation Warp Speed, is an immigrant from Morocco, and Anthony Fauci, director of the National Institute of Allergy and Infectious Diseases, descends from grandparents who immigrated from Italy. The University of Oxford and AstraZeneca, which jointly developed another COVID-19 vaccine, are based in England and BioNTech is based in Germany and was founded by Turkish immigrants. Without immigrants and foreigners, Americans and others would likely still be waiting for COVID-19 vaccines.

Through the looking glass of American history, there are some clear conclusions. The country was built by immigrants and continues to benefit from the work culture and drive of immigrant arrivals. Most immigrants arrived without money or education, and many arrived unable to communicate in English. They worked hard; and at least their children became fluent in their new language. Initially, the new immigrants congregated in communities populated by others from the same country where culture, religion, and language were familiar. Within a couple of generations, their descendants typically moved away and became integrated into the greater society and less connected to their countries of family origin.

Regardless of the era, the initial response of residents to new immigrants was opposition. Native Americans fought against the new European immigrants. Once the country was more established, new immigrants from different cultures such as the Irish, the Italians, and the Vietnamese were criticized and discriminated against.

The most recent wave of immigrants from Mexico and Central America face the same resistance and criticisms. They speak a foreign language, many are poor and unskilled, they tend to live in substandard housing and congregate together, and they did not receive permission or an invitation to come here. There is an old French saying translated into English, "The more things change, the more they are the same." So is it with immigration to America.

After introducing the time frame and conditions, the book is organized by ancestor and his or her family with historical context chapters interspersed. My father's ancestors including the McDonald's, immigrated largely to New England, Pennsylvania, and a few to Virginia. They moved to the Midwest when things became crowded in the East. My father was born in Chicago. His family is presented in Part Two.

My mother's ancestors largely immigrated to southern Virginia, and future generations moved to North Carolina and then to other southern states including Alabama, Louisiana, Arkansas, South Carolina, and Georgia. My mother was born in Louisiana and grew up in Arkansas. Part Three of this book focuses on my mother's ancestors including the Corsons.

My parents' respective ancestries are quite different. As noted, my father's ancestors generally lived in the north, and my mother's ancestors generally lived in the south. Some of my southern ancestors fought my northern ancestors in the U.S. Civil War. Some southern ancestors owned plantations and slaves while northern ancestors opposed slavery and fought a war to abolish slavery and preserve the nation.

One caution to keep in mind. Those ancestors who were better known, from important families, or involved in public life left a document trail for researchers. Those who were not public figures, who did not transact land or serve on public committees, left fewer clues to their lives. The stories and the ancestry charts that follow are more likely to portray those ancestors who were more visible and to under represent those with lower profiles.

The immigrants who are profiled in the chapters that follow are all direct ancestors—my grandparents, great-grandparents, great-great-grandparents, etc. unless noted otherwise.

Ancestry charts are included in the relevant chapters where possible but not shown in the Ebook versions. Key ancestry charts are also available at authorscottmacdonald.com.

Part One:
The Setting

Figure 2: Giving out soup tickets in London

Chapter 1:

Before America

Indentured Servitude

Emigrants from Europe began to come to North American in numbers in the early 1600s. They came for a variety of reasons. Most came from England, and most were poor. Estimates suggest between one half and two-thirds of early American immigrants came as indentured servants.[17] These individuals typically came because their living conditions in England were poor and hopeless, ships were readily available to transport them without need for cash payment, and they wished to improve their lives and were willing to take on the risks.

The population of England swelled from two million in 1520 to four million by 1600 due largely to increased births and decreased deaths.[18] At the same time, the economy lagged, harvests were poor, and changes in agriculture from open pastures available to tenant farmers to enclosed farms restricting such access led to wide-spread unemployment and rapidly rising prices for food and other necessities. Villagers left their hometowns and moved to the cities seeking work; many resorted to begging when work was unavailable. Some turned to crime, and streets were often over-crowded and dirty. Government authorities reacted harshly to crime and to begging by beating, imprisoning, or even hanging offenders.

Things improved a bit with the passage of the "Poor Law" under Queen Elizabeth designed to assist the "deserving poor."[19] But poverty, unemployment, and hopelessness among the poor continued through the 1600s.

Several of my ancestors sought to escape a life of poverty by emigrating to America in the 1600s. They agreed to serve a period of labor, typically five to seven years, in return for their passage to America. After serving their indenture, they generally went on to own property and achieve a standard of living not conceivable in England at that time. A few of the ancestors who served a term of indenture are introduced below.

Edward Milstead

Edward Milstead and his family came from Bethersden, in the county of Kent, England. He was born in 1656. Like most of England in the mid 1600s, Bethersden's poor people had few possessions and often little food.

When Edward was a teenager, he was arrested for theft and convicted of robbing two houses. From one house, he stole money and from the other house he stole food. Upon being found guilty by a jury, Edward appealed to an Anglican priest for intervention and was "reprieved under condition of transport," meaning he was deported.

Edward arrived in Maryland in 1674 at the age of eighteen. He was indentured as a shoemaker to William Chandler of Charles County, Maryland, for a term of five years. After earning his freedom in 1680, he married Susannah Clark around 1685 and later leased a fifty-acre tract of land and became a farmer raising primarily tobacco. His farming was successful, and he was able to lease and purchase other tracts over time. Susannah Clark died as a young woman, and Edward next married Elizabeth Ward around 1696.

Edward had at least two indentured servants of his own during his time in Maryland, which was a nice turnabout for him. He was also compelled to pay a fine of fifty pounds of tobacco for fathering a bastard child; apparently, he and Susannah had born a child before they were formally married.

Edward's transition from convicted thief in England to successful and respected farmer in Maryland is typical of the redemption and opportunity that was available in America for those struggling to survive in England during the 1600s.

Nathaniel Covell (Sr. and Jr.)

Nathaniel (Sr.), of Essex, England, emigrated to America shortly after the death of his father. The year was 1653, the height of Oliver Cromwell's power, when he dismissed the Parliament and began to dismantle the English government. There was significant chaos and strife in addition to the normal poverty-related issues, and with his father's death, Nathaniel likely felt it was timely to leave England and seek better opportunities in America.

Essex was an agricultural area, and Nathaniel was probably a tenant farmer. He did not have sufficient funds to pay for passage to America, so he agreed to an indenture. He was accompanied by his nine-year-old son, Nathaniel Jr., who was indentured to Massachusetts Governor Edward Winslow for seven years upon arrival.

When Nathaniel Jr. finished his indenture, he moved to Yarmouth and married Sarah Nickerson. They moved in with his father-in-law, William Nickerson, and the household petitioned for permission to move to Monomoit (later named Chatham). With his father-in-law's recommendation, Nathaniel Jr. became constable of the new town in 1674. He is listed as a founder of Chatham on the Founder's Plaque in that community.

William Pettypool

William Pettypool was born in 1630 in the village of Stepney near London. His father, Samuel, was a shoemaker and lived in one of the poorer areas of London. William emigrated to Virginia in the late 1650s as an indentured servant. He was sponsored by John Davis, to whom he was indentured, likely for five years. Another indentured servant of John Davis was Ann Smith, whom William married when their indentures ended. William then became a landowner and farmer in Maryland.

His descendants migrated over time to Virginia, North Carolina, Kentucky, Arkansas, and Louisiana (see Chapter 48 for more on the Pettypool family).

John Ford

Some immigrants came as small children, and some were kidnapped and brought against their will. According to the history of the Ford family, their original immigrant was John Ford:

> Somewhere on the coast of Ireland, a ship stood at anchor. A small boy was playing on the shore with other lads. His mother, in the usual crowd of onlookers, was intent on getting news of her home in Cheshire, a short day's sail across the Irish Sea. After a while, a man approached and invited the boys to come and see the ship. They were hesitant, but he offered a knife to each boy if he would come on board to get it. Those who did go aboard were seized, gagged, and hidden, and the ship sailed off with them. The story goes that one of the boys was named John Ford, and he was "about eight years old." The ship arrived at the port of Kicotan (now called Hampton), at the mouth of the James River. John was taken ashore and offered for sale (indenture).
>
> It was the custom in the colony for widows, orphans and abandoned children to be cared for by the vestry, under the charge of the minister of the local parish, following the Anglican practice in England. The Rev. Phillip Mallory was rector of Hampton Parish at this time. He recognized John at once, as he had known his family in Sandbach Parish in County Chester. The minister had been pastor of Moberly Parish, only a short distance from Abbeyfield Park, the Ford homeplace.
>
> The Rev. Phillip Mallory soon had the boy released, probably paying the cost of passage. From then on, John's home was in the Mallory household, where he was fed, clothed, and given an education.[20]

The Ford family became a prominent family in America with many descendants (see Chapter 45 for more on the Fords).

George Michael Ehret

George and his wife, Agnes, and their six children fled the Palatinate region of Germany in 1819. He did not have sufficient funds to pay for passage for the entire family and was not willing to leave any in Germany, so some of the boys were indentured. His son Ellis was so small that at first no one was willing to pay for his passage and take him as an indenture. Finally, a farmer and his wife took Ellis to watch their children and help with tasks around the farm. George's granddaughter Anna Marie was my great-grandmother (see Chapter 25).

Cromwell and the Parliamentarians vs. King Charles and the Royalists

Figure 3: Cromwell leading troops at the Battle of Marston Moor

King Charles I, son of King James I, ascended to the Crown in 1625, but he had an adversarial relationship with Parliament throughout his reign. He dissolved Parliament in 1627, but he convened a new Parliament in 1628 because he needed more revenue, and only Parliament could raise taxes. He then dissolved it again and operated without a Parliament from 1629 to 1640. At that point he needed money again to suppress a rebellion in Scotland, and he recalled Parliament, whose members were not pleased with the King's actions. Charles dissolved Parliament only three weeks later after considerable infighting. Six months later and in desperate need of funds, Charles convened Parliament once again. By then there was clear hostility between the King and the majority of Parliamentarians. In a further escalation of tensions, in 1642 Charles dispatched four hundred soldiers to enter the House of Commons and arrest five members who opposed Charles's policies. The attempt failed as the sought-after members were alerted and left before Charles and the troops arrived.

Following Charles's unsuccessful attempt to coerce Parliament, the country divided into cities and towns supporting the King, those supporting the Parliamentarians, and those attempting to keep both forces out. The supporters of Charles were often called "Cavaliers" and those opposed to the King were frequently called "Roundheads." The battles between these factions constituted the English Civil War which lasted from 1642 to 1651.

During the conflict, life in England for most residents became even more difficult. Neighbors choose sides and attacked others with opposing beliefs. Marauding bands favoring the Parliamentarians attacked country estates supporting the Crown. And forces favoring the Crown attacked villages supporting the Parliamentarians. Women and children were not spared. Hundreds of families fled England for America to escape the disorder and crime.

The King and his supporters left London for the more supportive East Midlands region north of London. Many of my family's more affluent ancestor emigrants were Cavaliers, including John Marshall, who raised a cavalry and fought for Charles in the first battle of the war — the 1642 Battle of Edgehill, which was indecisive. Royalist forces won most of the subsequent early skirmishes and marched to London later in 1642 seeking an early end to the war and victory for Charles.

Ancestor Nicholas Stevens and others organized "trained bands" of citizens to defend London from the Royalists. They stopped Charles's forces at Turnham Green and forced their retreat. Later Nicholas and his soldiers joined Oliver Cromwell's army. He fought at the Battle of Naseby in 1645 and in subsequent victories. Cromwell's army was often outnumbered by Royalist forces but won battle after battle.

Nicholas was a Captain, and some historians believe a Colonel or Brigadier General in Cromwell's army. When the Royalists returned to power with Charles II, retribution began against former leaders under Cromwell, and Nicholas departed England for America under a false name.

Another ancestor, George Denison, also fought with Cromwell's forces. At the crucial Battle of Marston Moor in 1646, the Parliamentarian troops confronted the king's forces in a major battle for control of York and northern England. George was wounded and captured but managed to escape as the battle continued. He was nursed back to health at the house of John Borodell by John's daughter Ann. Upon regaining his health, George married Ann; when the monarchy was restored and retribution began against Cromwell supporters, the couple moved to New London, Connecticut.

While many in England suffered from poverty, others (especially those descended from royalty) inherited wealth and lived a life of comparative luxury. During the English Civil War, these ancestors joined the Cavaliers in support of the Crown. Following the defeat of Charles I's forces and his beheading in 1649 — the first beheading of any English king — many ancestor Cavaliers emigrated to America. They likely worried about what life would be under Cromwell and the Parliamentarians and sought to find additional riches and success in the new world.

As Cromwell and the Parliamentarians took power in England, Virginia Governor William Berkeley, an avid supporter of the Crown, actively solicited Cavaliers and others from English society to emigrate to Virginia. According to one observer, "in a time of great insecurity for Royalist landed gentry, Virginia became a beacon of safety, comradeship, and opportunity."[21] It was "the only city of refuge left in His Majesty's Dominions, in those times, for distressed Cavaliers."[22]

The term "Cavalier" was originally a derogatory term for the King's wealthy supporters in England. With time and distance, however, the term became used in Virginia to describe men who were brave, chivalrous, and loyal. In Virginia, it came to convey a glorified past in which aristocrats provided leadership and social responsibility. In 1923, the term became associated with University of Virginia's athletic teams and continues to present times.

Ancestor immigrants to Virginia associated with the Cavaliers include William Norwood (who arrived in 1648), John Marshall (1650), Anthony Fulgham (1650), John Fleming (1652), George Bledsoe (1652), and William Randolph (1671).

Other immigrants from well-to-do English families were often the second- or third-born sons and not likely to receive significant inheritance, which generally went to the firstborn son. Examples include ancestors Owen Wynn who arrived from Wales in 1611, William Thornton who arrived from Yorkshire around 1641, and Nicholas Spencer who arrived in 1659 from Cople, in Bedfordshire, England.

The transplanted English aristocrats led to the creation of an English high society in Virginia, and members often became prominent planters and community leaders. They were typically from an area in southern England located between Kent, Devon, and Warwickshire counties and were typically active members of the traditional Anglican Church.

The Pilgrims

Figure 4: Pilgrim worship service in Plymouth, Massachusetts

While Anglican church members and Crown supporters emigrated to Virginia, Puritans, who supported Cromwell and sought to either reform the Church or separate from it typically moved to New England to establish their own religious practices. The Church of England (or Anglican Church) was created in 1534 after the pope refused to agree to a requested annulment of one of Henry VIII's marriages, so Henry expelled the Catholic Church and formed his own church under the direction of the Crown. Under newly passed laws, church attendance was required of everyone, the order of prayer and conduct of services was regulated, and preachers were encouraged to support the actions of the state from the pulpit. Puritans sought to reform the church and to reduce state regulations and persecution of non-conformers. Pilgrims were Puritans who had given up trying to reform the existing church and sought to separate and form their own churches, which was considered treason in England.

Plymouth Colony, the first settlement in New England, was founded by a group of English Pilgrims. The name of the colony was chosen because the group departed on the *Mayflower*, from the port of Plymouth, England. The core group at Plymouth Colony was part of a congregation led by William Bradford. This group of Puritan separatists, who had been holding weekly worship in the English village of Scrooby in Nottinghamshire, left England in 1608, after several members of the congregation were arrested and imprisoned at the behest of the Archbishop of York. The congregation first emigrated to the Netherlands, settling in Amsterdam and later in Leiden.

In Leiden, the congregation gained the freedom to worship as they chose, but Dutch society was unfamiliar to them. Scrooby had been an agricultural community, whereas Leiden was a thriving industrial center, and the new English residents found the pace of life difficult. The community remained close-knit, but their children began adopting the Dutch language and customs, and some entered the Dutch Army. They also were still not free from the persecutions of the English Crown. In 1618, English authorities came to Leiden to arrest William Brewster, a prominent member of the group, after he published comments highly critical of the king of England and the Anglican church. Brewster escaped arrest, but the events spurred the congregation to want to move farther from England.

While still in Leiden, the congregation obtained a land patent from the Plymouth Company in June 1619. They had declined the opportunity to settle in the Dutch colony of New Netherland because of their desire to avoid the Dutch influence. They sought to finance their venture through the Merchant Adventurers, a company of English merchants and investors who viewed the colony as a means of making a profit.

Using the financing secured from the Merchant Adventurers, the colonists bought provisions and obtained passage on the *Mayflower* and the *Speedwell*. They had intended to leave early in 1620, but they were delayed several months due to difficulties in dealing with the Merchant Adventurers, including several changes in plans for the voyage and in financing. The congregation and the other colonists finally boarded the *Speedwell* in July 1620, in the Dutch port of Delfshaven.[23]

Ancestors William Ring and his wife Mary Durant and their three children booked their passage on the *Speedwell*. Unfortunately, their ship returned to port in need of repairs, and William Ring died in Leiden before another ship was set to depart. Many of the other passengers from the *Speedwell* boarded the *Mayflower*, leaving the *Mayflower* with overcrowded conditions and inadequate food. Perhaps because Ring was not feeling well, he and his family waited for another ship instead of piling onto the *Mayflower*.

The Pilgrims, including ancestor Stephen Hopkins, arrived in America in 1620 in what is now Massachusetts, and soon thereafter many other ancestors immigrated in search of religious freedom from the Anglican Church. These ancestors included (with their approximate arrival dates): Edward Bangs (1623), John Wakeman (1628), Walter Palmer (1629), Alan Breed (1630), William Denison (1631), Ralph Smyth (1633), William O'Dell (1635), Ann Hutchinson (1636), William Nickerson (1637), Henry Adams (1638) and William Ludington (1639).

The Germans

Figure 5: Farm in Germantown, Pennsylvania, 1700s

The German immigrants came primarily from the Palatinate region of Germany along the Rhine River. The area had very fertile land, and the German farmers were industrious, leading to productive farms and affluent communities in the 1500s and early 1600s. There was minimal outmigration during these good times.

Everything changed with the onset of a series of wars and related religious strife beginning with the Thirty Years' War in 1618. Communities were part of principalities or states and ruled by local rulers or princes. While part of the Holy Roman Empire, the local rulers made the key decisions. With the emergence of Martin Luther and the Reformation, some principalities embraced Luther's teaching and some remained Catholic, leading to ongoing conflicts and ultimately resulting in the devastating Thirty Years' War, which was joined by many European nations.[24] The war, from 1618 to 1648, brought death and destruction to the Palatinate as opposing armies swept across the region in ongoing battles and accompanying raids and pillaging.

After the war, religious strife continued, and the area was hurt by the Nine Years' War from 1688 to 1697[25] and the War of the Spanish Succession from 1701 to 1714.[26] French army invasions were particularly devastating for local residents and farmers. Local men were often killed, women raped, and fields plundered. Over the period, an estimated 50 percent of the local population died through war, pestilence, and famine. In the Württemberg area, where many of my ancestors emigrated from, an estimated 75 percent of residents perished. What was once a prosperous area became an impoverished one.

To make matters worse, local rulers raised taxes to fund grand palaces and a high life-style striving to be more like the French royalty and other profligate German states. In Baden Württemberg, for example, the ruling Duke Eberhard Louis (also known as Eberhard Ludwig) built the 452-room Ludwigsburg Palace[27] — the largest palatial estate in the country. Construction started in 1704 and lasted beyond 1733.

Constant war, poverty, religious strife, and unsustainable taxes drove the Germans away beginning in the early 1700s. A few years earlier, William Penn had visited the area and preached the benefits of emigrating to Pennsylvania, an area of productive land and religious tolerance. This helped set the stage for German emigration to Pennsylvania. The English also promoted the idea of emigration to America, and ship owners promoted emigration to sell passage on their fleets of ships.

The first wave of emigrants from the Palatinate was in 1709, when seven thousand Palatines sailed for England. Later emigration accelerated. Between 1700 and 1775, an estimated eighty-five thousand Germans emigrated to America. John Peter Bloom (or Blum) and his family left Germany in 1752.

Typically, the emigrants packed all their possessions they could carry into a trunk and booked passage down the Rhine to Rotterdam in the Netherlands. It was usually a four- to six-week journey, and passengers were packed together and assessed tolls at various points along the way. From Rotterdam, the emigrants booked passage to Philadelphia via the seaport of Cowes in England. The journey to America was on ships typically so overloaded with passengers and merchandise that ship captains often left the chests and possessions of the emigrants on the dock, leaving the impoverished passengers with almost nothing, including food and substance for the long overseas journey.[28]

One observer at the time described the scene this way:

> *Sitting on boxes and bundles, which were piled high in the middle of the boat, could be seen Grey-haired men and women, old and feeble; yonder stood the young gazing in wonder at the shores as they slipped by. At times they were hopeful, and at others sad, and their glances would alternate, now to the north, now to the south toward their abandoned home, which had driven them out so unfeelingly, and yet those green hills and snow-capped mountains they cannot forget.[29]*

The German ancestors arrived over a long timeframe beginning around 1710 and ending around 1810. German immigrant ancestors included John Peter Bloom and Eve Bloom (1752), Johann and Anna Maria Schneider (1710), Hans Jung (1710) and George and Margarethe Knaus (around 1805–1810).

The Scots

Jared McDonald, the family's immigrant ancestor from Scotland, evidently came to America as a small boy after the Battle of Culloden, in which the English defeated the Scottish Jacobites (including the MacDonalds) in 1745. The Jacobites supported the restoration of the House of Stuart and Prince Charles to the English throne and fought unsuccessfully to overthrow King George. Similarly, ancestor David Halliburton emigrated in 1746, when the victorious English army swept through towns in Scotland, killing or arresting perceived opponents and raping and pillaging.

Around the same time but not directly connected to Culloden, Scottish tenant farmers were evicted in great numbers as landowners fenced in previously open pastures, and newly defined areas were leased to the highest bidder. In what has been called, "The Highland Clearances," many Scottish tenant farmers lost their properties and were forced to emigrate.

The Scotch-Irish, also called the Ulster Scots, including ancestor James Cunningham, emigrated between 1717 and 1776 from Ulster seeking economic opportunity. The promise of land ownership in America was not available in Northern Ireland. Also, many farmers in both Scotland and Ulster were Presbyterians and sought religious freedom from the church mandates which came increasingly from the Anglican Church authorities in England.

The Dutch

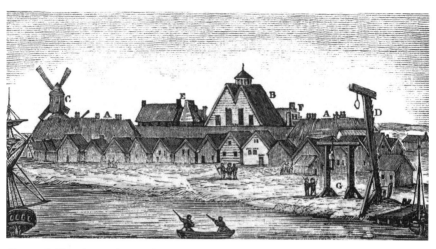

Figure 6: New Amsterdam, 1659

The major migrations to America before the 1776 revolution included the Scotch-Irish from the Ulster area, the Germans, the English, and the Scots. However, some came from the Netherlands including ancestors Egbert Sanderzen and Joost Adriansen Molenear.

The Dutch migration to America started later and was smaller in size than some of the other migrations. It was primarily motivated by commerce and profit and somewhat by a religious freedom. The Dutch involvement in America started when the Dutch East India Company, a private company, sponsored English explorer and captain Henry Hudson to find a northwest passage to the Indies. Instead Hudson found an abundance of wildlife and fertile fields along what was later named the Hudson River in what became New York. The Dutch East India Company set up trading posts and initiated trade with the local Native American tribe, the Iroquois. To accelerate trade and enhance profit, the Company traded firearms for furs. The Iroquois used the firearms against their enemies including the French, which was okay with the Dutch, but later used them against the Dutch as well.

In 1625, the Dutch East India Company's successor, the Dutch West India Company, with encouragement from the Netherlands' government, established the colony of New Amsterdam, which later became New York and New Jersey. To encourage immigrants, the company opened the new colony to anyone who wanted to come — not just to Dutch nationals — and offered free passage and land. The colony soon became a mix of nationalities including Walloons, Huguenots, Germans, Scandinavians, English, and African slaves. One observer in 1644 claimed, "that one could hear 18 different languages being spoken on the streets of New Amsterdam." [30]

The diversity of New Amsterdam surely contributed to the later emergence of New York City as an international city of many backgrounds and cultures.

In 1664, a British naval fleet entered the harbor and announced the English were taking control of the area from the Dutch. The Dutch defenses were too weak, and the Dutch gave way to the English. The British takeover of New Amsterdam effectively ended Dutch migration to America.

The Huguenots

The origin of the term "Huguenots" is not agreed upon. However, the term was used originally by Catholics as a derogatory description of the French Protestants at the time.

France was a Catholic country and was frequently at war with Protestant England. John Calvin, a French minister, was the leader in the Reformation movement to establish a religious presence different from the dominant Catholic Church in France and other nearby countries in the early to mid 1500s. The movement grew, and by 1572, there were about two million Protestants or "Huguenots" in France, much to the dismay of the Catholic church and the French government. Huguenots believed the Catholic church needed to be reformed and attacked Catholic churches and destroyed altars, relics, and sometimes even entire churches.

King Francis II and his wife, Mary, Queen of Scots, took the French throne in 1559. During their eighteen-month reign, many Huguenots were rounded up, charged with heresy, and put on trial in front of Catholic judges. Torture and burning at the stake were frequent punishments. During this timeframe, ancestors William and Mary Basse emigrated from France to London to escape the persecution. William Basse was born in 1520 in Champagne-Ardenne in northeastern France. His wife, Mary Carkin, was born around 1525 in the Loire Valley in central France. They married around 1560, and they were living in London by 1563.

Their son Humphrey was born around 1563 in London; he married Mary Bushier, who was also a Huguenot from the Loire Valley region. Their grandson Nathaniel Basse inherited his father's interest in the Virginia Company and emigrated to Virginia in 1619.

Back in France, conflict between Catholics and Huguenots continued including civil wars. Huguenots destroyed iconic Catholic symbols like the tomb of Saint Irenaeus, and Catholics attacked, killed, and wounded hundreds of Huguenots in the Massacre of Vassy in 1562. In 1572, in what is now known as "St. Bartholomew's Day Massacre," Catholics killed thousands of Huguenots in coordinated attacks throughout France.[31]

In 1598, Henry IV became king of France and issued the Edict of Nantes,[32] affirming Catholicism as the state religion but recognizing Huguenots and according them rights. This reduced the pressure to emigrate for a while.

But by the 1620s the Huguenots were under pressure again and persecuted by the Catholic Church and French government. The Huguenots revolted between 1621 and 1629, and the revolts were harshly suppressed. The number of Huguenots in France steadily declined from its 1572 high of about two million to less than one million by the mid 1680s. Against this background of conflict and persecution, ancestor Robert Brasseur emigrated, arriving in Virginia by 1638. He married Florence Elizabeth Fowke, another Huguenot. Their daughter Margaret was born in Virginia and married Thomas Jordan in 1658.

In 1643, Louis XIV ascended the throne and ratcheted up the pressure on remaining Huguenots. He closed Huguenot schools, excluded members from preferred professions, and allowed troops to loot Huguenot homes. Eventually, he issued the Edict of Fontainebleau, revoking the Edict of Nantes and forcing Huguenots to convert or leave the country.[33]

Ancestor Jan Letelier emigrated from Normandy, France, during this time. His specific departure date is not known; but he was living in Brooklyn, New York, in 1661 and was appointed magistrate of Bushwick on Long Island. His wife was Dutch, and their daughter married Dutchman Tunis Egbertzen.

In France, there were fewer than one hundred thousand Huguenots by 1700. The families had left France and settled throughout Europe, and some had come to America, including my ancestors.

Figure 7: The Mayflower at sea

Chapter 2:

Journey to America

Prior to 1606, it was illegal for Englishmen to emigrate except for "Lords and Other Great Men." [34] During the seventeenth century, about one hundred eighty thousand English men and women immigrated to America; about sixty thousand between the late 1620s and the early 1640s alone. [35] These were the risk-takers, unwilling or unable to stay at home and willing to suffer unknown dangers in hopes of a better life.

The early emigrants had little information about the risks and conditions that lay ahead. Later emigrants clearly had better access to information from those that had gone before, but they still left their homes and communities.

This was not an easy transition. Historian James Evans described it this way: "Aware as they were of the risks, their departure was often accompanied by an emotional farewell to a land, to everything and to everyone that emigrants had known: by the decision — as one emigrant wrote emotionally to his father from 'aboard a ship at Gravesend' — to 'bid adieu to the old world, or shake hands with my native soil forever.'" [36] They knew they were not returning.

While thousands of mostly British residents immigrated to America in the 1600s, crossing the Atlantic was a "gruesome, life-threatening endeavor for all travelers, regardless of wealth or seamanship." [37] Ancestors who emigrated were willing to take on the extraordinary challenges of an ocean crossing even before being confronted by the challenges of living in an undeveloped wilderness surrounded often by hostile natives.

Burton Derick, in his history of the Nickerson family and the settlement of Cape Cod, described the journey across the Atlantic as follows:

> We can only imagine the hardships the passengers endured. Ships of the time were not large and were poorly designed for speed and maneuverability. They were round bottomed and had a tendency to roll heavily in the swells of the open ocean. It is easy to visualize these Norwich landlubbers, probably seasick for days, trying to endure in cramped space without fresh foods, trying to survive on stale water and breads, and old vegetables. They certainly shared the space with some livestock… together with tools of their trade, looms and such. In addition, none of the passengers had any concept of the world they were about to enter. They left a comfortable city life, where amenities were available from the many shops, to come to a place that was sparsely inhabited, with a rudimentary commercial establishment, and no knowledge of what shelter they might find when they arrived. [38]

On December 20, 1606, the three ships *Susan Constant, Godspeed,* and *Discovery* set out from England for Virginia. The ship captains were Christopher Newport and ancestors Bartholomew Gosnold and John Ratcliffe. A few days after departing, gale-force winds forced the ships to anchor within sight of land off the north coast of Kent, England. The storms continued rocking the ships violently for six weeks, causing much sickness. After the convoy finally set sail again, there was friction among passengers and rising anger and unhappiness with limited provisions, widespread sickness, and bad weather. Storms forced ships off course and at times lost. John Smith, a key passenger, was imprisoned for mutiny, and Captain Ratcliffe wanted to turn back. The journey lasted four months before they arrived at what would become America's first permanent English settlement, Jamestown.

Two years after the first settlers arrived at Jamestown, the *Sea Venture* departed England with fresh supplies for the Virginia Colony. Unfortunately it sailed into a hurricane, which caused much damage. Water levels in the ship began to rise and the passengers took turns bailing but reached the point of exhaustion and could not continue. Passengers and crew prepared to die with the sinking ship, but the captain spied land just in time and drove the distressed ship onto the rocks of what turned out to be eastern Bermuda. The passengers, including ancestor Stephen Hopkins and John Rolfe, managed to reach land and later constructed two small ships to take them to Jamestown. The story of the *Sea Venture* apparently was the basis for the shipwreck scene in Shakespeare's *The Tempest*.

As referenced earlier, in July 1620, the *Mayflower* and the *Speedwell* were set to carry about one hundred pilgrims and others to the New World. After many delays and a false start, the *Speedwell* was judged unseaworthy, and most of her passengers boarded the *Mayflower* for the journey, creating overcrowded and under-supplied conditions.

The 102 passengers were crammed into a living space of eighty by twenty feet with five-foot ceilings; there was no privacy or relief from the odorous conditions caused by no baths, rudimentary sanitation, and widespread illness including seasickness. The weather turned bad with storms and gales, and the sailors were forced to reef the sails to save the mast, leaving the ship adrift. Huge waves crashed upon the decks, forcing the passengers to crouch below for days in poor light with poor air circulation. The ship's main support beam fractured, almost causing the ship to sink. This miserable and terrifying journey ended after about three months, when the ship reached land and the first Pilgrims disembarked at Plymouth Rock.

Many ships traveled from England to America in the following years. One account of such a journey was documented in a diary by Gottlieb Mittelberger, a German organ master and teacher, in 1750:

> *...during the voyage there is on board these ships terrible misery, stench, fumes, horror, vomiting, many kinds of seasickness, fever, dysentery, headache, heat, constipation, boils, scurvy, cancer, mouth rot, and the like, all of which come*

from old and sharply-salted food and meat, also from very bad and foul water, so that many die miserably.

Add to this want of provisions, hunger, thirst, frost, heat, dampness, anxiety, want, afflictions and lamentations, together with other trouble, as e.g., the lice abound so frightfully, especially on sick people, that they can be scraped off the body. The misery reaches a climax when a gale rages for two or three nights and days, so that everyone believes that the ship will go to the bottom with all human beings on board. In such a visitation the people cry and pray most piteously.

No one can have an idea of the sufferings which women in confinement have to bear with their innocent children on board these ships. Few of this class escape with their lives; many a mother is cast into the water with her child as soon as she is dead. One day, just as we had a heavy gale, a woman in our ship, who was to give birth and could not give birth under the circumstances, was pushed through a loophole (porthole) in the ship and dropped into the sea, because she was far in the rear of the ship and could not be brought forward.

Children from one to seven years rarely survive the voyage; and many a time parents are compelled to see their children miserably suffer and die from hunger, thirst, and sickness, and then to see them cast into the water. I witnessed such misery in no less than thirty-two children in our ship, all of whom were thrown into the sea. The parents grieve all the more since their children find no resting place in the earth but are devoured by the monsters of the sea. It is a notable fact that children who have not yet had the measles or smallpox generally get them on board the ship, and mostly die of them.

When the ships have landed at Philadelphia after their long voyage, no one is permitted to leave them except those who pay for their passage or can give good security; the others, who cannot pay, must remain on board the ships till they are purchased and are released from the ships by their purchasers. The sick always fare the worst, for the healthy are naturally preferred and purchased first; and so the sick and wretched must often remain on board in front of the city for two or three weeks, and frequently die, whereas many a one, if he could pay his debt and were permitted to leave the ship immediately, might recover and remain alive.

The sale of human beings in the market on board the ship is carried on thus: Every day Englishmen, Dutchmen, and High German people come from the city of Philadelphia and other places, in part from a great distance, say twenty, thirty, or forty hours away, and go on board the newly-arrived ship that has brought and offers for sale passengers from Europe, and select among the healthy persons such as they deem suitable for their business, and bargain with them how long they will serve for their passage money, which most of them are still in debt for. When they have come to an agreement, it happens that adult persons bind themselves in writing to serve three, four, five, or six years for the amount due by them, according to their age and strength. But very young people, from ten to fifteen years, must serve till they are twenty-one years old.

Many parents must sell and trade away their children like so many head of cattle, for if their children take the debt upon themselves, the parents can leave the ship free and unrestrained; but as the parents often do not know where and to what people their children are going, it often happens that such parents and children, after leaving the ship, do not see each other again for many years, perhaps no more in all their lives.

It often happens that whole families, husband, wife, and children, are separated by being sold to different purchasers, especially when they have not paid any part of their passage money.

When a husband or wife has died at sea, when the ship has made more than half of her trip, the survivor must pay or serve not only for himself or herself, but also for the deceased. When both parents have died over halfway at sea, their children, especially when they are young and have nothing to pawn or to pay, must stand for their own and their parents' passage, and serve till they are twenty-one years old. When one has served his or her term, he or she is entitled to a new suit of clothes at parting; and if it has been so stipulated, a man gets in addition a horse, a woman, a cow.[39]

As people learned of the dangers and discomfort of crossing the Atlantic, undeterred, they continued to come.[40] During the 1600s, about four hundred thousand people from Great Britain emigrated to America, constituting an estimated 85 to 90 percent of white immigrants. In the 1700s, prior to the Revolutionary War, an estimated three hundred fifty thousand to five hundred thousand Europeans arrived, including many from Scotland and northern Ireland. And about three hundred thousand Africans were forcibly brought to America during this time in even worse conditions. Most of the white immigrants came as indentured servants. Collectively, these were the immigrants and ancestors who began what became the United States of America.

Figure 8: Native American village on the move

Chapter 3:
The "Native" Americans

The Europeans were not the first immigrants to arrive in what later became known as America. The most prevalent theory is that people from north Asia in the area that encompasses present Siberia crossed into Alaska and North America about ten thousand years ago when the two land masses were connected by a land "bridge."[41] These Paleolithic hunter-gathers moved south over time and populated North, Central, and South America. They were the original immigrants.

When the Europeans arrived, they encountered a land occupied by then "natives" now commonly referred to as "Native Americans" although they were in fact immigrants from Asia who had been in the neighborhood a long time. Christopher Columbus called them "Indians," mistaking America for the Indian continent, and the name stuck. The Indians or Native Americans did not use either name, referring to themselves as members of their tribe.

When the Europeans arrived, natives occupied virtually all of North, South, and Central America. Estimates vary but recent studies suggest there were about sixty million native inhabitants when Columbus first visited.[42] In comparison, all of Europe probably had between seventy and ninety million inhabitants. Large American cities, especially in Central and South America were built and managed by peoples including the Inca, the Aztec, and Maya. In North America, areas were generally occupied by more dispersed tribes, and the population of North America may have been about four million at the time.[43] Some tribes, especially those on the Great Plains, focused on hunting and gathering and moved often following prey including buffalo herds. Others established permanent villages, cleared land, and grew crops including maize, supplemented by hunting and fishing.

There were some peaceful tribes, but others regularly were at war with their neighbors over territory. Defeating the enemy was an essential part of becoming an esteemed brave or warrior. Often the chiefs selected to lead the tribes were chosen because of their demonstrated bravery in battle. Conquering an enemy and forcing them to flee provided the victors more territory for hunting or growing, food stocks, and captives. Captive children and sometimes women were generally adopted into the conquering tribe and helped sustain the tribal population, but others were tortured. Treatment of captives varied, but treatment was often quite harsh as described below.[44]

> Warriors in combat could be quite vicious hacking injured members of other tribes, scalping, and torturing male captives. Men and women captives as well as teenage boys, would usually face death by ritual torture. The torture had strong sacrificial overtones, usually to the sun. Captives, especially warriors, were expected to show extreme self-control and composure during torture, singing "death songs", bragging of one's courage or deeds in battle, and otherwise showing defiance. The torture was conducted publicly in the captors' village, and the entire population (including children) watched and participated. Common tor-

ture techniques included burning the captive, which was done one hot coal at a time, rather than on firewood pyres; cutting with knives, beatings with switches or sticks, and jabs from sharp sticks. Captives' fingernails were ripped out. Their fingers were broken, then twisted and yanked by children. Captives were made to eat pieces of their own flesh, and were scalped alive. The genitalia of male captives were the focus of considerable attention, culminating with the dissection of the genitals one slice at a time. To make the torture last longer, the Native Americans and the First Nations would revive captives with rest periods during which time they were given food and water... By these means, the execution of a captive, especially an adult male, could take several days and nights.

It is not surprising that settlers feared Native Americans after hearing such stories and experiencing fierce attacks. Their response was often indiscriminate killing.

In most East Coast Native American cultures, land was not owned by any individual or group. It was to be used by and for all. When Europeans showed up and in many cases sought to buy or trade for what they saw as "Indian" land, the concept was utterly alien to the Natives. This led to many conflicts across America when settlers thought they had purchased property, and the Native Americans had a different understanding of the transaction and resented settler incursions.

When the Europeans settlers arrived in Virginia, they were a mystery to the local inhabitants. They looked to the Native Americans like the European traders who had become fairly familiar in the area — individuals who traded goods but established no permanent presence which would threaten the local territory. But when the new immigrants sought to establish permanent settlements and showed signs of moving in, they were more likely viewed as an encroaching new tribe and were attacked. European technology including guns allowed the settlers to fight off many such attacks, but the new settlers were generally outnumbered, and many died in the course of these conflicts.

The survival rate for new settlers was low — less than 50 percent survived a year in the early days of settlement. But there were many in Europe who immigrated to America, so the settler population was continually replenished while the native population was not. The settlers also brought new diseases with them for which the Native peoples had no immunity; and disease killed far more natives than warfare. Estimates of deaths mostly from disease, range from eighty to ninety-five percent of the Native population.[45]

Conflict and wars between settlers and Native Americans continued throughout the first two hundred years following the landing at Jamestown. Generally conflicts arose and intensified as English settlements continuously encroached on Native territory. And almost everyone was impacted. According to one account, "In the century and a half before 1776 it would have been difficult to find anyone born in the English colonies in North America who had not lost a loved one…to war."[46] "Civilians who dwelled on the exposed frontier in wartime lived with the constant fear of a surprise attack."[47]

My documented ancestors include members of four tribes: the Powhatan, Nansemond, Lenape, and Lumbee. They are introduced below and described in more detail in later ancestor chapters.

The first tribe encountered by the Jamestown immigrants were part of the Powhatan Confederacy. The dominant Powhatan tribe established a kind of empire in which the thirty surrounding tribes paid tribute and pledged loyalty. In return, the member tribes received protection from outsiders. The Powhatans did not appreciate the encroachment of the European settlers after they understood the settlers did not intend to leave. Repeated attacks during the first few decades of Jamestown were intended to drive the settlers away but without success. The Powhatan empire was finally broken in 1646 when the then-chief was captured and killed. Ancestor Pocahontas was the daughter of the previous Powhatan chief, the powerful Wahunsonacock (see Chapter 41).

The Nansemond lived along the Nansemond River south of Jamestown and were part of the Powhatan Confederacy. They were considered relatively peaceful and focused on farming and raising crops. Ancestor Elizabeth Keziah was from the Nansemond tribe and married John Basse in 1638.

When the early Jamestown settlers ran short of food, Captain John Smith led a raid on one of the Nansemond towns, burning houses and canoes, and demanded that the residents hand over four hundred bushels of corn or suffer total destruction from the better armed Europeans. The Nansemond complied. The following month, Smith and his party returned and demanded all of the remaining store of corn, leaving the tribe with little food to survive the winter months.

In 1609, after the chief of the Powhatans forbade further trading with the European settlers, Smith sent two colonists by ship and sixty by land to negotiate with the Nansemond. The two on ships never arrived, and the sixty armed colonists assumed the missing two men had been killed by the Nansemond. As a result, the colonists unleashed an attack on the Nansemond town on Dumpling Island, where the Nansemond chief lived and home to their sacred temples and buried ancestors. The Europeans' attack resulted in total destruction: they burned homes, looted and destroyed temples, dug up buried kings and stole the jewelry buried with them, and then burned the fields. More than half of the attackers were killed, and the event signaled the start of the first Anglo-Powhatan war, which lasted until 1614. It ended when Pocahontas, daughter of the Powhatan chief, married colonist John Rolfe.

In March 1622, the Powhatan tribe, led by Opechancanough, attacked Jamestown in what is now called the "Jamestown Massacre." In response, the colonists attacked Native villages everywhere including Nansemond towns, not distinguishing between tribes that had participated in the raid and others. Several Nansemond towns were destroyed and many natives killed. The second Anglo-Powhatan war lasted until 1632 when a treaty was signed.

The Lenape or Leni Lenape tribe lived primarily in present-day eastern Pennsylvania and New Jersey. They were farmers and hunters and stayed in the same place except for hunting parties and seasonal movements. They were generally peaceful, although occasional disputes and fighting erupted with neighboring tribes such as the Susquehannock. Disease from Europeans, especially smallpox, decimated the tribe. British authorities and settlers actually found benefit in their demise, and one British officer, Captain Simeon Ecuyer, commander of Fort Pitt, sent blankets and handkerchiefs from smallpox patients to the Lenape in hopes of propagating more infections and deaths.[48] Disease and the related loss of tribal members, coupled with the demand for land by new settlers, led to the establishment of a Lenape reservation in New Jersey. Eventually, the tribe split in two: those who converted to Christianity were forced to combine with other tribes in New York to survive. Others moved to Pennsylvania where the state conspired to steal their land, which resulted in wars between the Lenape and the settlers there. The Lenape lost these battles and they were forced to relocate to Ohio and then to Oklahoma with other tribes. Ancestor Julia Brotherton was from the Lenape tribe; more information about her is provided in a subsequent chapter. Life in the Lenape tribe is described in a book first published in 1938 and more recently republished in 1966, *The Indians of New Jersey: Dickon Among the Lenapes*.[49]

Probably the first tribe settlers encountered in what is now North Carolina were the Croatoan, who lived near Roanoke Island, where Sir Walter Raleigh attempted to establish a permanent colony in Virginia before Jamestown. It is commonly believed (although not proven) that these early European settlers merged into this friendly tribe and relocated to the Lumbee River area of North Carolina. As disease decimated the local tribes, the survivors merged into a single group that became known as the Lumbee; ancestor Elizabeth Bearfoot came from this people. See Chapter 27 on the Lost Colony.

The Native Americans in the 1600s, when confronted with settlers from Europe, did not have a chance. Most tribes, like the Lenape, were devastated by disease brought by the Europeans. Those that survived disease fought against the new immigrants and killed many, but the Europeans had superior technology and firepower and benefitted from a continual supply of new immigrants. The insatiable desire for more land to accommodate settlers' big families and thousands of new arrivals led to continual conflict; as the new arrivals gained the upper hand, they began to forcibly remove the Native inhabitants from their traditional homelands. The expansion of new settlers into areas like Ohio, North Carolina, and the South and Midwest always followed conflict with area tribes and their subsequent removal to more distant lands. As Native people were forced out, the new settlers moved in.

Those natives who survived, including the ancestors profiled in the chapters that follow, were typically the ones who converted to Christianity and adapted to the new lifestyles and culture brought from overseas. Those who did not adapt to this new lifestyle perished or ended up in distant reservations.

The final blow to Native American presence in many areas was The Indian Removal Act passed by Congress in 1830. The intention was to free up land for expansion of white settlements by forcing the Native tribes to vacate. The act gave President Andrew Jackson the power to negotiate the removal of many tribes throughout the South and Midwest to distant reservations primarily in Oklahoma and terminate their rights to long-held lands. Thousands of Native Americans died on their long journey from starvation and disease. The Cherokee called the trip *"nu na da ul tsun yi"* or "the place where they cried." It became known more widely in history as "The Trail of Tears." [50]

Figure 9: Colonial woman stirring cooking pot

Chapter 4:

Women in Colonial America

The documentation of early American history and ancestry records almost all focus on men. Women had few rights and were generally viewed through the prism of their husbands. Typically, women could not own property, vote, hold office, or otherwise participate in governmental affairs and offices.

Religion was an important part of early colonial life, especially in Puritan New England. Religious doctrine then viewed women as the weaker sex, more inclined to sin and make mistakes. Most witch trials in New England involved accusations that women had been seduced by the devil, and those found guilty were often hanged or burned at the stake. Women were taught God wanted them to be subservient, first to their fathers and then to their husbands. Women were often taught to read the Bible but not to write or be further educated.

But women were critical to the success of the American colonies. Women's responsibilities included bearing and raising children; domestic duties such as cooking, cleaning, and making clothes by spinning, weaving, and sewing; working the farm, including caring for and feeding animals and sometimes laboring in the fields; and often producing goods for use or sale such as dairy products, soap, candles, and clothing. They were responsible for entertaining, including hosting travelers, who often stayed in homes because hotels and inns were rare. The work was nonstop, especially when families often had ten or twelve children.

Being a woman on a farm in the colonial and post-colonial eras could be very lonely as husbands were often gone hunting, serving civic and military duties, etc. One account describes the life of women who moved to Ohio by wagon train such as ancestors Nancy McDonald, Susan Corson, Catherine Bloom, Elizabeth Corson, and Sarah Ludington:

> The trip to the Ohio Country in the late eighteenth century was very difficult for women. Many of them had no choice but to follow their husbands to the frontier. Most women traveled several hundred miles, often on foot, to get to Ohio. Because their wagons had very limited capacity, only absolute necessities were packed for the journey. Sentimental objects, like family heirlooms, china, and most furniture, often had to be left behind.

> Once these women arrived in Ohio, they faced numerous challenges. They and their families lived in primitive conditions until land could be cleared and a small, one-room cabin built. The climate could be very harsh, and settlers also dealt with annoying insects and dangerous animals. Having left friends and family behind in the East, many women faced homesickness and isolation. In the early years of settlement, women experienced many other challenges as well. Commonly, there were no close neighbors or nearby towns to provide much social interaction. Men were away from the home for long hours, working in the fields

or hunting and leaving their wives with no adult companionship. There were
numerous accounts of loneliness, depression, and even occasional suicides.[51]

Nathaniel Basse, an early colonial leader in Jamestown and who founded Basse's Choice (see Chapter 64) and his wife, Mary, had eleven children in thirteen years including three sets of twins. They also survived the Jamestown Massacre. However, Mary returned to England and died there at age thirty-nine. She is believed to have been suffering from acute depression from so much stress and relative isolation. Mental health facilities in England were well established, including Saint Mary's of Bethlehem asylum, while none existed in Virginia at that time. However, Mary Basse was an exception; colonial women almost always just suffered through setbacks and illness (both mental and physical) and continued forward with their family obligations.

Colonial women often died young, sometimes in childbirth. Typically, some of their children died young with the prevalence of disease and limited medical treatment. And often their husbands died, usually requiring surviving widows to remarry quickly to survive.

Women on the frontier lived in constant fear of Native attacks, and at times and in newly settled locations many if not most families experienced loss from such engagements. If not killed, women could be captured and taken hostage as slaves.

Against the background of incredibly challenging conditions, frontier women survived to build a nation. Their work and determination often went undocumented and uncelebrated but was critical to the survival of generations.

There were women who were able to achieve recognition despite the male dominance at the time. Ancestor Anne Hutchinson was famous for her preaching. Relative Penelope Baker organized the Edenton Tea Party and boycott in response to the British Tea Act, and during the Revolutionary War ancestor Sybil Ludington rode forty miles at night to alert the Minutemen in Danbury, Connecticut that the British were coming.

Other stories of brave colonial women emerged from the Revolutionary War. Casandra Bishop, who married ancestor Thomas Powell, was bold enough to confront British Colonel Banastre "the Butcher" Tarleton as later documented:

> *On the march of the British army from Wilmington to Virginia, in 1781, Col.*
> *Tarleton, near "Twanky Chapel," in Halifax County, either from a scarcity*
> *of provisions or from a malicious desire to destroy the property of American*
> *citizens who were opposed to the British, caught all the horses, cattle, hogs, and*
> *even fowls that he could lay hands on, and destroyed or appropriated them to*
> *his own use. The male, and most of the female inhabitants of the country fled*

from the approach of the British troops, and hid themselves in the swamps and forests adjacent; and, when they passed through the upper part of the country, while everyone else left the premises on which they lived, Mrs. Powell (then Miss Bishop) stood her ground and faced the foe fearlessly. But it would not do; they took their horses and cattle, and among the former, a favorite pony of her own, and drove them off to the camp, which was about a mile distant. Young as she was, she determined to have her pony again; and she must necessarily go to the British camp, and go alone, because no one would accompany her. And alone she went, on foot, at night, and without any weapon of defense, and in due time arrived at the British camp. By what means she managed to gain an audience with Tarleton is not known; but she appeared before him unannounced, and raising herself erect said, "I have come to you, sir, to demand restoration of my property, which your knavish fellows stole from my father's yard." "Let me understand you, Miss," replied Tarleton, taken completely by surprise. "Well, sir," said she, "your roguish men in red coats came to my father's yard about sundown and stole my pony, and I have walked here, alone, unprotected, to claim and demand him; and, sir, I must and will have him. I fear not your men; they are base and unprincipled enough to dare to offer insult to any unprotected female; but their cowardly hearts will prevent them from doing her bodily injury." And just then by light of a campfire, espying her own dear little pet pony at a distance, she continued, "There, sir, is my horse, I shall mount him and ride peacefully home; and if you have any of the gentlemanly feeling within you of which your men are totally destitute, or if you have any regard for their safety, you will see, sir, that I am not interrupted. But before I go I wish to say to you, that he who can and will not prevent this base and cowardly stealing from hen roosts, stables, and barn-yards is no better, in my estimation, than mean, good-for-nothing, guilty wretches who can do the dirty work with their own hands! Good night, sir." And without waiting further, she took her pony uninterrupted, and galloped safely home. Tarleton was so much astounded that he ordered that she should be permitted to do as she chose.[52]

Ancestors Smith and Margaret Johnson lived in Oglethorpe County, Georgia. During this time, Georgia was largely occupied by British troops. The area residents included Benjamin Hart, a Lieutenant in the Georgia militia, and his wife Nancy. One night when Benjamin was away, six loyalist soldiers broke into the Hart home, killed their prized turkey, and demanded Nancy cook it for them. They picked the wrong woman to try to intimidate. According to the oft-repeated story:

After ordering her to cook the turkey, the Tories entered the cabin, stacked their weapons in the corner, and demanded something to drink. Hart obliged them by opening her jugs of wine. Once the Tories began to feel the intoxicating effects of the wine, Hart sent her daughter Sukey to the spring for a bucket of water. Hart secretly instructed her to blow a conch shell, which was kept on a nearby stump, to alert the neighbors that Tories were in the cabin.

As Hart served her unwanted guests, she frequently passed between them and their stacked weapons. Inconspicuously, she began to pass the loaded muskets, one by one, through a chink in the cabin wall to Sukey, who had by this time slipped around to the rear of the building. When the Tories noticed what she was doing and sprang to their feet, Hart threatened to shoot the first man who moved a foot. Ignoring her warning, one Tory lunged forward, and Hart pulled the trigger, killing the man. Seizing another weapon, she urged her daughter to run for help. Hart shot a second Tory who made a move toward the stacked weapons and held off the remaining Loyalists until her husband and several others arrived.

Benjamin Hart wanted to shoot the Tories, but [Nancy] Hart wanted them to hang. Consequently, the remaining Tories were hanged from a nearby tree.

In 1912 workmen grading a railroad near the site of the old Hart cabin unearthed a neat row of six skeletons that lay under nearly three feet of earth and were estimated to have been buried for at least a century. This discovery seemed to validate the most oft-told story of the Hart legend.[53]

Today there is a Nancy Hart Highway (Georgia Route 77), a Lake Hartwell, and Hartwell County. Frontier women had a reputation for toughness, and Nancy was no exception.

Margaret Cochran Corbin was the first woman ever to receive an American military pension. She was born in Pennsylvania in 1751 and was orphaned at age five when her father was killed in Native American attack and her mother was captured and never able to return. Raised by an uncle, Margaret married John Corbin in 1772. He joined the military at the beginning of the Revolution, and, like many other wives, Margaret accompanied him and earned money working in the military camp doing laundry, cooking, and nursing. In the battle of Fort Washington on Manhattan Island, she dressed as a man and helped her husband load his cannon against the attacking British. When he was killed, Margaret continued loading and firing the cannon until she was severely wounded and then captured. After being released by the British, she continued to serve by aiding wounded patriot soldiers. The Continental Congress subsequently awarded her a lifelong pension equal to one half of a man's pension.[54]

Mary Ludwig Hays, aka "Molly Pitcher," also accompanied her husband to military camp, where she did laundry and cared for the injured and sick. During the Battle of Monmouth, as soldiers were dying of thirst, dehydration, and heat exhaustion in the high heat and humidity, Mary repeatedly moved around the battlefield with buckets of water from a nearby spring, saving lives. When her husband was injured and could no longer fire his cannon, she took his place. Reportedly, George Washington inquired who was the courageous woman on the battlefield and promoted her to sergeant, earning her the nickname, "Sergeant Molly." [55]

About two hundred years later, my mother, Bernice Corson MacDonald, after losing her husband and her only sister and brother, went to work to support her family. Despite lacking a college education, she eventually became only the second woman in the history of the prestigious Northern Trust Company to be promoted to be an officer of the bank. Her work ethic and success followed generations of other women who preceded her and whose success was obvious but often unrecognized.

Part Two:
My Father's Family

My father, Walter Bingham MacDonald

Chapter 5:

The MacDonald Family:
A Generational Journey from
Scotland to Chicago on Ships,
Horses, Wagons, and Trains

Pedigree Chart for Scott Douglas MacDonald

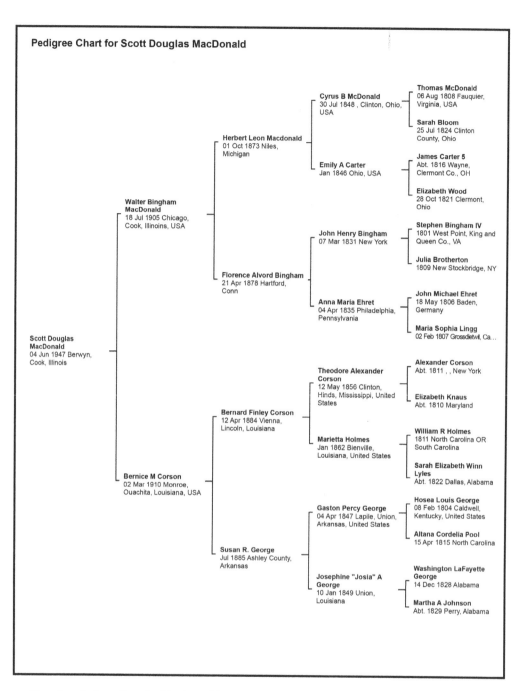

Genealogy 1: Scott Douglas MacDonald

Pedigree Chart for
Thomas McDonald

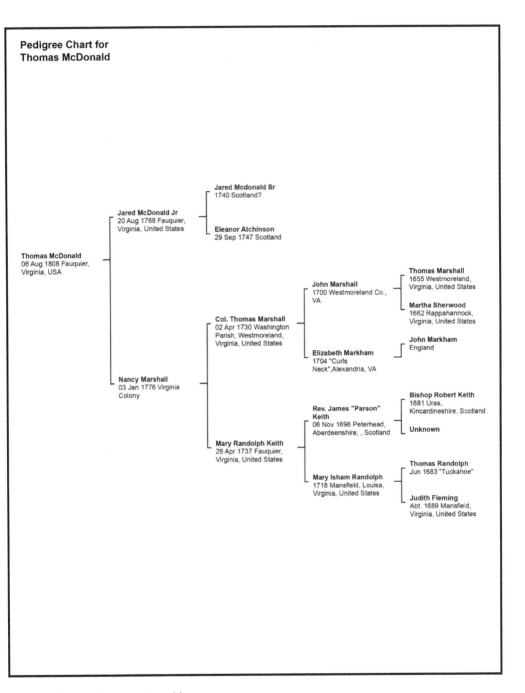

Thomas McDonald
06 Aug 1808 Fauquier, Virginia, USA

Jared McDonald Jr
20 Aug 1768 Fauquier, Virginia, United States

Jared Mcdonald Sr
1740 Scotland?

Eleanor Atchinson
29 Sep 1747 Scotland

Nancy Marshall
03 Jan 1776 Virginia Colony

Col. Thomas Marshall
02 Apr 1730 Washington Parish, Westmoreland, Virginia, United States

John Marshall
1700 Westmoreland Co., VA

Thomas Marshall
1655 Westmoreland, Virginia, United States

Martha Sherwood
1662 Rappahannock, Virginia, United States

Elizabeth Markham
1704 "Curls Neck",Alexandria, VA

John Markham
England

Mary Randolph Keith
28 Apr 1737 Fauquier, Virginia, United States

Rev. James "Parson" Keith
06 Nov 1696 Peterhead, Aberdeenshire, , Scotland

Bishop Robert Keith
1681 Uras, Kincardineshire, Scotland

Unknown

Mary Isham Randolph
1718 Mansfield, Louisa, Virginia, United States

Thomas Randolph
Jun 1683 "Tuckahoe"

Judith Fleming
Abt. 1689 Mansfield, Virginia, United States

Genealogy 2: Thomas McDonald

Jared McDonald (1740–1808)[56]

J ared was the first McDonald ancestor to arrive in America. According to later interviews,[57] he was born in Scotland. He was not listed on any ship's manifest, suggesting he immigrated as a child. He might have come with an adult or as a single child and then was sold as an indentured servant when he arrived. This was common for adults and children who lacked funds to pay for the passage.

It is believed he was born in 1740, and he married Eleanor Atchinson who is also thought to be from Scotland. They were apparently married in 1765 in Prince George's County, Maryland.

There are a couple possible origins for Jared McDonald that would fit the timing of his arrival in America. First, in Scotland, the MacDonald clan aligned with the Jacobites in support of the Stuarts and Prince Charles and against King George II of England. The revolt ended with the Battle of Culloden on April 16, 1746, in which the Jacobite army, including members of the MacDonald clan, was thoroughly defeated.[58] In the aftermath, the English army moved through Scottish towns imprisoning or killing Jacobite supporters. In advance of the English army, many Scots fled to the coast to emigrate. Young Jared would have been about six years old.

It is also possible that Jared's family was one of those Scottish families that had moved to Ulster in the early 1600s as part of King James I of England's plan to displace the Irish from parts of northern Ireland. Between 1717 and 1775, approximately 250,000 Scots from Ulster — commonly called Ulster Scots or Scotch Irish — migrated to America.[59] There were several factors behind this migration. Some left in search of better economic opportunities, especially when a change of feudal policies resulted in many Scotch-Irish losing the land they historically rented. A famine in Ireland in 1740–1741, in which about four hundred thousand people died, also led to increased migration. Some Ulster Scots emigrated for religious reasons as the Church of England displaced traditional Scottish Presbyterian practices per decree of the King of England.

The Scots and the Ulster Scots typically emigrated to Pennsylvania and Maryland. In the 1740s and later, as areas around Philadelphia filled up and land was less available for newcomers, they moved into the Shenandoah Valley in nearby Virginia. That is where Jared moved and raised his family. My DNA test results suggest that I have considerable Irish heritage as well; Jared's ancestors may have been Irish and moved to Ulster or to Scotland and intermarried before later emigrating to America.

There are many things that are unusual about Jared. His first name is not conventional for Scots or Irish. A traditional naming convention in Scotland held that the first son was named for the paternal grandfather, the second son for the maternal grandfather, and so forth. There is no Scottish or Irish record with the name Jared during this timeframe, according to professional researchers I have consulted in both places. It is therefore unlikely he was named for an ancestor.

Jared was literate; he wrote his name (which he spelled McDonald) clearly with good penmanship. He signed various deeds and marriage bonds for his daughters. Very few people were literate during these times. Typically, only ministers and religious officials could read and write. Jared must have been close to and most likely taught by a Presbyterian minister. I suspect he was indentured as a child to a minister upon his arrival in America, which would have not been uncommon.

Jared lived most of his adult life in Fauquier County, Virginia. Fauquier County was considered part of the frontier then, with scattered farms and few trails or roads. Today, the county is anchored by the historic town of Warrenton, Virginia, which was formally established in 1810.

Jared was most likely a farmer. He lived near the Blue Ridge Mountains, in the area near Upperville and the Lost Mountain. The area's soil was not as fertile soil as in other parts of the region and land was inexpensive, which is likely why they moved there. Life was hard, but Jared and his fellow settlers were up to the challenges.

He seems to have been in and out of court while in Virginia, because his name appears relatively often in court records. Apparently he was quite opinionated, as were many of the Scots who settled in the area. One record told the story of Jared who was accused of going to a neighbor's and beating him. He pleaded not guilty. When the trial started the judge asked Jared if he did it. Jared's reply was "yes." The judge asked why he pleaded "not guilty" if he did as charged. As recorded in the court's minutes, Jared replied "Because he had it coming." The judge found Jared guilty and fined him.

Jared and Eleanor were founders and active members of the Goose Creek Baptist Church near Upperville. The area was not densely populated, and there were few churches. As Presbyterians, including Scottish and Scotch-Irish settlers, moved further into the frontier, the Presbyterian Church had trouble providing ministers. The Presbyterians insisted their ministers be well educated and trained. By contrast, the growing Baptist movement required no formal education for their ministers; church members selected anyone who "felt the call" and was available and trusted.[60] The lack of a Presbyterian church presence likely led Jared and Eleanor to join in forming this rural Baptist church, which did not require a formally trained minister. The ease of establishing new congregations also likely contributed to the widespread growth of Baptist denominations in the South.

Typically people would travel for hours by horse to church on Sundays, remain the entire day, and then depart for home. The church became the central meeting place for those living spread out in the foothills and mountains. The Goose Creek Baptist

Church is no longer there, and its exact location and the location of its cemetery where Jared is likely buried are unknown.

Jared and Eleanor McDonald had eleven children; big families were customary then. Jared likely died in 1808; he was listed on the 1807 local tax roll but not subsequently. After his death, Eleanor moved in with one of their children. She died herself in 1832.

Jared McDonald Jr. (1768–1845)

Jared Jr. was Jared and Eleanor's second son. He was born August 20, 1768, in Fauquier County. He married Nancy Marshall, also of Fauquier County, in 1795. Generally, young men and women married neighbors because no one traveled much or had opportunity to meet strangers. The Marshall family also attended the Goose Creek Baptist Church and was a prominent family in the area. Nancy's brother was John Marshall, who became the Chief Justice of the U.S. Supreme Court. Jared's brother Samuel married Nancy's sister, Mary Ann Marshall.

When Jared was forty-four, he joined the Virginia Militia (the Fourth Regiment) to fight the English in the War of 1812, which ended after the December 1814 signing of the Treaty of Ghent (see Chapter 68). The Fourth Regiment was part of a larger group of Virginia militia that was sent to occupy and defend the strategic Craney Island near Norfolk. About eight hundred Virginians, likely including Jared Jr., were attacked by a British combined land and naval force of about 2,500 and successfully repelled the British. A few days later, the British attacked and defeated a different force of about five hundred Virginians at nearby Hampton. The War of 1812 ended in February 1815, and the Fourth Regiment of the Virginia Militia was disbanded on February 22, 1815.[61]

During the early 1800s the Shenandoah Valley where the McDonald's lived was becoming crowded as more settlers, including the Scotch-Irish, emigrated from Europe after the end of the Revolutionary War (1775–1783). Earlier settlers like Jared Sr. migrated into the valley from Pennsylvania and typically had large families. Usually the firstborn son inherited much of the parent's land, so other children looked elsewhere for farmland to rent or purchase. As available land in the valley became scarcer and more expensive, area residents moved into the Blue Ridge Mountains and then over the mountains into Native territory.

The Royal Proclamation of 1763 at the end of the French and Indian War prohibited settlers from moving west of the Appalachian Mountains, and that area was reserved for Native tribes. Some settlers moved there anyway despite the danger of raids.[62]

In response to land constraints in Virginia and the newly opened, abundant, and very inexpensive land in Ohio, Jared Jr. and his family explored the possibility of moving to Ohio. Early Ohio settlers sent letters to family and friends in Virginia often extolling the fertile soils available and inexpensive land in Ohio. The first wagon train from the area where Jared Jr. lived evidently departed in 1815 and almost certainly contained relatives and friends of the McDonald family. Moving to Ohio must have been a primary topic of conversation at Sunday church get-togethers in Virginia. Land companies and even the U.S. government actively promoted the opportunity associated with migration.

By 1825, Ohio was becoming settled with cities and commerce developing and even public education introduced in some areas. The journey was still arduous, but Native attacks were no longer a major threat and bridges had been built over some of the formidable rivers to be crossed. In 1825, the Ohio and Erie Canal was started, which would bring even more people and trade opportunities.[63]

Against this backdrop of history and conditions, Jared Jr., with his wife and twelve children, decided to pack up their possessions, say goodbye to family and friends, and leave the only area they had ever known for faraway Ohio. They were joined by Jared's younger brother Thomas and his family, and almost certainly some area friends (see Chapter 11).

The McDonald family would have joined others on the way to Clinton County. As a veteran of the Virginia militia, Jared could have been eligible to claim land in the Virginia Military District, a part of Ohio that Virginia reserved to use to pay its veterans in lieu of cash.[64] Jared would likely have had a land warrant "assigned" to him, meaning he was entitled to land because of military service, or he could have bought the warrant from someone who was entitled.

The McDonalds stopped in Greene County, Ohio, about fifteen miles north of the National Road and fifteen miles southeast of what was to become the city of Akron, which developed with the construction of the Ohio and Erie Canal beginning in 1825. It was close enough to transportation but also clearly an agricultural area away from higher priced commercial property. The McDonalds probably knew someone who had moved to the area who could welcome them.

The adjacent Clinton County, where Jared eventually moved, was established in 1810. At that time, there were only 2,674 residents. By 1820, immigration had increased the population to 8,085; and by 1830, the population was 11,436, including the newly arrived McDonalds of Fauquier County, Virginia.[65]

During their first few years in Ohio, Jared Jr. and his older sons probably focused on clearing the thickly forested land to create suitable farming land. They would have built a log cabin from the downed trees. It was grueling work but was customary and expected of new arrivals. Food came from hunting and later from gardens and crops. Some early settlers gave up and returned east, but most — including Jared Jr and his family — survived and stayed despite the challenges.

Thomas McDonald (1808–1888)

Thomas was the eighth child of Jared Jr. and Nancy Marshall. Like his brothers and sisters, he was born in Fauquier County, Virginia. When he was eighteen years old, he moved with his family to Ohio. Thomas would have been expected to work with his father and older brothers to clear trees, build a new home, and start the family farm.

In 1840, when he was thirty-two years old, he married Sarah Walker, a neighbor who was nineteen. They had a son, Bushrod, a year later; and Sarah died the same year. She may have died of complications arising from childbirth, which was not uncommon then. Years later, Bushrod died fighting for the Union army in the Battle of Shiloh[66] in Tennessee. It must have been heartbreaking for his father, Thomas.

On the frontier, men and women did not stay single long. Survival required both a husband and wife, and in Thomas's case, he had a newborn son. Two years after Sarah Walker died, Thomas married Sarah Bloom, whose family had moved to Clinton from the East Coast (see Chapter 12). Sarah was born in Clinton; she too was nineteen years old at the time of her marriage.

Thomas and Sarah Bloom had nine children, including Cyrus, their second-born. Thomas was a farmer, according to census records from 1850–1870. The 1880 Census lists him as a retired farmer.

Thomas joined the Union Army during the Civil War and served with the Thirteenth Ohio Cavalry Volunteers. He fought in several battles including the Battle of Cold Harbor, near Mechanicsville, Virginia, in 1864.[67] It is remembered as one of America's bloodiest battles, in which the Confederates won a lopsided victory with thousands of Union soldiers killed or wounded.

Late in the Civil War, his cavalry went on to fight in the Siege of Petersburg, where the Union army laid siege to Petersburg, Virginia, and fought a series of battles between June 1864 and April 1865. One of these battles — the Battle of Hatcher's Run[68] — was a hard-fought engagement with many back and forth attacks, retreats, and counterattacks. In another skirmish, the Battle of Fort Stedman, the Confederates launched the last significant attack on Union positions in an attempt to break the siege, but they were unsuccessful.[69]

After fighting in so many battles including Union loses and victories, Thomas McDonald and his cavalry were at Appomattox to witness the surrender of General Lee and the Confederacy. It must have been a tremendous relief to know the war was ending in victory. The Thirteenth Ohio Cavalry Volunteers mustered out of service August 10, 1865; [70] and Thomas would have returned home.

His obituary was published on April 12, 1888, in Warren County's newspaper, the *Western Star*. The article reveals more about his life.

Obituary of Thomas McDonald:

In the stillness of night on the 11th of February, one of our esteemed citizens, Mr. Thomas McDonald, was prostrated from a stroke of Paralysis, This being his third stroke, the family felt the grim messenger — Death — was near at hand and by telegram summoned the children from afar to his bedside. One son (Elmer of Iowa) was unable to come because of ill health and [a] married daughter living in California could not reach home in consequence of the severity of the weather and great distance; all the rest got home in time for a satisfactory recognition. Never after Mr. McDonald was stricken could he utter a sentence only an occasional word and by the movement of the head were the family enabled to administer to his wants. I would say here, that for 40 years he had been a sufferer from the effects of an attack of typhoid fever. He was a devout member of the Methodist church and a daily reader of the Scriptures and would read and reread the 14th chapter of St. John and the 27th Psalm. He always took active part in church work, especially in congregational singing. His gift of song lasted him to the last and his musical talent has descended to his children. He was born in the Shenandoah Valley, Virginia, August 6, 1808, and died after lingering ten days at his home in Harveysburg, Ohio Feb. 21, aged 79 years, 6 mo. And 15 days. When 18 years of age, he came with his parents to Greene county. After a few years the family removed to Clinton county near New Antioch. The remainder of his life was spent in Clinton and Warren counties. He experienced a great many hardships incident to pioneer life and at the age of 32 married Miss Sarah Walker, June 15, 1840. She died December 24, 1841, leaving an infant son 7 mo. Old. This babe lived to maturity, joined the army and gave his life for his country at the battle of Shiloh. Dec. 31, 1843 he was again married to Miss Sarah Bloom of Clinton county. As fruit of this union there were ten children. His widow, 8 children, 6 boys and 2 girls and several grandchildren survive him. Although the children sincerely mourn the loss of a dear old father, to the wife especially is the loss a deep one. They had trodden the matrimonial path hand-in-hand equally sharing care and prosperity, joy and sorrow for the past 45 years. Mrs. Ellen Cox, a sister of the deceased, is the only surviving member of eleven children, she lives with her son near New Burlington, and retains almost her youthful vigor, her age is 77 years. Mr. McDonald and family removed to Harveysburg eleven years ago where he has since resided. The funeral services were held at the home at 9:30 o'clock. Rev. R. K. Doern conducting the services delivered a brief but touching discourse. After prayer by Rev. Cleaver, the friends were allowed to pass through and see all that was mortal of him who had lived a long and useful life and had the love of his fellow man. His remains were interred at new Antioch Cemetery Thursday, Feb. 23. The funeral procession was joined by several acquaintances at Wilmington and at the cemetery there were numerous old friends and sympathizing neighbors of 30 years intimate association in waiting. There were no ceremonies at the grave save a short prayer and a few appropriate remarks by Col. Azirah Doan of Wilmington.

Cyrus McDonald (1845–1914)

Cyrus was the second of nine children from Thomas McDonald and his wife Sarah Bloom. He was born in 1845 in Clinton, Ohio, where he grew up. At some point, Cyrus decided he did not want to be a farmer but longed for a different and more interesting journey. And he did have a journey.

In 1869 he married Ruth McVay in Clinton. He was twenty-four years old, and she was twenty-five. They apparently had two children; one died as an infant and no record of the other one can be found. Perhaps the second also died young. They lived in Clinton and are listed in the 1870 Census. Ruth McVay died as a young woman in 1872.

The next year, in 1873, Cyrus married Emily (or Emma) Carter in St. Joseph, Indiana, where she was living at the time. Emily was the daughter of James Carter and Elizabeth Wood and had spent her early life in Cincinnati. She was born in 1846. He was twenty-eight years old and she was twenty-seven. They had one child, Herbert, in 1873. According to the 1880 Census, the three of them lived in Middleton, Ohio, which is just west of Clinton County. His occupation is listed as sewing machine agent.

In 1894 and 1895 Cyrus was listed in the Chicago city directory as a train conductor and working at the Passenger Station Hotel in Chicago's newly opened Grand Central Station. There must have been great excitement when the architecturally dramatic new train station opened in Chicago in 1893, and Cyrus was attracted at least for a while.

There is no mention of Emily in these directories, but she is listed as a widow in 1896 in Chicago, even though Cyrus was clearly still alive. Evidently Emily and Cyrus had a falling out, but no record of a divorce has been found. Cyrus was "dead" as far as Emily was concerned.

In 1897 Cyrus is listed as a hotel clerk and Emily as a widow. Herbert, their son, was living with Emily. The new train station and the adjacent hotel were not the success that was expected, and the hotel closed for good in 1901.[71] Before it closed, Cyrus had already moved on.

In 1898, Cyrus filed to incorporate the American Diamond Company with the Illinois Secretary of State, and later that year the Chicago city directory listed him as president of the American Diamond Company.

Also in 1898, Cyrus married Charlotte Rust in Milwaukee. Charlotte was the daughter of Daniel Moore and his wife Maria Roe. Cyrus's occupation was listed as diamond merchant. Emily continued to claim she was a widow, even though her son, Herbert, lived with her and worked for his father. Herbert's occupation was listed as a tailor before he joined his father in the diamond business; after he started working for Cyrus, he was listed as a bookkeeper. This branch of the McDonald family seems to have been adaptable and flexible when it comes to occupations and relationships.

In 1908, Cyrus married for the fourth time even though his third wife, Charlotte, appears to have still been alive. Perhaps taking a page from Emily, this time Cyrus claimed to be a widower. He married Helen E Moore, born about 1863.

Cyrus died in Chicago on February 13, 1914. The death record was signed by his sister, Mary Watrons. Emily died in Berwyn, Illinois, a suburb of Chicago, the next year. Her death record was signed by her son Herbert.

Herbert MacDonald (1873–1937)

Herbert, my grandfather, was the only child of Cyrus McDonald and Emily (or Emma) Carter. He was born in Michigan (probably Niles or Bay City) in 1873. He lived with his parents in Middletown, Ohio, before moving to Chicago sometime before 1894.

He married Florence Alford Bingham, my grandmother, in 1899 in Chicago; she was twenty-one and he was twenty-six. They had two children: Margaret MacDonald and my father, Walter Bingham MacDonald.

Florence was the daughter of John Henry Bingham, a lithographer of books and art in Philadelphia and then in Hartford, and Anna Marie Ehret, who was born in Philadelphia of a German father and Swiss mother, both of whom emigrated to Pennsylvania. John and Anna moved to Chicago around 1879. More on them in Chapter 25.

Around 1900, Herbert began spelling his name MacDonald instead of McDonald. His marriage certificate lists his name as "MacDonald" and the birth certificate of his son uses the same spelling. While it is not certain why he did this, I suspect it was response to the Irish immigration to America which began in large numbers with the potato blight in 1845. Between 1820 and 1930, about 4.5 million Irish emigrated to America.[72] They were typically poor, lived in overcrowded, subdivided dwellings in cities like New York; their neighborhoods generally lacked adequate sewage and running water, leading to disease such as cholera, typhus, and tuberculosis. Crime, violence, and alcoholism were common. When the Irish sought to move to better neighborhoods, the existing residents often moved out in fear of crime and disease. The Irish were Catholic in a mostly Protestant country and worked for wages far below what others would accept, depressing the labor market. It was not good to be considered Irish in the late 1800s, and discrimination was common. Then, as now, the "Mac" prefix was traditionally associated with Scottish heritage (as in Clan MacDonald) and "Mc" was more often associated with Irish heritage.

Herbert was likely told by his father and grandfather that his ancestry was Scottish. Perhaps he thought he could clarify that his family was Scottish and not Irish by simply changing the spelling of the last name. No matter the rationale, the name MacDonald has remained in the family ever since.

Margaret was born in 1902 and Walter in 1905 in Chicago. In the 1900 census, Herbert indicated he was an accountant, which was consistent with his job at the newly formed American Diamond Company. In 1900, he and Florence lived in Chicago, but they moved to nearby Berwyn by 1910. In the 1910 census, Herbert's occupation was listed as optician. In 1918, he registered for the Selective Service (draft) for World War I. He had blue eyes and red hair and was an optometrist. The 1920 census showed him as optometrist also. By the 1930 census, he was the owner of an optometry practice. He died before the 1940 census.

Prior to 1901, the practice of optometry was unregulated. In 1901, the state of Minnesota adopted the first state standards and Illinois followed later.[73] The first optometry courses were offered at Columbia University in 1910. Herbert almost certainly learned his practice by apprenticing with someone who was an optometrist.

Unlike his father, Herbert stayed married to one woman and did not move much. Once he discovered a profession he liked, he stayed with that. He lived his adult life in Chicago and the nearby suburb of Berwyn. His daughter married and remained in the Chicago area, eventually living in the northern suburb of Wilmette. His son, my father, remained in Berwyn until he died.

Walter Bingham MacDonald (1905–1954)

Walter, my father, was born in 1905 in Chicago. His family moved to the nearby suburb of Berwyn when he was two years old, and he continued to live in Berwyn until he died. He was too young to fight in World War I and too old for World War II. He registered for the Selective Service as was required, however. His registration said he had grey eyes and brown hair with a dark complexion. He had a mustache and wore glasses. Starting with the 1930 census, he listed his occupation as optometrist.

He attended Morton High School in Berwyn and then Northwestern University for two years. He graduated from Northern Illinois College of Optometry. Prior to his death he was a community leader in Berwyn, including president of the Kiwanis Club, a member of the Scottish Rite Temple, and a member of the board of directors of the local savings and loan. As a young child I remember going to the annual Kiwanis pancake breakfast and watching him cook and serve pancakes.

He owned an optometry practice in Berwyn and walked to and from work. Sometimes I would meet him on his way back and finish the walk home with him. He was an early adopter of new ideas. He joined with an optician to put a lab to produce eyeglasses in his optometry office so he could prescribe glasses and then have them made on-site. This was for patient convenience and quality control. Decades later, companies like Lenscrafters had the same idea.

He married my mother, (May) Bernice Corson in 1933 in Cook County, Chicago. She hated the name May and always went by Bernice. They had four children including Judith, Bing (Walter Bingham), Margot, and me.

My father died as a young man (forty-seven years old) from a stroke and related heart conditions. The morning of his death, the telephone rang and my mother answered, sitting at the telephone table in the hallway at the top of the stairs. I recall her wail and how I ran to her. I still remember the ring of that phone and my mother, with tears in her eyes, telling me "Your father has died."

Chapter 6:
The Marshall Family:
A Story of Ireland, the Magna Carta, a Pirate, and the Longest-Serving Supreme Court Chief Justice

**Pedigree Chart for
Nancy Marshall**

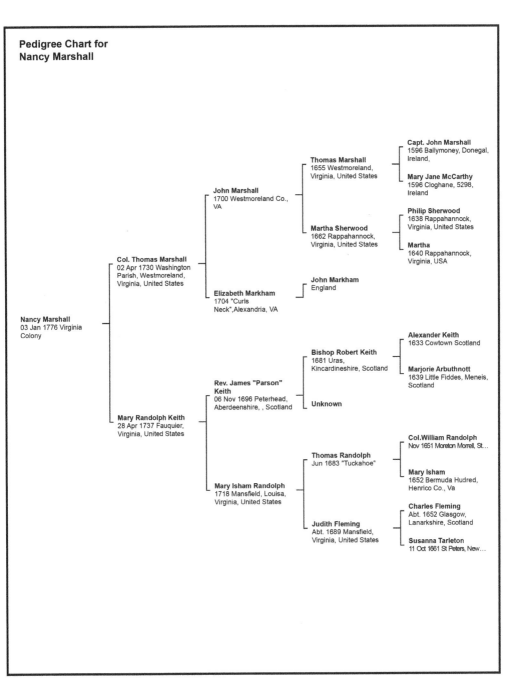

Nancy Marshall
03 Jan 1776 Virginia
Colony

Col. Thomas Marshall
02 Apr 1730 Washington
Parish, Westmoreland,
Virginia, United States

John Marshall
1700 Westmoreland Co.,
VA

Thomas Marshall
1655 Westmoreland,
Virginia, United States

Capt. John Marshall
1596 Ballymoney, Donegal,
Ireland,

Mary Jane McCarthy
1596 Cloghane, 5298,
Ireland

Martha Sherwood
1662 Rappahannock,
Virginia, United States

Philip Sherwood
1638 Rappahannock,
Virginia, United States

Martha
1640 Rappahannock,
Virginia, USA

Elizabeth Markham
1704 "Curls
Neck",Alexandria, VA

John Markham
England

Mary Randolph Keith
28 Apr 1737 Fauquier,
Virginia, United States

Rev. James "Parson"
Keith
06 Nov 1696 Peterhead,
Aberdeenshire, , Scotland

Bishop Robert Keith
1681 Uras,
Kincardineshire, Scotland

Alexander Keith
1633 Cowtown Scotland

Marjorie Arbuthnott
1639 Little Fiddes, Meneis,
Scotland

Unknown

Mary Isham Randolph
1718 Mansfield, Louisa,
Virginia, United States

Thomas Randolph
Jun 1683 "Tuckahoe"

Col.William Randolph
Nov 1651 Moreton Morrell, St...

Mary Isham
1652 Bermuda Hudred,
Henrico Co., Va

Judith Fleming
Abt. 1689 Mansfield,
Virginia, United States

Charles Fleming
Abt. 1652 Glasgow,
Lanarkshire, Scotland

Susanna Tarleton
11 Oct 1661 St Peters, New...

Genealogy 3: Nancy Marshall

Whedn Jared McDonald Jr. married Nancy Marshall in Fauquier County in 1795, he was twenty-six and Nancy was nineteen. She was the eleventh of thirteen children.

The Marshall Family had a long history in England and Ireland. Historians believe William le Mareschal went to England as commander of the invading army with the Norman conqueror in the eleventh century. From him descended William Marshall, the Earl of Pembroke, who owned considerable estates on the border with Wales. William and his descendants were supporters of the English kings and fought battles on their behalf.

William Marshall was a leader of English barons who forced King John to sign the Magna Carta. He married King John's youngest daughter, solidifying the Marshalls' influence.

The Marshall family involvement in Ireland deepened during the reign of Henry II, when Dermot, one of the Irish kings of Leinster (1110–1171) asked for help after being driven out of power. Henry declined because of his ongoing war with France, but he allowed one of his noblemen, Richard de Clare, often known as Strongbow, to help. Strongbow was a baron who had had most of his lands seized because Henry II distrusted his loyalty. With Strongbow's leadership, Dermot was restored to power. In exchange, Dermot agreed that Strongbow could marry Dermot's only child, his daughter Aoife, and that he would eventually inherit Dermot's vast lands. Strongbow's and Aoife's only child, also a daughter, married William Marshall (II), and inherited their remaining Irish estates.

William's grandson John Marshall was born in Ireland and was captain of the cavalry under King Charles I. After Charles's defeat, John decided to emigrate to America and arrived in Virginia in 1650. In America, he fought with valor in various conflicts with Native tribes.

Captain John Marshall married Mary Jane McCarthy, also from Ireland, and they had an unknown number of children in Virginia, including Thomas (1655–1704). Thomas became a wealthy farmer in Westmoreland County, Virginia. Between them, John and Thomas accumulated a large estate in Virginia — 1,200 acres as shown in deeds and wills. Thomas married Martha Sherwood and they had at least two children, including John Marshall (1732–1800) and another son named William. The Marshall lineage has lots of Johns, Thomases and Williams.

This John Marshall is sometimes referred to as "John of the Forest Marshall." The forest apparently refers to a wooded estate that was part of the acres he inherited. John of the Forest married Elizabeth Markham.

Elizabeth Markham has a most interesting story. Her father, John Markham, was an officer in the British Navy until he killed his captain in a duel. Markham fled and took refuge in Virginia to avoid facing British law. A Marshall family historian described John Markham as "A shrewd, money-getting, out-breaking, lawless, self-witted, large brained, devil-defying man… If all accounts of him be true, respecting neither God nor man, and fearing neither."[74]

According to one published account:

> There lived in Alexandria, Va., a merchant who had acquired a large fortune by trade. He was a married man, and he and his wife were elderly people. In their employ was a young man named John Markham. The old merchant died, and his widow inherited all his property. Markham persuaded her to marry him, and thus he acquired a large fortune. Sometime after the marriage, his business called him to England. The handsome but unprincipled young man, here met a beautiful young lady, attending a boarding school, and prevailed on her to elope with him, and a mock marriage was imposed upon her. Upon their arrival [in Virginia] the imposition was exposed, and great sympathy was expressed for the lovely girl. Regarding her as free, a gentleman proposed honorable marriage to her. Markham was incensed and challenged and killed him. [Markham's] real wife was greatly mortified, and soon died. Markham claimed and appropriated her whole estate, which he had not already squandered. He was now legally married to the young English girl, and a large family of children was born to them. But Markham died, and the widow found herself immensely wealthy. Her beauty was only matured, and her gayety made her a leader in society.

The story continues:

> At this time there appeared in Alexandria a handsome young Englishman, wearing a rich naval uniform. He seemed to have an abundance of money, and had the address to recommend himself to the good graces of the blooming widow. Infatuated with him, the widow married him, and placed all of her fortune under his control. When their honeymoon was ended, and the adventurer had possessed himself of all her property, he threw off restraint, and introduced into her house a set of rough and desperate companions, and made it the scene of boisterous revels. When his wife remonstrated, he struck her, and treated her with brutal contempt. Her children were purposely sent away [including Elizabeth who found a home with the widow of Thomas Marshall]. She had been finely educated, and possessed not only beauty, but the highest accomplishments of the day. [Eventually, she] discovered that she had married Blackbeard, the notorious buccaneer. When his identity was exposed, he gathered all and hastily departed to his ship. But female constancy clings to the most brutal and abandoned of husbands. She was often present at his orgies, and on one occasion, when two villains intended to assassinate Blackbeard, and were seated at table,

one on his right and the other on his left, she held two pistols beneath the table, and drawing a trigger with each hand at the same moment, the miscreants fell dead at the feet of her unworthy lord. But the ungrateful husband is said to have treated her with such cruelty that she died from the effects of a kick given her in one of his revels. But Blackbeard did not long survive his wife. Lieut. Maynard outwitted him on the North Carolina coast, and his riddled body, hung in chains, was suspended at Williamsburg as a warning to outlaws.[75]

Elizabeth was one of seventeen daughters and one son produced by John Markham and his young English wife (name unknown); Elizabeth married John Marshall in 1721 in Westmoreland, Virginia. Thomas Marshall, who would grow up to be a colonel in the Continental army, was the fourth of their nine children and the first boy. "He was of sound judgment and superior intellect."[76] With George Washington, he attended the school of Reverend Archibald Campbell, rector of Washington parish. He remained close friends with George Washington throughout his life.

Thomas assisted Washington on surveying excursions for Lord Fairfax and others and received several thousand acres of land in Henry County, (West) Virginia as compensation. During the French and Indian War, he was a lieutenant with General Braddock's army, and he later was a major and then colonel with the Continental forces under General George Washington in the Revolutionary War (see Revolutionary War chapter).

Thomas Marshall married Mary Randolph Keith in 1754; they had fifteen children including John Marshall, who became the longest-serving chief justice of the U.S. Supreme Court, and Nancy Marshall, who married Jared McDonald Jr.

Chapter 7:

The Keith family: From Robert the Bruce to a Scandal in Virginia

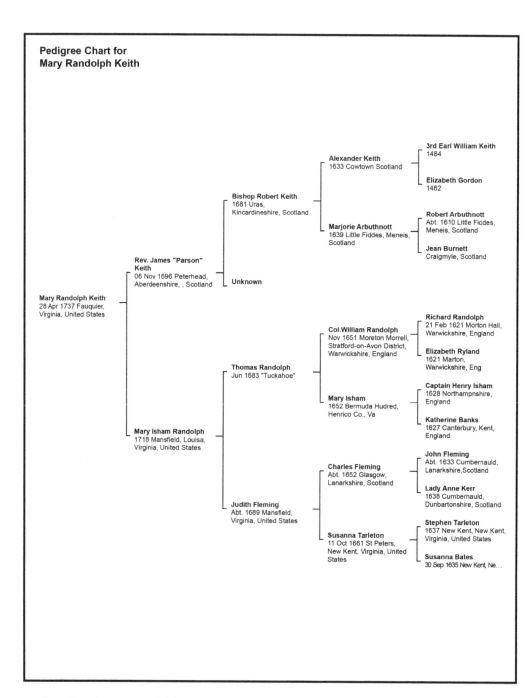

Pedigree Chart for
Mary Randolph Keith

Mary Randolph Keith
28 Apr 1737 Fauquier, Virginia, United States

Rev. James "Parson" Keith
06 Nov 1696 Peterhead, Aberdeenshire, , Scotland

Bishop Robert Keith
1681 Uras, Kincardineshire, Scotland

Unknown

Alexander Keith
1633 Cowtown Scotland

Marjorie Arbuthnott
1639 Little Fiddes, Meneis, Scotland

3rd Earl William Keith
1484

Elizabeth Gordon
1462

Robert Arbuthnott
Abt. 1610 Little Fiddes, Meneis, Scotland

Jean Burnett
Craigmyle, Scotland

Mary Isham Randolph
1718 Mansfield, Louisa, Virginia, United States

Thomas Randolph
Jun 1683 "Tuckahoe"

Judith Fleming
Abt. 1689 Mansfield, Virginia, United States

Col.William Randolph
Nov 1651 Moreton Morrell, Stratford-on-Avon District, Warwickshire, England

Mary Isham
1652 Bermuda Hudred, Henrico Co., Va

Charles Fleming
Abt. 1652 Glasgow, Lanarkshire, Scotland

Susanna Tarleton
11 Oct 1661 St Peters, New Kent, Virginia, United States

Richard Randolph
21 Feb 1621 Morton Hall, Warwickshire, England

Elizabeth Ryland
1621 Marton, Warwickshire, Eng

Captain Henry Isham
1628 Northampnshire, England

Katherine Banks
1627 Canterbury, Kent, England

John Fleming
Abt. 1633 Cumbernauld, Lanarkshire, Scotland

Lady Anne Kerr
1638 Cumbernauld, Dunbartonshire, Scotland

Stephen Tarleton
1637 New Kent, New Kent, Virginia, United States

Susanna Bates
30 Sep 1635 New Kent, Ne...

Genealogy 4: Mary Randolph Keith

**Pedigree Chart for
Princess Anabella Stuart**

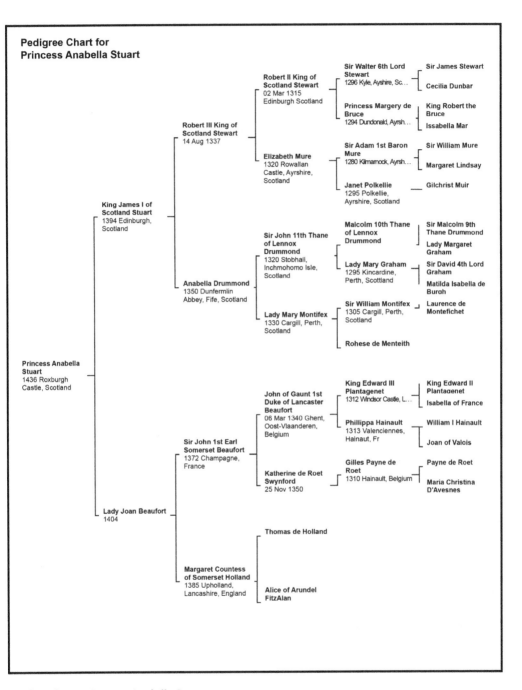

Genealogy 5: Princess Anabella Stuart

As mentioned earlier, Thomas Marshall married Mary Randolph Keith in 1754 in Fauquier County, Virginia. Mary's father was the Reverend James Keith who was born in Aberdeen, Scotland in 1696. He was thought to descend from Clan Keith and the Earls Marischal of Scotland, but this is unproven. He studied theology at Marischal College in Aberdeen and was ordained as a priest in the Church of England.

Reverend Keith supported the Stuarts and the Jacobites and was forced to flee to Virginia from Scotland after the failed Jacobite uprising in 1715. In Virginia, he had a reputation for being attracted to younger women and was removed from his church for licentiousness; but he was eventually able to resume preaching. He fell in love with Mary Isham Randolph, who was from a well-known and prosperous family, but the family did not initially approve and refused to give consent to marriage.

John Marshall described James Keith as follows:

> *A refugee from the abortive 1719 Jacobite uprising in Scotland, the Reverend Keith was particularly effective in the pulpit. He was a bachelor, but he was seventeen years older than Mary and, like much of the Anglican clergy in colonial Virginia, enjoyed a reputation for licentiousness. Mary and James had an affair and appear to have been discovered in flagrante delicto. The Randolphs, who held two seats on the vestry of Henrico parish, forced Keith's resignation and did their utmost to prevent the pair from seeing each other. Keith resigned as minister of the parish on October 12, 1733, and departed for Maryland immediately thereafter.*

> *The episode was handled gingerly by church authorities. Commissary James Blair, the Church of England's representative in Virginia, and a former minister of Henrico parish, wrote to the Bishop of London that "Mr. Keith has privately left this parish and Country, being guilty of fornication with a young Gentlewoman, whose friends did so dislike his character that they would not let her marry him." Blair, however, soon had second thoughts about the precipitate action against Keith. On March 24, 1734, he wrote a follow-up letter to the bishop stating that "I gave your Lordship an account of the misfortune which occasioned [Rev. Keith's resignation] tho' I did not then know what I have learned since that from some of the circumstances in his case, our Governor recommended him to the Governor of Maryland.*[77]

The circumstances are not mentioned in this account but presumably pertained to the fact that Reverend Keith and Mary Randolph were deeply in love. The following year Blair rescinded Keith's exile to Maryland and appointed him minister of the frontier parish of Hamilton in what subsequently became Fauquier County.

When Mary came of age, she and James Keith were married, but stories suggest the marriage was concealed from her family, and she stole away with Keith to England where he went to receive new orders from the church. After the couple eventually returned to Virginia, their marriage was accepted, and he continued to preach. They had eight children.

Another story about Mary adds further drama. When she was very young, she met a bailiff and was induced to elope with him. The Randolphs were outraged and hunted for the couple at length. Sometime later, the couple and their new child were discovered on an island in the James River. According to the story, Mary's brother and family members attacked and murdered the bailiff and the child and returned Mary to their home.

Late in life, Mary received a letter that purported to be from the bailiff, who claimed to be alive and living under a new name. The letter was probably written with evil intent or perhaps even as a sick joke. But Mary spent the rest of her days searching for her first lover and eventually suffered from what was described at the time as "insanity" or "lunacy."

The Keith lineage goes back many years and includes extraordinary Scottish nobility including Robert the Bruce, who is considered by many to be the founder of modern Scotland. Robert the Bruce fought the English in the First War for Scottish Independence and was King of Scotland from 1306 until his death in 1329. He remains a national hero in Scotland.

Robert the Bruce and his wife, Isabella Mar, had a daughter, Margery, in 1296. She married Walter Stuart, the sixth Lord High Steward of Scotland. They had a son, Robert, who became King Robert II of Scotland. His son became King James I of Scotland. James married Lady Joan Beaufort, and their daughter Princess Anabella Stuart married George Gordon, second Earl of Hundley. Their daughter, Elizabeth Gordon, married William Keith, the third Earl. Their son, Alexander, was Reverend James Keith's grandfather. Reverend Keith came from a very long line of famous Scottish ancestors including kings.

Chapter 8:
The Randolph Family: The Dynasty that Shaped Colonial Virginia

Pedigree Chart for
Mary Isham Randolph

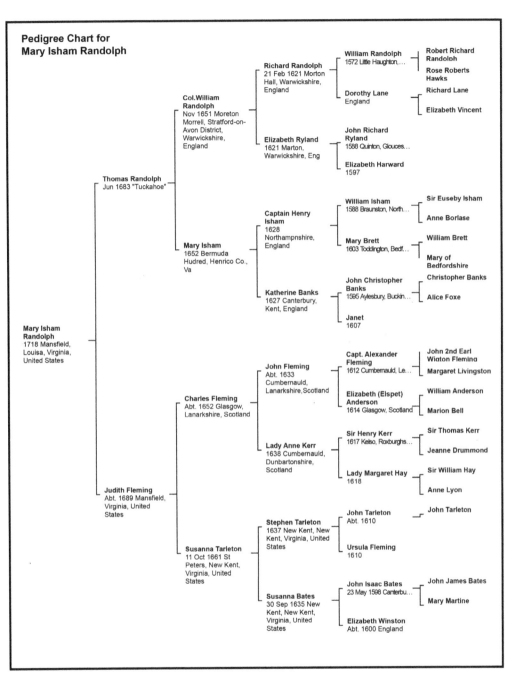

Genealogy 6: Mary Isham Randolph

Nancy Marshall (Jared McDonald Jr.'s wife) was the daughter of Thomas Marshall and Mary Randolph Keith. Mary's mother was Mary Isham Randolph. The Randolph family was one of the most prominent families in the American colonies.

The Randolph family also has a long history in Scotland and England. Thomas Randolph, Lord of Stratnith in Scotland, married Lady Isabel Bruce, sister of King Robert the Bruce, sometime around 1300.

In the 1600s, when William Randolph (1651–1711) was born, the family was still highly thought of in England and the king's court. They were key supporters of the Crown and were among the Cavaliers who supported King Charles I during the Civil War in England.

William Randolph was the son of Richard Randolph and Elizabeth Ryland and was born and raised in Warwickshire, England. Following the defeat of King Charles I by Cromwell and the parliamentarians, William's uncle, Henry, who had traveled to Virginia, sponsored William's emigration to Virginia. William arrived in Virginia in 1671 or early 1672.

William apparently arrived with little in the way of money or business connections. He made money initially by building houses and barns. Eventually, he saved enough to import several indentured servants and was given land grants. Over time he imported more servants and slaves and acquired more land. However, author Tess Taylor has pointed out William and others like him did have an advantage:

> [Historian H. J.] Eckenrode writes: "These were men who had fought on the royal side in the Civil War in England and now sought refuge in Virginia. They were known as 'Cavaliers,' and they gave Virginia a social atmosphere it never subsequently lost." William is praised for shrewdly accomplishing so much, but, extolling bloodline, Eckenrode implies more than once that his essential breeding gave William a knee up on his clamber toward greatness. The myths sit in uneasy tension: William Randolph may have pulled himself up by his bootstraps, but it also seems that his boots were better positioned than everyone else's.[78]

William made friends and was industrious. He was a merchant, planter, and ship owner and was also trained as a lawyer. He bought considerable land, including at Turkey Island on the James River. He married Mary Isham, a wealthy widow, whose parents were from the part of England where William had been raised; she owned land across the James River from William. They had nine children who survived to adulthood including Thomas, their fourth.

William Randolph was a founder and one of the first trustees of the College of William and Mary and served as Speaker of the House of Burgesses and Attorney General of Virginia. His descendants include Thomas Jefferson, John Marshall, and Robert E. Lee.

"All of the sons took active and prominent part in the affairs of the colony, and each received a large patrimony in the distribution of the great estate of their father. Most of them built fine houses and became known by the names of their estates."[79]

Thomas Randolph carried on in his father's tradition as a landowner, planter, and merchant, and he also served in the Virginia House of Burgesses. He was reportedly the first settler of Tuckahoe, Virginia and is sometimes referred to as Thomas Randolph of Tuckahoe. The main house of the Tuckahoe plantation where Thomas lived has been preserved and is a National Historic Landmark. One of Thomas's nephews, Thomas Jefferson, was a frequent visitor as a child. Thomas Randolph married Judith Fleming in 1712, and they had at least three children, including Mary Isham Randolph.

Thomas's brother John Randolph had a son John (Jr.), who would have been Thomas's nephew and first cousin to Mary Isham Randolph. John Jr.'s son Edmund became governor of Virginia, the first U.S. attorney general under President Washington, and the second U.S. secretary of state.

The Randolph family — among the most numerous and wealthiest first families of the colonies — has been called a dynasty that shaped colonial commerce and government for many years.

Chapter 9:

The Fleming Family: From King James to Colonial Virginia

**Pedigree Chart for
Judith Fleming**

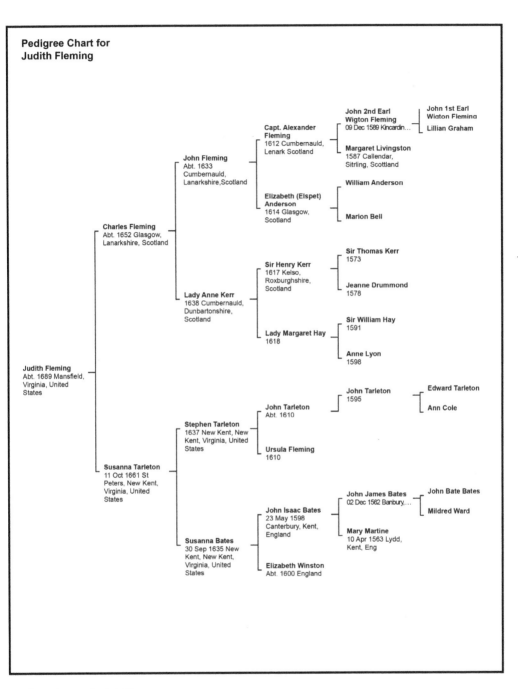

Judith Fleming
Abt. 1689 Mansfield,
Virginia, United
States

Charles Fleming
Abt. 1652 Glasgow,
Lanarkshire, Scotland

Susanna Tarleton
11 Oct 1661 St
Peters, New Kent,
Virginia, United
States

John Fleming
Abt. 1633
Cumbernauld,
Lanarkshire,Scotland

Lady Anne Kerr
1638 Cumbernauld,
Dunbartonshire,
Scotland

Stephen Tarleton
1637 New Kent, New
Kent, Virginia, United
States

Susanna Bates
30 Sep 1635 New
Kent, New Kent,
Virginia, United
States

Capt. Alexander
Fleming
1612 Cumbernauld,
Lenark Scotland

Elizabeth (Elspet)
Anderson
1614 Glasgow,
Scotland

Sir Henry Kerr
1617 Kelso,
Roxburghshire,
Scotland

Lady Margaret Hay
1618

John Tarleton
Abt. 1610

Ursula Fleming
1610

John Isaac Bates
23 May 1598
Canterbury, Kent,
England

Elizabeth Winston
Abt. 1600 England

John 2nd Earl
Wigton Fleming
09 Dec 1589 Kincardin...

Margaret Livingston
1587 Callendar,
Sitrling, Scottland

William Anderson

Marion Bell

Sir Thomas Kerr
1573

Jeanne Drummond
1578

Sir William Hay
1591

Anne Lyon
1598

John Tarleton
1595

John James Bates
02 Dec 1562 Banbury,...

Mary Martine
10 Apr 1563 Lydd,
Kent, Eng

John 1st Earl
Wigton Fleming

Lillian Graham

Edward Tarleton

Ann Cole

John Bate Bates

Mildred Ward

Genealogy 7: Judith Fleming

The Fleming family, like the Keith and Randolph families, has a long-documented history in Europe. The name "Fleming" means a native of Flanders. The wife of William the Conqueror was Matilda of Flanders. The Flemings were with the Normans at the Battle of Hastings in 1066.[80]

Like the Keiths, the Flemings came to America from Scotland. Cumbernauld Castle was in the custody of the Flemings for generations dating back to the fourteenth century. Robert Fleming, father of Malcolm, was a close colleague and supporter of Robert the Bruce, King of Scotland.

King James IV of Scotland was born in 1473. His father, James III, was much-hated and was overthrown in 1488, and James IV became king at the age of fifteen but deferred initially to the powerful nobles who led the rebellion against his father. Eventually he became a strong leader, spoke ten languages, and is regarded as one of the best of the Scottish kings. He had an arranged marriage with Margaret Tudor, eldest daughter of King Henry VII of England in 1502, and met her the following year when she turned thirteen.

About the same time, James IV had an affair with Isabel Stewart, daughter of James Stewart, first Earl of Buchan. They had an illegitimate child, Lady Janet Stewart, in 1502. Janet was called *"la belle Écossaise"* or "the beautiful Scotswoman." She served as governess to her half-niece, Mary Queen of Scots. She was briefly a mistress to King Henry II of France and later married her cousin, Malcom Fleming, third Lord Fleming. They had eight children.

A few generations later, the descendants of Lady Janet and James emigrated from Scotland to Maryland and Virginia. The first Scottish Flemings to immigrate to Virginia included Captain Alexander Fleming and his family. Alexander was born in 1612 in Cumbernauld, a town in Lanarkshire, Scotland, the second son of John Fleming, second Earl of Wigtown (or Wigton). Alexander became a merchant and married Elspet (Elizabeth) Anderson from Glasgow. Alexander and Elspet and their family, including their son John and his wife and child, emigrated to Virginia around 1653, ending up in New Kent County, Virginia. That was the year Oliver Cromwell was installed as lord protector of the commonwealth. The Flemings had always been supporters of the Crown, and John likely felt it was a good time to leave Scotland. Elspet died in 1658, and Alexander married Joyce Jones of Virginia.

Alexander and Elspet's son John Fleming was born about 1633 in Cumbernauld. He married a woman named Mercy or Mary, and she gave birth to Charles Fleming in about 1652 in nearby Glasgow. They emigrated to Virginia with Alexander's father and family the following year.

Land registers in New Kent County show that Alexander and his son John accumulated considerable land holdings.

The Flemings were very active and supportive of the colonists in the fight for independence. A cousin, also named John Fleming, was famous for giving his life in the American Revolution (see Chapter 31).

John's son and Alexander's grandson, Charles, married Susannah Tarleton in Virginia in 1684, and they had several children including Judith, who married Thomas Randolph and was the mother of Mary Isham Randolph and the grandmother of Mary Randolph Keith. Charles was also a large landowner and planter in Virginia.

Judith's brother, Colonel Thomas Fleming, led colonial troops in battles against the Natives including a particularly fierce fight in Point Pleasant on the Ohio River, that has subsequently been memorialized by a large monument near the site.

Colonel Thomas "commanded two hundred men in the battle of Point Pleasant, with the Indians, in 1774… Fleming's men hid behind trees and held out their hats. The Indians, mistaking the hats for white men's heads, shot at them. At this, Fleming's men would drop their hats and the Indians would rush forward to scalp their victims. When the Indians got near them, the whites would jump from behind the trees and tomahawk the unwary Indians. These men were all backwoodsmen and knew… the methods of Indian fighting. There were a thousand Indians and only four hundred whites [including Fleming's men], but the battle was a signal victory for the whites. Unfortunately, Fleming was severely wounded" but later recovered to fight in the revolutionary war.[81]

In Mary Randolph Keith, the well-regarded and historic families of Keith, Randolph, Isham, Fleming, and Marshall came together. And her daughter Nancy Marshall's marriage to Jared McDonald Jr. brought these families lines together with the McDonalds.

Chapter 10:
The Isham Family:
A Family Long Established in Pytchley, England, Disembarks in Jamestown, Virginia

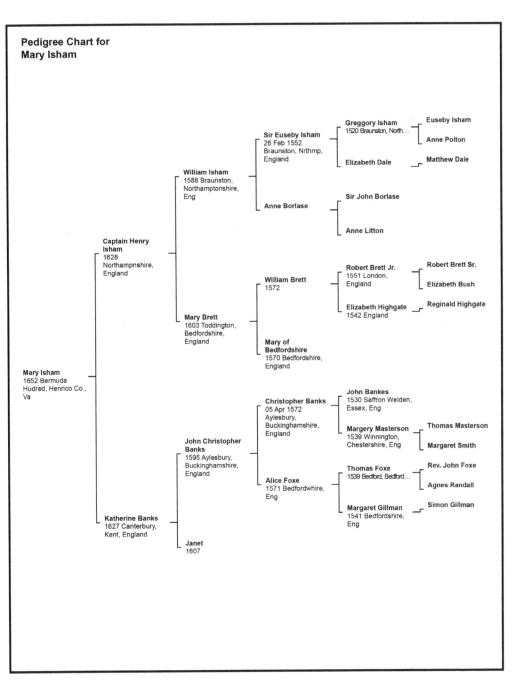

Pedigree Chart for Mary Isham

Mary Isham
1652 Bermuda Hudred, Henrico Co., Va

Captain Henry Isham
1628 Northampnshire, England

William Isham
1588 Braunston, Northamptonshire, Eng

Sir Euseby Isham
26 Feb 1552 Braunston, Nrthmp, England

Greggory Isham
1520 Braunston, North...

Euseby Isham

Anne Polton

Elizabeth Dale

Matthew Dale

Anne Borlase

Sir John Borlase

Anne Litton

Mary Brett
1603 Toddington, Bedfordshire, England

William Brett
1572

Robert Brett Jr.
1551 London, England

Robert Brett Sr.

Elizabeth Bush

Elizabeth Highgate
1542 England

Reginald Highgate

Mary of Bedfordshire
1570 Bedfordshire, England

Katherine Banks
1627 Canterbury, Kent, England

John Christopher Banks
1595 Aylesbury, Buckinghamshire, England

Christopher Banks
05 Apr 1572 Aylesbury, Buckinghamshire, England

John Bankes
1530 Saffron Welden, Essex, Eng

Margery Masterson
1539 Winnington, Chestershire, Eng

Thomas Masterson

Margaret Smith

Alice Foxe
1571 Bedfordwhire, Eng

Thomas Foxe
1539 Bedford, Bedford...

Rev. John Foxe

Agnes Randall

Margaret Gillman
1541 Bedfordshire, Eng

Simon Gillman

Janet
1607

Genealogy 8: Mary Isham

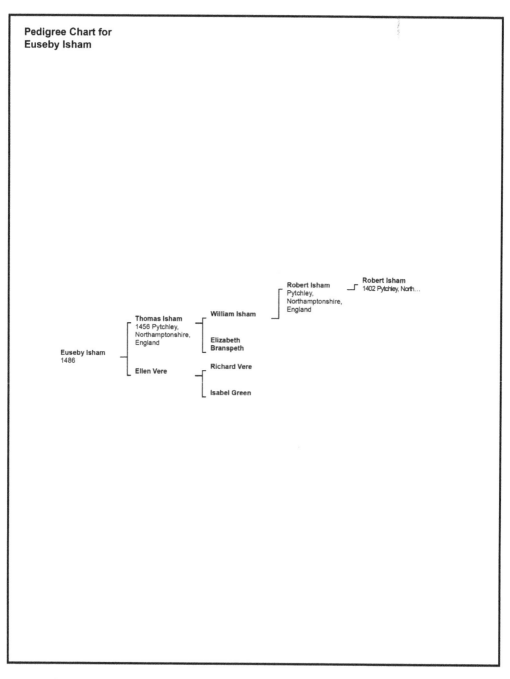

Pedigree Chart for
Euseby Isham

Robert Isham
1402 Pytchley, North...

Robert Isham
Pytchley,
Northamptonshire,
England

William Isham

Elizabeth
Branspeth

Thomas Isham
1456 Pytchley,
Northamptonshire,
England

Richard Vere

Euseby Isham
1486

Isabel Green

Ellen Vere

Genealogy 9: Euseby Isham

Immigrant and ancestor William Randolph came from a prominent English family, as did his wife, Mary Isham, whom he married in Virginia about six years after his arrival from England. The name Isham comes from the name of a Saxon village near Northamptonshire, England, which sits adjacent to the River Ise. Adding the suffix -ham to the name of the river led to the name Isham, or "town by the Ise." The Isham family in the area is documented back to 1086. Henry de Isham was named as a resident in the area in 1206 and another Henry de Isham appears as the local bailiff in records from the early 1300s.

Originally, the village developed around an abbey; the fields were used to grow crops to feed the abbey members, and the area was known for abundance of animals to hunt. Later the area became famous for English fox hunts. Today, the village of Pytchley has a population of about five hundred, a church, a school, and a pub. The nearest train station, Isham Station, lies about two and a half miles distant.

Robert Isham purchased the local manor house circa 1400, beginning what would become hundreds of years of Isham family presence and prominence in the Pytchley parish. Robert had a son, also named Robert (II), born around 1402. Robert (II)'s first son, William, inherited the family estates at Pytchley, which later passed to William's first born son, Thomas. Thomas married Ellen Vere, and they had at least two surviving sons, Euseby and John.

The family continued to live at Pytchley through the generations. Ancestor Sir Euseby Isham was knighted by King James I and built a magnificent manor house, which stood for two hundred years. He also served as Sheriff of Northamptonshire. Sir Euseby married Anne Borlase, daughter of Sir John Borlase and a descendant of the Scottish king William the Lion. Sir Euseby and Anne had at least three children. John, the oldest son, would have inherited the Pytchley estates. Henry, John's younger brother, married Katherine Banks, widow of Joseph Royall. Around 1656, with Oliver Cromwell in power and with most of the family inheritance going to his older brother, Henry decided to emigrate. Henry was the first Isham to leave England in at least seven hundred years.

Captain Henry and Katherine Isham settled in the newly formed area of Bermuda Hundred, near Jamestown, founded by Sir Thomas Dale. The town was named after Bermuda, where the Sea Venture had been shipwrecked in route to Jamestown. Henry was Justice of the Peace of Charles City County and Captain and High Sheriff of Henrico County subsequently. He was a wealthy and prominent member of Virginia society.

Henry and Katherine had at least three surviving children, including Mary, who married William Randolph. Mary bore nine children with William including a son, Isham Randolph, whose daughter Jane was mother to President Thomas Jefferson.

Mary and William's daughter Mary had a son named William Smith, who was the third President of William and Mary College.

While William and Mary were living in Henrico County, Mary's cousins lived in nearby Richmond County, Virginia. Ann Isham was born there in 1689 and married William Smith in 1716 in Surry County, Virginia (see Chapter 36). Isham descendants appear in both my mother's and father's ancestries.

Figure 10: Wagon train of pioneers moving west 1800s

Chapter 11:

The Wagon Trains to Ohio

F ollowing the death of her husband, John Corson, in 1812, Susan Benton Corson and her children joined friends and relatives moving from New York to Cincinnati, Ohio. Around the same time, George Knaus moved his family from Philadelphia to Montgomery, Ohio.

Sometime between 1815 and 1820, John William Bloom and his wife, Catherine, and several children packed their possessions in a wagon and joined other family and friends in a wagon train from Hunterdon County, New Jersey, west to Clinton, Ohio. Members of the Case and Jung families, John's cousins and aunts and uncles, moved with them.

A few years later, Thomas Ludington and his family packed their belongings in New York or Connecticut and joined a wagon train to Clinton County, Ohio. And in 1825, Jared McDonald and his family of twelve moved from Fauquier County, Virginia to Greene County, Ohio.

By the early 1800s occupied areas in more settled communities were becoming crowded and land was becoming more expensive. Colonial families typically had ten or twelve children, and the children who grew into adulthood needed land to farm and raise families. New immigrants were also constantly arriving increasing the demand for suitable land. And much of the land not already under colonial control was occupied by Native tribes and unavailable for new settlers.

The Treaty of Paris (1783) which ended the Revolutionary War, awarded the old northwest region, including lands in what is now Ohio, Indiana, Illinois, Michigan, Wisconsin, and part of Minnesota, to the new United States of America.[82] The area was largely occupied by Native tribes and French and English traders. In 1785, Congress passed the land ordinance providing for the surveying and sale of land in Ohio to new settlers.[83] The goal was to raise money for the federal government by selling frontier lands to migrating settlers looking for farmland. Eventually land was priced between one and two dollars per acre and terms were pretty generous to encourage migration from the more established colonies including Virginia. The Confederation Congress passed the Northwest Ordinance in 1787 establishing governmental administration in the area.[84]

Two issues slowed migration to Ohio and the Midwest, however. First, Native Americans in Ohio were not supportive of the idea white settlers would move in and take over the lands they traditionally used for growing crops and hunting. During the early history of the area, there were constant conflicts between Native tribes who had long lived in the area, and white settlers who moved in, cleared land, and started their own farms. The French generally aligned with the Natives, and from 1756 to 1763, the settlers and the English fought a war with France and their Native allies (the French and Indian War or the Seven Years' War) in which the English and settlers prevailed.

Later, during the American Revolution, most Native tribes in the area joined English forces to kill settlers and destroy their homesteads. Both Native raids on settlers and settler raids on Native villages were typically quite brutal with prisoners often killed and/or tortured; although white women and children were frequently kidnapped and forcibly integrated into the tribal culture. Living on the frontier in Ohio was dangerous.

The new American government sent troops to fight or pacify the Native Americans after the Revolution, but the Natives remained resistant, and tribes often united to fight and kill encroaching settlers and army troops. By 1788, there was widespread open warfare between Native tribes and white settlers, supported by the army and accompanying militias from Virginia and Kentucky. In 1792, Arthur St. Clair led an American force of almost 1,400 soldiers to confront the tribes led by the Miami war chief Little Turtle. In an overwhelming defeat, the Americans suffered 918 casualties including many hacked to death.[85]

The Native attacks and settler and militia counterattacks continued openly and unconstrained until the combined tribes were defeated in the Battle of Fallen Timbers in 1794. The resulting Treaty of Greenville, enacted in 1795, forced the tribes to largely vacate what became the state of Ohio, and made the area much safer for new settlers.[86] The state of Ohio was formed in 1804.

The second issue discouraging immigration to the Midwest was poor transportation. The journey from the east to Ohio followed largely unimproved trails and crossed five major rivers. In response to the transportation issues and with a desire to have more settlers move to Ohio and further areas west and buy federal land, Congress authorized and funded construction of the first federal highway, called the National Road, which was constructed between 1811 and 1837.[87] It included bridges over the rivers and a path through the mountains. By 1825, this road was open from Cumberland over the mountains to Wheeling, home of Fort Henry, on the bank of the Ohio River. This made travel by horse, oxen, and covered wagon easier although still daunting.

When my ancestors decided to move, the Native peoples had been mostly forced to vacate the area, the federal government was promoting cheap land and favorable terms, and a road was being constructed with bridges over major rivers. But the journey was still a challenge.

From published accounts, diaries, and journals, one of the worst feelings about traveling to the Midwest in the 1800s was saying goodbye to friends and families that the pioneers would never see again. The family planning to move stayed busy with all the preparations for the journey. This would have taken months. First, the home and farm had to be sold; decisions had to be made on which household items to select for the new home; and which items were necessary in case of injuries or breakdowns. And, how would everything fit into a wagon that was only ten feet long and three and a half feet wide? While father and grandfather haggled over the selling price of the property, mother and grandmother had to decide which family heirlooms stayed behind.

As members of this traveling group, the men in the party would have set forth rules and regulations for such things as camping, gathering firewood, and restrictions on gambling and drinking. Penalties would apply for infractions. These decisions were made before the trip began. The men worked together to pack the wagons for the best use of space with weapons and medical supplies in easy reach.

A typical covered wagon might contain the following items:

Bedding & Tent Supplies: *Tents, ground covers, poles, stakes, rope, blankets, quilts & pillows.*

Weapons: *Rifles, pistols, knives, hatchet, gunpowder, lead, bullet molds, powder horn, bullet pouch, & holsters.*

Food: *Flour, bacon, coffee, baking soda, corn meal, hardtack, dried beans, dried beef, dried fruit, molasses, vinegar, pepper, eggs, salt, sugar, rice & tea.*

Cooking utensils: *Kettle, skillet, Dutch oven, reflector oven, coffee grinder, coffee pot, tea pot, butcher knife, ladle, tin tableware, water keg, & matches.*

Medical: *Surgical instruments, liniment, camp stool, chamber pot, wash bowl, lanterns, candle molds, tallow, spyglasses, scissors, needles, pins, thread, & an herbal medicine kit.*

Clothing: *Wool sack coats, rubber coats, cotton dresses, wool pantaloons, buckskin pants, duck trousers, cotton shirts, flannel shirts, cotton socks, brogans, boots, felt hats, palm leaf sun hats, green goggles, & sun bonnets.*

Tools & equipment: *Set of augers, gimlet, ax, hammers, hoe, plow, shovel, spade, whetstone, oxbows, axles, kingbolts, linchpins, ox shoes, horseshoes, spokes, wagon tongue, heavy ropes, O&O chains.*

Luxuries: *Canned foods, plant cuttings, school books, music instruments, dolls, family albums, jewelry, china, silverware, fine linens, iron stove & furniture.*[88]

The wagons were much smaller than the Conestogas that would later carry commercial cargo to the West. The sides on the typical wagons were a mere thirty inches tall, topped with white canvas covers that were attached to metal braces. The front and backs could be opened or closed using drawstrings. There simply wasn't room for anyone inside of a wagon unless they were too old or too sick to walk. A mother would use a homemade sling to carry an infant on her back. Children were assigned to attend the livestock, find wood for nightly campfires, and fresh watering spots. An extra horse was tied to the back of each wagon so the father could ride out ahead to search for a suitable campsite each night. Sheep and cattle followed in herds along with the family dog who kept lookout for strays. The rooster and hens were in wooden cages that hung from the ceiling of the wagon to protect them from rain. The heavy wide-rimmed wheels kept the wagon from sinking into soft ground but caused many problems along muddy stream banks. The wagons were designed to carry 3,000 pounds, but experienced travelers advised strongly against trying to load that much weight. The bodies of dead horses and oxen along the edge of the trails attested to the value of that advice.

A typical journey could take one to two months of slow progress with oxen pulling heavy wagons and travelers walking. The distance from Virginia to Ohio was about four hundred miles; from New York, it was closer to five hundred miles. There must have been excitement and apprehension about going somewhere so far and unfamiliar.

Most pioneers found that their wagons were too heavy and unloaded unnecessary items along the trails. There were so many emigrants to Ohio that fresh water sources along the way became polluted, and many travelers died of cholera. Often, animals and people were loaded into barges to cross rivers; when animals panicked, they jumped into the fast-moving water and died, often along with the family member still holding the leash (usually a child). Sudden storms left deep ruts on the trails and caused broken wagon axles and abandoned wagons.

The average day on the trail began just before dawn, when the children gathered the animals, and mothers made breakfast of beans and rice. After cleaning up, the wagons moved out with a goal of fifteen miles a day. As the sun went down, the wagons formed a circle, and each family chose a section to start a fire and cook an evening meal. Then the women and older children typically helped the younger ones with reading and writing lessons while the men repaired the wagons by the light of lanterns.

When they finally arrived at the destination, the first thing to do was to register at the Land Office and get instructions on how to find or secure property. Then the family penned the livestock, secured the wagon, and looked for a hotel that offered a hot bath and, hopefully, a bed, even if many had to share.

Chapter 12:
The Blum or Bloom Family: German Refugees to Revolutionary War Heroes

Pedigree Chart for Sarah Bloom

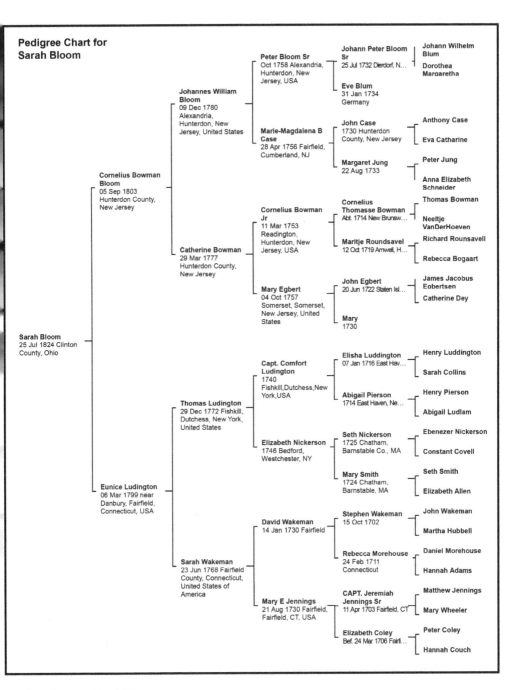

Sarah Bloom
25 Jul 1824 Clinton County, Ohio

Cornelius Bowman Bloom
05 Sep 1803 Hunterdon County, New Jersey

Eunice Ludington
06 Mar 1799 near Danbury, Fairfield, Connecticut, USA

Johannes William Bloom
09 Dec 1780 Alexandria, Hunterdon, New Jersey, United States

Catherine Bowman
29 Mar 1777 Hunterdon County, New Jersey

Thomas Ludington
29 Dec 1772 Fishkill, Dutchess, New York, United States

Sarah Wakeman
23 Jun 1768 Fairfield County, Connecticut, United States of America

Peter Bloom Sr
Oct 1758 Alexandria, Hunterdon, New Jersey, USA

Marie-Magdalena B Case
28 Apr 1756 Fairfield, Cumberland, NJ

Cornelius Bowman Jr
11 Mar 1753 Readington, Hunterdon, New Jersey, USA

Mary Egbert
04 Oct 1757 Somerset, Somerset, New Jersey, United States

Capt. Comfort Ludington
1740 Fishkill, Dutchess, New York, USA

Elizabeth Nickerson
1746 Bedford, Westchester, NY

David Wakeman
14 Jan 1730 Fairfield

Mary E Jennings
21 Aug 1730 Fairfield, Fairfield, CT, USA

Johann Peter Bloom Sr
25 Jul 1732 Dierdorf, N...

Eve Blum
31 Jan 1734 Germany

John Case
1730 Hunterdon County, New Jersey

Margaret Jung
22 Aug 1733

Cornelius Thomasse Bowman
Abt. 1714 New Brunsw...

Maritje Roundsavel
12 Oct 1719 Amwell, H...

John Egbert
20 Jun 1722 Staten Isl...

Mary
1730

Elisha Luddington
07 Jan 1716 East Hav...

Abigail Pierson
1714 East Haven, Ne...

Seth Nickerson
1725 Chatham, Barnstable Co., MA

Mary Smith
1724 Chatham, Barnstable, MA

Stephen Wakeman
15 Oct 1702

Rebecca Morehouse
24 Feb 1711 Connecticut

CAPT. Jeremiah Jennings Sr
11 Apr 1703 Fairfield, CT

Elizabeth Coley
Bef. 24 Mar 1706 Fairfi...

Johann Wilhelm Blum

Dorothea Margaretha

Anthony Case

Eva Catharine

Peter Jung

Anna Elizabeth Schneider

Thomas Bowman

Neeltje VanDerHoeven

Richard Rounsavell

Rebecca Bogaart

James Jacobus Egbertsen

Catherine Dey

Henry Luddington

Sarah Collins

Henry Pierson

Abigail Ludlam

Ebenezer Nickerson

Constant Covell

Seth Smith

Elizabeth Allen

John Wakeman

Martha Hubbell

Daniel Morehouse

Hannah Adams

Matthew Jennings

Mary Wheeler

Peter Coley

Hannah Couch

Genealogy 10: Sarah Bloom

Sarah Bloom (1824–1900)

Sarah Bloom was born in Clinton, Ohio. She was nineteen when she married Thomas McDonald, who had settled in the same town after moving with his parents and siblings from Virginia in 1826 (see Chapter 5). Thomas was thirty-five; he had been married once already but his first wife died two years before. Clinton was a small town then and both families were farmers. They probably were neighbors and likely attended the same church.

Thomas's family was Scottish, and Sarah's family was German in origin. Had the families not moved to Clinton, these two would never have formed a couple. In Pennsylvania (and nearby Virginia, Maryland, and New Jersey), German immigrants and Scottish immigrants did not mix. There were primarily German communities like Germantown, Pennsylvania, and Hunterdon County, New Jersey, where Sarah's family settled originally, and there were predominantly Scottish and Scotch-Irish communities like in Fauquier County, Virginia, where Thomas's family came from. Often, German and Scottish communities were located close to each other but had almost no interaction.

The Scots were typically independent and disliked rules and regulations. They often failed to register their land with local government authorities and typically were the first to encroach on Native lands. By contrast, the German immigrants typically followed the rules, were highly organized, and disciplined. Neither culture showed much respect for the other.

Johann Peter Bloom (1732–1814)

Johann Peter Blum arrived in Philadelphia from Germany on the ship *Two Brothers* in 1752. He traveled with his wife Eve, a son, and probably his father, who may have died in route. Two years later, the same ship capsized while transporting two to three hundred German Palatines, and they all drowned, underscoring the danger of the journey.

After arriving in Philadelphia on September 15, 1752, Johann Peter took the required oath of allegiance the same day. He then followed a path established by neighbors and possibly family before him to nearby Hunterdon County, New Jersey. Most immigrants from the Palatinate did not have the funds to pay for their passage and instead served two to five years indenture. It is likely but not certain that Johann Peter had to serve an indenture. At some point, he changed his German name Blum to a more American spelling, Bloom.

Johann Peter was married twice. His first wife, Eve, died in 1796 and was buried in Hunterdon County. Peter then married a woman named Sarah. He was an active member of the German Reformed Church and served as an elder. He died in 1814.

Peter Bloom Jr. (1758–1848)

Eve and Peter had many children — possibly fourteen — including Peter Bloom Jr., also known as Dr. Peter Bloom. Peter Jr. was born in 1758 in Hunterdon, New Jersey. He joined the Continental Army when he was nineteen years old and fought with the New Jersey Regiment in 1776 and again in 1777. During these times, there were many battles in New Jersey between George Washington's Continental Army and General Howe's British troops (see Chapter 31).

Peter married Marie-Magdalena Case in Alexandria Township, New Jersey, in 1780. They both attended the German Reformed Church in Hunterdon County and likely met at church. Their grandparents both immigrated from the Palatinate region of Germany and settled in the German community in Hunterdon County. I suspect the families were very close with so many shared stories and experiences.

Marie's parents were Johan (John) Kaes and Margaret Jung (after immigrating, the families Americanized their names to Case and Young). Both families descended from German Palatine immigrants, who were a substantial presence in Hunterdon Township; families owned farms nearby, worshiped together, and socialized. The family children often married within the group of descendants.

There are a few stories posted about the Kaes/Case family, and Johan Philip Kaes in particular:

> Johan Philip Kaes built a log cabin not far from the encampment of Chief Tuccamirgan with the help of Indian tribesmen. The childless chief and his wife grew fond of the Case children and had a gum log scooped out to use as a cradle. The chief's wife cared for the Case children as if they were her own. Upon the chief's death in 1750, he was buried in the Case family graveyard. His funeral took place at sunset when he was buried facing east in an upright position with blankets, pipes, knives, etc. — such things as he might need in the afterlife. His resting place is marked today by a stone monument.[89]

Johannes Wilhelm (John William) Bloom (1780–1851)

Peter Jr. and Marie-Magdalena had a son in 1780 named Johannes Wilhelm (or John William) Bloom. John William married Catherine Bowman in 1781 in their hometown in Hunterdon County. They had several children. Although their American experience and ancestry took place in the tight-knit German community in New Jersey, land was becoming less available and expensive. In 1771, for example, John Peter Bloom sold land for $75 an acre, whereas land in Ohio which selling for $1 to $2 per acre.

Sometime between 1815 and 1820, John William decided to move his family to Ohio for the same reasons Jared McDonald Jr. moved his a few years later from Virginia. John and his wife and several (probably six) children packed their possessions in a wagon and joined other family and friends in a wagon train west to Ohio. Around the same time, members of the Case family and Jung families moved also. The trip would have been a bit longer than from Virginia but the path would have been similar. The National Road would have been under construction and not yet completed to Wheeling on the Ohio River, making travel difficult. They likely spent a couple of months in route to Ohio.

John and Catherine Bloom choose to move to Clinton, Ohio; other relatives selected other nearby Ohio counties. By 1825 the German Blooms and the Scottish McDonalds found themselves neighbors in faraway Clinton, Ohio.

Chapter 13:

The Egbert and Molenear Families: Dutch Immigrants in New Amsterdam

Pedigree Chart for
Mary Egbert

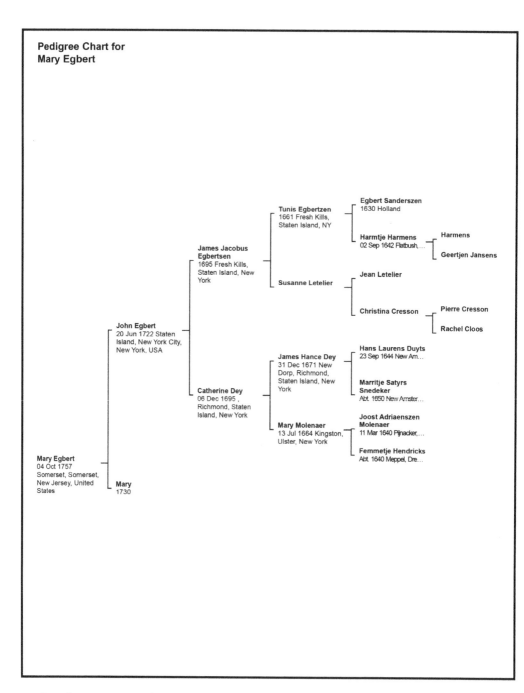

Mary Egbert
04 Oct 1757
Somerset, Somerset,
New Jersey, United
States

John Egbert
20 Jun 1722 Staten
Island, New York City,
New York, USA

Mary
1730

James Jacobus Egbertsen
1695 Fresh Kills,
Staten Island, New
York

Catherine Dey
06 Dec 1695 ,
Richmond, Staten
Island, New York

Tunis Egbertzen
1661 Fresh Kills,
Staten Island, NY

Susanne Letelier

James Hance Dey
31 Dec 1671 New
Dorp, Richmond,
Staten Island, New
York

Mary Molenaer
13 Jul 1664 Kingston,
Ulster, New York

Egbert Sanderszen
1630 Holland

Harmtje Harmens
02 Sep 1642 Flatbush,...

Jean Letelier

Christina Cresson

Hans Laurens Duyts
23 Sep 1644 New Am...

Marritje Satyrs Snedeker
Abt. 1650 New Amster...

Joost Adriaenszen Molenaer
11 Mar 1640 Pijnacker,...

Femmetje Hendricks
Abt. 1640 Meppel, Dre...

Harmens

Geertjen Jansens

Pierre Cresson

Rachel Cloos

Genealogy 11: Mary Egbert

The Dutch ancestors settled into what later became New York. The Egberts and Molenears moved to Staten Island after arrival in the mid 1600s before the British takeover. The ancestry is a bit hard to follow because of Dutch naming conventions. Instead of taking the last name of the father, the Dutch took the father's first name and added a suffix. So the first Egbert immigrant was named Egbert Sanderzen. His father's first name would have been Sander or Sanders and all of Egbert's brothers would have the last name Sanderszen: "sons of Sanders." Egbert Sanderzen's son Tunis became Tunis Egbertszen. The Dutch naming convention was so confusing to the English that they banned the practice after taking control of New Amsterdam in 1644. Tunis's son, James, born in 1695, would have become James Tunison but was given the family name of "Egbertsen" following the English convention of passing down the father's name.

The Egbert Family

Egbert Sanderzen immigrated to New Amsterdam by 1643, according to records in the local Dutch Reformed Church. He married Harmtje Harmens, whose parents had also immigrated from the Netherlands. They lived on Long Island and had three children including a son named Tunis.

Tunis married Susanne Letelier, whose father, Jan Letelier was a Huguenot who had immigrated from Normandy, France (see Chapter 1). They had eight children including James Egbertsen. They apparently lived first in Long Island and then Staten Island, where their children were born. Tunis served a number of public roles including as constable and supervisor.

James Egbertsen married Catherine Dey, whose grandparents had also immigrated from the Netherlands. Their son John was the father of Mary Egbert, who in turn was the mother of Catherine Bowman; Catherine married Johannes Bloom, and they moved to Clinton, Ohio, by 1820. Catherine and Johannes's daughter was Sarah Bloom, who married Thomas McDonald (see Bloom family chart).

The Molenaer Family

Mary Molenaer (Catherine Dey's mother)'s father, Joost Adriaenszen Molenaer, arrived in New Amsterdam from Holland on December 23, 1660, on the ship, *Trouw* ("Faith" in Dutch). He was listed as "Joost Adriaenszen Pynacker from Delft." He quickly moved to Esopus, New York, where he became a member of the militia in 1662 and was captain from 1678 to 1683.

He married Femmetje Hendricks (also born in the Netherlands) on May 4, 1663, at New Amsterdam Dutch Church. On June 7, 1663, a month after their marriage, the Esopus tribe launched a surprise attack on the Dutch settlement, killing most of the male defenders and capturing many children and women (including Femmetje) who had taken refuge in the stockade. It must have been terrifying for the women to be taken by hostile warriors into the wilderness. On the day of the attack, many of the militia were detailed to duty elsewhere, likely including Joost Molenaer, who otherwise may not have survived the attack. The incident is referred to as the "Esopus massacre." [90]

The Dutch forces, including a large contingent from New Amsterdam, searched for the captives and ultimately found and liberated them. A punitive campaign against all the Natives in the region followed.

Joost and Femmetje had one child, Marritje (or Mary), who was born in 1664. Femmetje died three years later in 1667. Marritje married James Hance Dey, and their daughter Catherine married James Egbertson, joining the Molenaer and Egbert family lines.

Jared McDonald Jr. and Sarah Bloom's children were the products of Scottish, Irish, English, German, Dutch, and French immigrants who came to America in the 1600s in search of a better life.

Figure 11: Pilgrims cutting forests and building houses at Plymouth Colony

Chapter 14:
New England

The Pilgrims on the *Mayflower* arrived at Cape Cod on November 11, 1620. The ship was originally intended to land in northern Virginia but had been blown off course. The passengers were forced to stay on board for thirty-nine days while leaders searched for a suitable settlement site along the shores of Cape Cod Bay. Each possible site had drawbacks: water too shallow to anchor the *Mayflower* and other arriving ships; no fresh water; and perceived vulnerability to Native attacks. Finally, the future site of Plymouth Plantation was selected: an area near the Plymouth Rock with a 165-foot hill offering spectacular views of the coastline, plus a freshwater brook and a channel to harbor boats. The best advantage of this location was that the land had already been cleared. Little did the exploring Pilgrims realize that the vacant land had been the home for about two thousand members of the Patuxet tribe until the years from 1616 to 1619. A disease much like Europe's Black Death had swept through the villages and reduced the population to less than five hundred. Survivors were believed to have scattered and blended in with other tribes of the Wampanoag. The 1605 map of this land drawn by the explorer Samuel de Champlain showed the banks of the harbor dotted with wigwams and fields of squash, beans and corn. Yet, the Pilgrims found only scattered bones whitened by the weather. With no explanation for the vacant land but a theory the land was cleared by Divine intervention, the English settlers decided to build their settlement here at Plymouth Rock and begin a new life.

In the spring of 1621, there were only fifty Pilgrims alive of the original 102 passengers on the *Mayflower*; the others had all died in a long and unforgiving winter. The Plymouth Colony inhabitants were not like many of the "gentlemen" original settlers of Jamestown: these were hardworking, determined settlers, not afraid of joining together to build the seventeen houses they needed. Single men moved in with families to save on labor and space. As the men kept building, the women tilled the fields, gathered winter berries, did the laundry, and cooked the meals. The children helped out by milking the goats, gathering herbs, and collecting eggs each morning. Often a child was tasked with the tedious chore of grinding corn (this was seed corn stolen from Patuxet caches buried in the dunes along the shoreline). Indian seed corn is colorful and pretty to look at, but the kernels are hard as rocks and can take hours to grind.

The arrival of the ship *Fortune* in 1621 with over one hundred new settlers meant that at least there were now more people who could take care of the sick and dying, but it also meant more mouths to feed. Life in early Plymouth Colony was difficult.

The Plymouth Colony settlers were not the first English to attempt a settlement in New England, as is commonly thought. In 1602, Bartholomew Gosnold visited the region and built a small fort on one of the Elizabeth Islands (Cuttyhunk) at the southwestern corner of the Cape. However, Gosnold decided not to try to establish a permanent settlement after an encounter with unfriendly Natives and instead sailed back to England. Later, Gosnold and his brother, Anthony, returned to America at Jamestown; and both died there.

William Ring's widow, Mary, and her three young children, Elizabeth, Andrew, and Susan, who had disembarked the *Speedwell* after its abortive trip but declined to set sail on the *Mayflower*, waited in Leiden for nine more years, and finally arrived in Plymouth Colony in 1629. In 1630, Elizabeth met and married Stephen Deane, who had arrived on the *Fortune* in 1621.

Elizabeth and Stephen had three children. Stephen was an original investor or "purchaser" in the group that financed the settlement and was entitled to certain privileges. In 1632, he was given exclusive rights to build a grist mill and supply the colony's needs. Unfortunately, Stephen died in 1634 at the age of twenty-nine. Elizabeth later married Josias Cooke and had three more children.

Stephen and Elizabeth Deane's daughter Susanna married Stephen Snow, son of Nicholas Snow, who had arrived in 1623, and his wife, Constance Hopkins, whose father Stephen Hopkins (see Chapter 15) arrived on the *Mayflower*. Stephen Snow and Susanna Deane's daughter Bethiah married John Smith (see Chapter 22).

Over time, more ancestors immigrated to New England. They generally came from England in search of religious freedom, flight from reprisals arising from the English Civil War, and economic opportunity. They usually chose to settle in Massachusetts and Connecticut, or occasionally adjacent parts of New York. They were merchants, farmers, preachers, landowners, fishermen, and craftsmen and often became successful businessmen, landowners and prominent members of the community serving in public roles including the militia. Some of the ancestors who immigrated to New England and their arrival dates include: Stephen Hopkins (1620), William Palmer (1621), Edward Bangs (1623), Alan Breed (1630), Christopher Avery (1630), John Wakeman (1630), William Denison (1631), Edward Payson (1633), Ralph Smyth (1633), Anne Hutchinson (1634), William O'Dell (1635), William Nickerson (1637), Henry Adams (1638), John Mayo (1638), William Ludington (1639), John Meigs (1639), and Nathaniel Covell (1653).

Chapter 15:
Stephen Hopkins:
The Only Person Who Was Both at Jamestown and on the *Mayflower*

The first European settlements in America were in Virginia. The first attempt to establish a permanent colony was in the area now called Roanoke Island (see Chapter 27). Sir Walter Raleigh tried to establish a colony there in 1584 and again in 1587. Neither attempt was successful. The colony at Jamestown, Virginia, was started in 1607 by the Virginia Company and attracted Englishmen seeking fortunes in the New World.

Whereas immigrants to the Virginia colony were typically motivated by potential financial gain, early settlers in New England were mostly motivated by religion, with the Puritans arriving in Plymouth on the *Mayflower* in 1620. One ancestor, Stephen Hopkins, was likely the only person to be both at Jamestown and on the *Mayflower* when it arrived in New England.

Stephen Hopkins was born and baptized in April of 1581 in the village of Upper Clatford in England. His parents were John Hopkins, a tenant farmer, and Elizabeth Williams. John was also an archer in the local militia. It is quite likely John gave his two sons including Stephen lessons in archery and fighting from an early age. John died suddenly in 1593; he was not a wealthy man and left very little inheritance. As was the custom for parents with children they could not support, Elizabeth most likely apprenticed out twelve-year-old Stephen.

When Stephen was about twenty years old, he married a woman named Mary (maybe Mary Machell but this is not confirmed). They had three children, but a few months after their baby, Giles, was born, they were forced to vacate the house they were staying in. Without owning land or having many assets or much income, Stephen found a job as minister's clerk for a group of investors and colonists heading for the new colony of Jamestown in Virginia.

Stephen boarded the *Sea Venture*, in Plymouth, England, on June 2, 1609. His wife and children stayed behind; how they managed to survive is not known.

The ship experienced terrible storms and nearly sank at sea (see Chapter 2). The crew managed to drive the *Sea Venture* aground in Bermuda just before the ship would have disappeared beneath the waves.

While shipwrecked in Bermuda, young Stephen questioned some of the decisions made by leadership as well as the authority of Thomas Gates, the incoming governor of Jamestown who was also aboard the *Sea Venture*. This was considered an act of treason, and Stephen was chained, brought before a court convened for this matter, found guilty, and sentenced to hang. He pleaded for his life and was pardoned. Having learned his lesson, he remained quiet for the rest of his time with the ship. About six weeks later, another crew member, Henry Paine, was charged with similar conduct and was hanged.

After living in Bermuda for ten months, the crew and passengers managed to construct two smaller ships and depart for Jamestown, arriving in May 1610. Jamestown was in terrible condition, with residents suffering and dying from starvation, disease, and Native attacks. On June 7, 1610, everyone in Jamestown boarded the two ships from Bermuda to evacuate back to England but returned to Jamestown when a supply ship arrived with provisions and new settlers.

In 1613, Stephen's wife Mary died back in England, effectively leaving their children as orphans. Stephen was able to depart Jamestown in 1614 to return to his family. On board his ship was John Rolfe, who had been on the *Sea Venture* with Stephen, and Rolfe's new wife, Pocahontas.

After returning to England, Stephen married a woman named Elizabeth, and they had a child, Damaris. As Stephen was settling into his new life in England, a group of religious separatists that had fled from England to Leiden, Holland, decided to move to Virginia and establish a home where they could maintain their religious purity without interference. They needed money and laborers, however, so they formed an investment company with wealthy English investors and offered shares of stock and free land to anyone who agreed to accompany them and work. Participants evidently felt the shares would be worth a fortune someday. It apparently did not take Stephen long to sign up and bring his wife and three children, including his two surviving children from his first marriage, for which he was given additional shares. They sailed aboard the *Mayflower*, which left England in August of 1620 but experienced many delays and returns before finally embarking in September, just before the winter storm season.

As described in the second chapter, it was a miserable voyage. The ship was overcrowded and under-provisioned. The weather quickly turned bad with fierce storms and big waves. Stephen's wife, Elizabeth, was pregnant and gave birth to a daughter, Oceanus, while in route. After two months at sea, the ship reached Cape Cod, instead of the intended destination of northern Virginia. They finally disembarked at Plymouth. Wintertime in what is now Massachusetts was a challenge and several who survived the passage died after reaching Plymouth, including Stephen's and Elizabeth's new baby and their daughter, Damaris.

Stephen was a leader in the new settlement, probably because of his prior experience in Jamestown. Eventually the settlers met two Native Americans who spoke English — an Abenaki named Samoset and the last surviving Patuxet, Tisquantum (or Squanto). Stephen Hopkins and these native guides were essential for establishing relationships with local tribes, including the Wampanoag, with whom the colonists celebrated a "Thanksgiving" feast in 1621, which is now viewed as America's first Thanksgiving.

Later that year, the ship, *Fortune*, brought more settlers, including Stephen Hopkins's boyhood friend William Palmer and his son. The Palmers moved into the Hopkins's house. In 1623, the ship *Anne* brought more settlers to the colony, mostly women, but also some men including Nicholas Snow, who came from the same town as Stephen and Elizabeth. Snow also moved into the Hopkins's house and later married their daughter Constance. Nicholas and Constance and their son Stephen were ancestors to Sarah Bloom through the Ludington line; Eunice Ludington was Sarah Bloom's mother.

As the colony grew, Stephen was elected and re-elected to the governing body called the Governor's Council. He served several years. However, in 1636 he was found guilty of beating up a younger man, John Tisdale. Details about the fight are not known, but Stephen was never elected again and ceased public service. He died in 1644 at the age of sixty-three having participated in much of early American history.

Chapter 16:
Anne Hutchinson and the Hutchinson Massacre

Anne Marbury was born in Alford, Lincolnshire England in 1591. She was the daughter of the Reverend Francis Marbury and Bridget Dryden. Reverend Marbury was a passionate Anglican minister with Puritan instincts who often challenged traditional Anglican doctrine. Before Anne was born, he was imprisoned for heresy for two years. Later he achieved favorable notoriety and advancement, and his views were softened a bit and thus tolerated by the Church.

He believed in a woman's education, and Anne received a better education than most girls at the time. She also learned scripture and Christian principles.

When she was twenty-one, she married William Hutchinson, a merchant in London. They were both passionate about their religious beliefs and began following a nearby minister, John Cotton, who believed man's salvation was tied to direct revelation with God. The Anglican archbishop did not approve of Cotton's teachings, and soon Cotton went into hiding and then emigrated to America. After the birth of their fourteenth child, the Hutchinsons followed Cotton to New England.

In New England, William Hutchinson became a very successful cloth merchant and bought and sold property. Anne became a midwife and offered women spiritual advice including hosting a weekly religious home study group for women. She expressed her belief in spiritual revelation, a conviction that stood in contrast to normal Puritan doctrine. Soon, men joined her classes, and they were well-attended, to the dismay of Puritan church leaders in Massachusetts.

In late 1636 and 1637, she was accused of heresy and related charges and found guilty. She was banished from the colony and expelled from her congregation. She and her family fled to the new settlement of Providence in the colony of Rhode Island, where there was more religious freedom than allowed in Puritan Massachusetts. About a year later, her husband was selected as the magistrate responsible for local government. Her husband died in 1641 at the age of fifty-five.

The Massachusetts Bay Colony (i.e., the Puritans who chased Hutchison out) threatened to take over Rhode Island; and Anne then moved the family to New Netherland, which was under the jurisdiction of the Dutch and safely distant from Massachusetts. She moved seven of her children including her daughter Anne, Anne's husband, William Collins, and several servants. Her daughter Anne and William Collins had a new baby (also named William) whom they left with Collins' parents in Connecticut until the move was settled.

Anne Hutchinson hired Captain James Sands to build her family a house; but the local Siwanoy tribe was displeased with the incursion into their lands. About the same time, the Dutch, led by Governor Willem Kieft, initiated attacks on Natives, including a particularly brutal attack on a neighboring village where eighty people, mostly women and children, were killed. The Siwanoy response was to attack white settlers including the Hutchinson-Collins homestead. According to one account of what became known as the "Hutchinson Massacre":

> *The Siwanoy warriors stampeded into the tiny settlement above Pelham Bay, prepared to burn down every house. The Siwanoy chief, Wampage, who had sent a warning, expected to find no settlers present. But at one house the men in animal skins encountered several children, young men and women, and a woman past middle age. One Siwanoy indicated the Hutchinsons should restrain the family's dogs. Without apparent fear, one of the family tied up the dogs. As quickly as possible the Siwanoy seized and scalped Francis Hutchinson, William Collins, several servants, the two Annes (mother and daughter), and the younger children.[91]*

During the attack, Hutchinson's nine-year-old daughter, Susanna [was found nearby]. She is believed to have had red hair, unusual to the attackers. She was taken captive and lived with the Native Americans for two to six years (accounts vary) until ransomed back to family members in Boston.

The Hutchinson-Collins family had lived in peace with Natives in their past and did not fear them. But they were unaware of the recent Dutch actions and the resulting anger held by the local tribe.

The baby (William) left with William Collins' parents was raised in Connecticut by his grandparents and later married Sarah Morrell. One of their children, Sarah, married Henry Ludington, whose descendants included Sarah Bloom.

Chapter 17:

The Ludington Family:
New England Pioneers and Leaders

Pedigree Chart for
Eunice Ludington

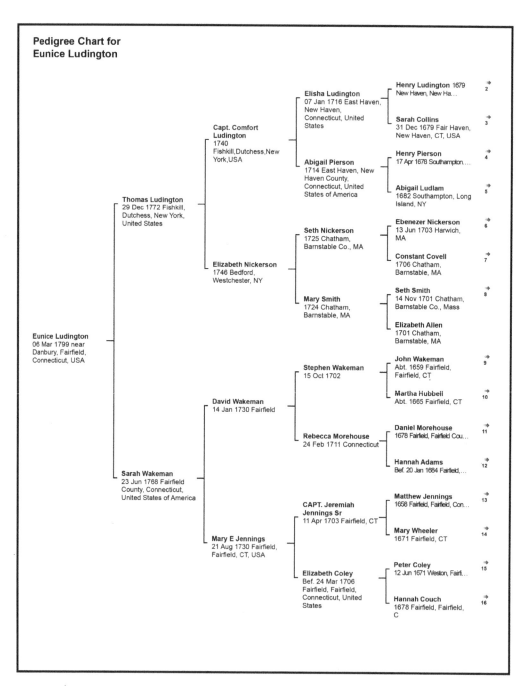

Eunice Ludington
06 Mar 1799 near
Danbury, Fairfield,
Connecticut, USA

Thomas Ludington
29 Dec 1772 Fishkill,
Dutchess, New York,
United States

Capt. Comfort Ludington
1740
Fishkill,Dutchess,New
York,USA

Elisha Ludington
07 Jan 1716 East Haven,
New Haven,
Connecticut, United
States

Henry Ludington 1679
New Haven, New Ha... → 2

Sarah Collins
31 Dec 1679 Fair Haven,
New Haven, CT, USA → 3

Abigail Pierson
1714 East Haven, New
Haven County,
Connecticut, United
States of America

Henry Pierson
17 Apr 1678 Southampton.... → 4

Abigail Ludlam
1682 Southampton, Long
Island, NY → 5

Elizabeth Nickerson
1746 Bedford,
Westchester, NY

Seth Nickerson
1725 Chatham,
Barnstable Co., MA

Ebenezer Nickerson
13 Jun 1703 Harwich,
MA → 6

Constant Covell
1706 Chatham,
Barnstable, MA → 7

Mary Smith
1724 Chatham,
Barnstable, MA

Seth Smith
14 Nov 1701 Chatham,
Barnstable Co., Mass → 8

Elizabeth Allen
1701 Chatham,
Barnstable, MA

Sarah Wakeman
23 Jun 1768 Fairfield
County, Connecticut,
United States of America

David Wakeman
14 Jan 1730 Fairfield

Stephen Wakeman
15 Oct 1702

John Wakeman
Abt. 1659 Fairfield,
Fairfield, CT → 9

Martha Hubbell
Abt. 1665 Fairfield, CT → 10

Rebecca Morehouse
24 Feb 1711 Connecticut

Daniel Morehouse
1678 Fairfield, Fairfield Cou... → 11

Hannah Adams
Bef. 20 Jan 1684 Fairfield,... → 12

Mary E Jennings
21 Aug 1730 Fairfield,
Fairfield, CT, USA

CAPT. Jeremiah Jennings Sr
11 Apr 1703 Fairfield, CT

Matthew Jennings
1658 Fairfield, Fairfield, Con... → 13

Mary Wheeler
1671 Fairfield, CT → 14

Elizabeth Coley
Bef. 24 Mar 1706
Fairfield, Fairfield,
Connecticut, United
States

Peter Coley
12 Jun 1671 Weston, Fairfi... → 15

Hannah Couch
1678 Fairfield, Fairfield,
C → 16

Genealogy 12: Eunice Ludington

Pedigree Chart for
Henry Ludington

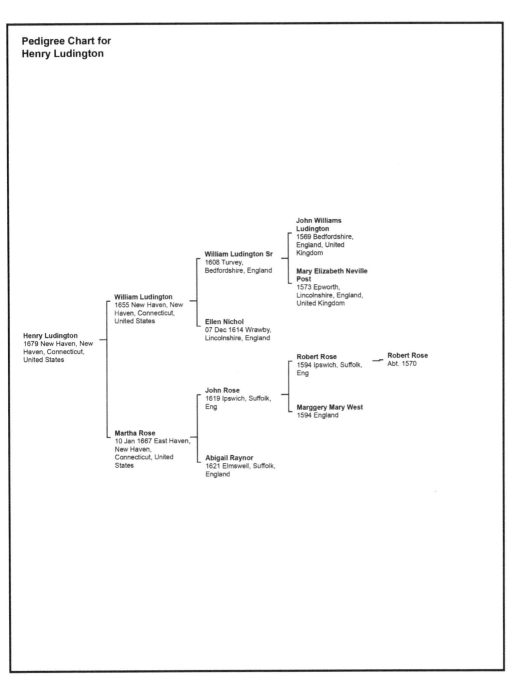

Henry Ludington
1679 New Haven, New
Haven, Connecticut,
United States

William Ludington
1655 New Haven, New
Haven, Connecticut,
United States

Martha Rose
10 Jan 1667 East Haven,
New Haven,
Connecticut, United
States

William Ludington Sr
1608 Turvey,
Bedfordshire, England

Ellen Nichol
07 Dec 1614 Wrawby,
Lincolnshire, England

John Rose
1619 Ipswich, Suffolk,
Eng

Abigail Raynor
1621 Elmswell, Suffolk,
England

**John Williams
Ludington**
1569 Bedfordshire,
England, United
Kingdom

**Mary Elizabeth Neville
Post**
1573 Epworth,
Lincolnshire, England,
United Kingdom

Robert Rose
1594 Ipswich, Suffolk,
Eng

Marggery Mary West
1594 England

Robert Rose
Abt. 1570

Genealogy 13: Henry Ludington

The Ludington family has a long history in England. One story, often quoted, says a Ludington was a follower of Richard the Lionheart in the Third Crusade and helped him escape prison. In return, the soldier was given nobility status and a family coat of arms. While often quoted, the story has never been proven.

The Ludington family was prominent in colonial America, with interests in commerce, banking, government, and as soldiers in the Revolutionary War. Family members were founding members of several American cities: Henry Ludington founded Kent, New York, in 1775; Lewis Ludington founded Columbus, Wisconsin, in 1844; James Ludington founded Ludington, Michigan, in 1859; and Nelson Ludington founded Escanaba, Michigan, in 1862. Harrison Ludington was active in the early development of Milwaukee and served as governor of Wisconsin.

William Ludington Sr. (1607–1661)

William Ludington (Sr.) and his wife Ellen Nichol, whom he married in 1635, immigrated together in the late 1630s — probably 1639— and were the first Ludingtons in America. The reason William and Ellen emigrated is not known for certain, but there was considerable emigration from England to New England during the period. Generally, the immigrants were seeking freedom to practice their religion instead of being forced to follow the dictates of the Anglican church.

William and Ellen emigrated from London to the Massachusetts Colony and settled initially in Charlestown, which years later became part of Boston. The Massachusetts Bay Company, which controlled Massachusetts, had strict boundaries on where one could build a house. They wanted to ensure a compact community to protect more easily against Native American attacks, make churches easier to get to, and minimize public expenditures. It was the antithesis of the sprawling Virginia colony. The company also limited the size of land grants given to new residents for the same reasons.

The first public record of William Ludington Sr. is a court record imposing a heavy fine for building his house outside the designated town boundary. Soon thereafter, however, the town permitted houses where Ludington had built, and the fine was rescinded. His good stature and reputation in the town likely helped him win expansion of the permitted building area and return of his fine, but he was a man who clearly pushed against limits and boundaries.

The family lived in Charlestown for twenty years where William Sr. was a weaver, a landowner, and a prominent citizen. He and Ellen had seven children including their son William.

In 1660, William Sr. and the family moved to New Haven, Connecticut, and settled in East Haven. New Haven had been established in 1638, around the time the Ludingtons first arrived in the more established Charlestown. New Haven and Connecticut were very similar to Massachusetts and very much a Puritan culture, but there were some differences. The New Haven residents appear to have worked to form a good relationship with the local Native tribes and paid them for any land to be settled. Unlike Massachusetts, New Haven did not require church membership for males to vote.

The New Haven colony eventually merged with the Connecticut colony but before then received a formal charter from King Charles II in 1662. In 1687, Sir Edmund Andros, the king's appointed governor for the Dominion of New England, led a company of British soldiers to New Haven and demanded the charter document be turned over to end the independence afforded by the New Haven Charter. As the story is told,[92] the two sides argued until dark, when candles were lit and the argument continued over the charter, which was displayed on a central table. Without warning, all the candles lost flame at the same time. When they were relit, the charter had disappeared. The colonists claimed no knowledge of what happened, but a furious Governor Andros returned to Boston empty handed. Two years later, Andros returned to England, and the charter reappeared and was returned to a visible location in the colony.

In East Haven, William Ludington became interested in the iron works, which was established in 1655 and was Connecticut's first iron works. William apparently established the first iron smelting plant in Connecticut, which was connected to the existing iron works. William died in 1661. At the time of his death, he owned considerable properties in the area.

William Ludington Jr. (1655–1737)

William Jr. was the sixth child of William and Ellen Ludington. He lived his entire life in New Haven and by all accounts was a successful businessman and community leader. According to the *New Haven Register,* "he was a man of means, intelligence, of ability, and of important standing in the community."[93]

He married Martha Rose, who was also from New Haven. They had three children including Henry. Martha died in 1690. William then married Mercy Whitehead in 1691 and had seven children with her.

Sybil Ludington's Not as Famous Ride

William's brother Henry had a daughter, Sybil Ludington, who became quite well known. In 1777, at the age of 16, she rode her horse for forty miles at night to summon the patriots to fight the British, who had attacked and were burning Danbury. She warned the militiamen — about four hundred — who were under the command of her father, that the British had attacked and were still coming. Her trip was similar to Paul Revere's ride from Boston, and she was formally recognized by George Washington; she was also the subject of a number of poems and books including the following 1940 poem by Berton Braley. There is a statue of her displayed at the Danbury library grounds and a statue in Washington DC. In 1975, the U.S. Post Office issued a commemorative stamp depicting her ride.

Sybil Ludington's Ride
By Berton Braley

Listen, my children, and you shall hear
Of a lovely feminine Paul Revere
Who rode an equally famous ride
Through a different part of the countryside,
Where Sybil Ludington's name recalls
A ride as daring as that of Paul's.

In April, Seventeen Seventy-Seven,
A smoky glow in the eastern heaven
(A fiery herald of war and slaughter)
Came to the eyes of the Colonel's daughter.
"Danbury's burning," she cried aloud.
The Colonel answered, "'Tis but a cloud,
A cloud reflecting the campfires' red,
So hush you, Sybil, and go to bed."

"I hear the sound of the cannon drumming"
"'Tis only the wind in the treetops humming!
So go to bed, as a young lass ought,
And give the matter no further thought."
Young Sybil sighed as she turned to go,
"Still, Danbury's burning — that I know."

Sound of a horseman riding hard
Clatter of hoofs in the manor yard
Feet on the steps and a knock resounding
As a fist struck wood with a mighty pounding.
The doors flung open, a voice is heard,
"Danbury's burning — I rode with word;
Fully half of the town is gone
And the British — the British are coming on.

Send a messenger, get our men!"
His message finished the horseman then
Staggered wearily to a chair
And fell exhausted in slumber there.

The Colonel muttered, "And who, my friend,
Is the messenger I can send?
Your strength is spent and you cannot ride
And, then, you know not the countryside;
I cannot go for my duty's clear;
When my men come in they must find me here;
There's devil a man on the place tonight
To warn my troopers to come--and fight.
Then, who is my messenger to be?"
Said Sybil Ludington, "You have me."

"You!" said the Colonel, and grimly smiled,
"You!" My daughter, you're just a child!"
"Child!" cried Sybil. "Why I'm sixteen!
My mind's alert and my senses keen,
I know where the trails and the roadways are
And I can gallop as fast and as far
As any masculine rider can.
You want a messenger? I'm your man!"

The Colonel's heart was aglow with pride.
"Spoke like a soldier. Ride, girl, ride
Ride like the devil; ride like sin;
Summon my slumbering troopers in.
I know when duty is to be done
That I can depend on a Ludington!"

So over the trails to the towns and farms
Sybil delivered the call to arms.
Riding swiftly without a stop
Except to rap with a riding crop
On the soldiers' doors, with a sharp tattoo
And a high-pitched feminine halloo.
"Up! up there, soldier. You're needed, come!
The British are marching!" and the drum
Of her horse's feet as she rode apace
To bring more men to the meeting place.

Sybil grew weary and faint and drowsing,
Her limbs were aching, but still she rode
Until she finished her task of rousing
Each sleeping soldier from his abode,
Showing her father, by work well done,
That he could depend on a Ludington.

Dawn in the skies with its tints of pearl
And the lass who rode in a soldier's stead
Turned home, only a tired girl
Thinking of breakfast and then of bed
With never a dream that her ride would be
A glorious legend of history;
Nor that posterity's hand would mark
Each trail she rode through the inky dark,
Each path to figure in song and story
As a splendid, glamorous path of glory —
To prove, as long as the ages run,
That "you can depend on a Ludington."

Such is the legend of Sybil's ride
To summon the men from the countryside
A true tale, making her title clear
As a lovely feminine Paul Revere!

Henry Ludington (1679–1727)

William and Martha's son Henry was born in New Haven in 1679 and lived his entire life there. Henry's profession was a carpenter. He married Sarah Collins, who was the granddaughter of Anne Hutchinson and William Collins, who both died in the "Hutchinson Massacre" in 1643. Her father was the baby that was raised by his grandparents in Connecticut after his parents were killed in the Siwanoy attack. Henry Ludington and Sarah Collins married in 1700 and had twelve children.

Elisha Ludington (1716–1793)

Henry's and Sarah's son Elisha was born on January 7 in East Haven, Connecticut, but the year is in dispute (1712 to 1716). He served with the Continental Army in the Revolutionary War in the New York Fifth Regiment (see Chapter 31).

After Elisha's marriage in 1738 in East Hampton, Connecticut, to Abigail Pearson, also from East Haven, they moved to Fishkill area of New York, about seventy miles to the west. The Fishkill area was originally part of the Dutch settlement; but from about 1730 it was settled mostly by New Englanders looking for more affordable land. The name "Fishkill" came from Dutch "vis kil" meaning "fish" and "stream or creek" Many years later, some residents proposed changing the name because of the connotation of dead fish, but the majority voted to keep the historical name.

Captain Comfort Ludington (1740–1805)

Elisha and Abigail's son Comfort Ludington was a farmer in Duchess County. At the age of nineteen, in 1760, he enlisted in the Duchess County militia. In February 1776, he was given command as captain of in a regiment of minutemen, to protect Duchess County and fight any British incursion.

Fishkill never saw any major battles but, as in most communities, the citizens were curious and anxious for news. According to an oft-quoted story, on one occasion when George Washington was the guest of a Dutchman named John Brinckerhoff, the host was trying earnestly to quiz the general on movements and operations of the Army. Growing weary of the questions, Washington interrupted the host with a question of his own. "Sir, can you keep a secret?" he asked. Brinckerhoff, hoping to hear an important revelation, replied, "Oh, yes, certainly." "So can I," said the General.[94] That was the end of the conversation.

Comfort married Elizabeth Nickerson in 1767. Elizabeth's parents were Seth Nickerson and Mary Smith. Comfort and Elizabeth had eleven children including Thomas.

Thomas Ludington (1772–1842)

Thomas was the fourth child of Comfort and Elizabeth and was born in Fishkill, Duchess County New York. He married Sarah Wakeman who lived in Fairfield, Connecticut.

Thomas and Sarah initially lived in Fishkill but at some point decided better opportunities awaited them in Ohio, presumably for the same reasons the McDonalds and the Blooms moved. By 1823, Thomas and Sarah packed up the family and took a covered wagon to Clinton, Ohio. The journey probably took two months and was very arduous. They travelled with nine children aged about twelve to twenty. The children would have been very helpful on the journey and clearing and planting the land in Clinton after their arrival. They also almost certainly travelled with friends and family as part of a wagon train.

The property Thomas bought in Clinton was adjacent to property owned by William Bloom, and both the Ludingtons and Blooms were Quakers. It is not surprising that Thomas's daughter married William Bloom's grandson Cornelius. And Cornelius and Sarah's daughter, also named Sarah, subsequently married Thomas McDonald.

Chapter 18:
The Wakeman Family: From England to New England

Pedigree Chart for Sarah Wakeman

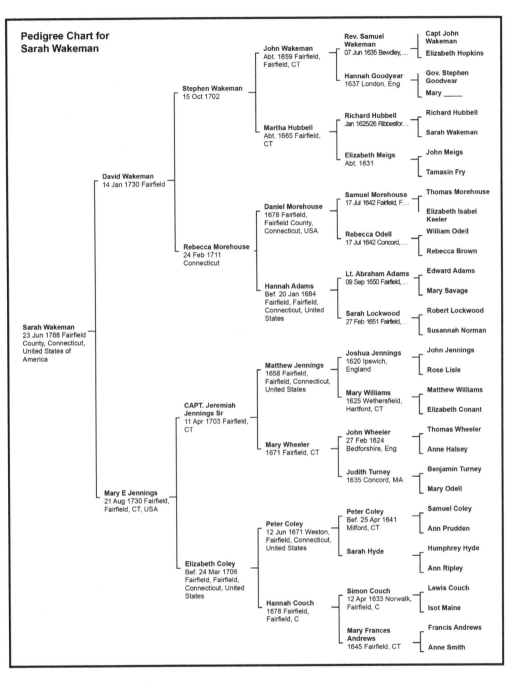

Sarah Wakeman
23 Jun 1768 Fairfield
County, Connecticut,
United States of
America

David Wakeman
14 Jan 1730 Fairfield

Stephen Wakeman
15 Oct 1702

John Wakeman
Abt. 1659 Fairfield,
Fairfield, CT

**Rev. Samuel
Wakeman**
07 Jun 1635 Bewdley,...

Capt John
Wakeman

Elizabeth Hopkins

Hannah Goodyear
1637 London, Eng

Gov. Stephen
Goodyear

Mary _____

Martha Hubbell
Abt. 1665 Fairfield,
CT

Richard Hubbell
Jan 1625/26 Ribbesfor...

Richard Hubbell

Sarah Wakeman

Elizabeth Meigs
Abt. 1631

John Meigs

Tamasin Fry

Rebecca Morehouse
24 Feb 1711
Connecticut

Daniel Morehouse
1678 Fairfield,
Fairfield County,
Connecticut, USA

Samuel Morehouse
17 Jul 1642 Fairfield, F...

Thomas Morehouse

Elizabeth Isabel
Keeler

Rebecca Odell
17 Jul 1642 Concord,...

William Odell

Rebecca Brown

Hannah Adams
Bef. 20 Jan 1684
Fairfield, Fairfield,
Connecticut, United
States

Lt. Abraham Adams
09 Sep 1650 Fairfield,...

Edward Adams

Mary Savage

Sarah Lockwood
27 Feb 1651 Fairfield,...

Robert Lockwood

Susannah Norman

Mary E Jennings
21 Aug 1730 Fairfield,
Fairfield, CT, USA

**CAPT. Jeremiah
Jennings Sr**
11 Apr 1703 Fairfield,
CT

Matthew Jennings
1658 Fairfield,
Fairfield, Connecticut,
United States

Joshua Jennings
1620 Ipswich,
England

John Jennings

Rose Lisle

Mary Williams
1625 Wethersfield,
Hartford, CT

Matthew Williams

Elizabeth Conant

Mary Wheeler
1671 Fairfield, CT

John Wheeler
27 Feb 1624
Bedforshire, Eng

Thomas Wheeler

Anne Halsey

Judith Turney
1635 Concord, MA

Benjamin Turney

Mary Odell

Elizabeth Coley
Bef. 24 Mar 1706
Fairfield, Fairfield,
Connecticut, United
States

Peter Coley
12 Jun 1671 Weston,
Fairfield, Connecticut,
United States

Peter Coley
Bef. 25 Apr 1641
Milford, CT

Samuel Coley

Ann Prudden

Sarah Hyde

Humphrey Hyde

Ann Ripley

Hannah Couch
1678 Fairfield,
Fairfield, C

Simon Couch
12 Apr 1633 Norwalk,
Fairfield, C

Lewis Couch

Isot Maine

**Mary Frances
Andrews**
1645 Fairfield, CT

Francis Andrews

Anne Smith

Genealogy 14: Sarah Wakeman

The name "Wakeman" comes from Middle English and has been translated as "watchman." It is also the title of the chief magistrate of the English town of Ripon, in Yorkshire. At Ripon, the office transferred from father to son and gave rise to the surname "Wakeman." The Wakeman family in New England traces its roots back to at least 1070 in England. The family was part of England's aristocracy with a coat of arms and various titles.

The first Wakeman to come to America was Samuel Wakeman, son of Francis Wakeman of Bewdley, Worcestershire. His brother John followed soon thereafter. Bewdley was the center of cap or hat manufacturing for many years in England.[95] At various times, hats were required by law to be worn on Sundays and holy days; hats had to be made by hand without use of machines, and imported hats were banned. At one time, there were an estimated one thousand people employed in the "cap" business in Bewdley. But laws were repealed and styles changed; and the cap business declined sharply in the mid-1600s. Whether Samuel and John emigrated because of declining business or in search of religious liberty, is not known. But Samuel came to New England in November 1631. He was killed in a battle in the Bahamas in the summer of 1641 where he and others went to assist English colonists under threat from the Spanish.

John Wakeman (1601–1661)

John Wakeman was born in Bewdley and married Elizabeth Hopkins there in January 1628. She was the daughter of Helen Vickaris and William Hopkins, also of Bewdley. John and Elizabeth moved to America shortly after their marriage and had six children including Samuel Wakeman, who was born in 1635. John is sometimes referred to by researchers as the "immigrant ancestor" from this branch of the family.

John Wakeman joined the New Haven Colony, being one of the original settlers and one of its prominent citizens. He was a deacon of the colony's first church (Center Church on the Green), and held various public offices including that of treasurer of the colony. In 1661 he moved to Hartford, where he died the same year. He was a signer of the New Haven Compact or Fundamental Agreement, which set out the rules for self-government in New Haven, and he served as Deputy to the General Court, Treasurer of the Colony, and captain of colonial forces.

Reverend Samuel Wakeman (1635–1692)

Samuel was the fifth of six children and was born in 1635. He graduated from Harvard University and married Hannah, daughter of Stephen Goodyear, in New Haven in 1656. They moved to Fairfield, where Samuel was ordained. He became a well-known minister at the Church of Christ in Fairfield, and some of his speeches were transcribed and saved, including a long sermon on the death of John Tappin of Boston which remains available to read today.

According to the Wakeman Genealogy 1630–1899:

> *Mr. Wakeman came to Fairfield with means, and by purchase and grant became owner of considerable real estate.*
>
> *His wife [Hannah Goodyear] was daughter of the Deputy Governor Stephen Goodyear, who was one of the first settlers of New Haven and was a man of prominence.*
>
> *It was supposed that [Stephen Goodyear] came from London, and that he had been a merchant there. He was engaged in commerce while in New Haven and was associated with Mr. John Wakeman [Samuel's father] in building or buying a ship and using it for commercial purposes. It started on its first trip in January 1646, Mr. Lamberton being master. Mrs. Goodyear [Stephen's wife and Hannah's mother] was a passenger, and the ship was never heard of, and as one consequence, Mr. Goodyear married Mrs. Lamberton. Mr. Goodyear was Deputy Governor of the Colony, elected annually from the first settlement, until he went to London, and was second only to Eaton [Governor]. When the latter died, Mr. Goodyear was in London, where he had gone to live, and this was the only reason for his not being elected Governor."* [96]

So many spouses died in early America that widows and widowers generally remarried fairly soon thereafter. Mr. Goodyear and Mrs. Lamberton were no exception.

Captain John Wakeman (1659–1709)

Captain John Wakeman was a son of Reverend Samuel Wakeman and Hannah Goodyear. He was born in 1659 in Fairfield, and he married Martha Hubbell in 1687. Her parents were Richard Hubbell who immigrated from England, and Elizabeth Meigs. John and Martha had seven children, including Stephen.

Martha Hubbell was actually a cousin of John Wakeman. It was not unusual for cousins to marry at the time; families were large and workdays were long, so opportunities to meet potential spouses were limited outside the families.

According to the *Wakeman Genealogy* 1630–1899:

> *Capt. John, son of Rev Samuel, was a prominent man in the Colony of Connecticut. He was appointed Deputy to the General Court, from Fairfield, and served at twenty-three sessions from 1690 to 1706. He was appointed Commis-*

sioner in 1695, 1696 and 1697; also Justice for Fairfield in 1698, and many times thereafter. He was appointed Lieutenant in May 1697 and Captain in May 1704 and 1705. He left an estate of about 1,000 pounds.[97]

John Meigs (1612–1658)

The Meigs also came to New England (Connecticut) from England. Elizabeth Meigs's father John was the immigrant. John was an active and well-known resident of New Haven. He was a member of the court, a Freeman (that is, a person with voting rights), a clerk in the New Haven "Trainband" (i.e. militia company) and had a desirable seat in church. But he was evidently not liked and could be argumentative and litigious. He was a shoemaker but apparently not a very good one and was frequently sued for faulty work. He was involved in multiple land disputes and reprimanded for breaking the Sabbath.

He may be best remembered for an incident involving "regicides." After restoration of the monarchy in England, King Charles II and his loyalists sought retribution against those who had supported Cromwell and parliamentary rule in England. They specifically targeted fifty-nine men who signed Charles I's death warrant and captured and hung many of them (including Gregory Clement, ancestor to Mark Twain). Those who had died before being caught, were dug up from their graves and hung anyway. Two regicides, Edward Whalley and William Goffe, managed to flee England before they were apprehended and went to Connecticut. But they were pursued in America by Royalists representing the Crown. Their escape from apprehension in America was facilitated by John Meigs.

After a long ride on horseback from the town of Guilford the night of May 12, 1660, John Meigs reached New Haven and notified the Reverend John Davenport, who was hosting Whalley and Goffe, that English agents were in route to capture the two men. Meigs led the two to a cave, where they hid for several weeks. Eventually the English agents finding no evidence that the two fugitives were in the area, departed for England. John Meigs is credited with saving Whalley and Goffe's lives.[98]

Chapter 19:

The Nickerson Family: Founders of Cape Cod Towns

Pedigree Chart for
Elizabeth Nickerson

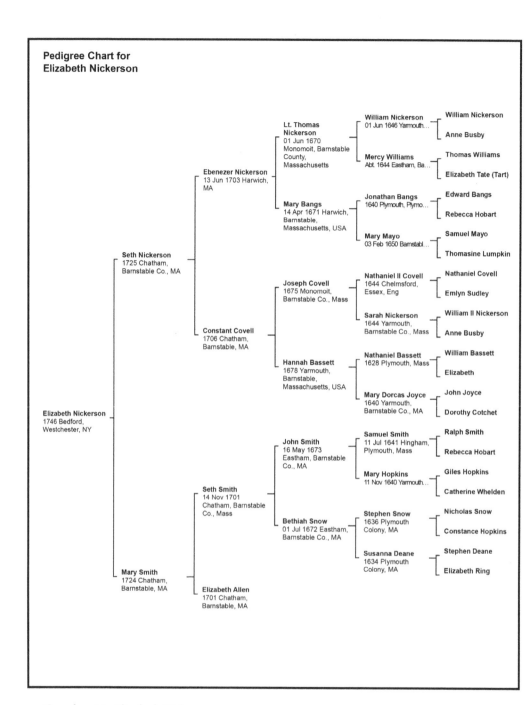

Genealogy 15: Elizabeth Nickerson

The Nickerson family immigrated to New England from England like many others; they chose to settle in Cape Cod and established a long-term presence there. Cape Cod was named by English explorer Bartholomew Gosnold. In 1602, Gosnold sailed from the Azores to Cape Elizabeth in Maine before proceeding to the Provincetown Harbor and renaming it "Cape Cod" because of the many cod-fishing boats in the area. Following the coastline, he named "Martha's Vineyard" after his deceased daughter, Martha, and the wild grapes that were prevalent in the area.

William Nickerson (1604–1690)

William Nickerson was born in 1604 in Norwich, England. His parents were William and Alice (maiden name unknown) Nickerson. The family had a long history in Norwich, with William's father, his grandfather (Thomas Nickerson 1542–1600), and his great-grandfather (Thomas Nickerson 1515–1584) all living their entire lives there. In about 1627, William married Anne Busby, also from Norwich.

Norwich was the second-largest city in England and the center of the wool and weaving industry. It was also a city which welcomed immigrants, especially those with weaving skills, including French Huguenots and Belgian Walloons. Many of the residents were Puritans or "nonconforming Protestants", which put them in conflict with the Church of England.

William and Anne had five children born in Norwich; they then moved the family to Massachusetts departing April 15, 1637 on the ship *John and Dorothy*. They came with Anne's parents, Nicholas and Bridget (Cocke) Busby, and three other siblings of Anne. In Norwich, William Nickerson and Nicholas Busby had been worsted weavers. It is not certain why they decided to depart, given their long family histories in Norwich, but the likeliest reason is conflict with the established Church and persecutions directed by Matthew Wren, then Bishop of Norfolk. During Wren's twenty-eight months as bishop, an estimated three thousand people left seeking freedom from religious persecution.[99] When William Nickerson and Nicholas Busby left England, Michael Metcalf, a fellow weaver, also departed Norfolk: he wrote his story and published it in a letter, which described the difficulty of being a Puritan in Norwich at the time. The challenges he described would likely have applied to Nickerson and Busby as well.

> *Metcalf was from Norwich, England and worked as a master weaver. He was persecuted by the Church of England for his Puritan beliefs and, upon fleeing to Massachusetts, wrote a long letter addressed to "all true professors of Christ's gospel" in Norwich. He spoke of the "great trouble" he had with the "Arch-Deacon's and Bishop's court at the hands of my enemies concerning the matter of bowing as well as for other matters of like consequence.*

Before the ecclesiastical court, Metcalf defended himself by quoting not only the Bible but also the church's own theologians. He related in his letter that their responses included "Blockhead, old heretic, the devil made you, I will send you to the devil." When his life was put in danger, his wife sometimes hid him in the thatched roof of their house.[100]

William Nickerson, Nicholas Busby, and Michael Metcalf and their families all departed from England and arrived in Massachusetts in June 1637, after about two months at sea. The journey was almost certainly a challenge as it was for other immigrants.

It is not certain where the Nickersons lived at first, but they probably lived with the Busbys who first settled in Newbury. The Nickersons then lived in either Boston or Watertown. No matter which neighborhood they settled in, they lived under the jurisdiction of the Puritan leaders of Massachusetts Bay. The Puritans could be just as intolerant and restrictive of non-conforming behavior as the bishop in Norfolk. The Nickersons evidently sought relief by moving to Plymouth Colony, which was led by Puritans who were more tolerant and more willing to accept newcomers, especially ones with needed skills such as weaving. Within the Colony, Nickerson lived in Yarmouth on Cape Cod, but there were frequent disputes with the town and neighbors about land ownership. Nickerson apparently tired of the disputes and the control the town authorities maintained over land transactions.

In 1656, William bought land from a Sagamore sachem, Mattaquason, in an area of Cape Cod that was called Monomoit. The authorities in Plymouth were outraged that William should buy land from a Native directly and initiated court actions to negate the purchase. The dispute was not resolved until 1665. William Nickerson subsequently moved his family to Monomoit, which was later named "Chatham." He and his family were the first European settlers in Chatham. William and Anne had five more children in Massachusetts for a total of ten. William died between August 1689 and September 1690.

In 1915, some of William Nickerson's descendants erected a large granite monument in the Nickerson family cemetery with the following inscription:

In memory of
William Nickerson
England 1604–
Massachusetts 1689–1690
Boston 1637 — freeman 1638 — Yarmouth 1640
Deputy to central court 1655
founder of Chatham
Religious teacher — useful citizen

William Nickerson (1646–1719)

William and Anne's son William (Jr.) owned land in the Cape Cod area and likely resided at the head of Ryder's Cove. He married Mercy Williams, from Eastham, Massachusetts, in 1668, and they had seven children including Thomas, who was born in 1670.

William and Mercy's lives were interrupted by a war with the local Native tribes that lasted from 1675 to 1676 in which many settlers and Native Americans were killed. Called "King Philip's War," [101] it was one of the deadliest wars in American history (see Chapter 20).

After the war, William returned to his home and became active in community affairs, serving on the grand jury and as a constable, inspector of whales, and selectman. He was also the first village treasurer and clerk. William and another resident were given responsibility for building the first village meeting house and church in 1700. William died in Chatham around 1719; his wife Anne lived to be more than ninety years old and also died in Chatham.

Thomas Nickerson (1670–1736) and Ebenezer Nickerson (1703–1762)

Thomas was the second child of William and Anne, born in Chatham about 1670. He lived in Chatham his entire life. In 1696, he married Mary Bangs. They lived at Cotchpinicut (Old Harbor) and Thomas held several public offices including selectman and town clerk. He also served as a lieutenant in the local militia. He is sometimes referred to in history books as "Nickerson of Chatham." He and Mary had at least four children including Ebenezer. Thomas died in 1735 or 1736.

Ebenezer was born around 1700 in Chatham and died in Chatham in 1762. He married Constant Covell, daughter of Joseph Covell and Hannah Bassett. He was a farmer and a captain in the militia. He was an active supporter of the Separatist religious movement that Anne Hutchinson had been involved in.

Ebenezer and Constant had eight children including Seth, all born in Chatham.

Seth Nickerson (1725–1801)

Seth was the second child of Ebenezer and Mary. He married Mary Smith, also from Chatham. Unlike most of their families who remained in Cape Cod, Seth and Mary moved to the Oblong area in Dutchess County, New York, shortly after marriage. The Oblong was a strip of land about 2.5 miles wide along the Connecticut–New York border. Connecticut had swapped that land with New York in 1731 in exchange for land along Long Island Sound. The Oblong was opened for settlement, and New York offered guaranteed titles and favorable land pricing. This became an "in" place to live and attracted many young couples and families from Cape Cod. Seth and Mary joined the movement. After moving, Seth served as road commissioner in 1773 and enlisted in the Third Regiment of the Dutchess County militia during the Revolutionary War.

Seth and Mary had nine children. Their daughter Elizabeth married Captain Comfort Ludington in 1767, uniting the Nickerson and Ludington ancestries.

Figure 12: Native American raid on settlers during King Philip's War

Chapter 20:

King Philip's War

King Philip's War,[102] fought in New England between 1675 and 1678, was one of the deadliest wars in American history. In proportion to area population, more people died than in any other war fought on American soil. More than six hundred colonists died, 1,200 homes were burned, and twelve colonial settlements were totally destroyed. Thousands of Native Americans were killed, died of disease and starvation, or were captured and sold into slavery in the West Indies and elsewhere.

King Philip's War was named after the local Wampanoag chief, Metacom (sometimes called King Philip by the English) and is sometimes referred to as Metacom's War or the First Indian War. There was considerable distrust between the New England colonists and local tribes including the Wampanoag. The colonists bought land for settlement from the local tribes, who became overly dependent on European goods and technology. As the Natives sold more land to sustain essential needs, they had less land for hunting, fur harvesting, trading, farming, and traditional activities. In 1662, King Philip, as he was called by the settlers, came to power when his older brother Wamsutta, the Wampanoag chief, died suddenly after being arrested by the English. The Wampanoag believed Wamsutta had been poisoned. Subsequently, the English forced King Philip to sign a treaty requiring the tribe to give up its arms, fearful the Wampanoag could revolt against English domination. Finally, three Wampanoag warriors were accused of murdering John Sassamon, a Christian and settler-friendly native, and were executed by the English. That was the last straw that triggered retaliation and the subsequent war.

Between June 20 and 23 in 1675, the Wampanog attacked the Swansea colony of Massachusetts, killing many settlers, burning homes, killing livestock, and destroying crops. In response, the settlers and their militia attacked Metacom's home village in Rhode Island and destroyed it, killing all residents. The war escalated as the summer passed, with other tribes joining the Wampanog attacking settlements throughout the colonies.

Ancestor Captain Avery was a military leader during this conflict and was viewed as a hero, fighting hostile Natives and defending settlers from massacre. According to historical records, a major battle occurred Sunday, December 19, 1675, between settlers with their Native allies (including the Pequot) and the Narragansett, who were allied with Metacom and his Wampanoag tribe.

The Narragansett fort was in South Kingston Rhode Island. It included five or six acres of dry land, was surrounded by a swamp, and was defended by palisades and felled trees. The only entrance was by a bridge made by a felled tree and commanded by a block house. Within, were not fewer that 3,500 warriors. The fight was desperate, for, on either side, it was a clear case of conquer or die. The final victory was with the English. It is said that 700 Indians were killed that day and that 300 of their wounded died. The power of the Narragansett tribe was broken. Capt. John Gallop, who commanded the Mohegans, was slain. The Pequot allies were under the command of James Avery.[103]

The defeat in Rhode Island effectively neutralized the Narragansett tribe and weakened the Wampanoags' capacity to fight. Metacom tried to recruit the Mohawks without success.

According to one historical account:

> *During the winter of 1676, King Philip's warriors continued to attack settlements throughout Massachusetts, Rhode Island, Connecticut, and Maine, proving there was no safe place for settlers in the region. The Indians attacked Plymouth Plantation and forced most of its citizens to the coast and, led by Chief Canonchet, destroyed Providence, Rhode Island.*
>
> *In an attack known as the "Nine Men's Misery" incident, Narragansett Indians ambushed around sixty colonists and twenty Christian Wampanoag Indians. The (attacking) Indians killed almost all the colonists; however, nine men were captured and gruesomely tortured to death.*[104]

By spring, the militia began to have more success. Chief Canonchet was captured and killed. About two hundred Narragansett were killed at the Battle of Turner Falls. The English offered amnesty to the war-weary Natives, but when they surrendered they were sold into slavery and shipped to the West Indies. Metacom was killed on August 20, 1767; his head was placed on a spike and displayed at Plymouth Colony for two decades. The war officially ended with the Treaty of Casco signed in 1678.

In addition to Captain Avery, ancestor George Denison served as captain, commanding troops from New London County and serving as second-in-command of the army in Connecticut. Other ancestors including William Nickerson served in the militia and fought to protect their homes and families.

Chapter 21:
The Mayo Family and the Old North Church

Reverend John Mayo (1597–1676)

John Mayo Jr. (or Reverend John Mayo as he became known) grew up during the turbulent times of Charles I, which was a time of great unrest, religious intolerance, and ultimately civil war in England. By 1618, John had departed England for Leiden, in the Netherlands, to join William Brewster and his congregation of Puritans. There he met and married Tamisen Brike.

John and his family followed William Brewster and the Puritans to Massachusetts, arriving in 1638. In the summer of 1638, at least twenty ships carrying an estimated three thousand colonists fled England and arrived in Massachusetts Bay, so John and his family had lots of company. He had attended Oxford in England, and in America he studied with Reverend John Lothrop and was ordained in 1640.

Reverend John and the family moved to Nauset (now Eastham) in 1646, and he became pastor of the church there. In November 1655, the family moved to Boston, and Reverend John became the first pastor of the Old North Church. This church became famous in colonial history when church sexton Robert Newman and Captain John Pulling Jr. climbed the steeple and held two lanterns high as a signal to Paul Revere to announce that British troops were on the move — an incident described in the famous poem by Henry Wadsworth Longfellow. This event, and the Battles of Lexington and Concord that followed, is generally considered the start of the Revolutionary War.

Reverend John Mayo retired from his post at the Old North Church in 1673 and died while living with his daughter in Barnstable in 1676. The church remains as Boston's oldest church and most visited historical site.

Paul Revere's Ride
by Henry Wadsworth Longfellow

Listen, my children, and you shall hear
Of the midnight ride of Paul Revere,
On the eighteenth of April, in Seventy-five;
Hardly a man is now alive
Who remembers that famous day and year.

He said to his friend, "If the British march
By land or sea from the town to-night,
Hang a lantern aloft in the belfry arch
Of the North Church tower as a signal light, —
One, if by land, and two, if by sea;
And I on the opposite shore will be,
Ready to ride and spread the alarm
Through every Middlesex village and farm
For the country folk to be up and to arm."

Then he said, 'Good night!" and with muffled oar
Silently rowed to the Charlestown shore,
Just as the moon rose over the bay,
Where swinging wide at her moorings lay
The Somerset, British man-of-war;
A phantom ship, with each mast and spar
Across the moon like a prison bar,
And a huge black hulk, that was magnified
By its own reflection in the tide.

Meanwhile, his friend, through alley and street,
Wanders and watches with eager ears,
Till in the silence around him he hears
The muster of men at the barrack door,
The sound of arms, and the tramp of feet,
And the measured tread of the grenadiers,
Marching down to their boats on the shore.

Then he climbed the tower of the Old North Church,
By the wooden stairs, with stealthy tread,
And startled the pigeons from their perch
On the sombre rafters, that round him made
Masses and moving shapes of shade,
By the trembling ladder, steep and tall
Where he paused to listen and look down

A moment on the roofs of the town,
And the moonlight flowing over all.

Beneath, in the churchyard, lay the dead,
In their night-encampment on the hill,
Wrapped in silence so deep and still
That he could hear, like a sentinel's tread,
The watchful night-wind, as it went
Creeping along from tent to tent
And seeming to whisper, "All is well!"
A moment only he feels the spell
Of the place and the hour, and the secret dread
Of the lonely belfry and the dead;
For suddenly all of his thoughts are bent
On a shadowy something far away,
Where the river widens to meet the bay, —
A line of black that bends and floats
On the rising tide, like a bridge of boats.

Meanwhile, impatient to mount and ride
Booted and spurred, with a heavy stride,
On the opposite shore walked Paul Revere
Now he patted his horse's side,
Now gazed at the landscape far and near,
Then, impetuous, stamped the earth,
And turned and tightened his saddle girth;
But mostly he watched with eager search
The belfry tower of the Old North Church,
As it rose above the graves on the hill
Lonely and spectral and sombre and still.
And lo! As he looks, on the belfry's height,
A glimmer, and then a gleam of light!
He springs to the saddle, the bridle he turns,
But lingers and gazes, till full on his sight
A second lamp in the belfry burns!

A hurry of hoofs in a village street,
A shape in the moonlight, a bulk in the dark,
And beneath, from the pebbles, in passing, a spark
Struck out by a steed flying fearless and fleet:
That was all! And yet, through the gloom and the light
The fate of a nation was riding that night;

And the spark struck out by that steed, in his flight,
Kindled the land into flame with its heat.

He has left the village and mounted the steep
And beneath him, tranquil and broad and deep
Is the Mystic, meeting the ocean tides;
And under the alders, that skirt its edge,
Now soft on the sand, now loud on the ledge,
Is heard the tramp of his steed as he rides.

It was twelve by the village clock,
When he crossed the bridge into Medford town.
He heard the crowing of the cock,
And the barking of the farmer's dog,
And felt the damp of the river fog,
That rises after the sun goes down.

It was one by the village clock,
When he galloped into Lexington.
He saw the gilded weathercock
Swim in the moonlight as he passed,
And the meeting-house windows, blank and bare,
Gaze at him with a spectral glare,
As if they already stood aghast
At the bloody work they would look upon.

It was two by the village clock,
When he came to the bridge in Concord town.
He heard the bleating of the flock,
And the twitter of birds among the trees,
And felt the breath of the morning breeze
Blowing over the meadows brown.
And one was safe and asleep in his bed
Who at the bridge would be first to fall,
Who that day would be lying dead,
Pierced by a British musket-ball.

You know the rest. In the books you have read,
How the British Regulars fired and fled,
How the farmers gave them ball for ball,
From behind each fence and farm-yard wall,
Chasing the red-coats down the lane,
Then crossing the fields to emerge again

Under the trees at the turn of the road,
And only pausing to fire and load.

So through the night rode Paul Revere;
And so through the night went his cry of alarm
To every Middlesex village and farm,
A cry of defiance and not of fear,
A voice in the darkness, a knock at the door,
And a word that shall echo forevermore!
For, borne on the night-wind of the Past,
Through all our history, to the last,
In the hour of darkness and peril and need,
The people will waken and listen to hear
The hurrying hoof-beats of that steed,
And the midnight message of Paul Revere.

Samuel Mayo (1625–1663)

Reverend John and his wife, Tamisen, had five children, including Samuel, who was born in 1625 in Leiden. He accompanied his parents to Massachusetts in 1638 when he was about eighteen years old and married Tamsen Lumpkin around 1644.

Samuel was attracted to the sea and became a mariner. He set up a fishing business, established a ferry service between Cape Cod and Barnstable, and was granted a deed to build a fish house on Cromwell's Point. He also became a minister and was referred to as Deacon.

In 1653, he joined two others and purchased the land which is now the village of Oyster Bay on Long Island from the local Lenape tribe. The purchase price was three coats, three shirts, two cuttoes (swords), three hatchets, three hoes, two fathom of Wampum, six knives, two pair of stockings, and two pair of shoes. Samuel, Peter Wright, and Reverend William Leveridge were the first European settlers at Oyster Bay. It seems like they cleaned out their closets and swapped it all for part of Long Island.

At some point, Samuel purchased a boat, *Desire,* and was hired by Reverend Leveridge to transport his goods to Oyster Bay. The ship was seized by a privateer captain, Thomas Baxter, who had permission to seize Dutch ships and ships doing business with the Dutch because of English-Dutch hostilities at the time. Privateers were authorized to act against enemies because the colonial governments did not have the resources to maintain a navy. But privateers were not the most reputable of people and often sought to take advantage and enrich themselves. Baxter claimed the *Desire* was transporting Dutch goods, which was not true; but it was an excuse to seize

Samuel's ship. The Connecticut court made Baxter return the ship to Samuel and fined Baxter for the illegal seizure.

In 1654, "Captain" Samuel Mayo and his ship were pressed into service against the Dutch. The *Desire* had an interesting history as just the third vessel built in Massachusetts. Her original captain, William Pierce, made his last voyage to the Bahamas, where he and some of the crew were killed by the Spanish, who were regularly in conflict with the English. The ship returned home, but its ownership group was in debt, and the ship was claimed by the president of Harvard University, acting on behalf of the John Harvard estate, because of unpaid debts. Subsequently, Captain Samuel Mayo and his investors took control.

Samuel and Tasmin had six children including daughter Mary, who married Captain Jonathan Bangs. Samuel died in 1663; his wife remarried and died in 1709.

Chapter 22:

Other New England Ancestor Families

The Smyth or Smith Family: Massachusetts Pioneers

Like many of his compatriots in early Cape Cod, Ralph Smyth (later changed to the Americanized Smith) came as a Puritan, likely arriving in 1633 on the *Elizabeth Bonaventure* from Norfolk, England. He probably came as an indentured servant, but this is not confirmed. He was a founder of Bare Cove, later named Hingham. A bell-tower monument was erected next to the Old Ship Church, the oldest church in New England today, to commemorate this event:

> To the memory of Ralph Smith — born at Hingham England 1610 — leading figure in founding Hingham, Massachusetts 1633 — Removed to Eastham about 1654. Died there 1685 — A pioneer of distinction, erected by the Association of Descendants of Ralph Smith, June 1946.

He was engaged in fishing and whaling from the shore and likely had his own boat. Notably, he was convicted and fined for "not seeing a whale for harvesting." He likely harvested a whale with his sons instead of registering it with the town and paying a required fee. It seems hard to hide an illegal whale, but he apparently tried.

Despite the laudatory memorial erected by his descendants, Ralph had issues while in Massachusetts. He was fined for "misorderly" behavior and disturbance, for breaking the peace, for striking a man named William Walker, for telling a lie and other transgressions.

His first wife died shortly after the birth of their seventh child, and he married Grace Hatch as his second wife. In her old age, Grace Smith narrated a book offering practical and spiritual counsel to her descendants, which was published in 1712.[105]

It is apparently the only recognized religious book written by a Calvinist woman that remains.

In 1646, the original Church of Nauset was formed, and that is likely where Ralph and Grace were married. The Reverend John Mayo was the minister.

Ralph Smyth became a popular figure and a wealthy landowner and merchant despite his run-ins with the church leaders. He served as a selectman and was regularly reelected for ten years. He died in 1685. He had seven children, including Samuel Smith who married Mary Hopkins. Their son John married Bethiah Snow (daughter of Stephen Snow and Susanna Deane); Bethiah and John Smith had ten children including Seth Smith, who was the father of Mary Smith (who went on to marry Seth Nickerson).

In 1734, a disease swept through New England, referred to as "pleurisy fever." Tragically, five of John and Bethiah Smith's children died that year, but Seth survived. Medical practices were primitive then, and the Puritan views were influenced by their belief of an all-present God whose eyes were on all places at all times; everything that happened in the world God created was because He wanted it to happen. He not only created prosperity and goodness in the world, but also death, wars, affliction, and diseases. Puritan preachers connected personal sin with the onset of a disease and implored each member of a congregation to search their soul and find out what they had done to displease God. Some ministers, like Cotton Mather, took this to extremes and tried to connect a certain sin to the area on the body which was painful. In other words, if someone had a toothache, it must have meant that they had been a glutton at the dinner table or that they had said something sinful.

The Smiths must have done considerable soul searching to understand why God chose to punish them and take so many of their children.

The O'Dell Family: Connecticut Pioneers and Witnesses to Witch Trials

Rebecca Morehouse married Stephen Wakeman in 1727 in Fairfield, Connecticut. Her father was Daniel Morehouse and her mother was Hannah Adams. Her paternal grandmother, Daniel's mother, was Rebecca O'Dell. The O'Dells have a long English history.

The first generation O'Dell in America was William, born around 1601 in Odell, Bedfordshire England. O'Dell generally means "of Dell," so William Odell would have originally meant William from Dell or Odell.

William and his family and friends were Puritans; they did not get along with Church of England leaders and ministers and decided to move to New England. But it was difficult to leave at that time; before embarking, emigrants to America from England had to provide a certificate from the justice of the peace and the minister of the parish where they lived. People not in good standing, including Puritans and especially Puritan ministers, would have difficulty obtaining the required documentation. They would also be required to pay a tax.

Odell, his minister (Peter Buckley) and friends and family boarded the *Abigail* in 1635. They were not listed on the manifest submitted to authorities before departure but are listed upon its arrival in America. Apparently they sneaked aboard likely with the consent of (and a payment to) the ship's captain. Up until the moment the ship departed, they were probably very afraid the authorities would find them.

The new immigrants founded Concord, the second town in Connecticut, in 1639. In the summer of 1644, with the town of Concord struggling and many residents dissatisfied with the high taxes and relatively poor soil for farming, sixteen families including William Odell (called Odle in the records) moved and founded the town of Fairfield.

Witch Trials

Figure 13: Witchcraft trial in Salem 1692

During this time, Massachusetts and Connecticut experienced a series of witch trials where someone, usually a woman, was accused of being a witch and placing curses on others. Usually someone in the community suffered a calamity or illness, and relatives and neighbors blamed someone else who was unpopular or acting strangely.

Witch trials in Salem, Massachusetts have been much discussed, but witch trials also happened in Fairfield.

The typical trial started with an accusation. The accused would be interrogated by the court officials and sometimes by unsympathetic neighbors; often the accused would confess under the stress of interrogation. Other times a trial would be held; the accused would be inspected for "marks of the devil" which were often found by accusers. Those found guilty were generally hanged, and some were burned at the stake. Others whose guilt was not so conclusively determined were given the water test. In a water test, the accused would be bound and thrown in a lake or pond. If she did not sink or if she "rose into the air," she would be declared a witch. If she sank, she would be declared innocent. Unfortunately, innocent people often drowned.

In 1671, one of Odell's neighbors, Elizabeth Knapp, was convicted of witchcraft in Fairfield and hanged. Her hanging was witnessed by William Odell's wife, Rebecca. William Odell remained in Fairfield until his death in 1676.

Witch trials also happened in England. John Garner (1633–1702), the future brother-in-law of ancestor William Keene (1641–1683) arrived in Virginia as a four-year-old with his father Richard and uncle Thomas in 1637. Both men were fleeing the aftermath of witch trials. In 1635, the year that William Odell and his family left England, Thomas's wife Mary Lacye Garner, who had been accused of witchcraft in Shropshire, England was given a water test in which she drowned, proving her innocence but with little consolation. The next year, Richard's wife was accused of being a witch and also drowned, thereby establishing her innocence. Both Thomas and Richard were awarded two pounds to pay for their wives' Christian burial. Not surprisingly, the two widowers departed England the next year for America, distant from the religious authorities in England. John Garner would go on to marry William Keene's sister Susanna.

The Adams Family: Family of Presidents

Henry Adams was born in Barton St David in Somerset, England, around 1583. His parents were John Adams (1555–1604) and Agnes Stone (1556–1616). He married Edith Squire in 1609 in Somerset. Edith's two sisters married men who emigrated to New England; and in 1638 Henry and Edith, Henry's brothers, and Henry's and Edith's eight sons and one daughter sailed from their home England, for Massachusetts, arriving in 1638.

Henry was one of the first settlers of the Massachusetts Bay Colony and was granted land in what later became Braintree, Massachusetts, named for Henry and Edith's English home. He was a farmer, planter, and leading citizen.

His descendants include Presidents John Adams and John Quincy Adams. There is a granite column in Braintree, Massachusetts, placed by President John Adams with the following inscription:

> *In Memory of Henry Adams who took his fight from the Dragon persecution in Devonshire in England, and alighted with eight sons, near Mount Wollaston...*[106]

One of Henry and Elizabeth's eight sons was named Edward. There were several Edward Adams in the area at the time, and it is not always clear which one was being mentioned in the records. My Edward was born in 1629 in Somerset, England and died in 1671 in Fairfield, Connecticut. He was living in New Haven by 1640 and married Mary (possibly Mary Savage or Mary Patchen) in 1647. In about 1646, he received a land grant in nearby Milford subject to the condition "that he will both learn to dress Leather and Skins and alsoe follow His trade in the town."[107] The good citizens of Milford appeared willing to give a land grant but only if Edward filled their need for a leather tanner.

Edward and Mary's granddaughter Rebecca married Stephen Wakeman in 1727. With Rebecca's marriage to Stephen, the family lines of Adams, Morehouse, Odell, Lockwood, Hubbell, Meigs, Goodyear, Hopkins, Goode, and others were brought together. And their son David married Elizabeth Nickerson, bringing even more of New England's prominent families together. The history of the family is very much the history of New England.

Chapter 23:
Elizabeth Wood Carter:
A Challenging Life in the Midwest

Emily Carter married Cyrus McDonald in St. Joseph, Indiana in 1873. Not much is known about Emily's family, but most of what is known suggests a life filled with tragedies.

Emily was born in 1846 in Ohio — probably in Hamilton County. Neither of her parents appear to have been successful or notable. As a result, there is little written about them. No obituaries, no news articles, no online family ancestry documentation. Her mother, Elizabeth Wood, was born in 1821 in Ohio, possibly in Carthage. Her father, James Carter, was born in New Jersey. Elizabeth and James married on Sept 26, 1840; she was nineteen years old and he was twenty-four.

Elizabeth and James had three children: Sarah Jane, Seth, and Emma. James Carter died August 1, 1846 at the age of thirty, leaving Elizabeth a widow with three young children. In the 1850 Census, Elizabeth was living in the same household as a John Carter, who may have been James' brother. He is listed as a pattern maker, and Elizabeth is listed as a seamstress. Clearly, she was taking in work to pay the bills.

Sometime after 1850, Elizabeth moved the family to South Bend, Indiana, and she married Daniel Cushaw (or Cushway) in 1858. A short time later, Daniel deserted her. She had another baby, Clara Isabelle, in 1859; Clara was almost certainly Daniel's child, but the child was given the last name of "Carter," suggesting Daniel had left before the birth.

Elizabeth's son Seth helped support the family after the death of his father. But with the outbreak of the Civil War, Seth enlisted in Company C of the newly formed Ninth Regiment of the Indiana Volunteer Infantry in August 1861. He was seventeen or eighteen years old. After a few minor skirmishes, the Ninth Regiment was part of the Battle of Shiloh in April 1862.

The Battle of Shiloh took place on the western front of the Civil War. Most of the Union and Confederate troops were in the East under Generals George McClellan and Robert E. Lee, but General Ulysses Grant led Union troops through Kentucky and Tennessee defeating Confederate troops and securing territory including Nashville. To stop Grant and his march through the region, Confederate General Albert Johnson led 45,000 troops in a surprise attack against Grant and Union General Don Buell. The dawn attack near Shiloh Church forced the Union troops back, but fighting raged all day with many casualties including General Johnson himself, who became the highest ranking officer to die on either side during the Civil War.

The next day, Grant counterattacked and drove the Confederates back. The Confederates disengaged and retreated back to Corinth, giving the Union Army an important victory. But the casualties were very high on both sides with thirteen thousand Union soldiers and ten thousand Confederate soldiers dead, wounded, or captured. Seth Carter survived the Battle of Shiloh but died a few months later in an army hospital in Nashville, apparently of dysentery. More Civil War soldiers died of disease than of bullets, and Seth was not an exception. Seth's death must have been heartbreaking for Elizabeth.

She applied for a pension related to Seth's death and was awarded eight dollars per month. In 1870, Elizabeth married Thomas Strong, who died in 1891, leaving her a widow again. Her daughter Emily married Cyrus McDonald. Elizabeth died Nov 20, 1911 at the age of ninety and after a very challenging life.

Chapter 24:
The Bingham Family and the Lenape Tribe

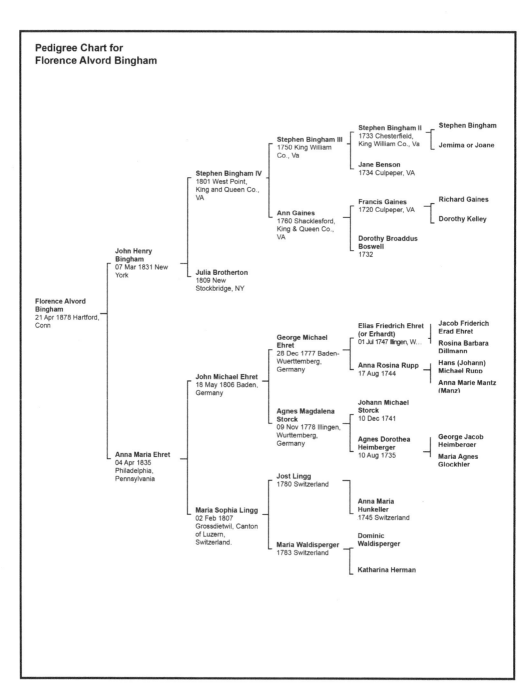

**Pedigree Chart for
Florence Alvord Bingham**

Florence Alvord Bingham
21 Apr 1878 Hartford, Conn

John Henry Bingham
07 Mar 1831 New York

Stephen Bingham IV
1801 West Point, King and Queen Co., VA

Stephen Bingham III
1750 King William Co., Va

Stephen Bingham II
1733 Chesterfield, King William Co., Va

Stephen Bingham

Jemima or Joane

Jane Benson
1734 Culpeper, VA

Ann Gaines
1760 Shacklesford, King & Queen Co., VA

Francis Gaines
1720 Culpeper, VA

Richard Gaines

Dorothy Kelley

Dorothy Broaddus Boswell
1732

Julia Brotherton
1809 New Stockbridge, NY

Anna Maria Ehret
04 Apr 1835 Philadelphia, Pennsylvania

John Michael Ehret
18 May 1806 Baden, Germany

George Michael Ehret
28 Dec 1777 Baden-Wuerttemberg, Germany

Elias Friedrich Ehret (or Erhardt)
01 Jul 1747 Illingen, W…

Jacob Friderich Erad Ehret

Rosina Barbara Dillmann

Anna Rosina Rupp
17 Aug 1744

Hans (Johann) Michael Rupp

Anna Marie Mantz (Manz)

Agnes Magdalena Storck
09 Nov 1778 Illingen, Wurttemberg, Germany

Johann Michael Storck
10 Dec 1741

Agnes Dorothea Heimberger
10 Aug 1735

George Jacob Heimberger

Maria Agnes Glockhler

Maria Sophia Lingg
02 Feb 1807 Grossdietwil, Canton of Luzern, Switzerland.

Jost Lingg
1780 Switzerland

Anna Maria Hunkeller
1745 Switzerland

Maria Waldisperger
1783 Switzerland

Dominic Waldisperger

Katharina Herman

Genealogy 16: Florence Alvord Bingham

There were many Binghams in colonial America who went on to achieve great success. Many descend from the immigrant Thomas Bingham, who moved to Connecticut from Sheffield, England, as a young man around 1635. Several members of another Bingham family emigrated from Ireland later in 1793. It is unknown where the Bingham line in my ancestry originated: England, Ireland, or even (as one report suggests) Scotland.

Stephen Bingham (1680–1759)

The earliest documented Bingham ancestor in my line, Stephen Bingham (I), was born about 1680 in King William County, Virginia, near Jamestown. He was an early resident in the newly developing town of West Point, Virginia. West Point lies on a narrow strip of land where the Pamunkey and Mattaponi rivers join to create the larger York River and has an interesting history. During the early days of settlement, the site was inhabited by members of the Mattaponi tribe, an Algonquian-speaking tribe affiliated with the Powhatan Confederacy, who called the village Cinquoteck.[108] After a "massacre" in 1644, during the third Anglo-Powhatan war, Governor Berkley drove the Mattaponi off this stretch of land. Captain John West assembled first two thousand acres and then an additional twelve thousand acres as the "West Plantation." The point of land on the plantation where the ships docked to deliver and pick up goods was called "West Point." It became a very active port in the Virginia Colony.

In 1701, an act was passed to establish a town at the port to be called "Delaware Town," and a surveyor laid out a town with lots of one-half acre each. Stephen Bingham bought some of these lots and moved there as one of the earliest residents. He died there in 1759.

Stephen Bingham (II) (1733–1794) &
Stephen Bingham (III) (1750–1808)

Stephen (II) was born in 1733, the second child and only son of Stephen Bingham (I) and Jemima Bingham. He married Jane Benson, and they had at least three children: Leah, Stephen, and Alice.

Stephen (II) apparently owned a well-known store in West Point in 1774. A notice in the local paper, the *Virginia Gazette,* on July 26, 1774, indicated someone broke into Stephen Bingham's store the previous night and stole considerable merchandise. The list of items taken gives a glimpse of what gentlemen were wearing or possessing at the time: a silver watch, leather snuff boxes, a superfine black coat and waistcoat, velvet breeches, a light colored drab coat with silver buttons, black doeskin breeches, twenty white shirts (most of them ruffled), a scarlet cloak, aprons, ruffles, handkerchiefs, linen waistcoat and breeches, silk and thread stockings, a small trunk, etc.

In June 1776, as the Revolutionary War approached, Stephen was called upon by local officials to serve as a commissioner to examine the channel of the York River for navigation and the adjacent shores for placement of batteries in defense of the King William County region against the British. The commission was further directed to build small ships that would become part of the first American navy.

Stephen's son Stephen Bingham (III) was born in 1750 in the West Point area of King William County and died there in 1808. He married Ann Gaines, daughter of Francis Gaines. Stephen and Ann had five children including a son also named Stephen (IV) in 1801.

Stephen Bingham (IV) (1801–1858)

Stephen (IV) was in the shipping business and frequently sailed between West Point, Virginia and New York. While in New York, Stephen met and subsequently married Julia Brotherton. They had three children together, all born in New York, including John Henry Bingham, who was born in 1831.

Julia Brotherton (1809–1861) and the Brotherton Indians

Julia Brotherton was a Native American descended from the Leni Lenape ("Lenape") tribe, which had lived in the Delaware watershed in New Jersey and extended into parts of New York and Pennsylvania. They were a mostly peaceful tribe made up of many clans.

In 1594, the Lenape first began to trade with European explorers who were seeking fish, furs, and timber. As trading increased, wildlife diminished, as did fish and forests. During the seventeenth century, the Lenape moved their settlements in search of more furs, fish and timber they could trade to satisfy their desire for European goods including iron tools.

During the French and Indian Wars and the American Revolution, the Lenape generally sided with the British, hoping the British would help protect them from settler incursions and let the Lenape live in peace. During the Revolutionary War, in an attempt to manage the conflict and protect settlers, the state of New Jersey set aside a "reservation" for the Lenape in 1780 and called it "Brotherton." The Native Americans who lived there, who traditionally did not use family names, were given the last name of Brotherton.

By then, the Lenape had been joined by other Native people whose tribes had been decimated by disease and war including Pequot, Narragansett, Montaur, and others. Without benefit of a common tribal language, the use of English became common at Brotherton.

The leader or chief of the Brotherton Indians was Samson Occum, chief from the Mohegan tribe, who converted to Christianity and became a Christian minister. An English settler, Eleazer Wheelock, was Occum's minister and mentor and later convinced him to go to Europe and raise money for the development of an Indian school to be built in Connecticut. Occum spent eighteen months in Europe and raised twelve thousand pounds. Wheelock took the money, moved to New Hampshire, and used the funds to establish Dartmouth college for the education of English settlers.[109]

By 1790, conditions on the reservation had deteriorated to the point that most Brotherton Indians moved to Wyoming Valley, Pennsylvania. Those who had converted to Christianity remained in New Jersey for a while but were unable to sustain themselves. They also faced indiscriminate attacks from settlers.

In 1799, the Oneida tribe of New Stockbridge, New York, invited the Brotherton Indians to join them. By 1802, seven years before Julia's birth, Occum led the remaining members at Brotherton out of New Jersey for New York.

Stephen Bingham met Julia and they were married sometime before 1831 in New York. Their first child, John, was born in 1831, followed by Charles and Julia. In 1858, Stephen's ship, *New York*, sank while in route to New York, and Stephen was lost at sea. Julia died a few years later.

John Henry Bingham (1831–1910)

John Bingham was born in New York in 1831; but by 1850, he lived in a boarding house in Philadelphia and listed his occupation as "painter." While in Philadelphia, he met Anna Marie Ehret; and they married in 1854 (see Chapter 25).

By 1855, John and Anna moved to Hartford, Connecticut. They had twelve children some of whom died very young. John was interested in a new technology for printing called lithography which was invented in Germany in 1796 and became available in America about twenty years later. Color lithography became popular around the 1880s and 1890s. Lithography was used in printing maps and pictures because it offered greater clarity and contrast quality.

In 1860, John joined with W.H. Dodd and formed Bingham & Dodd, a firm specializing in lithography. The firm became quite well known for quality works, and there remain several historical books with maps, drawings, and pictures made by Bingham & Dodd. Their portrait of Abraham Lincoln is considered exceptional and is held by the U.S. Library of Congress.[110] Among the many works they published that achieved recognition are: *The Last Men of the Revolution* and a portrait of

President Andrew Johnson. The partnership lasted fourteen years and was dissolved in 1884.

While in Hartford, Bingham began to invent things and obtained a series of patents including one for manufacturing pipes (1874), a pack of playing cards (1877), a bronzing machine (1881), and a printer's damping roller (1884).

Sometime before 1891, John and Anna Marie and four of their children, including Florence, moved to Chicago. Unlike earlier travelers to the Midwest, they did not take a covered wagon and trek for two months. They almost certainly took a train from the East Coast. They likely took the New York, New Haven and Hartford Railroad to New York. Then, they may have taken the Pennsylvania Railroad to Philadelphia and visited Anna's family for a few days before taking the Pennsylvania "Limited" to Chicago — about a twenty-hour trip. A fellow named George Pullman had developed a railroad sleeper car in 1864, and the Binghams likely tried out a Pullman sleeping car on their journey; John's successful career would have provided the necessary resources for the trip.

It is unknown why they moved, but I suspect it was curiosity about the Columbia Exposition or World's Fair that would be held in Chicago in 1893.[111] The Exposition was famous for demonstrating new technology and new products and was a "must-see" for those interested in the latest technology and inventions.

In Chicago, John continued to tinker and experiment and received a patent for a new type of tire for vehicle wheels (1891). About a year after Anna died, John became ill and died in the Resthaven Sanitarium in Elgin, Illinois, on June 11, 1910.

Florence Albord Bingham (1878–1945)

John and Anna Marie had ten children. Their youngest, Florence, was born in 1878. She taught music in 1897, according to the Chicago city directory, and then married Herbert MacDonald in October 1899, in Chicago. They had two children, Margaret and Walter. Walter was my father.

I never met my grandmother, Florence. She died in 1945, two years before I was born. Florence lived in Berwyn, a suburb just west of Chicago, a few blocks from where my parents and I lived. According to my mother, her mother-in-law Florence or "Mother MacDonald" would frequently call and tell my mother that she was in the mood to go out for dinner and have chicken or some other dish; she would ask Mom to pick some up at the grocery store and cook it so that she could join Mom and Dad for dinner that night. She said she would pay for the chicken but never did. This irritated my mother because it was during the Depression, and money was tight. But Florence was a bit pushy and used to getting her way.

Florence's and Herbert's other child, my aunt Margaret, married Charley Tuttle and moved to the northern Chicago suburb of Wilmette. They had two children: Nancy who married Ken Ragland, a professor of astronautical engineering at the University of Wisconsin, and had three children, and Carolyn, who married Al Menzel, had two children, and then later married John Mellor. I remember Nancy and Ken especially as kind and interested people, even though I was much younger.

Chapter 25:
The Ehret Family:
Swiss and German Immigrants
to Philadelphia

Pedigree Chart for
Anna Maria Ehret

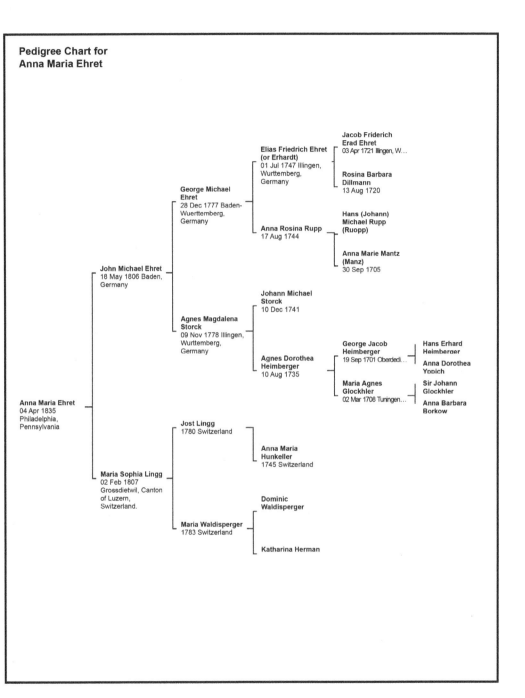

Anna Maria Ehret
04 Apr 1835
Philadelphia,
Pennsylvania

John Michael Ehret
18 May 1806 Baden,
Germany

Maria Sophia Lingg
02 Feb 1807
Grossdietwil, Canton
of Luzern,
Switzerland.

**George Michael
Ehret**
28 Dec 1777 Baden-
Wuerttemberg,
Germany

**Agnes Magdalena
Storck**
09 Nov 1778 Illingen,
Wurttemberg,
Germany

Jost Lingg
1780 Switzerland

Maria Waldisperger
1783 Switzerland

**Elias Friedrich Ehret
(or Erhardt)**
01 Jul 1747 Illingen,
Wurttemberg,
Germany

Anna Rosina Rupp
17 Aug 1744

**Johann Michael
Storck**
10 Dec 1741

**Agnes Dorothea
Heimberger**
10 Aug 1735

**Anna Maria
Hunkeller**
1745 Switzerland

**Dominic
Waldisperger**

Katharina Herman

**Jacob Friderich
Erad Ehret**
03 Apr 1721 Illingen, W…

**Rosina Barbara
Dillmann**
13 Aug 1720

**Hans (Johann)
Michael Rupp
(Ruopp)**

**Anna Marie Mantz
(Manz)**
30 Sep 1705

**George Jacob
Heimberger**
19 Sep 1701 Oberdedi…

**Maria Agnes
Glockhler**
02 Mar 1708 Tuningen…

**Hans Erhard
Heimberger**

**Anna Dorothea
Yonich**

**Sir Johann
Glockhler**

**Anna Barbara
Borkow**

Genealogy 17: Anna Maria Ehret

John Henry Bingham's wife, Anna Marie Ehret, was born in Philadelphia, but her grandparents (like the Germans who settled in Germantown and Hunterdon County, New Jersey) immigrated from the Palatinate region of Germany. The Ehret family was from Württemberg along the Rhine. As many of their friends fled the Palatinate, with its constant and debilitating wars, to emigrate to America, George Michael Ehret and his wife Agnes (Storck) stayed until 1819. As wars continued, the government enacted a mandatory conscription for young men. George's and Agnes's oldest son turned fifteen and soon would be drafted; many who were drafted never returned. France was headed toward a revolution and "rabble-rousers" were infiltrating into Württemberg, making the situation more uncertain. It was time to make a move.

George Michael Ehret (1777–1858)

According to an Ehret family bible, "The Ehret family came to America to avoid European armies as they were part of the Anabaptist religious movement that opposed the killings in war."[112] George Michael Ehret, his wife Agnes (also called Magdalene), and their six children left Germany via Amsterdam in 1819 and arrived in Philadelphia aboard the ship *Recovery* on July 26, 1819.

George had been a shoemaker in Germany and was a shoe cobbler in Philadelphia. Some of the boys were indentured to pay for their passage, including the smallest child, Elias. Elias was so small, no one wanted to pay for him. Finally, a farmer and his wife took the small child to watch their children and help with tasks around the farm. Elias was playful and enjoyed spooking the animals; he and the serious farmer did not get along. One day a big storm approached, and the farmer told Elias to close the barn doors, but the boy was too short to reach the latches. The angry farmer attempted to close the doors himself, but the rising wind tore the doors off the hinges, landing on the farmer and killing him. Relieved of his indenture, Elias moved back to Philadelphia and became an apprentice to his father making shoes.

Soon thereafter, there was a cholera epidemic in Philadelphia, and a doctor advised Elias to drink port wine to ward off the disease. Elias spent all of his savings buying and consuming large quantities of port wine. He did avoid illness and likely attributed this to his consumption. Such was the state of medical advice in the 1830s.

During the financial crisis later called the "Panic of 1837,"[113] banks closed, businesses failed, unemployment soared. The financial depression lasted until the mid-1840s and it affected the Ehrets and everyone else. Elias met Sophia Henning, whose family was also from Württemberg, at a dance social; they were married and, following the Panic, packed their wagon and few possessions and moved to Elkhart, Indiana, where they lived the rest of their lives.

John Michael Ehret (1806–1889) and Sophia Lingg (1807–1874)

George and Agnes also had a son named John Michael Ehret, who was born in 1806. John married Maria Sophia Lingg (or Ling), who was Swiss. She was born in 1807 in Grossdietwil, in the Swiss canton of Luzern and emigrated with her family in 1816; she was nine years old at the time. The area the Linggs emigrated from was undergoing significant turbulence at the time with a change in government and war with France. The Treaty of Paris in November 1815 established the concept of permanent Swiss neutrality, but turmoil continued for a while. Like other Swiss immigrants, the Linggs settled in Pennsylvania, which was tolerant and accepting of various religions; and the Swiss and German immigrants often intermarried, as was the case of John Ehret and Sophia Lingg.

In the 1860 census, John's occupation was listed as a carpenter. By 1862, he was a member of the Seventy-second Pennsylvania Infantry in the Union Army. He fought in the epic Seven Days Battles[114] near Richmond where the newly designated commander of ninety thousand southern troops, General Robert E. Lee, faced one hundred thousand Union troops commanded by General George McClellan. The weather was extremely hot, and wounded soldiers often died quickly from gangrene and other diseases. Lee drove McClellan back from Richmond but at a huge cost of lives. Lee suffered twenty thousand causalities and McClellan sixteen thousand. Historians have praised Lee for his tactics and criticized McClellan for retreating when he had superior forces. Eventually, President Lincoln replaced McClellan for his lack of aggressiveness and picked Ulysses S. Grant as his new general.

The largest of the Seven Days Battles was at Gaines's Mill,[115] previously owned by the Gaines family (Ann Gaines was the wife of Stephen Bingham [III]). General Lee sent waves of Confederate troops against Union positions attempting to drive the Union troops into the Chickahominy River. The Confederates finally broke through as night descended, and the Union troops retreated across the river under cover of darkness. As a result of the battle, General McClellan abandoned the attempt to take Richmond and left the area. About fifteen thousand soldiers perished at Gaines's Mill.

Part Three:
My Mother's Family

My mother, Bernice Corson MacDonald

Chapter 26:
The Corson Family:
From Sweetheart Abbey and an Embalmed Heart in Scotland to a Small Town in Arkansas

Pedigree Chart for
Bernice M Corson

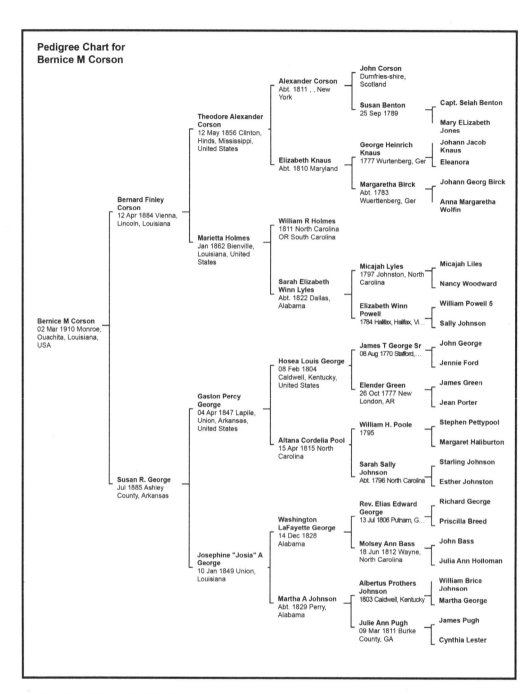

Bernice M Corson
02 Mar 1910 Monroe,
Ouachita, Louisiana,
USA

Bernard Finley Corson
12 Apr 1884 Vienna,
Lincoln, Louisiana

Susan R. George
Jul 1885 Ashley
County, Arkansas

Theodore Alexander Corson
12 May 1856 Clinton,
Hinds, Mississippi,
United States

Marietta Holmes
Jan 1862 Bienville,
Louisiana, United
States

Gaston Percy George
04 Apr 1847 Lapile,
Union, Arkansas,
United States

Josephine "Josia" A George
10 Jan 1849 Union,
Louisiana

Alexander Corson
Abt. 1811 , , New
York

Elizabeth Knaus
Abt. 1810 Maryland

William R Holmes
1811 North Carolina
OR South Carolina

Sarah Elizabeth Winn Lyles
Abt. 1822 Dallas,
Alabama

Hosea Louis George
08 Feb 1804
Caldwell, Kentucky,
United States

Altana Cordelia Pool
15 Apr 1815 North
Carolina

Washington LaFayette George
14 Dec 1828
Alabama

Martha A Johnson
Abt. 1829 Perry,
Alabama

John Corson
Dumfries-shire,
Scotland

Susan Benton
25 Sep 1789

George Heinrich Knaus
1777 Wurtenberg, Ger

Margaretha Birck
Abt. 1783
Wuerttenberg, Ger

Micajah Lyles
1797 Johnston, North
Carolina

Elizabeth Winn Powell
1784 Halifax, Halifax, Vi…

James T George Sr
08 Aug 1770 Stafford,…

Elender Green
26 Oct 1777 New
London, AR

William H. Poole
1795

Sarah Sally Johnson
Abt. 1796 North Carolina

Rev. Elias Edward George
13 Jul 1806 Putnam, G…

Molsey Ann Bass
18 Jun 1812 Wayne,
North Carolina

Albertus Prothers Johnson
1803 Caldwell, Kentucky

Julie Ann Pugh
09 Mar 1811 Burke
County, GA

Capt. Selah Benton

Mary ELizabeth Jones

Johann Jacob Knaus

Eleanora

Johann Georg Birck

Anna Margaretha Wolfin

Micajah Liles

Nancy Woodward

William Powell 5

Sally Johnson

John George

Jennie Ford

James Green

Jean Porter

Stephen Pettypool

Margaret Haliburton

Starling Johnson

Esther Johnston

Richard George

Priscilla Breed

John Bass

Julia Ann Holloman

William Brice Johnson

Martha George

James Pugh

Cynthia Lester

Genealogy 18: Bernice M. Corson

There are several Corson family lines that emigrated to America, but the one that produced my mother came from Dumfriesshire, Scotland. The known family history begins with an Italian artisan named Corsani or Corsini. He and others were brought to Scotland by Queen Dervorguilla. After her husband's death, Dervorguilla had his heart embalmed and carried it with her in a silver casket. She commissioned the construction of Sweetheart Abbey in memory of her husband and brought artisans (including the ancestor Corsani) to Scotland to work on the project. She and the heart of her husband are buried in the Abbey, which was completed around 1273 and lies in what is now called the village of New Abbey, about eight miles south of Dumfries.

The first of this line of Scots to emigrate to America was John Corson (Sr.) who left Scotland in 1807 and settled in New York. He died in New York in 1812.

John Corson and his wife, Susan Benton had at least two children including Alexander Corson, who was born in New York about 1811. Shortly after John Corson died in 1812, his widow and children moved to Ohio. It is unclear why this family moved so soon after death of the husband and father. Most likely, other family members were moving, and Susan decided to go with them and take her sons. Living as a single mother in New York would have been challenging then. But there may have been another reason to move as well.

At the time of John Corson's death in 1812, it had only been twenty-nine years since the Treaty of Paris recognized the independence of the United States. And yet, this independence was being threatened again by Great Britain, whose actions and perceived actions led to an American declaration of war against the English in June, 1812.

By 1812, the economy in America was beginning to rival that of England, and at the center of that growth was New York City. Its harbor held hundreds of merchant ships loaded with goods for buyers in Europe. The cobblestone streets rumbled from the sounds of oxen and horse-drawn carts and wagons carrying homemade and manufactured goods to the ships waiting to sail.

Certainly, Susan Corson heard the stories of the British Navy harassing American merchant ships all along the Atlantic coast, confiscating the ships and cargo, and impressing American sailors who were taken prisoner and forced to man British warships during England's war with Napoleon. It was not surprising that New York citizens worried that they might fall under British rule again.

While Susan Corson was caring for her husband and her infant children, the original fort south of Manhattan, known as the Battery, had been dismantled and turned into a park, leaving the harbor generally defenseless. Reports to the governor warned that the British could invade, and the mayor appealed to citizens to defend their city.

Hundreds of citizens picked up shovels and picks and began working to build new defenses. Blockhouses, batteries and forts were built hurriedly on almost all islands and reefs along New York's coast. But none of this likely relieved the fears of those who lived there.

It must have been harrowing times for an ailing John Corson and his wife. His death in 1812 may have released Susan Benton Corson from her ties with New York and given her the courage to seek a safer life in Ohio for her and her children.

Captain Selah Benton (1740–1812)

Susan Corson was the daughter of Captain Selah Benton and Mary Elizabeth Jones. Selah Benton fought with the Continental Army in the Revolutionary War in many of the significant battles early in the war (see Chapter 31).

Alexander Corson (1811–1860)

After growing up in Ohio, Susan's and John's son Alexander married Elizabeth Knaus in 1832. Her family had emigrated from the Württemberg area in the German Palatinate and lived in Philadelphia before moving to Ohio. Her father was a bricklayer in Philadelphia. They moved after 1811, but no specific date has been established. Marriage between Scottish and German immigrant descendants was not typical, but on the frontier families quickly became "Americanized" with less distinction accorded to ancestry and past family history.

By 1846, Alexander and Elizabeth had moved from Ohio to Hinds County, Mississippi. Hinds County was created following the Treaty of Doak's Stand in 1821,[116] where Andrew Jackson and Thomas Hinds convinced the Choctaw to vacate the area and relocate to Arkansas. During the negotiations, a chief of the Choctaw's complained to Jackson about his proposal for the tribe to relocate.

> *"I know the country well... The grass is everywhere very short... There are but few beavers, and the honey and fruit are rare things." Jackson finally resorted to threats to pressure the Choctaw to sign a treaty. He shouted, "Many of your nation are already beyond the Mississippi, and others are every year removing... If you refuse... the [Choctaw] nation will be destroyed.[117]*

As an incentive to the Choctaw, Jackson promised protected land in Arkansas, Indian schools to be built, an annuity of $6,000 for sixteen years, and supplies including corn, blankets, kettles, rifles, ammunition, and a blacksmith. The promised land in Arkansas was already occupied by the Quapaw people, but that was not Jackson's concern.

The U.S. negotiators used a combination of threats and incentives to cause the Native American leaders to vacate their historic homeland. After the treaty was agreed and the Choctow had vacated, new settlers moved in, including Alexander and Elizabeth Corson.

Soon plantations growing cotton with slave labor proliferated. The first railroad connecting to Jackson opened, and industrial and processing facilities were developed leading to growth and opportunity for new residents. The area is central in the state of Mississippi; and its largest city, Jackson, subsequently became the state capitol.

Alexander and Elizabeth had three more children in Hinds including Theodore. Alexander died in Hinds sometime before 1860, and Elizabeth died after 1880.

Theodore Alexander Corson (1856–1926)

Theodore Corson, or T.A. as he was called, was an interesting man who pursued varied interests and accomplishments. He was born in the town of Clinton, Hinds County, Mississippi in 1856 and he lived there until at least 1880. He met Marietta Holmes, who was from Louisiana, and they were married in Lincoln, Louisiana on June 21, 1883. They lived in Louisiana until Marietta's death in 1892.

In 1894, T.A. married Martha "Mattie" Brooks in Chicot, Arkansas. They lived in Portland, Arkansas, until his death. In Arkansas, T.A. was the town telegraph operator for twenty years, working officially for the Missouri Pacific Railroad.

T.A. was an active member of the Baptist church. In 1908, T.A. edited a new newspaper that was created for the town of Portland called the Portland Index. Unfortunately, it did not survive long.

In 1907, T.A. was granted a patent for a railroad train car door. As the railroad telegraph operator, he must have realized a problem with the train freight doors and sought to invent a new type of door. It is unclear if railroads ever adopted T.A.'s door design.

He died in 1926, and the notice of his death appeared in the local newspaper:

Portland Telegraph Operator Is Found Dead in Bed.
Special to the Gazette

Pine Bluff, Feb 3 — T. A. Corson, aged 70, telegraph operator for the Missouri Pacific railroad at Portland for the past 20 years, was found dead in his bed about 6 o'clock this morning, when his wife attempted to awaken him for breakfast.

He is survived by his wife and one son, who lives in Chicago [Bernard], and a daughter in Russellville.

Bernard Finley Corson (1884–1957)

T.A. and Marietta's son Bernard, my maternal grandfather, was born in 1884 in Vienna, Louisiana. He lived with his family in Louisiana until his mother died and his father remarried. Then he moved with the family to Ashley County, Arkansas. In 1905, at the age of twenty-one, he married Susan (Susie) George. She was twenty years old and was born in Ashley County. Her parents were Gaston Percy George and Josephine George.

Bernard was a telegraph operator like his father, but his job was eliminated with the advent of the telephone. He moved his family to Louisiana to take extension courses in accounting at LaSalle University. Susie and Bernard's three children, including my mother, were born in Monroe, Louisiana.

They moved back to Ashley County for a while, and Bernard apparently served as town clerk. His father-in-law, Judge Percy George, ran the town and likely facilitated Bernard's appointment. After receiving his accounting degree, Bernard applied for a job as an accountant and was offered a job in Detroit. According to my mother, times were tough in Arkansas and Bernard was unwilling to compromise his ethics and work in a corrupt county environment. The family moved from the mostly rural South to the urban North by 1920. After three years in Detroit, Bernard was transferred to Chicago, where he and Susie lived until moving back to Arkansas sometime around 1950 to take over management of Judge Percy George's hotel, the Palace Hotel, in downtown Hamburg.

Bernard became a Christian Scientist, much to the dismay of his wife, Susie, who was an avid Methodist, and they argued often about religion. Susie was an active member of the Women's Christian Temperance Union, which supported prohibition.

They had three children: Francis, Bernice (my mother), and Bernard Jr. Francis married Frank Stanicek, and they lived in Hinsdale and Clarendon Hills, western suburbs of Chicago. They had four children: Frank Jr., Blair, John, and Jean. I still keep in touch with Jean, who lives in Steamboat Springs, Colorado.

Bernard Jr. (Barney) and his wife Wynne Rinnman had four children: Natalie, Susie, Wynne, and Bernard (Barry). They lived in Shenandoah, Iowa, and then Evanston, Illinois, a suburb of Chicago. I keep in touch with Wynne, who is an avid Chicago Cubs fan.

Bernard, my grandfather, died in Arkansas in 1957. His wife Susie, my grandmother, moved back to Chicago to be closer to her daughter Bernice (my mother) and died there in 1966. Susie was very social. When she was in her seventies she had a hysterectomy at a Chicago hospital. My mother was worried about her and went to visit often. On the first visit, Granny, as I called her, was missing from her room, much to the alarm of my mother and the nursing staff. It turned out that Granny had gotten out of bed and walked down the hall, pushing her IV bag holder, and was visiting other patients and chatting with her newfound friends.

Bernice Corson (1910–2000)

My mother was born in Monroe, Louisiana, in 1910. She and her parents lived much of their formative lives in the small town of Hamburg, Arkansas, but, as noted previously, the family also lived in north for many years, first in Detroit and then in Chicago.

After graduating high school in Chicago, my mother worked at a department store and spent her spare time studying dance. One year she was invited to go to New York City for an audition with the Radio City Rockettes, but her father refused permission because he did not feel dancing on a stage was an appropriate activity for a young woman. She was crushed. She attended the University of Arkansas for one semester but dropped out because she could not afford to continue.

She married Walter in 1933; she was twenty-three and he was twenty-eight. They were both living in Berwyn at the time and had been introduced by a mutual friend, Doug Scott. According to her notes, she was not attracted to him at first, but over time she fell in love. It was during the Great Depression and life was challenging. And when they had their fourth and last child, they named him after Doug Scott — Scott Douglas MacDonald — that's me.

Bernice was very close to her sister, Fran, and later to her younger brother Barney. The two sisters each had four children the same ages, and the families often spent holidays together. Unfortunately, Fran died of cancer in 1952 at the age of forty-two. Her husband, Frank, later married Dorothy Guy, who I remember fondly. She had one son, John Guy, from her prior marriage, and I keep in touch with him through Facebook. John lives in Indiana.

Barney moved to Riverside from Iowa and lived with our family until he could bring his family to Chicago. While he lived with us, Uncle Barney became a surrogate father to me. He took the job as station manager of WLS radio in Chicago. Not long after the family moved to nearby Evanston, Barney died suddenly of walking pneumonia at the age of forty-six (1958), leaving a wife and four children. He died on my mother's birthday, and I remember the call from his wife to my mother, and her anguish upon learning her brother had died so young and so suddenly. We cried a lot that night.

After my father's death, my mother took a clerical job at Liberty Mutual life Insurance and then at the Northern Trust bank in Chicago. She rose through the ranks in the male-dominated bank and retired as the second female vice president in the bank's history.

She was short in stature, about five foot four, and had red hair and a steely determination. She was often described as a dynamo, always in motion and never at rest. She was determined that her children would all graduate from college, which she was never able to do. She never had much money after her husband died, and we children mostly raised ourselves and worked every available hour to pay our own bills, even as youngsters. Later in life, she relied too much on alcohol to relax and likely bury the memory of family losses. She died of dementia-related problems at the age of ninety.

My grandparents, Bernard and Susie Corson

Figure 14: Roanoke Colony found abandoned

Chapter 27:

The Lost Colony and
the Lumbee Tribe

Establishing a European colony on the mid-Atlantic shore of America in the 1500s amidst unfriendly Natives and untamed and uncharted land was a challenge. The Spanish tried it first, having realized wealth and gold from South American expeditions and hearing of tales of similar riches available in North America. The Holy Roman Emperor Charles V authorized Lucas Vázquez de Ayllón, a well-connected judge who owned considerable land in Hispaniola (Dominican Republic), to establish a colony on the southeast coast of the North American mainland. The colony was initially referred to as Chicora, after the Spanish name given a native who was captured and taken to Spain, where he told of vast gold and riches in the area. Six ships carrying six hundred people sailed from Hispaniola to the Outer Banks of what is now North Carolina, arriving in July 1526. By October, the colonists had suffered Native attacks, illness, hunger and starvation, rebellion and desertion by African slaves, and many breakdowns and accidents. When Vázquez de Ayllón died about three months later, the remaining colonists sailed back to Hispaniola.

French Huguenots tried to find refuge in the same area in the early 1560s; their leader was captured and the others quickly abandoned the land to return to Europe. Three years later, another group of French landed and were attacked and massacred by the Spanish, who claimed the area as their possession.

Then came the English, led by the knighted Sir Walter Raleigh. Raleigh was a favorite of Queen Elizabeth, who granted Raleigh the right to establish a settlement in what is now known as Virginia. In 1584, Raleigh sent explorers Philip Amadas and Arthur Barlowe to North America in search of a potential site for an English colony. They selected Roanoke Island and returned to England with Manteo, chief of the Croatan tribe, and Wanchese, a leader of the Roanoke tribe. Raleigh quickly put the two Native men on display and used them to raise money for the proposed settlement.

In 1585, Raleigh sent an expedition to Roanoke Island under the direction of Ralph Lane and Raleigh's cousin Richard Grenville. Manteo became their interpreter and guide. Grenville returned to England in June of that year, and Lane and the remainder of the group departed in July 1586, having suffered from conflicts with the native tribes, illness, hunger, and difficult living conditions.

Sir Walter Raleigh was convinced vast riches awaited, so he sent another expedition led by John White in 1587 to establish the city of Raleigh by the Chesapeake Bay. However, they only made it as far as Roanoke and remained there. The next year, White agreed to sail back to England to secure needed supplies for the new colony. His return to Roanoke from England was delayed a couple years due to the Anglo–Spanish War. Three years after departing Roanoke, White returned but found no colonists, no bodies or graves, and no sign of conflict. The colonists had just disappeared.

The only sign left at the site was a carving at the entrance of the abandoned fort, "CROATOAN," and a carving in a nearby tree, "CRO." White and the colonists had agreed if the colonists had to move from the settlement, they would leave a sign about where they were going; and if they were leaving under duress, they would also leave a Greek cross; but neither carving showed the distress sign. This has led many historians to believe the remaining colonists joined the remnants of the local Croatan tribe, which spoke a language associated with Algonquian tribes.

The colonists may have split into two or more groups. Pottery fragments have been found on Hatteras Island, about fifty miles south of Roanoke, suggesting one group may have moved there.

The Croatans apparently moved west and joined other tribes who had suffered significant losses due to disease and war and were unable to sustain themselves alone. Many retreated to a swampy area along the Lumbee River in North Carolina which offered protection from other tribes and white settlers. Over time, they were joined by escaped slaves. Later they became referred to as the Lumbee tribe.

When the early European settlers came into the area, they were surprised that some of the Lumbee spoke English. They were also surprised to find European artifacts such as dishware and utensils, suggesting the Lumbee had a past relationship with Europeans.

Tribal history was oral; North American Natives did not use writing before contact with settlers. Lumbee history taught that the tribe originally came from the coastal area and included English settlers. Whether some or all of the Roanoke settlers ended up as part of the Lumbee tribe cannot be proved or disproved, but the Lumbee believe it is so.

In the 1880s, the North Carolina legislature enacted a series of Jim Crow laws to re-segregate the state, dividing Black and mixed race people from Whites. Hamilton McMillan, a Democratic State Representative, led the fight to ensure the Lumbee were not considered Black or mixed race, in part due to the Lumbees' presumed history of saving the early settlers at the Lost Colony. The Legislature agreed and provided the Lumbee with their own school system and did not impose the restrictions they imposed on "Negroes."

Ancestor Elizabeth Bearfoot (last name also recorded as Ox or Oxendine) was born about 1702. As indicated in Chapter 34, she was from the Lumbee tribe, and her ancestry was most likely from the Oxendine family, a Lumbee family that included remnants of the Roanoke, Croatan, Cheraw, and Creek peoples. She may well have been a descendant of a Lost Colony survivor.

Figure 15: Colonists arriving at Jamestown 1607

Chapter 28:
Jamestown

Many ancestors, including the Lyles and their various spouses and associated families, emigrated from England and arrived in Virginia beginning in the early 1600s. Jamestown was the first permanent English settlement in America, and emigrants from England around this time typically moved to the Jamestown area in Virginia or to New England.

In June, 1606, King James I gave the Virginia Company in England a charter to establish an English colony in the Chesapeake region of America. An expedition with three ships (*Susan Constant, Godspeed,* and *Discovery*) largely organized by Bartholomew Gosnold, set sail from England on December 20, 1606 with 144 crew and settlers. After a long journey plagued by bad weather, including a hurricane, they landed at Jamestown in May 1607. The *Discovery* was captained by John Ratcliffe, an ancestor.[118]

Jamestown was selected because it had access to the navigable James River just south of the Chesapeake Bay and was located upriver in a harbor protected from the Atlantic Ocean. It was easily reached by ocean-going ships but not readily visible to passing Spanish warships.

The settlers were a mixed lot. Many were "gentlemen" from upper-class families. They were more accustomed to being taken care of than doing manual labor. Others were craftsmen and laborers selected because their skills would be needed in the new world. The settlers were attracted by the prospect of finding gold and becoming rich. If they knew the challenges ahead, it is most unlikely any would have volunteered for the adventure.

On May 14, 1607, the three ships were unloaded at Jamestown, councilors were announced and Edward Maria Wingfield became the first president of the Virginia colony according to written instructions from the Virginia Company.

All men were now needed to build a fort and stockade, so John Smith, who had been imprisoned for mutiny while on the ship (see Chapter 2) was released to help with construction and defense. However, the Native attacks, sickness, disease, lack of food and Wingfield's inadequate leadership all took their toll on the colony. By August 1607, nearly half of the 105 settlers had died. Yet Wingfield seemed healthy which prompted Smith to investigate. Smith alleged that Wingfield had kept private stores for himself including beef, oatmeal, eggs, and wine, all the while allowing the colonists only insect-infested gruel and polluted water. Edward Wingfield was soon sent back to England.

John Ratcliffe was elected second president of the Virginia Colony. He put Smith in charge of finding food supplies, but Smith was more focused on fighting the Powhatan in retaliation for their savage attacks. Ratcliffe gave up his position as president to Smith in July 1608.

The first year of Jamestown was marked by disease, starvation, and Native attacks. By January 1608, only forty settlers remained alive. They survived only because some of the local Natives occasionally traded food for European goods.

John Ratcliffe sailed back to England in 1609 but returned later to Jamestown aboard the *Diamond*, serving as its commander. He should have stayed in England.

On his return to Virginia, Ratcliffe thought his trading skills would be useful with the Native tribes, so he accepted the invitation from the Powhatan chief to attend a gathering where corn would be traded for trinkets and tools. As Ratcliffe and his men returned to the settlement, Powhatan fighters hiding in the tall grasses ambushed them. Ratcliffe, the leader of the expedition, was singled out for a horrible fate. He was tied naked to a stake before a fire where his skin was scraped off by Powhatan women using seashells. The skin was thrown into the fire. Afterwards, they burned him alive.

Captain Christopher Newport arrived with supplies and sixty new settlers the next January. In April, Newport sailed back to England; by then more settlers had died including some of the newer arrivals. A fire destroyed much of the new supplies and food, leaving the settlers more dependent on food provided by the local tribes. Most historians would likely agree that only John Smith's strong leadership and his ability to trade with the local tribes for food kept the colony from failing.

Francis Nelson arrived shortly after Newport's departure with additional supplies and more settlers. The new settlers soon fell sick to the same diseases that afflicted the original settlers including dysentery, salt poisoning (from drinking river water), and typhus.

The local Native tribes were part of the Powhatan Confederacy. At times they supported the English settlers by providing food and trading; at other times they were hostile, killing settlers who strayed outside the fort at Jamestown.

By winter of 1610, the settlers had run out of food, and the relations with the Powhatan had devolved into open conflict. It is often referred to as "the starving time." [119] Desperate, the settlers slaughtered all the animals they could find for food from horses, dogs, cats, and rats and mice. There was even some cannibalism. Whenever anyone ventured out of the fort looking for anything to eat, Powhatan warriors quickly killed them.

Thomas Gates and two ships arrived at Jamestown in May of 1610 with some supplies and healthy men. By this point most of the settlers in the colony were too weak to stand, and the newly arrived ships were under-provisioned for the need. The leadership decided to load the survivors on the ships and sail for England, abandoning Jamestown. Before they crossed into the Atlantic, however, they turned back because three new ships under Lord De La Warr arrived with new supplies and men. Jamestown was saved, at least for a while.

De La Warr took charge and installed a military-like discipline in Jamestown. His men fought back against the Powhatan, driving them away from the perimeter of the fort, using superior firepower including the ships' cannons. In March 1611, De La Warr returned to England.

In 1611, Thomas Dale sailed to Jamestown with three ships, three hundred new settlers, livestock, and supplies, arriving in May. With fresh men, food, and armaments, the settlers began attacks against Powhatan villages in response to continued killings of settlers.

After the Royal Charter of 1609, when King James I granted more territory and more rights including the ability to raise money and sell land, promoters of the Virginia colony in England raised considerable sums to sponsor more ships; and more settlers arrived authorized to own land. The colony was also permitted self-government with a legislature. A second English settlement called Henrico was established just to the north. The new settlement was ferociously opposed by the Powhatan, who saw it correctly as a further incursion into their traditional lands and resulted in considerable conflict over time.

In 1612, colonist John Rolfe arranged to plant some mild West Indian tobacco in the Virginia soil, and the result was transforming. The favorable tasting new tobacco caught on in London and became the cash crop that would fund the colony for years to come.

There continued to be confrontations and killings between Natives and settlers, and in 1613, amidst a major confrontation between hundreds of Powhatan warriors and heavily armed settlers, a peace treaty was negotiated by John Rolfe and another settler and Opechancanough, brother of Wahunsonacock, leader of the Powhatans. Shortly thereafter John Rolfe married the Wahunsonacock's daughter Pocahontas (see Chapter 41). Relative peace followed and allowed further development of the Jamestown community.

With self-government, land grants to newly arriving settlers, fewer conflicts with local Native tribes, and a profitable cash crop, the settlement thrived at last. Between 1618 and 1621, almost four thousand new settlers arrived in Jamestown.[120]

The Powhatan and their allies were not pleased with the expansion of Jamestown and further incursions into their traditional lands. On March 22, 1622, about five hundred fighters from several tribes under the Powhatan leadership attacked Jamestown area settlements and killed about one-third of all the settlers in Virginia. The new community of Henrico was destroyed. The day is now referred to as "The Jamestown Massacre." The Powhatan war leader, Opechancanough, believed the English would leave. He apparently said to the assembled chiefs, "Before the end of two moons, there should not be an Englishmen in all their countries." [121] He was very much mistaken.

The Jamestown Massacre in Isle of Wight County

The houses were building, when, in March, 1622, occurred the great massacre by the Indians. In the course of a very few hours one-fourth of the white population perished. The mortality in the plantations in Warrascoyack reached a total of fifty-three. Some miraculous escapes are recorded. The Indians came to one Baldwin's house and wounded his wife, but Baldwin by repeatedly firing his gun so frightened them as "to save both her, his house, himself and divers others."

At about the same time they appeared at the house of Master Harrison, half a mile from Baldwin's, where was staying Thomas Hamor, brother of Capt. Ralph Hamor, who also lived near-by. The Indians pretended that they came to escort the captain to their king, who was hunting in the woods. The message was sent to the captain, but, he not coming as they expected, they set fire to a tobacco house, and murdered the white people as they rushed out of Harrison's building in order to quench the flames. Many were killed, but Thomas Hamor was saved by a chance delay. He remained to finish a letter, which he was engaged in writing. After concluding the letter, he went out, but seeing the commotion, and receiving an arrow in his back, he returned and barricaded the house. Then the savages set the house on fire, whereupon Hamor, with twenty-two others, fled to Baldwin's house, leaving their own burning.

In the meantime, Capt. Ralph Hamor was in utmost peril. He was on his way to meet the king, who had invited him, and came upon the savages chasing some of the whites. He returned to his new house, where, armed with only spades, axes, and brickbats, he and his company defended themselves till the enemy gave up the siege and departed. At the house of Capt. Basse, however, in the same neighborhood, everybody was slain. Basse, who was in England at the time, escaped.

The consternation occasioned by the massacre was such that the determination was taken to abandon all the plantations but seven or eight, viz., Jamestown… All Warrascoyack, from Hog Island down the river shore for fourteen miles, was abandoned. But vigorous efforts were made by the authorities to dislodge the Indians from the locality. In the fall succeeding the massacre an expedition was sent out under the command of Sir George Yeardley against the savages down the river. He drove out the Nansemonds and Warraseoyacks, burned their houses, and took their corn.

In the summer of 1623 the governor sent companies in all directions against the Indians. Capt. William Tucker, of Kecoughtan (Hampton), commanded the expedition against the Nansemonds and the Warrascoyacks. On the same day, August 2, 1623, all of these commands fell upon the Indians, slaughtered many, cut down their corn, and burnt their houses. A week after, Capt. Tucker went down a second time against the Nansemonds. The proprietors of the abandoned settlements took heart and were allowed to return to them. The census of February 6, 1623–24 showed as then living at "Warwicke Squeake" and "Basse's Choice" fifty-three persons; twenty-six had died "since April last."[122]

The settlers responded just as ruthlessly as the Natives, and a second Anglo-Powhatan war commenced and lasted for two years. The war resulted in the Powhatan Confederacy defeated, their towns burned, and their crops destroyed. With the Powhatan driven out, the settlement of Virginia expanded to nearby lands, giving rise to the Virginia Colony and then the Commonwealth of Virginia.

Many ancestors were part of the Jamestown story. Stephen Hopkins arrived on one of the original supply ships, the *Sea Venture*, in 1610 with John Rolfe. He played a prominent role in the colony's early days. Bartholomew Gosnold, a cousin, was the driving force behind the expedition, and both he and his brother, Anthony, died at Jamestown. In an attempt to reduce tensions between the Powhatan and the colonists, Captain Newport and John Smith offered a teenage boy from the colony, Thomas Savage, another ancestor, to live with the Powhatan tribe, learn their language and lifestyle. He lived with the Powhatans and became fluent in their language and later became a primary interpreter.

Other ancestors in Jamestown at the time included John and Ann (Gooch) Johnson who lived in Jamestown and had five children born there between 1620 and 1628. Elizabeth Powell and her husband, Thomas Garnett, lived and died there, and their first son was born there in 1625.

With the defeat of the Powhatan, other lands opened up for settlers, including Isle of Wight County, which was across the James River and a few miles to the south. Many of my ancestors emigrated from England to Isle of Wight County.

But the 1622 Jamestown massacre and aftermath did not end the conflict between settlers and members of the local tribes. Fighting continued until 1628 when peace was declared, but that peace was short-lived and hostilities resumed in 1629. A "final" peace was reached in 1632. In 1638, settler John Basse, an ancestor, married the daughter of a Nansemond chief, further cementing the peace.

In 1644, however, the Powhatan under Chief Opechancanough attacked again trying to drive the settlers away. About four hundred settlers were killed including ancestors Godfrey Ragsdale, his wife Mary Cookney, and her parents John Cookney and Jean Smithe. Godfrey and Mary left a three-month old baby, Godfrey (II), who survived. That baby grew up and had a son, Godfrey (III) who married Rachel Rowlett; their daughter Martha Ragsdale married Seth Pettypool.

In August 1645, Opechancanough was captured and killed, and his warriors were deported to an island in the Chesapeake Bay. A boundary was established formally separating the Powhatan from settlers as part of the Treaty of 1646, which ended the Anglo-Powhatan wars at last.

Figure 16: A log cabin in North Carolina

Chapter 29:
North Carolina

Immigrants to colonial America generally came from England, Scotland, Ireland, Wales, the Netherlands, and Germany. Those seeking religious freedom or identifying with a Puritan form of religion typically emigrated to New England. Those seeking economic opportunity often choose to go to Virginia, either through Pennsylvania and Maryland or directly to the Jamestown area. The Germans and the Scots generally went through Philadelphia and the Shenandoah Valley, and the English often choose southern Virginia around Jamestown.

Over time, the Shenandoah Valley and Philadelphia become crowded and land less available. Families had many children, and new immigrants were arriving steadily. As described in Chapter 11, many residents there opted to go to Ohio and the Midwest by wagon train over the National Road. Others, including many Scotch-Irish, instead opted to go south to North Carolina. Often, the original immigrants settled in Pennsylvania, then moved to Virginia which offered more available and affordable land. Then their descendants migrated to the Midwest or North Carolina.

Many of my mother's ancestors started in England, emigrated to Virginia, and had children and grandchildren who emigrated to North Carolina. Family lines including Lyles, Jones, Woodward, Earp, Powell, Smith, Johnson, Winn, and others all made this journey. Some were Quakers leaving an oppressive religious environment in England.

In 1663, eight English lords were granted a charter as the "lords proprietors" to develop and run the colony referred to as the Province of Carolina. They incentivized immigrants with generous land grants including thirty to one hundred acres to new immigrants, depending on their status. To encourage large plantations, masters and owners were given headrights for each slave imported, leading to the widespread importation of slaves.

By 1735, the Scotch-Irish in particular were immigrating into North Carolina in significant numbers. They typically settled in the northeastern part of the state, closest to the Virginia border, in an area referred to as Albemarle due to its proximity to the Albemarle Sound. Over time they moved into adjacent counties including Chowan and then Johnston. By the mid 1700s, more German families moved from Pennsylvania and Virginia to North Carolina, also in search for available and affordable land for their large families.

As the Jamestown area became crowded and land less available, the easiest access to open land was over the Great Wagon Road, which started in Philadelphia and continued through Virginia and into North Carolina. Originally this road was a Native trail, but as settlers travelled it, more trees were cut and it was widened. From the 1750s on, the Great Wagon Road was critical to the development of North Carolina.

The constant pressure to move to new lands was also due to the nature of tobacco farming at the time. Repeated planting of the same crop exhausted the soil, and without suitable fertilizer, the land became less productive. So the farmers moved to new lands which had not been planted previously with tobacco.

Documenting ancestors along the Virginia–North Carolina border is extremely challenging. A formal boundary between the states was not defined until William Byrd and Edward Moseley surveyed the area beginning in 1728. When tax collectors from Virginia came to record property and taxes owed, local residents typically claimed they lived in North Carolina, and when the taxmen from Carolina showed up, the same residents claimed they were in Virginia, leaving early local tax records missing many residents completely.

Generally, Virginians like Byrd did not hold North Carolinians in high esteem. His description of life in North Carolina must be viewed with a touch of sarcasm and humor.

> *Surely there is no place in the World where Inhabitants live with less Labour than in N Carolina. It approaches nearer the Description of Lubberland that any other, by the great felicity of the Climate, the easiness of raising Provisions, and the Slothfulness of the People.*

> *The Men, for their Parts, just like the Indians, impose all the Work upon the poor Women. They make their wives rise out of their Beds early in the Morning, at the same time that they lye and Snore, till the Sun has run one third of his Course, and disperst all the unwholesome Damps. Then, after Yawning for half an Hour, they light their Pipes, and, under the Protection of a cloud of Smoak, venture out into the open Air; tho', if it happens to be never so little cold, they quickly return Shivering into the Chimney corner. When the weather is mild, they stand leaning with both their arms upon the corn-field fence, and gravely consider whether they had best go and take a Small Heat at the Hough; but generally find reasons to put it off until another time.*

> *Thus they loiter away their Lives, like Solomon's Sluggard, with their arms across, and at the Winding up of the Year Scarcely have Bread to Eat.*

> *To speak the Truth, tis a through Aversion to Labor that makes People file off to N Carolina, where Plenty and a Warm Sun confirm them in their Disposition to Laziness for their whole lives.*[123]

The Edenton Tea Party

In contrast to Byrd's perception, there are many examples of North Carolina residents' engagement especially in the Revolutionary War and events leading up to the War. Most Americans are familiar with the story of the Boston Tea Party, where Sons of Liberty dressed as Native Americans and threw boxes of tea from the British East India Company into Boston Harbor in protest against the Tea Act of 1773. In October of 1774, fifty-one women from Chowan County, North Carolina, led by Penelope Barker, wrote and signed a petition to protest the Tea Act and the related tax and vowed to boycott British tea. It is now referred to as the "The Edenton [NC] Tea Party." Barker was the second wife of Thomas Barker of Bertie, North Carolina. His first wife was ancestor Pheribee Savage.

Women's activism and protest was virtually unheard of in 1774 anywhere in the American colonies. Women were busy raising large families and expected to focus on the needs at home. The petition promised to continue the boycott "until such time that all acts which tend to enslave our native country shall be repealed." According to Penelope Baker's biography, she stated at the time, "Maybe it has only been men who have protested the King up to now. That only means we women have taken too long to let our voices be heard. We are signing our names to a document, not hiding behind costumes like the men in Boston did at their tea party. The British will know who we are." The Edenton Tea Party was a landmark for women in politics and was well publicized and praised by American patriots but dismissed and ridiculed in London.[124]

Figure 17: Slaves picking cotton

Chapter 30:
The Slaves

The founding and early development of America cannot be told without acknowledging the role of slavery, especially in the South. I have been unable to identify any ancestors who descended from slaves; but with several southern ancestors living on plantations in Virginia, North and South Carolina, Georgia, Alabama, Louisiana and other places, it is likely some white male ancestors impregnated female slaves, and there are unknown ancestors which resulted.

Initially, the need for labor in early America was satisfied by immigrants and indentured servants, who usually worked for five to seven years to pay back for their passage to America. The first African slaves actually arrived at Jamestown in 1619. A Portuguese slave ship was captured by the privateer *White Lion*, and that ship docked in Jamestown with some of the seized slaves. Some of these slaves were traded to the colonists for food.

Those slaves and others who followed initially were viewed and treated as indentured servants. After working for their indenture period, they were free and were given basic possessions to restart their lives. Early settlers were familiar with the indentured system but unfamiliar with a system that kept people in servitude forever.

In the north, African servants were used in the cities to complement trades and fill industrial roles in additional to traditional farming activities. They often learned a trade and were freed after serving their indenture. In the south, slaves were used on farms to plant and harvest crops; female slaves also worked in the fields but typically did household chores on larger farms or plantations.

Then things changed in the South. In 1640, a Virginia court sentenced a rebellious African servant, John Punch, to a life of indenture or slavery. Unlike white indentured servants, Africans were easily recognized and more easily put into a caste system when slavery become more widespread.

In the mid and late 1600s, England's economy was doing better and fewer indentured servants were emigrating. At the same time the tobacco economy in Virginia and North Carolina was booming, requiring more labor. Natives were enslaved, but they often escaped and made their way back to their home communities. They also did not adjust to the confined lifestyle and were considered less immune to some tropical diseases than recent African immigrants.

To accommodate the thriving tobacco economy and supply the need for labor, Virginia legalized slavery in 1661. And in 1662, a Virginia court ruled that children followed the status of their mothers. An enslaved mother would have enslaved children; a free mother would have free children. Previously, children were viewed as tied to their father; but white men who impregnated African women did not want legal responsibility for those offspring, so the state simply changed the rules. Tying children to fathers also inhibited sales of male slaves, potentially lowering their value.

The southern colonies had considerable land occupied only by Native Americans. The states wanted more settlers and provided incentives to accomplish this. Any settler coming into a state received a "headright" which entitled him to a specified number of acres for him and anyone he brought with him. If a family of eight immigrated, for example, the head of household would be entitled to eight parcels of property. Indentured servants and slaves were counted as part of the household. Typical headrights varied but probably averaged fifty acres per person, which created a significant incentive to bring indentured servants and slaves into southern colonies such as Virginia and North Carolina. A family of eight, for example, would have been granted four hundred acres. And if that family brought ten slaves, the four hundred acres became nine hundred, even if the family sold some of the slaves after collecting their headrights.

As planters and landowners acquired more land, they needed more laborers. Big plantations growing tobacco (and later cotton) needed many farmworkers, which led to greater pressure to import more slaves. Essentially, the southern states subsidized and rewarded settlers for bringing in slaves. The North did not face the same conditions and were not as dependent on quantities of cheap labor to realize financial success.

The treatment of slaves varied greatly by location. Most of the African slaves brought to North America were shipped to the Caribbean to work on sugar plantations. Plantation owners there typically remained in England and other European countries and hired managers to run the Caribbean plantations. The owners and their managers often sought short-term profits and drove their slaves very hard, leading to high death rates and poor longevity. New captives were imported regularly to replace those who died.

By contrast, in much of the American South slaves were viewed as assets and were highly valued. This is not to say they were treated humanely: there was no permitted freedom of expression, and the consequences of resistance were often whipping or death. But those who did what was ordered at least lived longer and healthier lives than their Caribbean counterparts.

In Alabama, for example, most cotton moved by steamship along local rivers. Warehouses were typically located at the top of bluffs overlooking the river landings. Rolladores, who were typically slaves, moved the cotton at the top and put it on wooden slides propelling it to the landing at the bottom, where Stevedores would catch and load the bales. Stevedores performed work considered too dangerous to risk valuable slaves; they were often Irish immigrants, who were considered more expendable.[125]

In later-developing areas like southeastern Arkansas, slaves often fared worse. According to one report:

> *The most capable male slaves were often separated from their families and relocated to the swamps of southeast Arkansas. These swamplands were poorly drained, and many planters required their slaves to work long hours clearing trees from the swamps by hand. Slaves were forced to live in cramped slave quarters in the densely forested swamps, surrounded by disease-carrying mosquitoes. Conditions were brutal; slaves often received only one pair of clothes per year, given on Christmas by the planter family. Diets consisted of only fatback and cornmeal, usually lacking in vegetables and other necessities to stave off deficiencies.* [126]

About four hundred thousand Africans were forcibly imported to North America. [127] They lived disproportionately in the South. With population reproduction, which was encouraged and often forced, there were almost four million slaves in America when the Civil War started in 1860. [128]

Only about one-third of white residents owned slaves, [129] but those that did not own slaves usually aspired to do so. Owning slaves was a sign of class and achievement. Some of my ancestors owned slaves, and others did not. The richer ones that are better documented owned slaves, and the poorer ones, about whom less is known, almost certainly did not.

Enslaved Africans and their American descendants played an essential part in the economic growth and development of the South. The agricultural economy in the 1700s and early 1800s was largely dependent on an institution that violated basic human rights and was unfair and immoral by any measure.

Many slavery policies adopted by southern states had significant long-term consequences. The African American community became more matriarchal, with children attached to the mother and not the father. Families were often split with men being sent to other plantations and forced to abandon their families. Marriages between slaves were specifically not recognized or actually forbidden by the states. And it was illegal to teach a slave to read and write. When slavery did end with the Emancipation Act in 1863 and the subsequent end to the Civil War, freed slaves did not have much of a chance to compete. The legacy of slavery continues to affect American society hundreds of years later.

Figure 18: The Battle of Kings Mountain, South Carolina

Chapter 31:
The Revolutionary War
(1775–1783)

Almost no one wanted a war between the American colonies and Britain; well maybe a few "patriots" but not many others. Like many wars, this one started by accident, but there were many contributing factors that led to a receptivity for war when it did come.

The end of the French and Indian War (or Seven Years' War) in 1763 was celebrated throughout the colonies because it forced removal of the French and their Native American allies, ended many attacks on settlers who lived on the frontier, and opened land for colonial expansion. However, the English Proclamation of 1763 forbid colonial expansion into Native American territories, including what became the Midwest and much of the South. The colonists were not consulted, and they were angered that their sacrifices did not result the increased access to land that they had hoped for and expected.

The French and Indian War also left Britain with considerable debt, and the English economy suffered from recession and high unemployment at the time. The English Parliament needed to raise taxes and thought taxing the colonies would help alleviate these financial burdens. Also, there were about ten thousand British soldiers then in the colonies with no war to fight, but there was no desire to bring them home to England and add to the unemployment. As a result, the Parliament passed a series of acts without consulting their colonies. These included a tax on sugar and molasses (The American Revenue Act of 1764), the Currency Act (1764) requiring use of English currency despite its limited availability in the colonies, the Stamp Act (1765) requiring all paper used to be stamped showing payment of tax, and the Tea Act (1773) allowing direct sale of tea by the East India Company.

The Stamp Act especially was met with widespread opposition in the colonies. The Act demanded that all colonial printed materials be produced on stamped paper from London which carried the official embossed revenue stamp. This included all legal documents, newspapers, magazines, and even playing cards. The stamped papers had to be purchased using British currency instead of the colonial paper money, even though Americans typically no longer used British currency. Those who disobeyed the demands of the Stamp Act could have their personal property of value confiscated at the discretion of British soldiers in the colonies.

The Stamp Act Congress was held in New York City and became the first significant joint colonial response to any British demand. It created the Committee of Correspondence to try legal negotiations as a solution. However, the Sons of Liberty were more effective.

Colonial newspapers reported on the state by state demonstrations by the Sons of Liberty, and membership in the group increased quickly. Their most effective action and one widely supported was to confront and threaten the stamp distributors. As the confrontations became more violent, more stamp distributors resigned their commissions. When a distributor in Westmoreland County, Virginia, boasted that he would continue to sell stamped paper when and where he chose, ancestor Richard Henry Lee gathered his militia men, went to the man's home, forced him to resign, then burned all of the stamped papers in a bonfire on his lawn.

Other acts followed to raise revenue for Britain, despite the English tradition of avoiding taxation without representation and the fact that the colonies had no members in Parliament to represent them. The Tea Act was not actually intended to raise revenue directly but to help the financially stressed East India Company dispose of its large tea inventory by giving them a monopoly in the colonial market. This was a "last straw" for the colonial activists and resulted in the Boston Tea Party, where Sons of Liberty members dressed as Native Americans and threw a shipload of tea into the Boston Harbor before the tea could be offloaded. Less well known were other Tea Act protests including the Edenton Tea Party (see Chapter 29).

With tensions rising, particularly in Boston and New England, the English decided to arrest perceived colonial leaders who opposed British taxes and related policies. In April 1775, British General Gage dispatched nine hundred soldiers from Boston to Lexington, where he thought John Hancock and Samuel Adams were staying, to capture them and then proceed to Concord to seize an arsenal of weapons. The timing was a poorly kept secret but the route was not known in advance. The plan was to send the troops before midnight, complete the mission in Concord by eight o'clock in the morning and be back in Boston by noon without any significant opposition.

Patriots Paul Revere, Charles Dawes, and other riders rode to Lexington and Concord beginning at midnight to alert citizens, militia, and Hancock and Adams that the British soldiers were coming (see Paul Revere's Ride Chapter 21). The British ran well behind schedule but did not encounter serious opposition on their march to Lexington; there were too many soldiers and too few colonists prepared to try to stop the formable army. But after not finding Hancock or Adams, they marched to Concord and were confronted by a group of patriots at the town's north bridge. Shots were fired leaving two colonists and three English soldiers dead. These shots became known as "the shots heard around the world" in the opening stanza of Ralph Waldo Emerson's poem, *Concord Hymn*:

> *By the rude bridge that arched the flood*
> *Their flag to April's breeze unfurled*
> *Here once the embattled farmers stood*
> *And fired the shot heard round the world.*

The British march back to Boston late in that day was devastating: an estimated one thousand colonial farmers, militia, and other locals from Massachusetts, Connecticut, and even Rhode Island gathered and fired from behind trees, fences and rocks at the bright, red-coated marchers on their way back to Boston. There is no roster of which patriots fought, but it is almost certain that some of the many area ancestors would have joined battle. There were causalities on both sides, including civilians that British soldiers killed in their homes believing they were part of the enemy. But the British suffered more with sixty-five dead and 207 wounded. And with the shots fired, the Revolutionary War began.

Each colony had its own militia, usually formed to defend against Native American attacks. The militias were the colonies' military before the establishment of the Continental Army. When the War of Independence broke out, ancestor Thomas Marshall was part of the leadership of the original Culpeper (Virginia) Minutemen, formed in July 1775, a year before the Declaration of Independence. The Minutemen, so called because they could be called upon with a minute's notice, fought the British in the earliest battles. They were known for their flag, a white banner depicting a rattlesnake, and their phrases, "Liberty or Death" and "Don't Tread on Me."

A couple months after Concord and Lexington, in June, 1775, patriots occupied Breed's Hill overlooking Boston Harbor (see Chapter 58) and fought the first major battle of the war. Thereafter, George Washington was formally appointed Commander of the Continental Army and ancestor Selah Benton joined him in Boston for a siege that led to the British withdrawal from that city.

Washington and his troops moved on to New York; as did the British under General Gage. Both sides felt the war would be won in New York City; whomever controlled New York controlled the American economy. The Declaration of Independence was issued in July 1776, and General Howe moved twenty thousand additional British soldiers and several warships to New York City to confront and defeat the colonials. Washington split his troops between Long Island and north of the city; Selah Benton was an ensign with the troops on Long Island. The major battle on Long Island occurred in August, and nine thousand American troops, representing most of the Continental Army, were forced to retreat to Brooklyn Heights and backed against New York Bay, which was blocked by British warships. The British forces were led by General Sir William Howe who decided to pause the attack and give Washington time to surrender. Instead, the Americans appealed to small boat owners across the bay to rescue the Americans under cover of darkness. In one of history's greatest escapes, surrounded on land by the British army and blocked by British warships in the bay, nine thousand Continental troops evacuated in small boats under cover of darkness, with wagon and cannon wheels muffled and everyone quiet so as not to attract British attention. In the morning, fog miraculously descended providing protection for the last of the troops including General Washington, to leave. This daring retreat saved Washington, Selah Benton and the Continental Army.

Selah Benton and his regiment fought battles in New Jersey including the famous Battle of Trenton. After losing many battles in New Jersey and losing the effort to protect Philadelphia, the capital, George Washington and his troops wintered in Pennsylvania in 1776. Morale was very low, troops were leaving, and the general population was questioning whether the drive for independence would end soon. General Washington led his depleted Continental troops across the Delaware River on Christmas evening and launched a surprise attack on 1,500 Hessian troops in Trenton, scoring a major American victory and giving hope to the troops and patriots throughout the colonies.

Soon thereafter, General Washington launched an attack on the British troops at nearby Princeton. An ancestor (cousin), John Fleming, played a key role in the Princeton battle, as reported in *Finding Your Forefathers in America*:

> *This young man [John Fleming] was a Captain in the First Virginia Regiment of the Continental Line. Toward the end of the year 1776 his regiment marched northward and joined the American forces about Philadelphia under [George] Washington. He commanded his regiment in the Battle of Princeton, January 3, 1777. The Americans were being forced back, several companies broke and fled, and there was a danger of a general stampede. Washington was alarmed, and rode forward, in great peril, to attempt to stem the retreat. He rode his horse between his men and the British, who were only about thirty yards apart, and became the target for the enemy's fire, but was providentially preserved. It was just at this moment when disaster seemed imminent, that the First Virginia, led by its heroic young Captain Fleming, came out of the woods, cheering and shouting.*

> *Stopping on a line with Washington, just 30 yards from the British, the brave young officer of 22 coolly ordered his men to "dress the line before they fired." Whereupon, the British exclaimed with curses "We will dress you," and poured deadly fire. Then the British engaged in a bayonet duel with the Virginians in the course of which Captain Fleming and Lieutenant Bartholomew Yates (aged 19) were mortally stabbed.*

> *The British were forced back, and the example of the First Virginia had a saving effect.*

> *On January 24, 1777, a notice appeared in the Virginia Gazette: "By accounts from the northward, we have the melancholy news of the death of Captain John Fleming of the First Virginia Regiment, who proved himself to be a gallant officer, and nobly fell on the 3rd instant, near Trenton, at the head of his company, in defense of American freedom. He was universally esteemed by those who were acquainted with him, and his loss is much regretted."[130]*

The two American victories after so many losses reinvigorated the American colonies and enabled further recruitment of soldiers to the Continental Army. Selah Benton was promoted to lieutenant and then later to captain due to his leadership and heroism in battle.

The Bloom family, having immigrated to New Jersey from Germany not that long before, supported the Continental Army. Peter Jr. and his siblings enlisted in a New Jersey regiment and fought under Washington in both losing battles and victories in 1776 and 1777. One of Peter's brothers, Issac, died in battle in New Jersey. During the winter quarters both years, conditions were dreadful, with Continental soldiers suffering from inadequate clothing and shelter, malnutrition, hunger, and disease.

Ancestors Major Thomas Marshall and enlisted man Lewis Lyles fought with General Washington in key battles in New Jersey including at Brandywine and Germantown. At Brandywine the main Continental Army led by Washington faced the main British Army led by General Howe. While outnumbered, the colonials fought a particularly intense fight, as described by historian John Ferling:

> The fighting was savage. One Redcoat was amazed by the "most infernal fire" on this field, as balls whistled and set "trees crackling over one's head" and "leaves falling as in autumn." Much of the combat was at close quarters, "almost Muzzle to Muzzle," according to one rebel. A private in the Bucks County militia remembered "bombshells and shot fell round me like hail, cutting down my comrades on every side, and tearing off the limbs of trees like a whirlwind."[131]

According W.M. Paxton, at Brandywine:

> The third Virginia Regiment, under command of Col. Thomas Marshall, which had performed severe duty in 1776, was placed in the wood on the right, and in front of Woodford's Brigade and Stephen's division. Though attacked by superior numbers, the regiment maintained its position until both its flanks were turned, its ammunition nearly expended, and more than half its officers, and one third of its soldiers killed, or wounded… Among the wounded in the battle, were Lafayette and Woodford. It has been said that at Brandywine, Col. Marshall saved the patriot army from destruction."[132]

During the battle, Thomas Marshall's horse was shot out from under him, but he found another mount and continued the fight. The battle resulted in a British victory and the loss of one thousand Americans, but most of the Continental Army escaped to regroup and fight again.

Not long after, Washington and his remaining army fought another battle at Germantown. The Continentals suffered their second major defeat within a month, losing about another one thousand men. In the battle, Thomas Marshall succeeded Brigadier General Mercer who had died earlier, and ancestor Lewis Lyles and his North Carolina regiment were tasked with covering the American retreat, holding off the British so the Continental Army would survive. In the heavy fighting during the retreat, North Carolina's commander, General Francis Nash, was killed; but Lewis Lyles survived.

In 1776, ancestor Comfort Ludington was a captain of the Dutchess County (New York) militia, protecting a major Continental supply depot, providing medical facilities to army soldiers including those injured in the battle for New York, and fighting loyalists and hostile Native tribes. In nearby Connecticut, ancestor Henry Ludington commanded another militia company; he later joined the Continental Army as a colonel and served for a time as aide-de-camp to George Washington. His daughter Sybil was the heroine who in 1777 rode through the night to alert the militia the British were coming after burning Danbury (see Chapter 17).

Colonel Ludington also was instrumental in helping establish America's first secret service by recruiting spies to gather information on British activities. Enoch Crosby was one of the first spies that Henry collaborated with. Crosby was apparently the basis for James Fenimore Cooper's character Harvey Birch in the novel, *The Spy.*

While sequestered in New Jersey and having recently suffered military loses in New York, George Washington sent "Mad" Anthony Wayne and a small force including Captain Selah Benton, to attack the British military base at Stony Point, New York, in 1779. According to one description of the raid:

> *The fort sat on a point that rose 150 feet above the Hudson and was surrounded by water on three sides. A swamp, passable by foot only during low tide, lay on the fourth side. It was garrisoned by nearly seven hundred enemy soldiers and its fortifications were daunting — two abatis, three redoubts, and cannon trained on every approach. The plan…was so risky that the advance parties were labeled 'forlorn hope'…or 'suicide squads' in today's lexicon. Wayne was to lead two hundred carefully chosen volunteers, daredevils who were to strike after midnight… Each man was to wear a piece of white paper in his hat to signify that he was a comrade to other rebels.*

> *The attack came off flawlessly… Once inside, the fighting was hand to hand, with the rebels wielding bayonets, swords, and spontoons (a half-pike). The Americans suffered 100 casualties…but the British lost 676 killed, wounded, and captured.*[133]

Another theater of war was in upper New York state and Pennsylvania. The British organized, supported, and armed Loyalists and Natives, primarily from the Iroquois League, to attack, plunder, and destroy settlements that potentially supplied men to patriot forces and food supplies to the Continental Army. The attacks were widespread and often savage. The leader of these troops, Joseph Brant, became known as a "monster" because of alleged atrocities by his Mohawk warriors. Local militia responded but were unable to contain the attackers. In one battle, eight hundred militiamen from Tryon County engaged a large force of Loyalists and Native fighters; about 465 militiamen died as well as many Loyalists and Natives on the British side. Finally, General Washington sent General John Sullivan with four thousand Continental soldiers to the area to confront the British and their allies. The British troops left the area to defend against a rumored attack against Canada, leaving the Loyalists and Natives, who were no match for Sullivan's troops. Ancestor Elisha Ludington fought under Sullivan as they destroyed Iroquois villages and killed loyalists. After the war, the Iroquois were forced completely out of the area, opening the land for colonial settlers.

The Americans did win a significant battle at Saratoga in 1777, with the defeat of British General Burgoyne, the loss of one thousand of his soldiers, and surrender of almost six thousand others. But subsequently, neither side made much progress, and the British still held New York. The French entered the war in 1778, making Britain's prospects of an early victory less likely.

In 1779, the British adopted a new strategy — launch a major campaign in the South where, aided by a strong Loyalist population and opposed by few Continental troops, the English could take control of Georgia and South Carolina and then move into North Carolina and Virginia. Taking the South and destroying the Continental Army, they thought, would carry over and result in victory in the North. And even if the war ended in a settlement, the new United States would become a small country, limited to the New England colonies, and Britain would control Canada, the South, New York, Philadelphia and nearby regions.

Britain already controlled Savannah so the next move in the South was Charleston. The siege of Charleston is described as follows:

> In December 1779, the British Commander-in-Chief in America, General Sir Henry Clinton left New York City with a fleet of ninety troopships, fourteen warships, and more than 13,500 soldiers and sailors. Sailing for Savannah, Georgia, Clinton planned to rendezvous with a force commanded by Lieutenant Colonel Mark Prevost and march overland to Charleston, South Carolina. Defending the city was a grossly outnumbered American army under the command of General Benjamin Lincoln.

In March 1780, Clinton, Prevost, and General Charles Lord Cornwallis whose force had accompanied Clinton from New York, descended on Charleston. By early April, the combined British forces had successfully trapped the Americans in the beleaguered city.

To make matters worse for the defenders, British warships successfully ran past Fort Moultrie at the mouth of Charleston Harbor, further isolating Lincoln's position by effectively closing off any means of escape or reinforcement. The noose only grew tighter as more British forces converged on the Charleston area and began to bombard the Americans' hastily prepared defensive works.

On April 21, hoping to preserve his army, Lincoln offered to surrender the city if his men were allowed to leave unharmed. Clinton refused to accept these terms and quickly resumed his artillery bombardment.

Over the next two weeks, the British moved closer and closer to the American lines. By May 8, only a few yards separated the armies. Clinton demanded that Lincoln surrender unconditionally. The American general refused, so Clinton ordered the city bombarded with heated shot. As Charleston burned, Lincoln had no choice but to accept the inevitable.

The siege of Charleston finally came to a close on May 12, 1780. With General Lincoln's surrender, an entire American army of roughly 5,000 men ceased to exist.[134]

Among the prisoners was ancestor Major John Ford.

After the American surrender at Charleston, South Carolina, on May 12, 1780, the British had effective military control of Georgia and South Carolina. British General Cornwallis next set his sights on North Carolina and the ultimate control of the American South. However, Cornwallis wanted more troops and turned to Loyalist officers, Lieutenant Colonel John Moore and Major Nicholas Welch, to raise a loyalist army and support the pending British invasion of North Carolina. British troops aided by Loyalists moved on to Charlotte, taking the city with little opposition in the fall. However, the British and their Loyalist allies did not give much credit to the militias, especially in South Carolina, who did not go quietly. The militia did not fight in the Battle of Charleston, typically feeling the local residents there were rich, high society, and plantation owners with little in common with the back country and small towns from which the militia members were generally drawn. But when the British and the Loyalists moved through the back country pillaging and killing, the militia boys decided it was time to respond. The fighters included ancestors Joseph Breed, his brother Nathan, and his son-in-law Richard George, all of whom were part of Colonel Thomas Brandon's regiment of the South Carolina Militia.

Battle of Ramsour's Mill

Moore and Welch recruited 1,300 Loyalists and on June 20, 1780, they assembled on a hillside at Ramsour's Mill in Lincoln County, North Carolina. The Patriots found out about the Loyalist camp and marched in four hundred poorly trained and ill-equipped militia under the leadership of Colonel Francis Locke and Colonel Thomas Brandon.

In a thick fog, the Patriots launched a surprise attack despite being outnumbered. They sneaked up on the Tories and fought them hand-to-hand two hours. Neither side had uniforms, so there was considerable confusion. When the fog lifted, both sides had lost an equal number of soldiers, but the Loyalists fled. The Patriots, including the Breeds and ancestor Richard George, dug a mass grave for the hundreds of dead soldiers. Local support for the Loyalists waned after the battle, and General Cornwallis never received the Loyalist support he needed to prosecute the southern war as he had planned. For their part, the Patriots were inspired to fight more battles including the Battle of Kings Mountain four months later.

Battle of Musgrove Mill

Four weeks after a small battle and victory against Loyalists at Stallion's Plantation in central South Carolina, Joseph Breed Jr. and relatives found themselves again taking on the Loyalists in a surprise raid at Musgrove's Mill, which controlled the local grain supply. The Patriots were not happy that the Loyalists were camping there. Even though a local farmer had warned the Little River Regiment that the British had been reinforced with three hundred militia and provincial regulars, the hour-long battle took place anyhow. Sixty-three Tories were killed and seventy taken prisoner. This victory reinforced the Patriots' belief that the South Carolina backcountry could not be held by the Tories.

Battle of Kings Mountain

American pioneers who chose to settle their families west of the Appalachian Mountains were known as the "Overmountain Men" and were accustomed to the rough life and dangers of living in the wilderness. Colonel Isaac Shelby commanded a group these men and led them over the range of mountains into North Carolina to join Colonel William Campbell's Patriot forces. Together they were 1,400 strong. Both Shelby and Campbell knew that Charlotte, North Carolina, had surrendered to the British and that British General Cornwallis was using the city as his center of command.

When British Major Patrick Ferguson found out about the joint forces of Patriots, he requested reinforcements from Cornwallis. There was no reply. By October 1, Ferguson had reached the Broad River in North Carolina and issued a public letter demanding the local militia to join him "lest they be pissed upon by a set of mongrels" (the Overmountain Men).[135]

When spies reported to Shelby and Campbell that the British were camped at Kings Mountain, the Patriots chose to use the element of surprise to surround the British troops and open fire. The entire battle would have been comical if it hadn't been so deadly: the British had camped at the steepest part of the ridge. The Patriots had to run up the hill while they were shooting. Ferguson ordered his men to charge down the hill and use their bayonets. Having no bayonets, the Americans had to run back down the hill and hide in the woods. The British ran back up the hill followed by the Americans shooting at them. Again and again the two armies chased each other up and down the mountain. Finally, Ferguson was attacked from behind and his horse dragged him behind Patriot lines, where a Patriot demanded his surrender. Ferguson shot him. The Patriots returned fire, and Ferguson died of seven bullet wounds.

The American victory significantly reduced Loyalist support in the South and is considered the beginning of the end of Britain's Southern strategy. Twenty-eight Americans died and fifty-eight were wounded in the battle; about two hundred fifty Loyalists died, 163 were wounded, and 668 captured.

The Battle of Cowpens

The last battle that ancestor Joseph Breed Jr. and his relatives participated in was the Battle of Cowpens, on January 17, 1781. Many historians considered this battle a turning point in the Revolutionary War.

General Cornwallis planned on returning to the Carolinas and leading the invasion that he had postponed after the defeat at Kings Mountain. He ordered his most capable commander, Lieutenant Colonel Banastre Tarleton, to pursue General Daniel Morgan's forces and wipe them out. Tarleton led a legion of Loyalist cavalry and light infantry called Tarleton's Raiders that won numerous battles and inspired fear by civilians and patriot forces. His nickname was "the Butcher." He was accused of massacring Patriot soldiers after they surrendered, treating civilians harshly, and advocating repression of the civilian population.

Morgan did not want to risk having his troops ambushed while trying to cross the two rivers in his path, swollen with high flood waters, so he decided to make a stand in a lightly forested area called "Hannah's Cowpens." Scouts had relayed to Morgan that Tarleton was marching his men throughout the night without stopping for rest or food. Morgan anticipated that the twenty-six year-old Tarleton, with all his youthful aggression, would make a headlong assault, which he did. The Americans were waiting and responded aggressively, overwhelming Tarleton's army. The Patriots killed 110 British soldiers and Loyalists and captured 829.

While almost all the ancestors were Patriots and fought the British and their Loyalist allies, ancestor Mary Cunningham's brother, Bill, is a different story. Bill Cunningham had originally enlisted with the Patriots, joining the South Carolina Regiment of Horse Rangers, whose captain was family friend John Caldwell. There was a falling out between Bill and the regiment, and Bill was court-martialed and whipped in public. After being humiliated, Bill Cunningham deserted and fled to Florida. Captain Caldwell ordered Bill's old and feeble father evicted in an increasingly hostile feud. Bill then began his tour of vengeance.

He raised an army of Loyalists which traveled from Florida to Laurens County, South Carolina, where they stopped at Captain Caldwell's home and shot him. Bill then proceeded to the home of William Richie, who had carried out Caldwell's order to evict Bill's father, and shot and killed Richie in front of his family and then burned his house. For the entire year of 1781, "Bloody Bill" Cunningham and his Loyalists killed any Patriot they encountered. No one commanded more fear and hatred in South Carolina than Bloody Bill and his band of Loyalists. By the end of the Revolution, Bloody Bill and his followers retreated back to Florida, where he was arrested by Spanish authorities and deported to Cuba. Bill died in Nassau, the Bahamas, in 1787.[136]

While the South Carolina militia and some Continental troops were fighting British and Loyalist troops in South Carolina, Cornwallis moved into North Carolina, and General Washington appointed General Nathanael Greene to take over the Continental troops in the South. Ancestor Elisha Woodward and his friends and relatives joined the North Carolina militia and fought in many battles during the war. Elisha was likely a member of the Johnston County regiment which primarily fought battles against Loyalists and their Cherokee allies but also against British troops. They were in at least thirteen known battles.

The North Carolina militia fought alongside troops of the Continental Army commanded by General Greene. Greene's few troops and the relatively inexperienced militia were no match for the professional British troops under General Cornwallis. Greene tried to avoid major confrontations with the more numerous and better equipped British, instead engaging in small battles and hit-and-run tactics to wear down the British. According to Greene, "We fight, get beat, rise, and fight again."[137]

In one typical battle, the Battle of Cowan's Ford in January 1781, the British troops moved forward during a heavy rain in the hopes of catching and destroying Greene's outnumbered troops and militia. The Patriots waited in hiding across the Catawba River. When the British began to ford the river, Patriot troops opened fire, killing

British soldiers in the water. When British troops managed to reach the bank and establish a beachhead, the Patriots retreated into the woods and disengaged.

Elsewhere, ancestor Lewis Lyles' enlistment period expired and, he returned home from New Jersey and Pennsylvania to North Carolina in late 1778. He was still there when the British took Charleston in 1780. He re-enlisted in 1781, and his new regiment was hastily assembled to join General Greene in South Carolina:

> *Reconstituted from April to July of 1781, with detachments being hurriedly sent to South Carolina to support Maj. Gen. Nathanael Greene. As men were recruited, they were assembled and marched southward, usually with no uniforms and with no arms or ammunition. Ultimately, the 2nd NC Regiment again became part of the NC Brigade (one and only one), an element of the Southern Department.*[138]

Battle of Eutaw Springs

The North Carolina men fought valiantly under General Nathanael Greene in the Battle of Eutaw Springs[139] against much more seasoned British troops led by General Alexander Stewart. This battle, fought in September 1781, was the last major Revolutionary War engagement in the Carolinas. The brutal battle ranged all day with almost 1,200 casualties. Both sides claimed victory, but the British retreated to Charleston after suffering many casualties.

Battle of Yorktown

Frequent battles, constant marches, and the frustrating inability to defeat the less numerous and less well-equipped Patriots weakened the British troops. Later in 1781, General Cornwallis and the British troops moved out of North Carolina to Yorktown, Virginia, and waited for resupply, additional troops from the north, and arrival of more British navy ships. General Washington moved down from the North and brought additional troops and, supported by French soldiers and the French navy, surrounded Cornwallis and begin a siege and shelling. On October 19, 1781, Cornwallis surrendered his eight thousand troops and much equipment. The devastating British loss at the Battle of Yorktown lead to the end to the Revolutionary War and the Treaty of Paris in 1783. Ironically, Britain's Southern strategy, designed to win the war, led to its defeat.

Going Home

Many ancestors fought in the Revolutionary War in many battles and in many locations. Generally, their service was for one year (militias often shorter) but many extended their terms. Some re-enlisted after putting their farms in order; later in the war, some enlisted for a full three years in exchange for a bigger bonus. Eventually all who survived returned to their farms and families, like ancestor David Wakeman, who went home following his discharge from the Fifth Connecticut Regiment:

He returned [home] with John Hendrick, and arrived first at the home of the Hendricks, and found the house vacant. They continued across the fields to the Wakeman house, where they found the two families together, Mrs. Henrick helping Mrs. Wakeman in spinning woolen yarn, and the boys and girls of both families were harvesting buckwheat. David Wakeman had much ground prepared for corn in the spring, before he was obligated to start for the front, and as Jeremiah [the oldest son] could not take care of so much, if planted, he utilized some of the ground for buckwheat. While David did not leave the plow in the furrow, he did leave much corn unplanted. The two families had worked together, and helped each other during the season [when the fathers were gone doing military service], and it was not strange that Jeremiah Wakeman and Phebe Hendrick should have become attached to each other. When David arrived home from the army, he was so fatigued, he was unable to help much in gathering in the crops. Jeremiah was anxious to enlist in his country's cause, but Mr. Wakeman would not give his consent to joining the Militia, because of the great hardships he endured. But when the call came for mounted men, he allowed Jeremiah to enlist.[140]

Chapter 32:
The Lyles Family: England, North Carolina, and Alabama

Pedigree Chart for
Sarah Elizabeth Winn Lyles

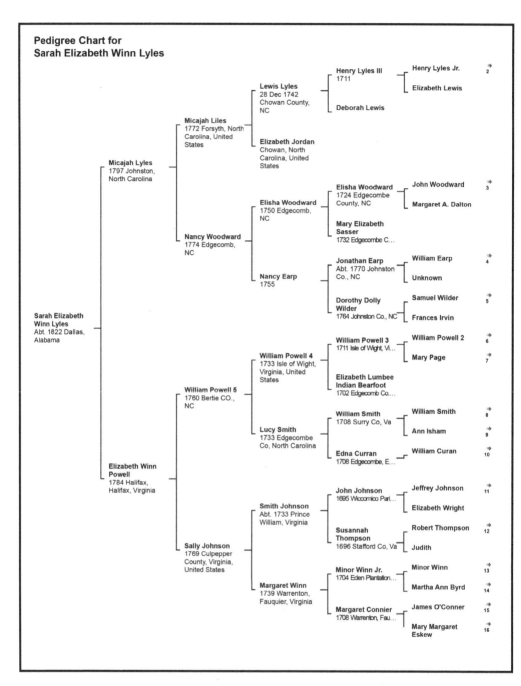

Sarah Elizabeth Winn Lyles
Abt. 1822 Dallas, Alabama

Micajah Lyles
1797 Johnston, North Carolina

Elizabeth Winn Powell
1784 Halifax, Halifax, Virginia

Micajah Liles
1772 Forsyth, North Carolina, United States

Nancy Woodward
1774 Edgecomb, NC

William Powell 5
1760 Bertie CO., NC

Sally Johnson
1769 Culpepper County, Virginia, United States

Lewis Lyles
28 Dec 1742 Chowan County, NC

Elizabeth Jordan
Chowan, North Carolina, United States

Elisha Woodward
1750 Edgecomb, NC

Nancy Earp
1755

William Powell 4
1733 Isle of Wight, Virginia, United States

Lucy Smith
1733 Edgecombe Co, North Carolina

Smith Johnson
Abt. 1733 Prince William, Virginia

Margaret Winn
1739 Warrenton, Fauquier, Virginia

Henry Lyles III
1711

Deborah Lewis

Elisha Woodward
1724 Edgecombe County, NC

Mary Elizabeth Sasser
1732 Edgecombe C...

Jonathan Earp
Abt. 1770 Johnston Co., NC

Dorothy Dolly Wilder
1764 Johnston Co., NC

William Powell 3
1711 Isle of Wight, Vi...

Elizabeth Lumbee Indian Bearfoot
1702 Edgecomb Co....

William Smith
1708 Surry Co, Va

Edna Curran
1708 Edgecombe, E...

John Johnson
1695 Wiccomico Pari...

Susannah Thompson
1696 Stafford Co, Va

Minor Winn Jr.
1704 Eden Plantation...

Margaret Connier
1708 Warrenton, Fau...

Henry Lyles Jr. [2]

Elizabeth Lewis

John Woodward [3]

Margaret A. Dalton

William Earp [4]

Unknown

Samuel Wilder [5]

Frances Irvin

William Powell 2 [6]

Mary Page [7]

William Smith [8]

Ann Isham [9]

William Curan [10]

Jeffrey Johnson [11]

Elizabeth Wright

Robert Thompson [12]

Judith

Minor Winn [13]

Martha Ann Byrd [14]

James O'Conner [15]

Mary Margaret Eskew [16]

Genealogy 19: Sarah Elizabeth Winn Lyles

**Pedigree Chart for
Henry Lyles Jr.**

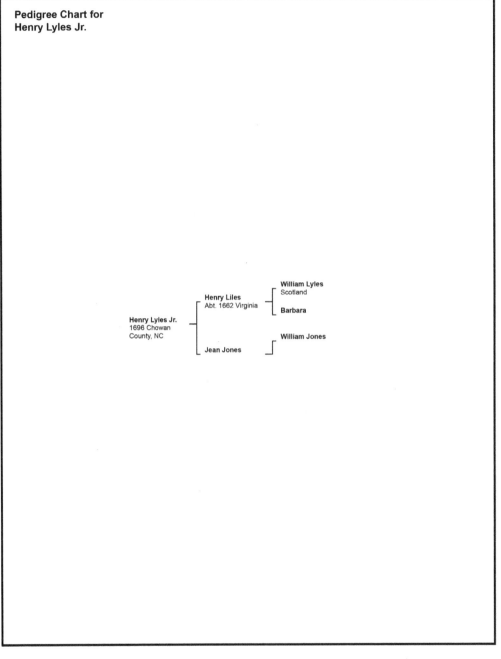

Henry Lyles Jr.
1696 Chowan
County, NC

Henry Liles
Abt. 1662 Virginia

Jean Jones

William Lyles
Scotland

Barbara

William Jones

Genealogy 20: Henry Lyles Jr.

The Lyles (or Liles) family came from England or Scotland. Henry Lyles was born about 1662. Some researchers believe he was born in Virginia but emigrated to Chowan County in North Carolina by 1692. He had property holdings of one thousand acres in 1712 and is listed in various land transactions and as a witness on deeds and wills from 1693 to 1722 in Chowan County.

Henry's son Henry Lyles (II) was born sometime between 1684 and 1690 in Chowan County. He married Elizabeth Lewis, who was born in 1683 in York, Virginia; her parents were from Wales. Their son Henry (III) was born in 1711; it is not known how many other children they had. Henry (II) died around 1723.

Henry Lyles (III) (1711–1790)

Henry (III) was born in 1711 in Chowan County and died about 1790 in nearby Johnston County. He married Deborah in 1730, and they had eleven children including Lewis. According to North Carolina archives:

> Henry Liles moved into Eastern Wake County from Rocky Hock Community of Chowan County in the 1750s. He was the father of Lewis Liles since the hand copied math book of the Jordans and Liles (original at State Department of Archives and History) gives dates of birth of the Liles and others when they lived in Chowan and Johnston County.

> In 1761 Henry received a land grant from the Earl of Granville of 600 acres along Buffalo Swamp that was near Powell's Creek that runs from south of the Folesville community into the Neuse River near Milbourne. In 1762, he received permission to build a mill pond where Powell Creek divides.

> Henry Liles was a member of Captain Edward Powers soldiers … during the French and Indian Wars…

> We have no record of Henry Liles' death but he probably lived with his son Lewis Liles until his death around 1790.[141]

Lewis Lyles (1742–1795)

Lewis Lyles was also born in Chowan County in 1742. He married Elizabeth Jordan in Forsyth, North Carolina in 1761, and they had four children including Micajah. In 1777, Lewis enlisted in the Fourth North Carolina Regiment in the Continental Army. The regiment fought under George Washington in several major battles including Brandywine and Germantown (see Chapter 31).

In 1781, Lewis re-enlisted and fought in the Battle of Eutaw Springs, the last major battle in the Carolinas. After the war, he returned to Johnston County, where he lived until his death.

Micajah Liles (1772–?) and Micajah Liles (II) (1797–1868)

Micajah Liles was born either in Forsyth County, North Carolina, or in Johnston County, where his family lived and where he married Nancy Woodward. He and Nancy had at least two children — Micajah and Nancy Rose. They must have liked the name Micajah, because Nancy had a brother named Micajah also. The marriage record lists Micajah's family name as "Liles." Previously, it was spelled a variety of ways but "Lyles" seems the most common.

Nancy and Micajah's son Micajah (II) was born in 1797 in Johnston County. By 1820, he was living in Dallas County, Alabama, as a single man. He married Elizabeth Winn Powell, who had been married to Thomas Traylor and had five children with him. In his will, Traylor named his wife as executrix with instructions on how to divide household items among his children as they came of age. He also gave instructions that his wagon and horses should be sold "after my family is done moving to Alabama country." This suggests he may have known and approved of the plan that Elizabeth and Micajah would marry following his death and of their intended move to Alabama.

Elizabeth and Micajah were married in 1820 in Dallas County, Alabama; he was about twenty-three and she would have been about thirty-six years old. Dallas County was created in 1818 from lands vacated by the Creek people in 1814. Soon after its creation and with considerable newly available land, Micajah and Elizabeth likely moved there to take advantage of the opportunity. Before the birth of their third child in 1825, they moved about seventy miles northeast to Talladega County, Alabama.

The area was booming at the time with cotton the dominant crop. The invention of the cotton gin in 1794 and the invention of the steamboat in 1807 and its introduction on the Alabama River in 1818 created a very favorable local economic environment (see Chapter 47). During their time in Alabama, they would also have experienced the development of "showboats," which transformed steamboats from mundane transportation into floating palaces with ballrooms, theatres, saloons, and card players.

Micajah and Elizabeth Lyles lived in Talladega until their deaths. They would have witnessed and participated in the area transformation from remote Creek territory to highly developed plantations and advanced transportation. When Micajah died in 1868, the following obituary appeared in the local newspaper:

We regret to learn that our old friend Micajah Liles died at his residence in this county on Sunday last. Mr. Liles was one of the early settlers, a substantial and true man and a most excellent citizen. He had been often elected tax collector for our county and proved a faithful and efficient officer. [Our] old men are rapidly passing... [142]

Elizabeth had died a couple years before Micajah; they had five children together including Sarah, the mother of Marietta Holmes, who would become the wife of T.A. Corson.

Chapter 33:

The Woodward Family:
Bath, North Carolina and
Blackbeard the Pirate

**Pedigree Chart for
Nancy Woodward**

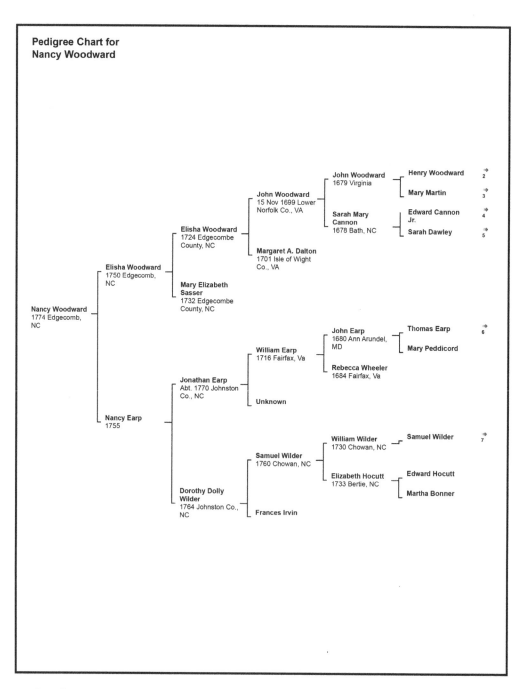

Genealogy 21: Nancy Woodward

Pedigree Chart for
Henry Woodward

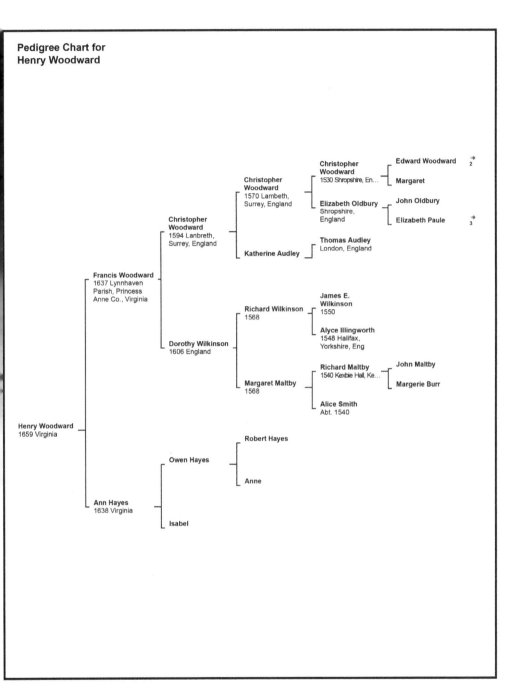

Genealogy 22: Henry Woodward

icajah Lyles (II)'s mother was Nancy Woodward, who married Micajah (I) in 1793 in Johnston County, North Carolina. The Woodward family's documented ancestry goes back to Kent, England.

Christopher Woodward (III) (1594–1650) and Francis Woodward (1637–1679)

Christopher Woodward, whose father and grandfather were also named Christopher, was the first Woodward to immigrate to America. He was born in Lambeth, in the English county of Surrey, in 1594; and in 1620, at the age of twenty-six, he sailed to Virginia aboard the ship *Tryall*, arriving on Hog Island near Jamestown. His first wife was named Margaret. They survived the Jamestown Massacre, but she died as a young woman. In 1637 Christopher sponsored the immigration from England of Dorothy Wilkinson, whom he married when she arrived.

He petitioned and was awarded six hundred acres of land in Charles County: headright for himself, his late wife, and for his new wife and four others. He likely was one of the few to be given land grants for two wives. He was a tobacco farmer, and upon acquiring his property, neighbors would have joined him in a community barn-raising to erect the necessary buildings for a tobacco farm, including a main barn for the livestock, a smokehouse for the meat, a tobacco-curing barn, various tool sheds, and a family home.

At that time, tobacco was critically important for the economy and livelihood of almost all settlers. Because of the absence of a colonial currency and unavailability of British coin, tobacco was also used as legal currency in Virginia for almost all transactions.

One document also referred to Christopher as a "Burgess," which at the time meant an elected or unelected official in the community. Dorothy and Christopher had five children including Francis. Francis was born in 1637, married Ann Hayes in 1656, and they had four children. They lived in Lower Norfolk County, in the area where the city of Norfolk is today.

Henry Woodward (1659–1734) and Bath, North Carolina

Francis and Ann's son Henry was born in 1659. Times in southern Virginia were good, but with so many large families and new immigrants, land was becoming expensive. Henry's brother, John, was the oldest boy and most likely heir, so Henry began to explore options as he matured. He married Mary Martin in 1678; he was nineteen years old and she was eighteen. They had three children. At some point, Henry and Mary packed up their possessions and moved to Bath, North Carolina. They would have been among the earliest settlers there. They were active members of the St. Thomas Episcopal Church, which is now the oldest church in North Carolina.

Bath at the time was a small town with quite a reputation. It was the first incorporated town in North Carolina in 1705, and it was also the seat of government under three North Carolina governors. When the first governor, Edward Hyde, displaced his predecessor, Deputy Governor Thomas Cary, Cary and his supporters rebelled (the Cary Rebellion). Eventually, Cary lost, and he and his colleagues were sent to England to stand trial. However, no one showed up to testify against them, and the case was dismissed.[143]

Government in the colony was not dignified. When South Carolina sent troops to help North Carolina counter attacks by the Tuscarora, a dinner arranged to celebrate the arrival of the reinforcements got quite out of hand. Several of the guests, including Governor Hyde, North Carolina Councilman Thomas Boyd, and other members of the party became quite intoxicated and argumentative. They stripped naked and conducted a boxing match on the site. It is not known who won, and it was possible the participants did not know who won either.[144]

Blackbeard, the pirate, used Bath as his local residence beginning sometime after 1714 (and after his presumed stay in Alexandria, Virginia, see Chapter 6), when he befriended Governor Charles Eden, married a local woman, and settled at nearby Plum Point. He used Bath as a place to dispose of his spoils, and Governor Eden is believed to have shared in the loot in exchange for offering protection. The pirate was killed in a battle with the Royal Navy off the coast of North Carolina in 1718. Tobias Knight, secretary of the colony, was charged with receiving stolen merchandise from Blackbeard, but he was acquitted, likely due to the influence of the governor.[145]

Henry Woodward died in Bath in 1734; his wife pre-deceased him.

Elisha Woodward Jr. (1750–1792)

Elisha, son of Elisha Sr. and great-great-grandson of Henry and Mary, was born in 1750 in Edgecombe County, North Carolina. He married Nancy Earp, whose ancestry dates back to Ireland. They had a daughter, Nancy, who was born about 1774 and married Micajah Lyles in 1793, connecting the Woodward line with the Lyles line.

Elisha was a member of the North Carolina militia (see Chapter 31), which fought many battles during the Revolutionary War. After the war ended, Elisha returned home to Johnston County where he died in 1792.

Chapter 34:
The Lawrence Family: Quakers in Colonial Virginia

**Pedigree Chart for
Elizabeth Lawrence**

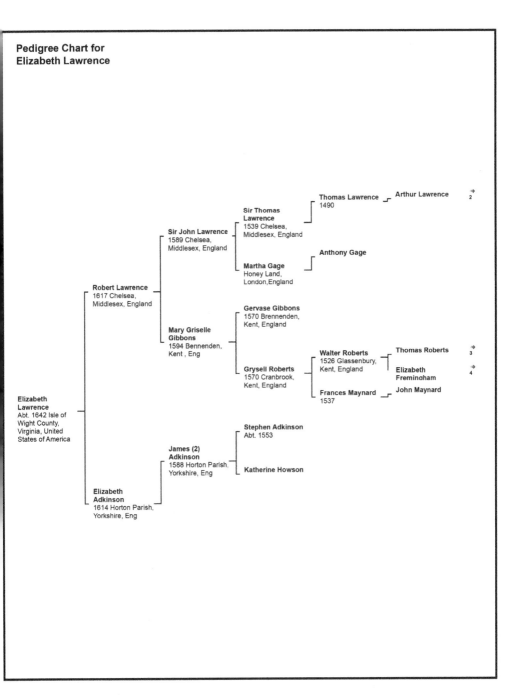

Genealogy 23: Elizabeth Lawrence

Elizabeth Lawrence married William Powell around 1668 in Isle of Wight, Virginia. The Lawrence family originated in Normandy, France, and settled in England following the Norman invasion in the eleventh century. In 1150, Robert Lawrence was a silversmith to the Lord of Lancaster Castle. His son, also Robert, accompanied Richard the Lionheart in the Third Crusade to Jerusalem where they defeated the Muslim leader Saladin at the Siege of Acre. At the siege, Robert apparently scaled the walls and opened the gates for the arriving British armies. As a result, Robert was knighted and awarded lands by the king to build Ashton Hall in 1191. King Richard also awarded Robert with his family a coat of arms for his bravery.

A few centuries later, Sir John Lawrence emigrated to James City, Virginia, where he secured land to allow a settlement one hundred fifty miles north of Jamestown on Long Isle, Virginia. He evidently missed his life in England and returned there and died in 1638 in Chelsea.

Robert Lawrence (1617–1682)

After John's death, his son Robert left Oxford University, collected his inheritance, married Elizabeth Adkinson, and sailed to Virginia, arriving near Jamestown in Nansemond County. He acquired lands in Lawne's Creek Parish, and he and Elizabeth had five children, including their daughter Elizabeth.

Robert served as Justice of the Peace from 1659 to 1660. He also became a Quaker. The Quakers were in frequent conflict with members of the more established Anglican Church in Virginia and were widely discriminated against. The Quakers were mostly pacifist and did not fight back. However, some Quakers adopted an interventionist character: barging into other churches, disturbing public worship, and exhorting ministers and congregations with fevered railings and reproaches. These actions did not aid their popularity. Beginning around 1660, Virginia Governor William Berkeley expelled the Quakers, and many went to more accommodating Maryland while others moved to nearby North Carolina.

Elizabeth Lawrence married William Powell, and they lived their entire lives in Isle of Wight Virginia, but their son Thomas Powell moved to North Carolina.

Chapter 35:
The Powell Family and the Lumbee Tribe

Pedigree Chart for Elizabeth Winn Powell

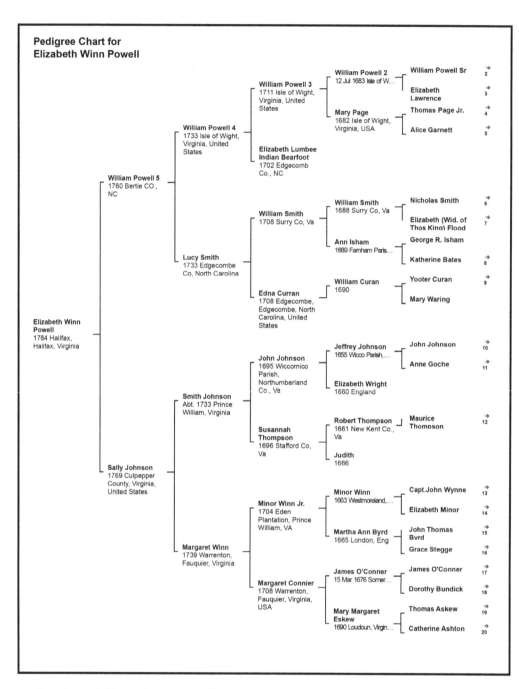

Genealogy 24: Elizabeth Winn Powell

Thomas Powell (1599–1687)

Thomas Powell was an early resident of the Jamestown area. He most likely came from Suffolk, England, but he may have come from Wales.

His wife likely died as a young woman. They had two sons, Nathaniel and William who were born in Isle of Wight, Virginia. Thomas evidently came with money and paid for an indentured servant as well as his own passage. When in Virginia, he acquired a number of estates and would have been considered a wealthy planter in colonial terms. He owned hundreds of acres on different parcels throughout the region when he died in 1687.

William Powell (I) (1640–1695)

William was the younger brother of Nathaniel and was born in Isle of Wight, Virginia, in 1640. He married Elizabeth Lawrence in 1668. They had seven children and lived in the Isle of Wright until William's death in 1695. He was a Quaker and a planter.

William was a substantial landowner. In William's will in 1695, he left his current plantation to his wife and then (after her death) to his son John. He left other properties to each of his children including Nathaniel, Jacob, William, Thomas, and Elizabeth. He clearly owned considerable land.

(Thomas) William Powell II (1680–1757) and William Powell (III) (1711–1792)

William's and Elizabeth's son Thomas William (II) was born around 1680 in Isle of Wight. He married Mary Page about 1700; Mary's family was from Hunston in West Sussex, England. Either she emigrated with her father to Isle of Wight or she was born in Virginia. Thomas and Mary had nine children. Both Thomas William and Mary's families were Quakers. At some point, Thomas and family moved to Albemarle in North Carolina, and he died there in 1757.

Thomas and Mary's son William (III) was born around 1711, probably in the Isle of Wight, although he may have been born in North Carolina. He married Elizabeth Bearfoot, who was a member of the Lumbee tribe. They had eleven children and apparently lived in the Isle of Wight before moving to Edgecombe County, North Carolina.

Elizabeth Bearfoot and the Lumbee Tribe (1702–1771)

The Bearfoot (or Barefoot) family history extends back to at least 1093 in England. The Norwegian King Magnus, surname Barefoot, succeeded King Edgar of Scotland. His descendants likely include Thomas Bearfoot.

Thomas Barefoot immigrated from England to the Jamestown area in Virginia in 1616. Noah Bearfoot, who died in 1710 in Surry County, Virginia, was the progenitor of many Bearfoots throughout the South. One descendant of Noah, also named Noah Bearfoot, is listed in local records as Elizabeth's father. The North Carolina Barefoots were known to intermarry with Native Americans.

Elizabeth was a Lumbee Indian and may well have descended from a mixed marriage. Apart from the Bearfoot connection, her ancestry is believed to be from the Oxendine tribe, and some local records show her name as Elizabeth Ox or Oxendine (see Chapter 27).

The Lumbees were a combination of survivors from multiple tribes and others. They were discriminated against and despite being from many tribes and places, retained a certain cohesiveness. The North Carolina state government recognizes the Lumbee as a tribe, but the federal government does not.

One well known story of the Lumbee occurred in 1958. The Ku Klux Klan began a campaign of harassing and terrorizing the Lumbee including burning crosses in the front lawns of residents at night. The Klan leader, James W. "Catfish" Cole, called for a big rally of the Klan in Robeson County, the home of the Lumbee, "to put the Indians in their place and to end race mixing."

That night the Klan brought large banners and a portable generator for lighting and sound in a large field. Over a hundred Klansmen showed up in their white costumes. The lighting was not very good, however, and the Klan members failed to notice about one thousand Lumbee people moving in to surround them. At some point, the Lumbee began yelling and firing their guns in the air, and the Klansmen panicked and ran away into the woods or to nearby police begging for protection. The Klan was so humiliated and the news coverage so widespread, the Klan was never active in Robeson County again.[146]

Chapter 36:

The Smith Family:
Halifax, North Carolina, and the
First Presidential Tour

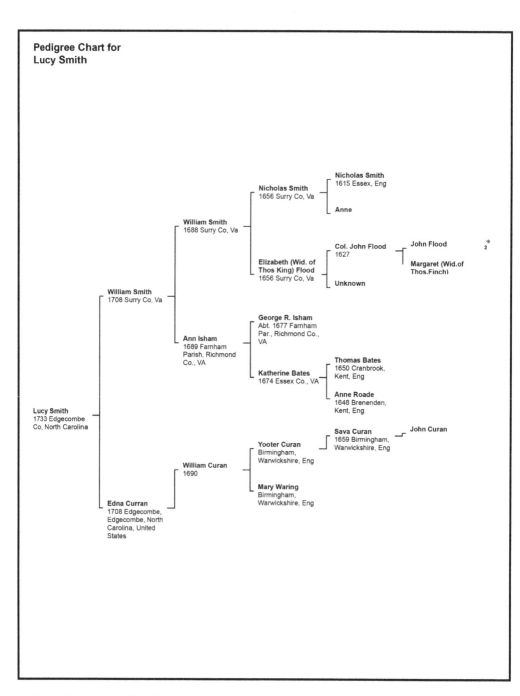

**Pedigree Chart for
Lucy Smith**

Lucy Smith
1733 Edgecombe
Co, North Carolina

William Smith
1708 Surry Co, Va

Edna Curran
1708 Edgecombe,
Edgecombe, North
Carolina, United
States

William Smith
1688 Surry Co, Va

Ann Isham
1689 Farnham
Parish, Richmond
Co., VA

William Curan
1690

Nicholas Smith
1656 Surry Co, Va

Elizabeth (Wid. of
Thos King) Flood
1656 Surry Co, Va

George R. Isham
Abt. 1677 Farnham
Par., Richmond Co.,
VA

Katherine Bates
1674 Essex Co., VA

Yooter Curan
Birmingham,
Warwickshire, Eng

Mary Waring
Birmingham,
Warwickshire, Eng

Nicholas Smith
1615 Essex, Eng

Anne

Col. John Flood
1627

Unknown

Thomas Bates
1650 Cranbrook,
Kent, Eng

Anne Roade
1648 Brenenden,
Kent, Eng

Sava Curan
1659 Birmingham,
Warwickshire, Eng

John Flood

Margaret (Wid.of
Thos.Finch)

John Curan

2

Genealogy 25: Lucy Smith

Nicholas Smith (Sr.) was born around 1615 in Essex, England. He arrived in Virginia in 1637, settled in Isle of Wight, and married a woman named Anne. They had at least three children in Virginia including Nicholas (Jr.). In 1645, Nicholas Sr. bought seven hundred acres of land along the James River, indicating he had ample financial resources. In 1667, he served as a justice in Isle of Wight, so he was well regarded also. He died in 1695 in Isle of Wight.

The Smith family descendants lived in Isle of Wight until William Jr., who was born in 1708 in Surry County. He married Edna Curran, and they moved to Halifax, North Carolina, where they lived until their deaths in 1791. They were part of the Virginia migration to nearby areas of North Carolina that included many ancestors in search of land and some looking for more religious freedom, especially the Quakers.

A smallpox epidemic decimated local North Carolina Native tribes (especially the Waxhaw) around 1740; the survivors the area and joined the Catawba. This opened considerable land for new settlers.

Halifax was becoming a booming center of economy and politics in the mid-1700s when William and Edna migrated there. In 1759, the town of Halifax became the county seat. North Carolina's Fourth Provincial Congress (set up by the residents and independent of British rule) met in Halifax in April 1776, and adopted the Halifax Resolves,[147] which called for American independence. This was the first official action for independence taken in the colonies before the American Revolution.

Both William and Edna reportedly died in Halifax in 1791 for unknown reasons but likely due to disease such as smallpox or typhoid fever. Otherwise, 1791 was an auspicious year for Halifax. President George Washington decided to tour the southern states; and his first stop in North Carolina in 1791 was in Halifax, where he spent the night. It was part of the first presidential tour in American history and set the precedent for many future presidents.

Several stories emerged from the North Carolina tour which underscore how difficult it was to plan and manage such a tour and also show the character of the first president.

> *Washington's own diary gives accounts of accidents while the group crossed the Chesapeake and Occoquan Creek. In North Carolina, the entourage stopped for breakfast one morning at a private home, mistaking it for an inn. Not until Washington went to pay the bill did he realize the mistake; the president was so flustered he reportedly gave the lady of the house a kiss on the cheek.*

...

A widely-known story from near Salisbury, North Carolina is that Washington concealed his identity during a stop at the Brandon farmstead where only a young girl, Betsy Brandon, was present. Betsy lamented that the rest of the family had gone to town to see President Washington, while she had been left behind to do chores and tend to the house. Washington assured her that he would make sure that she, too, would see the president if she would just serve refreshments to the travelers. The story goes that Betsy served up milk and snacks and that just before taking his leave, the old Virginian revealed to Betsy that she had been in the company of the President of the United States.[148]

William and Edna's daughter Lucy married William Powell in 1755 in Edgecombe County, North Carolina.

Figure 19: Burning of Jamestown during Bacon's Rebellion

Chapter 37:
William West and Bacon's Rebellion

B eginning in the 1650s, Virginia colonists began moving into territory occupied by the Doeg tribe and other Native groups. Conflicts resulted between encroaching settlers and the natives. Nathaniel Bacon led the militia in a series of raids killing Natives not only from the Doeg tribe but all others he encountered. The killings were popular with settlers, including indentured servants who needed land to farm when their indenture was completed. Bacon feuded with, Governor William Berkeley (whose wife was Bacon's aunt), accusing him of being soft on the Natives, corrupt, and not responsive to settler safety. In 1676, Bacon and his followers decided to overthrow the Governor by force; Bacon's Rebellion is considered the first rebellion in the American colonies. Bacon and his men took control of the state government for a time and later burned the Virginia capitol of Jamestown when their opponents began to strengthen. Many of the rebels came from Isle of Wight and included ancestors William West, Michael Fulgham, and others. The rebels were defeated after Bacon's untimely death due to dysentery.

Besides Bacon, a key leader of the rebellion was ancestor William West. William had witnessed Native Americans murder his father and maintained a hatred of all Natives subsequently. Late in the rebellion, West led a force of rebels to retake a large home that had been a Bacon headquarters but had been captured by forces loyal to the governor. The home, later called "Bacon's Castle," is a historic landmark in Surry County and is the oldest brick dwelling in North America.

The governor's forces, led by Colonel Bridger, captured West and his colleague William Drummond, who was the colonial governor of Albemarle Sound in the province of Carolina. Bridger promised the leaders would not be executed if they surrendered; but after their surrender, the captured leaders were immediately sentenced to hang. Drummond was made to walk barefoot to the scaffold before they hanged him. West somehow escaped and went into hiding. Many others were also hung.

Henry West, William's brother, along with seventy others (including many Isle of Wight residents), petitioned to have William West pardoned and his properties restored. The pardon was granted, and William West emerged from hiding and returned to Isle of Wight and resumed his role as planter.

William's wife, Rebecca Bracewell, was born around 1648 in Isle of Wight and died there fifty-two years later. Her parents were Robert and Rebecca Bracewell. Robert was born in London around 1605, attended Oxford College and graduated from there at the age of fifteen. He became a minister in the Church of England and emigrated from London in 1651. In 1653, he was elected to Virginia's House of Burgesses but was soon suspended because he was a minister and was forbidden to serve in a public capacity because of England's policy separating church and state. Reverend Bracewell died in 1668.

This English concept of separating church and state became part of the First Amendment to the United States Constitution, which reads "Congress shall make no law respecting the establishment of religion, or prohibiting free exercise thereof..." But, unlike the English, the Americans believed religion should not preclude a person from serving in public office. This principle was documented in the Sixth Amendment, which states, "no religious test shall ever be required as a qualification to any office or public trust under the United States." Robert Bracewell would have been a welcome member of the House of Burgesses (or its successor, the House of Delegates) had he lived under the U.S. Constitution.

Chapter 38:
John Mottrom: The First White Man in Northumberland, Virginia

The main settlement areas around James City (Jamestown) began to fill up by the mid 1600s. New immigrants were entitled to land grants based on how many people they brought into the colony. To accommodate the demand, arriving ships from Europe typically began to disembark their passengers along the northern neck of Virginia; and the new settlement there became known as Northumberland.

At the same time, nearby Maryland experienced considerable conflict and even military battles between Puritans and Catholics vying for control of that colony. Northumberland lay directly across the Potomac River from Maryland and was a convenient destination for Marylanders seeking to escape the conflict.

Probably the first white man to leave Maryland for the Northumberland area was Colonel John Mottrom (1590–1655), who emigrated originally from Cheshire, England, to Maryland. He was a successful trader and merchant and moved across the Potomac River to Virginia to an area called "Chicacone" around 1645. His house became a refuge for Protestants escaping from the wars with Catholics in Maryland.

Mottrom earned the respect of the local Native tribes. He was also respected by incoming white settlers and was the first representative from the area to serve in the Virginia House of Burgesses.

There was considerable resentment throughout the local Native tribes about English encroachment on their Virginia lands, which led to frequent conflict. John Mottrom was the one person all sides trusted, and he negotiated with Machywap, chief of the Chicacoan tribe, to secure land for the settlers. In 1650, Mottrom and the Chicacoan took six settlers to court for stealing two Native women, six deer skins, and three beaver skins from the Patuxet tribe and secured acceptable compensation —

records do not disclose the compensation for stealing the two women as compared to stealing the animal skins. As pressures for land increased with the arrival of more settlers from Europe, Mottrom spearheaded a plan to designate fifty acres for every Native "bowman" to preserve good lands for the natives and protect them against total encroachment. John Mottrom died in 1655, and the Natives eventually were forced out by disease and relentless pressure from settlers, unable to defend their property in court and lacking an advocate for their rights.

John Mottrom married Mary Spencer, and their daughter Frances married Nicholas Spencer, who immigrated from England (see Chapter 46). The Spencers were ancestors to the George family including my maternal grandmother, Susie George.

John's and Mary's son John Jr. was involved indirectly in the first legal separation/ divorce in Virginia. Richard Wright, a London merchant, was master of a ship trading between Virginia and England. Eventually, he settled in Virginia and married Anne Mottrom, daughter of John Jr. and his wife. Richard and Anne's son Mottrom Wright grew up to marry Ruth Griggs, his grandfather John Jr's widow (she was probably not his grandmother by blood, but was possibly his step-grandmother). After ten years of marriage to Mottrom Wright, Ruth Wright became "horrified at the sinfulness of her union" and secured a separation. Keeping it in the family, Mottrom Wright then apparently married the widow of his mother's brother (his aunt). Marrying a cousin was not uncommon in colonial America, but Mottrom Wright took family relationships to the extreme.

Chapter 39:

The Johnson Family and the Jamestown Massacre of 1644

Pedigree Chart for
Sally Johnson

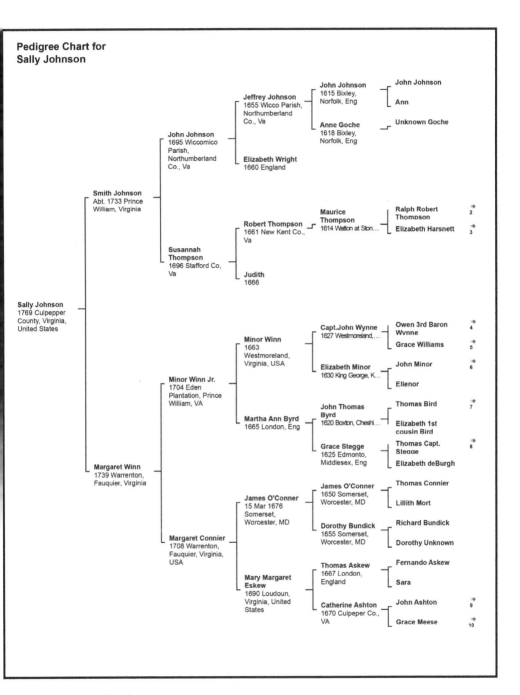

Sally Johnson
1769 Culpepper
County, Virginia,
United States

Smith Johnson
Abt. 1733 Prince
William, Virginia

John Johnson
1695 Wiccomico
Parish,
Northumberland
Co., Va

Jeffrey Johnson
1655 Wicco Parish,
Northumberland
Co., Va

John Johnson
1615 Bixley,
Norfolk, Eng

John Johnson

Ann

Anne Goche
1618 Bixley,
Norfolk, Eng

Unknown Goche

Elizabeth Wright
1660 England

**Susannah
Thompson**
1696 Stafford Co,
Va

Robert Thompson
1661 New Kent Co.,
Va

**Maurice
Thompson**
1614 Watton at Ston...

**Ralph Robert
Thompson** 2

Elizabeth Harsnett 3

Judith
1666

Margaret Winn
1739 Warrenton,
Fauquier, Virginia

Minor Winn Jr.
1704 Eden
Plantation, Prince
William, VA

Minor Winn
1663
Westmoreland,
Virginia, USA

Capt.John Wynne
1627 Westmoreland,...

**Owen 3rd Baron
Wynne** 4

Grace Williams 5

Elizabeth Minor
1630 King George, K...

John Minor 6

Ellenor

Martha Ann Byrd
1665 London, Eng

**John Thomas
Byrd**
1620 Boxton, Cheshi...

Thomas Bird 7

**Elizabeth 1st
cousin Bird**

Grace Stegge
1625 Edmonto,
Middlesex, Eng

**Thomas Capt.
Stegge** 8

Elizabeth deBurgh

Margaret Connier
1708 Warrenton,
Fauquier, Virginia,
USA

James O'Conner
15 Mar 1676
Somerset,
Worcester, MD

James O'Conner
1650 Somerset,
Worcester, MD

Thomas Connier

Lillith Mort

Dorothy Bundick
1655 Somerset,
Worcester, MD

Richard Bundick

Dorothy Unknown

**Mary Margaret
Eskew**
1690 Loudoun,
Virginia, United
States

Thomas Askew
1667 London,
England

Fernando Askew

Sara

Catherine Ashton
1670 Culpeper Co.,
VA

John Ashton 9

Grace Meese 10

Genealogy 26: Sally Johnson

The Johnsons of Northumberland first came to America with John Johnson who was born in Bixley, in the English county of Norfolk, around 1615. He emigrated with his parents, John and Ann Johnson, possibly around 1624, to the Jamestown area. He married Ann Goche, who was also from Bixley.

The Johnsons moved to Northumberland County in the 1630s and would have been among the early settlers there. In 1653, John purchased land in Northumberland and was exempt from taxes due to injuries suffered in a massacre — likely the 1644 attack by the Powhatan under Chief Opechancanough in which almost five hundred settlers died — more than died in the Jamestown Massacre of 1622. (See Chapter 28.)

The Jamestown Massacre of 1644

The 1644 surprise attack was carefully planned. Powhatan Chief Opechancanough was growing old and this was likely his last chance at controlling the expansion of European settlements. His followers were supportive because they sought an opportunity to demonstrate their wartime bravery and achieve warrior status after twelve years of relative peace. The British were preoccupied with the English Civil War, and the timing in the spring would be when food stocks were low and therefore not susceptible to settler theft and destruction, and the tribes would be dispersed on hunting parties.

In this assault, the Powhatan did not attack the more populated and better defended Jamestown; instead they attacked outlying plantations and lightly defended settlements. While initially successful in their attacks, the settlers and their militia responded forcefully destroying villages and killing Natives over the next two years. Chief Opechancanough was captured and killed and the remnants of the Powhatan Confederacy were expelled to the north side of the York River in a treaty signed in 1646.

Chapter 40:

The Wynn or Gwynn Family: From Wales to Historic Gwynn's Island

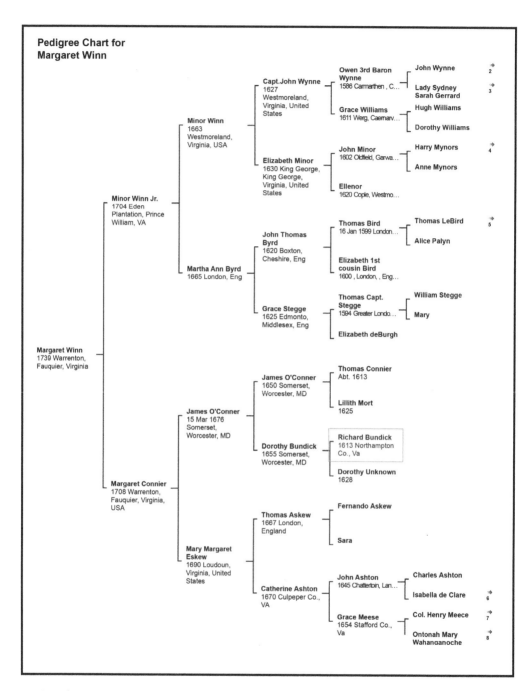

Pedigree Chart for Margaret Winn

- **Margaret Winn** 1739 Warrenton, Fauquier, Virginia
  - **Minor Winn Jr.** 1704 Eden Plantation, Prince William, VA
    - **Minor Winn** 1663 Westmoreland, Virginia, USA
      - **Capt.John Wynne** 1627 Westmoreland, Virginia, United States
        - **Owen 3rd Baron Wynne** 1586 Carmarthen , C...
          - **John Wynne** →2
          - **Lady Sydney Sarah Gerrard** →3
        - **Grace Williams** 1611 Werg, Caernarv...
          - **Hugh Williams**
          - **Dorothy Williams**
      - **Elizabeth Minor** 1630 King George, King George, Virginia, United States
        - **John Minor** 1602 Oldfield, Garwa...
          - **Harry Mynors** →4
          - **Anne Mynors**
        - **Ellenor** 1620 Cople, Westmo...
    - **Martha Ann Byrd** 1665 London, Eng
      - **John Thomas Byrd** 1620 Boxton, Cheshire, Eng
        - **Thomas Bird** 16 Jan 1599 London...
          - **Thomas LeBird** →5
          - **Alice Palyn**
        - **Elizabeth 1st cousin Bird** 1600 , London, , Eng...
      - **Grace Stegge** 1625 Edmonto, Middlesex, Eng
        - **Thomas Capt. Stegge** 1594 Greater Londo...
          - **William Stegge**
          - **Mary**
        - **Elizabeth deBurgh**
  - **Margaret Connier** 1708 Warrenton, Fauquier, Virginia, USA
    - **James O'Conner** 15 Mar 1676 Somerset, Worcester, MD
      - **James O'Conner** 1650 Somerset, Worcester, MD
        - **Thomas Connier** Abt. 1613
        - **Lillith Mort** 1625
      - **Dorothy Bundick** 1655 Somerset, Worcester, MD
        - **Richard Bundick** 1613 Northampton Co., Va
        - **Dorothy Unknown** 1628
    - **Mary Margaret Eskew** 1690 Loudoun, Virginia, United States
      - **Thomas Askew** 1667 London, England
        - **Fernando Askew**
        - **Sara**
      - **Catherine Ashton** 1670 Culpeper Co., VA
        - **John Ashton** 1645 Chatterloin, Lan...
          - **Charles Ashton**
          - **Isabella de Clare** →6
        - **Grace Meese** 1654 Stafford Co., Va
          - **Col. Henry Meece** →7
          - **Ontonah Mary Wahanganoche** →8

Genealogy 27: Margaret Winn

218

**Pedigree Chart for
Grace Meese**

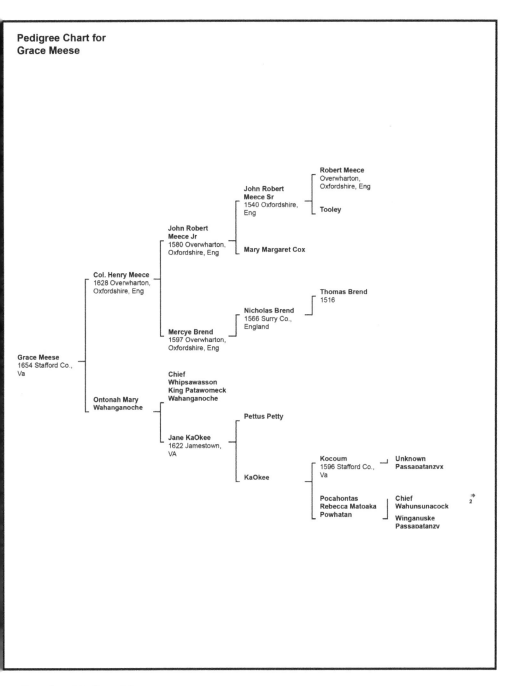

Grace Meese
1654 Stafford Co.,
Va

Col. Henry Meece
1628 Overwharton,
Oxfordshire, Eng

Ontonah Mary
Wahanganoche

John Robert
Meece Jr
1580 Overwharton,
Oxfordshire, Eng

Mercye Brend
1597 Overwharton,
Oxfordshire, Eng

Chief
Whipsawasson
King Patawomeck
Wahanganoche

Jane KaOkee
1622 Jamestown,
VA

John Robert
Meece Sr
1540 Oxfordshire,
Eng

Mary Margaret Cox

Nicholas Brend
1566 Surry Co.,
England

Pettus Petty

KaOkee

Robert Meece
Overwharton,
Oxfordshire, Eng

Tooley

Thomas Brend
1516

Kocoum
1596 Stafford Co.,
Va

Pocahontas
Rebecca Matoaka
Powhatan

Unknown
Passapatanzvx

Chief
Wahunsunacock

Winganuske
Passapatanzv

→
2

Genealogy 28: Grace Meese

Like many families in colonial America, last names were often spelled different ways by government and church officials including tax collectors and census takers. Most early immigrants were illiterate, and when names were spelled out they appeared as an interpretation of a verbalized name. Also, last names were sometimes combined with family names of spouses. The Wynn or Winn family also appears as Gwynn as some ancestors who likely took the G from Owen Winn's mother's name, Gerrard or Garred, and added it to Winn.

The Wynn family came from Caernarfonshire, Wales, and had a long history there with documentation dating back to the fourteenth and fifteenth centuries. Sir John Wynn was the first of the baronets whose ancestral home was Gwydir in northern Wales. Gwydir Castle was built around 1500, primarily using materials taken from the dissolved Maenan Abbey. Gwydir remained the seat of the Wynn/Gwynn family until 1678.

The first of the family line to emigrate to America was Owen Wynn, who had been well educated at Westminster, Eton, and St. John's Cambridge before he arrived in Jamestown in 1611. When his brother Richard, the second baronet, died in Wales, Owen became the third baronet. He married Grace Williams in England in 1625; she was the daughter of Owen's patron John Williams, the Lord Keeper of the Great Seal and later Archbishop of York. After returning to Virginia, John and Grace's second child, also named John, was born in 1627 in Isle of Wight, Virginia.

John Winn, also known as Captain John Winn, was born in Westmoreland, Virginia and married Elizabeth Minor in 1650. Her father, John Minor, emigrated to Virginia with his mother and siblings from Oldfield, Garway England before 1627 and was a successful planter and attorney. Captain John's and Elizabeth's descendants include Jonathan "Stonewall" Jackson, the famous Confederate War general.

Gwynn's Island

The Virginia Winn family is best known for Gwynn's Island and its early colonial history. Hugh Gwynn, Owen Wynn's brother, was another early immigrant to the Jamestown area. According to legend, around 1611 Hugh was exploring the Chesapeake Bay and stopped by a small island at the mouth of the Piankatank River. He heard a girl's desperate calls; a Powhatan girl had fallen from her canoe and could not swim. He pulled her to safety, saving her life.

Her father was chief of the mighty Powhatan tribe and as a reward for saving his daughter gave Hugh Gwynn the island, which became known as Gwynn's Island. Hugh subsequently secured formal title to the Island from Virginia authorities and settled there with his family.

The island became part of the history of the American Revolution. In 1776, John Murray, Lord Dunmore, the last colonial governor of Virginia, stationed naval ships in the Norfolk harbor. Dunmore was very unpopular with Virginians because of his arrogant ways including suspending the Virginia legislature and ruling by decree. When sailors of the Royal Navy at Norfolk developed smallpox, American patriots planned an attack even though the American Revolution had not yet begun.

Dunmore and the navy ships retreated to Gwynn's Island, along with area loyalists. He built two batteries and a stockade on the island as defensive measures. He tried to continue his rule over Virginia from Gwynn's Island. Five days after the Declaration of Independence, American General Andrew Lewis opened fire from Gloucester County, Virginia, using cannons. The battle become one of the bloodiest of the war. The British loyalists were all killed, and Dunmore fled and was not heard of again.

Figure 20: John Smith saved by Pocahontas 1607

Chapter 41:

The Story and Ancestry
of Pocahontas

The Powhatan girl Hugh Gwynn saved, according to legend, was Pocahontas, the favorite daughter of the Powhatan chief. Her story and ancestry follows.

Jamestown was founded in 1607 with the arrival of three ships. The settlement was located in an area dominated by an Algonquian-speaking tribe, and that tribe was part of a larger Powhatan Confederacy led by the great chief Wahunsonacock. The Powhatans operated like an empire, with the constituent tribes paying tribute and pledging loyalty in return for protection from other hostile tribes. War among tribes was frequent as tribes regularly tried to expand their territory, secure more food and goods, acquire more members by kidnapping women and children, and achieve personal warrior status by exhibiting bravery in battle. Protection afforded by membership in the Powhatan group was important.

In the Powhatan culture, any young woman was eligible for marriage after she had gone through puberty. When a man sought a woman and then made her an offer, she could refuse it or accept it. If she accepted his proposal, which typically had nothing to do with love, the man would go to her parents and prove that he could provide for her. He also had to present them with a "bridewealth." This was a dowry of supplies and food that would compensate the parents for the lost labor when their child left the household. The prospective husband also had to have gone through the ritual of "Huskanaw," which was required to become a warrior in the tribe.[149]

Huskanaw was a rite of passage which initiated young men into adulthood. This ritual was held each year for teenage boys and young adult men. As the boys were gathered together, the adult guides made a big to-do about separating them from their families and then led them off into the forest where the elite men of the tribe sat in a circle on the ground. Their faces were painted black and they wore antlers on their heads.

For the first two days the boys danced and chanted in a circle around the elite, as instructed by their guides. Each boy was painted either red, black or white and carried green boughs. Meanwhile, back in the village, the mothers of these boys painted their own faces black. For days, the mothers would wail and cry at the "death" of their sons and prepare their homes for a "funeral." Most of the men of the village followed the boys to observe the first three days of Huskanaw.

In the afternoon of the third day, the boys, clad only in loincloths, sat beneath the trees and were guarded by their guides. They did not mingle with the adult men and the elite, as they were not yet worthy. Shamans were assigned to boys according to the color paint they wore. The adults formed a gauntlet from the tree the boys were under to another tree in the distance. A shaman would grab a boy in his group and run the boy thru the two rows of men, trying to protect him from the whips and clubs the men would use on the boy. After each boy had made it to the next tree, the adults would form another gauntlet to another tree, and so on.

If the boys made it to the third tree, the men tore it down to make head wreaths for them. The werowance then held a feast, but the boys were not allowed to attend. They had to lie on the ground like corpses. Afterwards, they were whisked away and into a pen under the supervision of elders for nine months to suffer the elements and prove to their guides that they were worthy of adulthood. During this time in seclusion, a tradition was that the shamans often gave the boys a potion which caused hallucinations. It is said that they did this in order to summon their god, Okee, to receive blessings. Some boys did not survive the Huskanaw, but those that did were received back into the village with much rejoicing.

If a Huskanaw initiate made an offer to a young Powhatan woman and she accepted, and if her parents were pleased with the bridewealth the man had presented, then they could marry. The man returned home where the women in his family prepared a new home for the couple. Family and friends gathered at the bride's home, and the couple joined hands while someone broke a chain of shells over their heads. The ceremony completed; the couple left for their new home.

Chief Wahunsonacock had several wives, but per custom, his marriage to his first wife (Winganuske) was a lifelong partnership, while subsequent wives stayed in the household until their first child was born and then returned to their families and could marry someone else if they chose. Winganuske was the daughter of Japazaws, chief of the Patawomeck tribe and his wife, who was Wahunsonacock's sister. As a result of the intermarriage, the Patawomeck would be loyal allies with the Powhatan forever.

Wahunsonacock and Winganuske had a number of children, including Matoaka Amonute Powhatan (note names are English transliterations of the Algonquian). Matoaka became known as Pocahontas by the colonists. Those that met her claimed she was favored by the chief over all his other family members. There is disagreement among historians about Pocahontas and her descendants, and written records are minimal and inconclusive. The following story is supported by many historians, but others disagree or are unsure.

As a teenager, Pocahontas married Kocoum, who became chief of the Patawomeck and was the younger brother of her grandfather, Japazaws, keeping relationships in the family. She had two children, a son (called little Kocoum) and a daughter Ka-Okee. The Patawomeck tribe likely kept the children protected and secluded to avoid kidnapping and forced marriage by others seeking status and power.

Prior to her first marriage, she became quite famous to the colonists and to a great many later in history. According to the settlers' legend, Captain John Smith was exploring and seeking a meeting with Wahunsonacock in the hopes or procuring food for Jamestown. Smith was captured by Powhatans and eventually brought before Wahunsonacock. After much discussion and a shared meal, the chief had two large, flat stones placed before him, and Smith was dragged forward and his head placed on one of the stones with Indians with clubs standing ready to bash his head. Pocahontas jumped between Smith and the Indians with clubs and pleaded to spare his life, which Wahunsonacock did.[150] There are theories why she intervened and why the chief spared Smith's life, but no one will ever know for certain.

In April 1613, Pocahontas, by then a young woman and mother, was visiting the Patawomeck tribe when Captain Samuel Argall coincidently stopped there on a mission to trade. Argall managed to kidnap Pocahontas and offered to ransom her in exchange for seven Englishmen being held by the Powhatans. The negotiations went on for months, during which Pocahontas was well treated and mentored in English, English culture and Christianity. Around the same time, her husband Kocoum was killed, possibly by Argall's troops, who feared he would attack seeking return of his wife.

After the exchange was finally agreed and the prisoners released, Pocahontas decided she liked the English culture and Christianity and, with permission of her father, married John Rolfe, a colonist, and went to England with him.

Her two children were raised by the Patawomeck tribe. The daughter, Ka-Okee, had a daughter, Jane Ka-Okee, born about 1628; she married Patawomeck Chief Whip-sawasson Wahanganoche. They had a daughter, Ontonah Mary Wahanganoche, who married settler Colonel Henry Meece. Their daughter Grace Meece married John Ashton, and their descendants lead to ancestors Elizabeth Powell and Sarah Lyles. And this is how Pocahontas became my ancestor.

Some historians believe Pocahontas did not marry Kocoum or had children with him. If this were true, most likely another daughter of Wahunsonacock and Winganuske married Kocoum and would be my direct ancestor. In this case, Pocahontas would be my aunt and not my grandmother. It is impossible to ever know for certain.

Chapter 42:
The Hosea George Family: England to Kentucky and Daniel Boone

Pedigree Chart for
Hosea Louis George

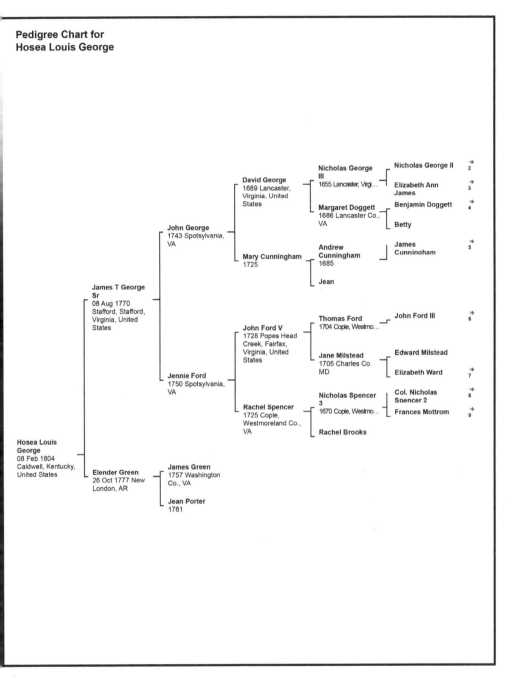

Hosea Louis George
08 Feb 1804
Caldwell, Kentucky,
United States

James T George Sr
08 Aug 1770
Stafford, Stafford,
Virginia, United
States

Elender Green
26 Oct 1777 New
London, AR

John George
1743 Spotsylvania,
VA

Jennie Ford
1750 Spotsylvania,
VA

James Green
1757 Washington
Co., VA

Jean Porter
1761

David George
1689 Lancaster,
Virginia, United
States

Mary Cunningham
1725

John Ford V
1728 Popes Head
Creek, Fairfax,
Virginia, United
States

Rachel Spencer
1725 Cople,
Westmoreland Co.,
VA

Nicholas George III
1655 Lancaster, Virgi...

Margaret Doggett
1686 Lancaster Co.,
VA

Andrew Cunningham
1685

Jean

Thomas Ford
1704 Cople, Westmo...

Jane Milstead
1705 Charles Co.
MD

Nicholas Spencer 3
1670 Cople, Westmo...

Rachel Brooks

Nicholas George II →2

Elizabeth Ann James →3

Benjamin Doggett →4

Betty

James Cunningham →5

John Ford III →6

Edward Milstead

Elizabeth Ward →7

Col. Nicholas Spencer 2 →8

Frances Mottrom →9

Genealogy 29: Hosea Louis George

Pedigree Chart for
Nicholas George II

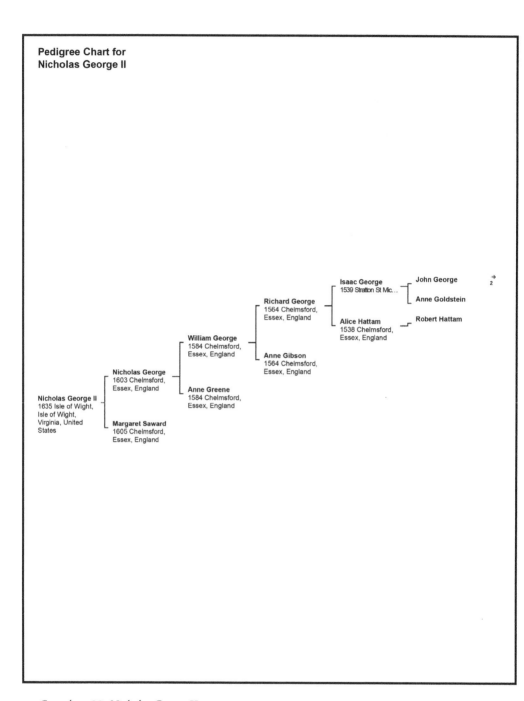

Nicholas George II
1635 Isle of Wight,
Isle of Wight,
Virginia, United
States

Nicholas George
1603 Chelmsford,
Essex, England

Margaret Saward
1605 Chelmsford,
Essex, England

William George
1584 Chelmsford,
Essex, England

Anne Greene
1584 Chelmsford,
Essex, England

Richard George
1564 Chelmsford,
Essex, England

Anne Gibson
1564 Chelmsford,
Essex, England

Isaac George
1539 Stratton St Mic…

Alice Hattam
1538 Chelmsford,
Essex, England

John George

Anne Goldstein

Robert Hattam

2

Genealogy 30: Nicholas George II

228

My maternal grandmother, Susie George, descended from a long line of Georges dating back to England. This family emigrated to Virginia, and subsequently relocated to Kentucky and then Arkansas. The first known ancestor was Richard George, who lived in Gloucestershire, England and was born about 1385. His descendants lived primarily in Gloucestershire.

Nicholas George (I) (1603–1661); (II) (1635–1700); and (III) (1655–1733)

Nicholas George, son of William George and Ann Greene, was born in Essex in 1603, and he married Margaret Saward, who was also from Essex, in 1621. Either in 1635 or 1638, the family arrived in Virginia. Nicholas became a planter and had fairly extensive land holdings.

Nicholas (II) was born in Isle of Wight, Virginia, around 1635 and married Elizabeth Ann James, who was from Lancaster, Virginia, in 1655. They had five children including Nicholas (III). Nicholas (II) was appointed constable of Lancaster County in 1663 and served to 1664. He died around 1700. In his will, Nicholas left a number of items to a Negro boy named Dick including a feather bed with blanket and sheets, a case of pistols and a sword, a chest, two tables, a kettle, and two cows. For a planter to leave so much in a will to a Negro boy was highly unusual; I suspect Dick was Nicholas's illegitimate son.

Nicholas (III) was born in 1655 in Lancaster, Virginia. He married Mary Fowler, from Richmond County, in 1680. They had seven children including David, who was born in 1689 in Lancaster. David married Mary Cunningham (see Chapter 43), and they had four children including John.

John George (1743–1813)

John George was born in 1743 in Spotsylvania, Virginia. In 1765 he married Jennie Ford, who was also from Spotsylvania (see Chapter 45). They had nine children.

John was a sergeant with Virginia's Fifth Regiment in the Revolutionary War. His unit fought in several major battles including the Battle of Brandywine, the Battle of Germantown, and the Battle of Monmouth (see Chapter 31).

Sometime prior to 1777, John and Jennie and their young family moved to Caldwell, Kentucky; they would have been among the first settlers in Kentucky along with the more famous Daniel Boone. In 1776, there were only two hundred settlers living in Kentucky, partly due to the presence of hostile Native tribes including the Shawnee and Cherokee, who disliked the settlers moving into their lands and fought on the side of the British against the settlers in succeeding wars. During the Revolution and immediately afterwards many more settlers arrived. The trip from Virginia was hazardous; settlers traveled by horse and wagon along the Wilderness Road, and travelers were always on the lookout for Native war parties.

Kentucky became the location for several Revolutionary War battles in the "western theater" including the Battle of Blue Licks. As the war continued, John enlisted as a lieutenant with the Continental Battalion of Artillery in 1779 in Kentucky. Many of the major battles near the end of the war were heavily influenced by the destructive impact of artillery, and Lieutenant George was there, surrounded by smoke, sound, and intense fighting.

John George died in 1813 at Eddy Creek in Caldwell in his adopted state of Kentucky. His wife Mary passed in 1825.

James T. George (1770–1847) and Elender Green (1777–1849)

John and Jennie's son James T. George Sr. was born in Stafford, Virginia, in 1770. He moved with the family to Kentucky when he was a young boy. In 1794, he married Elender Green; like James, her family had moved to Kentucky when she was a child.

Around the same time, a Lewis Green lived near the border of Virginia and Kentucky. Lewis was likely related to Elender's family but the direct relationship has not been documented. Daniel Boone was said to have often repeated a story about Lewis that talks about the challenges of living on the Kentucky frontier:

Lewis and a brother-in-law resided near Blackmore's on the Clinch River in southwest Virginia bordering on Kentucky. They lived about 15 miles below Captain Cass's place, where Boone was sojourning, and they went out some considerable distance into the mountains to hunt. One day when Green was alone, his companion being absent on the chase, a large bear made his appearance near camp, upon which Green shot and wounded the animal, which at the moment chanced to be in a sort of a sink-hole at the base of a hill. Taking a roundabout way to get above and head off the bear there being a slight snow upon the ground covered with sleet, Green's feet slipped from under him, and in spite of all his efforts to stop himself, he partly slid and partly rolled down the hillside until he found himself in the sink hole where the wounded bear had fallen. The wounded bear enraged by his pain charged at Green, tore and mangled his body in a shocking manner, totally destroying one of his eyes, When the bear had sufficiently gratified his revenge by gnawing his unresisting victim as he wished, the bear suddenly departed, leaving the unfortunate seriously wounded hunter in a helpless and deplorable condition, all exposed, with his clothing torn in tatters, to the severities of the cold temperatures.

His brother-in-law returned at length, found and took Lewis to camp. After a while, thinking it impossible for Lewis to recover, his companion went out on pretense of hunting for fresh meat, and unconcerned abandoned poor Lewis to his fate. He reported in the settlement that Lewis had been killed by a bear. Alone in the camp the small fire soon died away from his inability to provide fuel. Lewis dug with his knife a hole like a nest beside him in the dirt floor in his cabin. He managed to reach a bundle of wild turkey feathers which had been saved, and with them lined the excavation a made himself quite a comfortable bed, and with the knife fastened to the end of a stick, he cut down, from time to time, bits of dried bear meat hanging over head Upon this he sparingly subsisted and recovered slowly, He at length managed to get about.

When Spring opened, a party of whom Daniel Boone appeared to have been with, went from Blackmore's settlement to bury Green's remains, with the brute of a brother-in-law for a guide. To their surprise and astonishment they met Lewis plodding his way towards home, and learned the sad story of his suffering and desertion by his brother-in-law. The party were so indignant that they could scarcely refrain from laying violent hands on the monster guilty of so much inhumanity to a helpless companion. Lewis although scared and disfigured lived for many years, dying in 1784 in Kentucky.[151]

James and Elender had ten children. In late 1813 or early 1814, they moved the family to Perry, Alabama. Sometime between 1840 and 1847, James and Elender moved to Union County, Arkansas, where James died in 1847. As he aged, James may have moved to Arkansas to live with some of his children who had moved there and their families.

Hosea George (1804–1859)

James and Elender's son Hosea was born in 1804 in Caldwell, Kentucky. He moved as a child with his family to Perry, Alabama, and married Louisa Pool in 1829. The Pool family had moved to Perry from North Carolina when Louisa was a youngster (see Chapter 48).

Hosea and Louisa had one child in 1832, and Louisa died the next year. There was a cholera epidemic at the time, and she may have died as a result.

Hosea married Louisa's sister, Altana Cordelia Pool, the next year. They had two daughters while living in Perry, but the older died at the age of five. Within a few years, they moved to Union County, Arkansas, where other members of the George family were gravitating as well. Hosea is listed in the census as a farmer, and they had two more children in Arkansas including Gaston Percy George. Hosea had eight thousand acres of land under cultivation at one time, demonstrating the considerable size of his plantations.

The George family were early settlers in Arkansas. In 1830, Union County only had 640 residents. This increased to 2,889 by 1840. The largest growth spurt came in the 1840s when the Georges arrived, and by 1850 there were 10,298 residents. Growth slowed after 1850.[152]

Immigrants came mostly from Alabama, Georgia, and Mississippi and were attracted by the availability of productive farmland and the absence of hostile Native Americans at the time. Primary crops were cotton, corn, peas, beans, and sweet potatoes. Many large plantations were developed, and slaves constituted more than half the population by 1860.[153]

Gaston Percy George (1847–1909)

Gaston Percy George was born in 1847 in Union County, Arkansas. He lived with his family on a plantation and was remembered as a wild and likely spoiled child growing up. Once in a fit of temper, he rode a horse into the main house, according to my mother who passed on stories from her parents.

When he was thirteen or fourteen years old, he took his slave and ran away from home to join the Confederate Army. He lied about his age claiming to be sixteen, but someone found out and he and his slave were assigned the task of making bullets in the rear. He was later discharged because of his age but apparently rejoined when he did turn sixteen.

After the Civil War, Gaston went to Tennessee and attended school for two years and then returned home to farm. He owned three acreages totaling more than one thousand acres.

In 1868, he married a cousin, Josephine or Josie George, in Louisiana. They returned to Arkansas and had six children. In 1898, at the age of fifty-one, Josie died. The next year, Gaston married Jessie Liddell. Gaston died in 1909, and Jessie sometime later.

Susie George (1885–1966)

Gaston and Josie's daughter Susan was known as Susie, and she was born in 1885 in Ashley County, Arkansas. She was my grandmother. As a young woman, she was sent away to attend a girl's school in Virginia. The George family was well-to-do and could afford to send their children away for schooling.

One day she was returning from school and at the train station in Hamburg, when the telegraph operator, Bernard Corson, saw her and immediately fell in love, according to my mother. Within a year, despite Susie's family's objections — apparently they did not think a telegraph operator was worthy of their daughter — Susie and Bernard were married in 1905.

Susie and Bernard had three children including my mother. Despite living in Arkansas, the children were born in Louisiana where Bernard was studying accounting (see Chapter 26). During the Depression, they moved north to Detroit and then Chicago. Susie's brother, Percy George, remained in Arkansas, where he became a powerful county judge and bought the elegant Palace Hotel in downtown Hamburg. He offered to leave the hotel to Susie and Bernard if they would return to Hamburg and run the hotel, which they did. Judge Percy would sit at the entrance to the hotel in a straight chair and approve anyone entering his hotel. When he died in 1941, however, his will did not mention leaving the hotel to Susie and Bernard. After Bernard's death in 1957, Susie moved to Chicago to be close to my mother, and she died there in 1966.

I have been to Hamburg, Arkansas. It is a very small town distant from every significant city or employment center. When Bernard and Susie were managing the relatively upscale Palace Hotel, across town in the Black neighborhood, Ethel and Preston Pippen were raising their family of twelve. In 1965, their youngest child, Scottie, was born and went on to win multiple NBA championships playing with Michael Jordan and the Chicago Bulls.

Several ancestor families are connected to the Georges directly through marriage. Three families in particular merit mention: Cunningham (Mary Cunningham married David George), Doggett (Margaret Doggett married Nicholas George [III]), and Ford (Jenny Ford married John F. George).

Chapter 43:

The Cunningham Family: Scotland to Northern Ireland and then on to America

Pedigree Chart for
Mary Cunningham

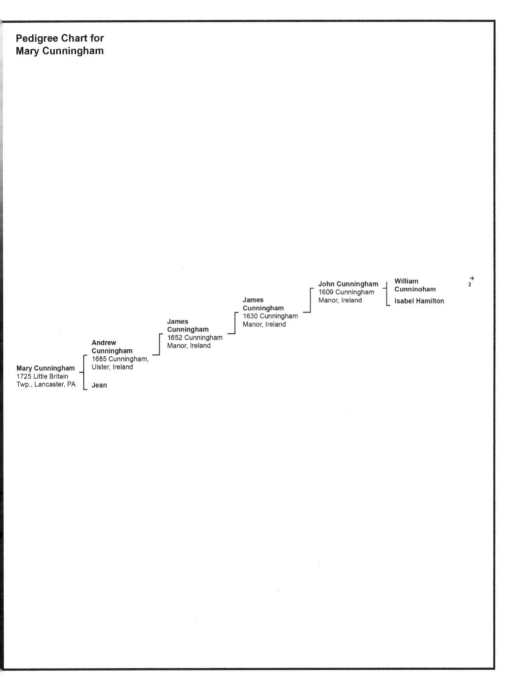

Mary Cunningham
1725 Little Britain
Twp., Lancaster, PA

Andrew
Cunningham
1685 Cunningham,
Ulster, Ireland

Jean

James
Cunningham
1652 Cunningham
Manor, Ireland

James
Cunningham
1630 Cunningham
Manor, Ireland

John Cunningham
1609 Cunningham
Manor, Ireland

William
Cunningham

Isabel Hamilton

2

Genealogy 31: Mary Cunningham

Pedigree Chart for
William Cunningham

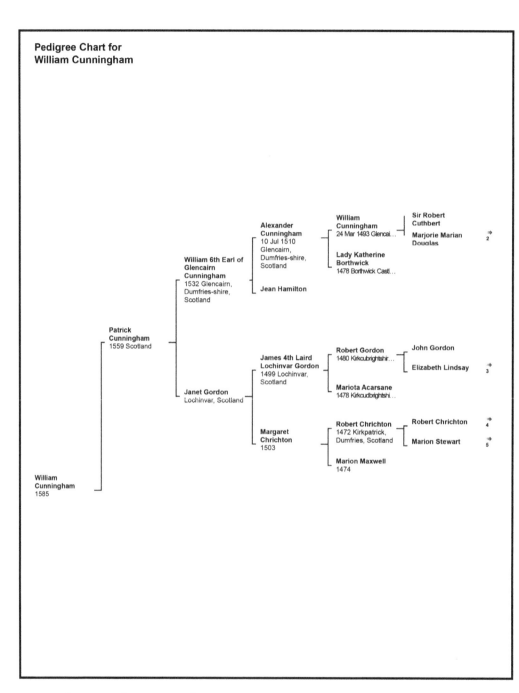

William Cunningham
1585

Patrick
Cunningham
1559 Scotland

William 6th Earl of
Glencairn
Cunningham
1532 Glencairn,
Dumfries-shire,
Scotland

Janet Gordon
Lochinvar, Scotland

Alexander
Cunningham
10 Jul 1510
Glencairn,
Dumfries-shire,
Scotland

Jean Hamilton

James 4th Laird
Lochinvar Gordon
1499 Lochinvar,
Scotland

Margaret
Chrichton
1503

William
Cunningham
24 Mar 1493 Glencai...

Lady Katherine
Borthwick
1478 Borthwick Castl...

Robert Gordon
1480 Kirkcubrightshir...

Mariota Acarsane
1478 Kirkcudbrightshi...

Robert Chrichton
1472 Kirkpatrick,
Dumfries, Scotland

Marion Maxwell
1474

Sir Robert
Cuthbert

Marjorie Marian
Douglas

2

John Gordon

Elizabeth Lindsay

3

Robert Chrichton

4

Marion Stewart

5

Genealogy 32: William Cunningham

Mary Cunningham married David George around 1740. She was born in Pennsylvania but moved with her family to Virginia as did many new immigrants during these times. Her family history is centered in Cunningham Manor (or Manorcunningham) a small village in the County Donegal in Northern Ireland. Several generations of Cunninghams lived in Manorcunningham, beginning with Patrick Cunningham, who moved there from the ancestral home in Glencairn in the Scottish county of Dumfriesshire, prior to 1644.

Queen Elizabeth I sought to subdue the unruly Irish by encouraging Englishmen to settle in the northern part of Ireland, closest to England and Scotland. Her efforts were unsuccessful partly because those who moved there often became friends and intermarried with the local Irish and became sympathetic to the Irish viewpoint. Others moved back to England to flee Irish hostilities.

King James I, an ancestor and a Scotsman, realized to subdue the Irish he needed to move Scots into Ireland. Scots, he felt, were accustomed to hardship, stubborn, slow to adapt and make friends, and would protect their newly acquired property with the ferocity needed to survive the Irish attacks and harassment. The Plantation of Ulster was born. James seized about three million acres from the Irish landowners and gave grants to Scottish and some English settlers. Patrick Cunningham relocated from Scotland to take advantage.

The relocation of Scots to northern Ireland and the forced expulsion of Irish from there led to periodic conflicts lasting almost four hundred years. The "Troubles" between Irish Catholics and English/Scottish Protestants lasted from 1968 to 1998. Since 1921, Ulster and Northern Ireland has been part of Great Britain while the rest of Ireland is an independent country.

In the years that followed Patrick's move to Manorcunningham, his descendants were born, lived, and died in or near the town. James (Jr) was born there in 1652 but by 1730, like many others at the time, he had emigrated to America. Conditions in Ulster deteriorated in the early 1700s. Landlords raised land rents and evicted long-term Scottish tenants for higher rent paying Irish. The English Parliament, seeking to protect English merchants from competition, passed laws restricting the export of goods from Ireland, and the king of England sought to impose religious practices that were at odds with practices of the Presbyterian Church in Scotland and northern Ireland. These factors, coupled with economic recession caused by drought, led about 250,000 people to emigrate from Ulster to America, and some estimates are much higher.

The Cunningham and Caldwell families emigrated together and stopped in Pennsylvania first. Soon they moved to Virginia, which was less crowded and offered more available land. John Caldwell and three Cunningham brothers — Thomas, Andrew, and James — began buying land in Brunswick County, Virginia. Some family members moved to Laurens County, South Carolina, while others stayed in an area called Cub Creek, then in Lunenburg County, Virginia. The neighborhood around Cub Creek was known as Caldwell Settlement, named for John Caldwell.

There were 17 founders of Cub Creek, led by John Caldwell and the Cunningham brothers. The settlement was formally approved by the Presbyterian Synod, which provided religious guidance and ministry.

The Cunninghams evidently brought goods from Manorcunningham packed in old chests and papers attached to at least one of them. The papers which survived provide ancestry details.

Andrew Cunningham, son of James, was probably born around 1685 and moved to Cub Creek between 1738 and 1745. He had acquired considerable land and left property and assets to his wife Jean, his oldest daughter Mary, and others. His will was written in 1760 and probated in 1761.

Chapter 44:
The Doggett Family:
A Reverend with Books

Pedigree Chart for
Margaret Doggett

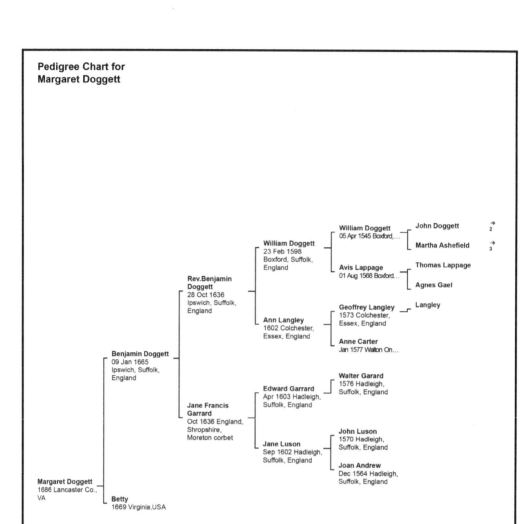

Genealogy 33: Margaret Doggett

oggett family records go back at least to Richard Doggett, who was born in 1481 in Groton, in the English county of Suffolk. There were Doggett's living in the Babergh area of Suffolk for hundreds of years before Richard, but few written records have survived. Richard married Sarah Le Gris, who was from Suffolk England also and was the daughter of Rev. John LeGris and Elizabeth Lappage. Richard apparently was a prosperous resident of Suffolk.

Their son John Doggett was born in 1510 in Bures St. Mary, in the Babergh district of Suffolk. He married Martha (Ashefield?).

John is referred to as a "gentleman." He and Robert Doggett, presumably John's brother, were likely the most prominent residents of Groton at the time. John died in 1564 in Suffolk.

John Doggett had a son named William born in 1545. Some key information comes from William's tombstone in St. Mary's Church in Boxford. The stone is imbedded in the floor next to an exterior wall and protected by a carpet which covers it. It is an elaborately carved black marble slab with an inscription on a brass plate:

> *Here lyeth William Doggett, marchant adventerer Citizen and mercer of London and free of the East India Company, who tooke to wife Avis Lappadge ye Daught. of Thomas Lappadge of Boxford, with who he lyved 19 years & had Issue by her 6 sonnes & 6 davgters. Ye said William departed this life ye 10th of October 1610 beinge of the age of 53 years.*

At the four corners of the stone are four brasses in the form of shields, each bearing the coat of arms of an organization of which William was clearly proud to be a member. These organizations are: the City of London; the Worshipful Company of Mercers; the Company of Merchant Adventurers; and the East India Company.

Reverend Benjamin Doggett (1636–1682)

William's grandson Reverend Benjamin Doggett was born in 1636 in Ipswich, in the county of Suffolk, England. He attended private school in Westminster and later graduated from St. James College and the University of Cambridge. He was admitted to the college as a "sizar," meaning he did not pay full tuition but served as a servant to an upperclassman who became his tutor and mentor. His mentor was William Twyne, who received a Bachelor of Divinity degree and undoubtedly influenced young Benjamin.

Benjamin received a Bachelor of Arts degree and then a Master of Arts Degree. Instead of following his family's path as merchants and a prosperous future, Benjamin was ordained as an Anglican minister. His first post was in the small village of

Stoke-by-Clare in 1661. He moved to a much larger church in Hadleigh, Suffolk, in 1664. The same year, he married a young widow, Jane Garrard.

Benjamin's brother, Richard, was a merchant and had established an active trade with merchants from Lancaster County, Virginia. Through Richard, Benjamin likely learned of an opening for a minister in Lancaster. In Hadleigh, Benjamin did not have permanent tenure because another minister still served as the more senior living rector. With limited near term opportunities at home and the opportunity to build a congregation in the New World, Benjamin emigrated in 1668 or 1669.

In Virginia, Benjamin served as minister to Christ Church and shortly later founded and also served as the minister to St. Mary's Whitechapel Church. He ministered to both congregations at the same time and became quite well known and respected as a minister. Rev. Benjamin Doggett died in 1682 in Lancaster and was buried under the chancel of St. Mary's as he had requested. He was a man of strongly held views as was evident in his will which included:

> For son Benjamin, one hundred fifty acres of land unless he chooses to marry before the age of twenty-two, for which he shall forfeit the land; For son Richard, one hundred acres of land unless he should marry before twenty-two years of age; For son William one hundred acres unless he should marry before twenty-two years of age; and a similar provision applied if daughter Ann married before the age of eighteen.

The Reverend had a personal library and had accumulated a great number of books, which was unusual in colonial Virginia, since most people were illiterate. Sensing there was no market to sell the books in Virginia, in his will Benjamin directed that a great chest be acquired and filled with his cherished books. The chest was to be shipped to England and the books sold to pay debts. The chest of books was one of the most valuable possessions Benjamin owned when he died, according to the appraisal conducted following his death.

Chapter 45:
The Ford Family:
An Abducted Child, an Officer Captured in the Revolutionary War, and Many Others

**Pedigree Chart for
Jennie Ford**

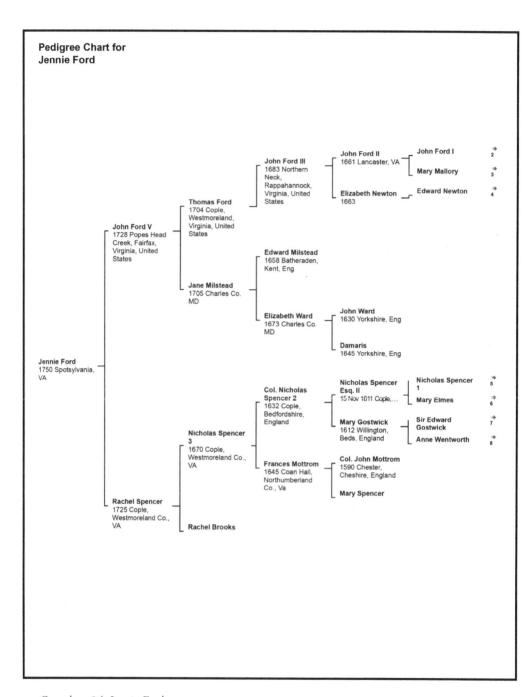

Jennie Ford
1750 Spotsylvania,
VA

John Ford V
1728 Popes Head
Creek, Fairfax,
Virginia, United
States

Rachel Spencer
1725 Cople,
Westmoreland Co.,
VA

Thomas Ford
1704 Cople,
Westmoreland,
Virginia, United
States

Jane Milstead
1705 Charles Co.
MD

Nicholas Spencer
3
1670 Cople,
Westmoreland Co.,
VA

Rachel Brooks

John Ford III
1683 Northern
Neck,
Rappahannock,
Virginia, United
States

Edward Milstead
1658 Batheraden,
Kent, Eng

Elizabeth Ward
1673 Charles Co.
MD

Col. Nicholas
Spencer 2
1632 Cople,
Bedfordshire,
England

Frances Mottrom
1645 Coan Hall,
Northumberland
Co., Va

John Ford II
1661 Lancaster, VA

Elizabeth Newton
1863

John Ward
1630 Yorkshire, Eng

Damaris
1645 Yorkshire, Eng

Nicholas Spencer
Esq. II
15 Nov 1611 Cople,...

Mary Gostwick
1612 Willington,
Beds, England

Col. John Mottrom
1590 Chester,
Cheshire, England

Mary Spencer

John Ford I → 2

Mary Mallory → 3

Edward Newton → 4

Nicholas Spencer
1 → 5

Mary Elmes → 6

Sir Edward
Gostwick → 7

Anne Wentworth → 8

Genealogy 34: Jennie Ford

Jennie Ford married John F. George in 1765, probably in Spotsylvania County, Virginia: both were born and grew up there. Jennie's parents were John Ford and Rachel Spencer. Jennie and John lived in Stafford County, Virginia, which is adjacent to Spotsylvania County, had nine children, and moved subsequently to Caldwell County, Kentucky.

The Ford family history is documented back to the 1500s in England. In about 1585, John Ford was born in Sandbach, in the English county of Cheshire, and he died around 1639. A famous English playwright, John Ford, was born in Ilsington, Devon, in 1586 and died around 1639. It is unlikely but possible this could be the same person.

Regarding the Ford family of Sandbach, the following is taken from *Historical Southern Families*:

> *The Ford family of Abbeyfield Park in Sandbach Parish, Cheshire, England, came into prominence during the reign of Henry VIII, by acquisition of monastery lands near Sandbach. The dissolution of the smaller monasteries was completed by the year 1540. It is a historical fact that "Bluff King Hal" disposed of these church properties only to his favorites; thus it is highly probable that one of his Ford intimates had the good fortune and the necessary means to become the owner of a very desirable estate.*
>
> *A family receiving benefits from the monarch would naturally adhere to the ruler's church-state policies. Even three generations later, the Fords of Cheshire continued in the royalist party. As the struggle for power grew to a crisis under the Stuart kings, loyalty assumed an ever increasing importance.*[154]

John Ford (1636–1699)

Sixteen years later after arriving as a child (see Chapter 1), John Ford married the niece of the Reverend Phillip Mallory, the man who had taken him in and paid for his passage when John arrived in Jamestown as an unaccompanied child. She was Mary, daughter of the Reverend Thomas Mallory, Dean of Chester Cathedral in England.

John was active in county affairs. He held five hundred acres of land in King and Queen County, Virginia. This may have been his wife Mary's legacy from her father's estate. He served on the county grand jury in 1685, also in 1693, and was under contract to operate a ferry over the nearby river.

John and Mary Ford's descendants, including John (II) born in 1661, and John (III), born 1683 lived in Virginia and had plantations primarily growing tobacco. Thomas

Ford, son of John (III), was born around 1704 and married Jane Milstead in 1724 in Maryland. Jane and Thomas's first child, Catherine, was born in Maryland the following year.

Thomas and Jane moved to Fairfax County, Virginia, shortly thereafter. Thomas received the first of three land grants in Virginia in 1725 with others received in 1730 and 1744. He was very active in the local Anglican Church and was elected vestryman multiple times as was his neighbor, George Washington. He practiced law and had clients across many nearby counties. He had a plantation near the head of Pope's Creek, just downstream from what became Mount Vernon Church.

Major John Ford (1728–1803)

John Ford (IV) was the first son and fourth child of Thomas and Jane Ford. He was born in Fairfax, Virginia, around 1728. In 1748 he married Rachel Spencer in Fairfax; she was the daughter of Nicholas and Mary Spencer. They had six children.

With the end of Native hostilities and the opening of Cherokee lands, young people were attracted to the good farmland available in the western Carolinas where they could use government bounties and land grants to acquire farmland. John, Rachel, and their children moved to Mecklenburg County, North Carolina, by 1765 and then to nearby Spartanburg County, South Carolina. Rachel died in 1770 at the age of 45 years.

With the commencement of the Revolutionary War, John enlisted as a lieutenant with the Third North Carolina Regiment and was later promoted to captain and then major. The regiment fought several battles including the defeat in Charleston — the worst American defeat in the Revolutionary War. Major John Ford surrendered with the Continental Army and five thousand troops in Charleston in 1780 and became a British prisoner. Typically, officer prisoners were allowed to stay at home or in a hotel with other captive officers until they were exchanged for equivalent British officer captives. Captured enlisted men were treated more harshly, and many died in British custody.

After the war, John lived in South Carolina. South Carolina Governor William Moultrie recognized John's abilities and appointed him judge and tasked him with other public duties. But eventually John moved his family to the frontier of Kentucky, possibly in 1786. His daughter and her family had previously moved to Kentucky, and perceived better economic opportunities were available on the frontier as the Carolinas were becoming increasingly developed and crowded. John moved to Shelby, Kentucky, and there married Catherine Grace, a widow, in 1792. He died in 1803.

Chapter 46:

The Spencer Family:
The Family of Churchill and
Princess Diana

**Pedigree Chart for
Rachel Spencer**

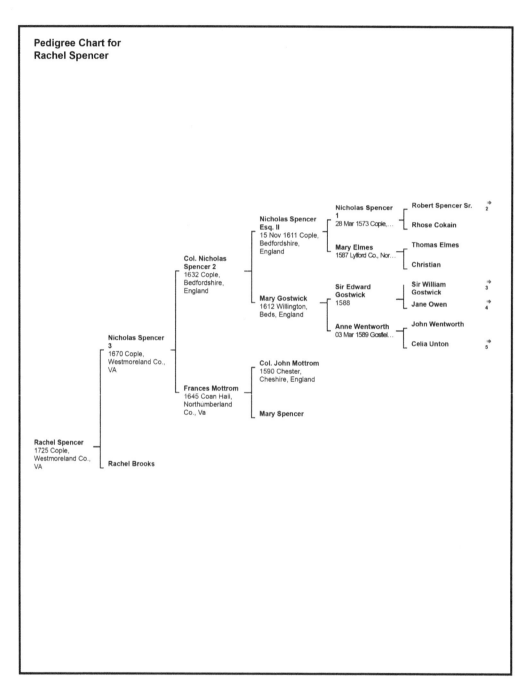

Genealogy 35: Rachel Spencer

Rachel Spencer married John Ford (IV) in 1748 in Fairfax Virginia. She came from a prominent English family based in Cople, Bedfordshire. The Spencer family lineage in England includes Winston Churchill and Diana Spencer, Princess of Wales.

The Spencer family acquired the manor of Rowlands in 1531 in Cople, and the family remained anchored there until the property was purchased by Sarah Churchill, Duchess of Marlborough, in the 1700s.

Nicholas Spencer (I) was part of the English aristocracy; he was born in 1611 in the family estate in Cople and died there in 1644 at the age of thirty-three. He married Mary Gostwick, who was also from a prominent family. Her brother inherited the title Baronet of Bedfordshire, which was handed down from her grandfather originally.

Nicholas and Mary had several children. The oldest, William, inherited the family fortune. Without the prospect of inheritance, Nicholas (II) and Robert, the second and third sons, emigrated to America. Nicholas (II) was a London-based merchant before he emigrated to Westmoreland County, Virginia, in the 1650s. His brother, Robert, emigrated to Surry County, Virginia; he later moved to Talbot County, Maryland, and established what became the Spencer family plantation or "Spencer Hall."

Nicholas (II) settled in Westmoreland County and was the agent for his cousin, John Colepeper, who had considerable investments in Virginia including having inherited his father's share of ownership in the Virginia Company. Colepeper never visited Virginia, preferring the aristocratic life in England and knowing that his investments in Virginia were being well taken care of.

Nicholas Spencer was appointed customs collector for Virginia in addition to his duties for his cousin. Apparently, he was very good at the job and he was appointed to other public positions because of his administrative abilities and prominence. He was President of the Council of the Virginia Colony and he served as acting governor of Virginia from 1683 to 1684.

Together the lands belonging to John Colepeper that Nicholas administered and his own extensive holdings amounted to an estimated five million acres, an unprecedented amount of land which caused some resentment in the colony.

Nicholas was good friends with the Washington family, and he and Lt. Colonel John Washington together bought five thousand acres at Mount Vernon, which later became George Washington's estate.

Nicholas married Frances Mottrom, daughter of John Mottrom (see Chapter 38), a well-respected leader and early pioneer in Virginia. They had five sons including Nicholas (III) and at least one daughter. Nicholas (II) died in 1688.

Nicholas (III) was born in 1670 at the homestead in Cople Parish, in Westmoreland County, Virginia. Nicholas's brother William returned to England for his schooling and remained there, serving as a Whig member of the Parliament from Bedfordshire. William handled the Spencer estates in England and married Lady Catherine Wentworth.

After William died around 1695, Nicholas (III) returned to England to take care of the family possessions and estates, but he returned to Virginia prior to the birth of his daughter Rachel in 1770. There is no record of Nicholas's death yet discovered, which is unusual, so he may have returned to England again.

Figure 21: Picking, baling, and ginning cotton

Chapter 47:
The Southern States

A s North and South Carolina became more settled, settlers looked further south for available land and economic opportunity. Some ancestors moved to Kentucky while others followed a path to Georgia and then Alabama. Arkansas and Louisiana came later.

Kentucky

Kentucky was occupied by many Native tribes prior to the arrival of European settlers. They frequently fought with each other for land, status, and captives but no one tribe achieved dominance. The French had an influence with French traders working throughout the area.

A series of events led to the area attracting English settlers. Following the Seven Years' War and the Treaty of Paris (1763), the French gave up all claims to North American lands east of the Mississippi, including what became the State of Kentucky. Around the same time, the powerful Iroquois tribe from New York moved into the area and began actively raiding local tribes, killing warriors, and seizing captives to take back home and replenish their tribal losses. They also sought to take over the fur trade with the English as supplies diminished further east.

To make matters worse for the local tribes, European diseases including smallpox hit the area, wiping out most tribal members. Kentucky was not such a great place to live anymore if you were a member of the Catawba or Shawnee or other tribes.

Englishman James Harrod arrived with settlers in 1774 and purchased substantial land from the local tribes who, with diminished members, agreed to vacate. The town of Harrodsburg was founded and immigrants from Virginia and the Carolinas were encouraged to take advantage of available land and favorable soil conditions. Joseph Breed and his family moved to what is now Monroe County, Kentucky, in 1773 to preach the gospel; and John George and his family moved to Caldwell County, Kentucky between 1770 and 1777 to begin farming. After the Revolutionary War, around 1786, Major John Ford and his family moved to Shelby County, Kentucky, seeking future land and opportunity for his family.

There continued to be conflict between settlers and the tribes of the Western Confederacy until the Battle of Fallen Timbers and the following Treaty of Greenville in 1795, which required Northwestern tribes to move out of most of Ohio and Kentucky. In 1820, Stephen Pool moved to Breckinridge County, Kentucky from North Carolina, taking advantage of a less threatening environment and available and productive land.

Georgia

Georgia was the youngest and least populated of the original thirteen colonies. The impetus to establishing the Georgia colony came from James Oglethorpe, a member of Britain's Parliament and an advocate for social reform. He chaired a Parliamentary committee on prison reform and advocated a plan to send inmates from Britain's overcrowded debtor jails to Georgia, giving them a new start and reducing Britain's burden at home. The British government quickly endorsed the plan; they also viewed Georgia as a potential buffer between their colony in South Carolina and the Spanish, Britain's arch enemy at the time, who were based in Florida.

Unlike the other colonies, Georgia was run by a board of trustees in London with no governor or legislature in the new colony. The Georgia colony was established in 1732 and explicitly banned slavery, rum, lawyers, and Catholics. The formal ban on lawyers was a novel concept. According to Oglethorpe, Georgia was to be "free from that pest and scourge of mankind called lawyers." [155] He believed settlers were capable of pleading their own cases. The ban on Catholics was an attempt to prevent Spanish spies from infiltrating Georgia from Florida.

The area was largely occupied by Native American peoples including the Creeks and Cherokees. The tribes were rivals, and the Cherokees defeated the Creeks in a major battle in 1755, forcing the Creeks to abandon considerable territory.

The first English settlers to come to Georgia were typically from over the border in South Carolina. They engaged in buying Natives who had been captured in inter-tribal battles and selling them as slaves. Later, they found more profit in buying and selling deer skins.

The Georgia colony did not prosper initially. The first goods were not exported back to England until 1749, sixteen years after the colony was started, and there was pressure from England for the colony to become self-sufficient following the costly wars in Europe. In 1751, the prohibition against slavery was rescinded, in an attempt to make agriculture more profitable. The prohibition on rum, incidentally, had been rescinded in 1742 after many complaints by settlers, and the ban on Catholics faded away as the threat from Florida abated. But the ban on lawyers lasted until 1755.

In 1752, the trustees gave the colony back to the king, and it became a royal colony operated like the other American colonies.

In 1773, Georgia signed the Treaty of Augusta with the Creek and Cherokee which, coupled with earlier treaties, caused the tribes to vacate much of Georgia and opened the area to colonial settlement. Some of the Creek did not agree to the terms of this treaty but later reaffirmed the provisions in 1790.

Georgia grew, and plantations proliferated as the Creek and the Cherokee departed. Cotton became the dominant crop, and slaves provided the primary labor. In 1783, when the Revolutionary War ended, Joseph Breed Jr. and his family moved from South Carolina across the border to Wilkes County, Georgia. Shortly afterwards, Smith Johnson and his family moved from Halifax County, Virginia, to Oglethorpe County, Georgia, which is next to Wilkes County. In 1798, Richard George and his family relocated from South Carolina to nearby Warren County, Georgia, where he married Priscilla Breed, daughter of Joseph Breed Jr.

In 1792, Eli Whitney moved to Georgia after graduating from college. He stayed on a plantation near Savannah and soon learned about cotton, the dominant crop in the area. Working with plantation staff, he invented the cotton gin, which allowed cotton to be processed much faster than it could be by hand. This revolutionized cotton farming and the economy of the South. By the mid-nineteenth century, cotton was America's leading export.[156]

The introduction of the cotton gin led to accelerated growth, more profits, larger plantations, and more slaves. Ancestors such as James Pugh and his family moved from North Carolina to Burke County, Georgia, in 1804 in response to better economic opportunities.

Alabama

Alabama became the twenty-second state in 1819, but much happened before then in the area. The Treaty of Paris (1763) ended France's claim on the area. The Treaty of Madrid formalized the southern U.S. boundary with Florida, which was still under Spanish rule, and U.S. troops expanded that boundary with an 1812 annexation. The Mississippi Territory was organized in 1798. Georgia ceded its western half (what is now Mississippi and Alabama) in 1802 and paid $1,125,000 to the federal government, which paid the Creeks to leave and extinguished all Native property claims. The Mississippi Territory was split between Mississippi and Alabama in 1817, and the Alabama Territory was formed.

Like other areas, Alabama was largely occupied by native tribes including the Creeks and the Cherokee but also the Chickasaw, Choctaw, and Seminole. As white settlers moved in from nearby states, disputes and fighting between these Native peoples and settlers were not uncommon. The Treaties of Augusta and New York in 1783 and 1790 required the Cherokee and the Creek to vacate considerable land in Georgia and parts of Alabama.

The United States and Britain went to war from 1812 to 1815 (see Chapter 68), and the British provided Native tribes, especially the Creek, with arms they could use to attack U.S. settlers. In 1813, a Creek faction called the "Red Sticks" attacked Fort

Mims in southern Alabama. The "Fort Mims Massacre" resulted in the deaths of about 250 Americans and Native allies; afterwards the Red Sticks destroyed nearby farms and plantations killing livestock and settlers and burning crops and buildings.[157] These actions spread considerable alarm to settlers elsewhere.

Federal troops were all engaged in fighting the British and unavailable to fight the Creek in Alabama. General Andrew Jackson led a Tennessee militia, supported by militias from Georgia and the Mississippi Territory (including Alabama), and defeated the Creek Red Sticks after a series of battles in 1814, becoming an American military hero. The Creek, including the Red Sticks and other Creeks not involved with the fighting, were forced to sign the Treaty of Fort Jackson, which required the tribe to cede twenty-three million acres opening up half of what became the State of Alabama.

With the Creek evicted, cotton farming lucrative, and vacant land readily available, Alabama grew quickly. Cotton farming became very productive with the introduction of the cotton gin and then the steamboat. Roads in Alabama were poor and it was difficult to move cotton to market until the steamboat was introduced to Alabama in 1818.[158] With shallow drafts and powerful engines allowing the barge-like ships to move upriver against the current, cotton warehouses and river landings were soon commonplace. Cotton and other goods moved downriver to the port city of Mobile, and other goods moved upriver from Mobile. In 1819, Mobile had less than one thousand residents. With the introduction of the steamboat and expansion of cotton production, Mobile had over twenty thousand residents by 1850.

While steamboats were very efficient at moving goods during the 1800s, they suffered some disadvantages including the tendency for their boilers to blow up, causing ships to sink and often killing and maiming passengers. Mark Twain's brother, Henry Clemens, died in Twain's arms from such an explosion. In 1865, the steamboat *Sultana* exploded, killing 1,800 Union soldiers recently released from prison camps. Eventually, railroads replaced steamboats, but for most of the nineteenth century the boats were essential for the development of the central part of the United States.

Richard Bass and his family moved from North Carolina to Perry County, Alabama, in 1813. Around the same time, Richard George and his family moved to Perry County from Georgia. A bit later, James George (unrelated to Richard) moved to Perry County from Kentucky. A few years after that William Poole moved to Perry County from North Carolina. The attraction of Perry County, which was not formally recognized as a county until 1819, was its location in Alabama's "Black Belt" and the availability of considerable land vacated by the Creek. The Black Belt is a large swath of land characterized by rich, black topsoil with high content of clay and minerals. Evidently, it was very good for growing cotton. Later the term "Black Belt" was also used to refer to the predominately African American population in this region both before and after the Civil War.

Arkansas and Louisiana

Arkansas and Louisiana followed a different path and timetable than other southern states. French traders and trappers were the first Europeans to settle in the area and the first successful French settlement was in 1686. This area was claimed by France until France conveyed the area to Spain in a secret treaty in 1762 (Treaty of Fontainebleau). The Treaty of Paris awarded the land east of the Mississippi River to the United States, but the land west of the river remained nominally French, although France had already secretly given it to Spain.

In 1800, the Spanish gave the land, including what is now Arkansas and Louisiana, back to France. With England and France at war in 1803, Napoleon sought to raise funds and sold the returned land and much more that lay to the north to the United States for $15 million as part of the Louisiana Purchase. President Jefferson made the purchase despite much criticism because he wanted control of the Mississippi River and land for future American expansion.

The primary Native tribe in the area was the Quapaw, who generally got along with the French but were threatened by new English immigrants. They signed a treaty in 1818 relinquishing most of their traditional lands in return for a guarantee they would retain thirty-two million acres along the Arkansas River in south Arkansas. The United States reneged on the treaty a year later and reduced the Quapaw land to one million acres.

The federal government also negotiated treaties with other tribes in Georgia and Alabama to move onto Quapaw land west of the Mississippi River, which helped clear land east of the river but created conflicts to the west. The Indian Removal Act of 1830 required all the tribes to remove to designated areas later called reservations, and these removals occurred throughout the 1830s and later. This led to considerable deaths and suffering by natives and has been called "the Trail of Tears." Most of the reservation lands were in Oklahoma, far from the tribes' ancestral homes. This cleared the land for new settlers in Arkansas, Louisiana, and the south and Midwest.

In 1819, the territory of Missouri applied for statehood as a slaveholding state. There was much debate in Congress including bills introduced to prohibit slavery in Missouri; and many plantation owners in Missouri moved their operations and their slaves to the territory of Arkansas out of fear that slavery would soon be outlawed in Missouri. Finally, in 1836 Arkansas was admitted as a slave state and Michigan was admitted as a free state shortly thereafter to keep the balance of slave and non-slave states in the Union.

The following year, the Panic of 1837 greatly damaged the national economy and especially the economy of southern states. Governmental policies intended to dampen land and commodity speculation instead led to a sharp drop in prices and recession. Banks were stressed and stopped lending, businesses without credit failed, and farms which relied on loans against future harvests were bankrupted. The price of cotton plunged, destroying the value of southern farms and plantations and creating a situation where owners could not repay their debts. The economy did not recover until 1843.

With the Native tribes expelled, the economic panic over, and available and inexpensive farmland readily available, ancestors Hosea George and his family moved from Alabama to Union County, Arkansas in the mid 1840's, as did William Poole and his family. Hosea married William Poole's daughter; their granddaughter was my grandmother, Susie George, and her daughter Bernice was my mother, born in Louisiana and initially raised in Arkansas.

Chapter 48:
The Pool or Pettypool Family: Indentured Servant to Confederate Leader

Pedigree Chart for Altana Cordelia Pool

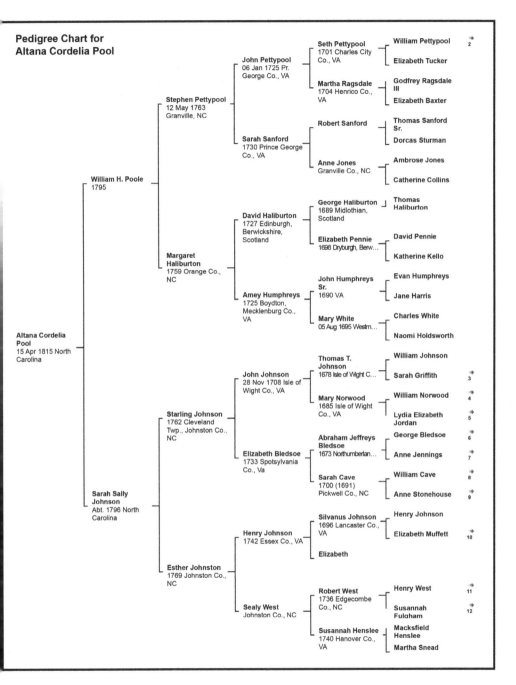

Altana Cordelia Pool
15 Apr 1815 North Carolina

William H. Poole
1795

Stephen Pettypool
12 May 1763
Granville, NC

Margaret Haliburton
1759 Orange Co., NC

Sarah Sally Johnson
Abt. 1796 North Carolina

John Pettypool
06 Jan 1725 Pr. George Co., VA

Sarah Sanford
1730 Prince George Co., VA

David Haliburton
1727 Edinburgh, Berwickshire, Scotland

Amey Humphreys
1725 Boydton, Mecklenburg Co., VA

Starling Johnson
1762 Cleveland Twp., Johnston Co., NC

Esther Johnston
1769 Johnston Co., NC

John Johnson
28 Nov 1708 Isle of Wight Co., VA

Elizabeth Bledsoe
1733 Spotsylvania Co., Va

Henry Johnson
1742 Essex Co., VA

Sealy West
Johnston Co., NC

Seth Pettypool
1701 Charles City Co., VA

Martha Ragsdale
1704 Henrico Co., VA

Robert Sanford

Anne Jones
Granville Co., NC

George Haliburton
1689 Midlothian, Scotland

Elizabeth Pennie
1698 Dryburgh, Berw...

John Humphreys Sr.
1690 VA

Mary White
05 Aug 1695 Westm...

Thomas T. Johnson
1678 Isle of Wight C...

Mary Norwood
1685 Isle of Wight Co., VA

Abraham Jeffreys Bledsoe
1673 Northumberlan...

Sarah Cave
1700 (1691) Pickwell Co., NC

Silvanus Johnson
1696 Lancaster Co., VA

Elizabeth

Robert West
1736 Edgecombe Co., NC

Susannah Henslee
1740 Hanover Co., VA

William Pettypool → 2

Elizabeth Tucker

Godfrey Ragsdale III

Elizabeth Baxter

Thomas Sanford Sr.

Dorcas Sturman

Ambrose Jones

Catherine Collins

Thomas Haliburton

David Pennie

Katherine Kello

Evan Humphreys

Jane Harris

Charles White

Naomi Holdsworth

William Johnson

Sarah Griffith → 3

William Norwood → 4

Lydia Elizabeth Jordan → 5

George Bledsoe → 6

Anne Jennings → 7

William Cave → 8

Anne Stonehouse → 9

Henry Johnson

Elizabeth Muffett → 10

Henry West → 11

Susannah Fulgham → 12

Macksfield Henslee

Martha Snead

Genealogy 36: Altana Cordelia Poole

T he Pool family originally came from England and went by the name Pettypool. Over time, European names evolved and were frequently Americanized after immigration. "Pettypool" became "Petty Pool" with Petty as a middle name and then the name just became Pool or Poole.

William Pettypool (1630–1668)

William Pettypool emigrated to Virginia in the late 1650s as an indentured servant to John Davis (see Chapter 1). John Davis did not get along with his neighbors, Emmanuel Alvis and John Raughn. In November 1660, William testified in court that Davis had ordered him to steal Alvis's and Raughn's tobacco plants, which he did. Other witnesses testified that they heard Davis instruct William to steal the plants and promise him land and cattle if he was successful. Ann Smith, another indentured servant, was also asked to help in the theft but declined. The Court found Davis guilty but it also ordered William and Ann to be committed to the sheriff's custody for their "scandalous and dangerous behavior."

The following year, William and Ann were released from their indenture and were married. Then they moved to Talbot County, Maryland. Most likely they needed a new start away from the controversies in York County, Virginia. Maryland was also offering free land to new settlers. William died at the age of thirty-eight, but he had accomplished what would have been unimaginable if he had stayed in England; he was a landowner. His wife Ann and a child, William, survived him.

William Pettypool Jr. (1665–1726) and Seth Pettypool (1701–1773)

William and Ann's son William Pettypool was born around 1665 in Virginia before his parents moved to Maryland. At some point, he moved back to Virginia and purchased land south of Petersburg along Monk's Neck Creek. William Jr. was also apparently involved in trade with local Natives; he seems to have been involved in various activities which may have been necessary to supplement his income as a small planter of tobacco at the time. He and his wife Elizabeth Tucker had at least four children including Seth.

Seth Pettypool was born by 1701, most likely in Charles City County, Virginia. He married Martha Ragsdale in 1720. He began acquiring land in areas that recently opened for new development including along Aarons Creek in what became known as Halifax County.

John Pettypool (1725–1803) and Stephen P. Pool (1763–1841)

John Pettypool was born in Prince George's County, Virginia; he was the first son and third child of Seth and Martha. He married Sarah Sanford, daughter of Robert Sanford and Ann Jones. John, Sarah, and their young family moved to Granville County, North Carolina, around 1762. The area had been first settled by Europeans around 1715 and had reached sufficient population to become a county, splitting off from Edgecombe County in 1746. The area was soon characterized by tobacco plantations and slaves. For planters, land was more available and less expensive than in Virginia and had not been exhausted by repeated plantings; this likely was the primary attraction for the Pettypools.

John and Sarah had nine children including Stephen, who was born in Granville and married Margaret Halliburton, whose father was from Scotland (see Chapter 49). They lived in Granville until around 1790, when they relocated to Johnston County, North Carolina, south of Granville. I suspect that Stephen found an attractive farm available in Johnston County and moved to take advantage.

Around 1820, the family moved to Breckinridge County, Kentucky, and Stephen died there in 1841. Stephen also began spelling his name Stephen P. Pool with the middle initial P standing for Petty.

William Poole (1795–1860)

William Halliburton Poole, son of Stephen Pool and Margaret Halliburton, was born around 1795 in Johnston County, North Carolina. He dropped his father's middle name of Petty and added an e to the end of Pool. So in three short generations, "Pettypool" became "P. Pool," and then "Poole."

William married Sarah Sally Johnson, daughter of Starling and Esther Johnson in Johnston County in 1812. The family moved to Perry County, Alabama, sometime between 1822 and 1828; perhaps right after the death of his mother in 1823 in Johnston County. His father had died a few years earlier. This timing also closely followed defeat of the Creek in Alabama and the beginning of their rapid removal, opening land for new settlers.

Sometime between 1847 and 1850, the family moved again, this time to the town of Franklin in Union County, Arkansas. Arkansas had become a state in 1836, and Congress nullified Native land titles and forced the removal of Native communities. William died in 1860 in Union County; his wife Sarah died there nine years later. They had eleven children including their first two children, Louisa and Altana. Both Louisa and Altana would go on to marry Hosea George.

The Poole family, being from the South, supported the Confederacy during the Civil War. Louisa and Altana's brother Thomas was a leader of the Twenty-eighth Louisiana Volunteers. Their story is typical of the contest between the North and the South, from a Southern perspective.

The Twenty-eighth Louisiana Volunteers

Figure 22: Louisiana brigade in combat

By the spring of 1862, New Orleans, Baton Rouge, and Natchez, Louisiana, had fallen under control of the Yankees. Those living in northern Louisiana, leery of invasion, gathered together to organize Confederate companies and regiments. Joining up as a volunteer was much preferable to being labeled as a "conscript" under the new Conscription Act. That label could last a lifetime and be the very reason a soldier could be shunned by his whole hometown community. After all, any Southern gentleman who did not voluntarily protect the Southern cause was forever looked down upon and his reputation ruined.

Even though the Twenty-eighth Louisiana Volunteers are hardly mentioned in most history books, their participation along the Bayou Teche was an important part of the Confederate effort. Ten companies made up the regiment, and after two grueling months of training (using sticks in place of real weapons), the men were assigned to Monroe to protect the vital railroad that went to Vicksburg.

After a year of never seeing the enemy, the Rebels finally engaged when the Union gunboat Diana sailed up a channel of the Atchafalaya River. The Confederates opened fire and continued shooting for three hours at the surprised Yankees on board. After the white flag of surrender was raised, the Rebels then took over the vessel and the 150 men on board, thirty of whom were dead.

The fighting moved to an area near Fort Bisland, where twelve thousand Northerners outnumbered the men of the Twenty-eighth. Under the cover of darkness, the Rebels left their trenches and followed Colonel Gray to join General Richard Taylor's troops near a plantation called Irish Bend. They waited there together in the thick woods when suddenly 375 Yankee soldiers appeared. The Rebels ambushed them, killing 115 by using a deadly combination of ammunition called "buck and ball" — a type of musket round including one rifle ball and three buckshot.

The Confederate forces retreated from these engagements, enduring months of forced marches with the Yankees not far behind, until the Union commander got tired of the pursuit and returned to southern Louisiana. Meanwhile, in December 1863, the men of the Twenty-eighth got orders to return to the area of Monroe and wait for a shipment of arms. This was a dream come true — the soldiers were going home.

Only a few of the rebels were allowed passes to spend Christmas with their families, however: the rest of the Twenty-eighth had to live outdoors in the freezing rain, unable to light campfires for warmth. As was typical at the time, more soldiers likely died of sickness than being killed in battle. After spending several weeks in Monroe, news came that the arms shipment had been confiscated by the Yankees on the other side of the Mississippi. All of their suffering had been in vain.

On April 8, 1864, the Louisiana Rebels found a location near Mansfield where their nine thousand men would take on thirty thousand Yankees. This battle was similar to the Battle of the Crater during the siege of Petersburg, only this time it was the Rebels who were caught in the ravine and had to struggle to climb up the opposing hill to face the enemy within gunshot. The route of the Twenty-eighth could be followed by the dead and dying men that lay strewn across the bloodstained slope. But the Louisiana men continued to fight despite the surrounding carnage. The Union commander found that nearly all of his officers were wounded or killed and half of his division was left on the field.

On the ninth of April the Confederate regiment came under the command of Major Thomas Poole, brother of ancestor Altana Poole, who ordered the remaining men of the Twenty-eighth to encamp and rest while other units pursued the enemy. While recuperating, Thomas Poole was promoted to colonel and the unit was then referred to as Colonel Poole's Regiment.

Finally, the unit marched out of camp and quickly caught up with the retreating Union soldiers near Mansura on May 15. The two armies disengaged before any real fighting could take place. However, the next day, the Rebels discovered the Union army in thick woods. The command was given to enter the dense forest at a full charge using their "Rebel yell." But, as fast as they charged, back out they came, having been blasted by cannon fire. A second attempt to meet the enemy found the two armies in hand-to-hand combat in the middle of the forest. Empty muskets became deadly clubs, and the clang and thwack of musket butt against bayonet rang out across the woods. It was a vicious struggle with each side refusing to yield. The men of the Twenty-eighth were finally beaten back, but the firing of weapons had set the thick woods on fire with walls of fire driving both sides back. The Twenty-eighth withdrew, and the Yankees crossed the Atchafalaya River. This was the last battle fought by Poole's Regiment.

Even though orders were received to head towards Arkansas, the summer heat was too much. The drinking water was polluted, soldiers were collapsing from heat stroke, and smallpox had broken out in camp. In light of these problems, Colonel Poole kept the men of the Twenty-eighth in the area of Boeuf Prairie until September 1864.

Little is known of the regiment thereafter except that they did spend the winter camped on Bayou Cotile near Alexandria. When word arrived in Louisiana that Robert E. Lee had surrendered in April, the military regiments had already begun to fall apart. Whole units dissolved overnight. The men of the Twenty-eighth were paroled on May 16, 1865.

Chapter 49:

The Halliburton Family: Coming to America after Seven Hundred Years in Scotland

argaret Halliburton was born in Orange County, North Carolina, around 1759. She married Stephen P. Pool (formerly Pettypool) prior to 1795. Her parents were David Halliburton and Amy Humphreys. David's family has a long history in Scotland. In the twelfth and thirteenth centuries, the Halliburtons lived in Berwickshire in the Scottish lowlands. They remained in the Scottish lowlands for many centuries showing up in Berwickshire, East Lothian, Lanarkshire, and nearby towns.

The first of the family to leave Scotland and emigrate to America was David Halliburton, who arrived in Virginia in 1746. He emigrated as a young man and probably was accompanied by his brother, Thomas. They left Scotland at a time when many Scots were fleeing the harsh tactics of the Duke of Cumberland, who was determined to subdue Scotland after his victory over the Jacobites at the Battle of Culloden in 1746. They appear to have been the first of the family to leave Scotland in seven hundred years.

After arriving in Virginia, David met and married Amey (or Amy) Humphries in 1752. Amey's grandfather emigrated from Wales to Virginia before 1670. David and Amey moved to Orange County, North Carolina, by 1763. They both died in North Carolina; David in 1767 and Amey in 1790. They had seven children including Margaret.

Chapter 50:
The Isle of Wight Johnsons: from Scotland to Virginia

Pedigree Chart for
Sally Johnson

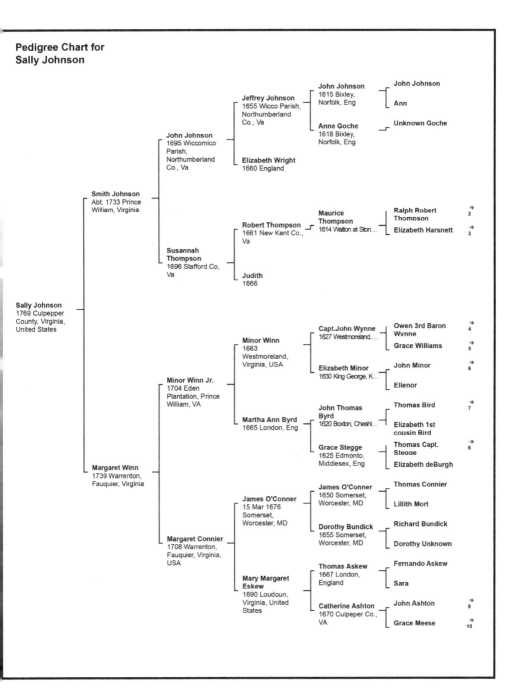

Sally Johnson
1769 Culpepper County, Virginia, United States

Smith Johnson
Abt. 1733 Prince William, Virginia

Margaret Winn
1739 Warrenton, Fauquier, Virginia

John Johnson
1695 Wiccomico Parish, Northumberland Co., Va

Susannah Thompson
1696 Stafford Co, Va

Minor Winn Jr.
1704 Eden Plantation, Prince William, VA

Margaret Connier
1708 Warrenton, Fauquier, Virginia, USA

Jeffrey Johnson
1655 Wicco Parish, Northumberland Co., Va

Elizabeth Wright
1660 England

Robert Thompson
1661 New Kent Co., Va

Judith
1666

Minor Winn
1663 Westmoreland, Virginia, USA

Martha Ann Byrd
1665 London, Eng

James O'Conner
15 Mar 1676 Somerset, Worcester, MD

Mary Margaret Eskew
1690 Loudoun, Virginia, United States

John Johnson
1615 Bixley, Norfolk, Eng

Anne Goche
1618 Bixley, Norfolk, Eng

Maurice Thompson
1614 Watton at Ston., Va

Capt.John Wynne
1627 Westmoreland,...

Elizabeth Minor
1630 King George, K...

John Thomas Byrd
1620 Boxton, Cheshi...

Grace Stegge
1625 Edmonto, Middlesex, Eng

James O'Conner
1650 Somerset, Worcester, MD

Dorothy Bundick
1655 Somerset, Worcester, MD

Thomas Askew
1667 London, England

Catherine Ashton
1670 Culpeper Co., VA

John Johnson

Ann

Unknown Goche

Ralph Robert Thompson →2

Elizabeth Harsnett →3

Owen 3rd Baron Wynne →4

Grace Williams →5

John Minor →6

Ellenor

Thomas Bird →7

Elizabeth 1st cousin Bird

Thomas Capt. Stegge →8

Elizabeth deBurgh

Thomas Connier

Lillith Mort

Richard Bundick

Dorothy Unknown

Fernando Askew

Sara

John Ashton →9

Grace Meese →10

Genealogy 37: Sarah Sally Johnson

Sarah Sally Johnson was Altana Pool's mother. Unlike the Johnson family of Northumberland, Virginia, her family likely originated near Dumfriesshire, Scotland. There is no indication the Johnson family of Northumberland was related to the Johnsons who emigrated from Scotland to Isle of Wight.

Johnson is a very common name in England and Scotland; the derivation is from "son of John." Before most people had two names, a male child of a father named John was often called Johnson or sometimes Johnston. In the United States, Johnson is the second most common name after Smith.

William Johnson was born about 1648. He was probably born in Virginia but may have been born in Scotland or England.

The earliest definitive record of ancestor William Johnson is from December 21, 1687, when he paid Philarette Woodward, daughter of Thomas Woodward, four thousand pounds of tobacco as an indemnity and for future maintenance of his illegitimate child. Philarette later married John Giles, who left his stepdaughter Jane four hundred acres in his will. Jane was almost certainly William's child. William was married at the time, which likely accounts for the heavy fine.

William married Sarah, the daughter of Owen Griffin (or Griffith) around 1670. Owen Griffin had immigrated to Isle of Wight from Caernarfon in Wales prior to 1665. He was an insurgent in Bacon's Rebellion. They had four children, including Thomas Johnson (I), born around 1680.

The Johnson descendants continued to live in Isle of Wight until John Johnson (1708–1780 moved to Johnston County, North Carolina, around 1755.

John Johnson married his first wife prior to 1730, and they had seven children. He married for a second time to Elizabeth Bledsoe, and they also had seven children, including Starling Johnson.

Starling Johnson was born in 1762; he grew up to marry Esther Johnson, a daughter of Henry Johnson and Sealy West. Starling and Esther had seven children including Sarah Sally Johnson, who married William Halliburton Poole, the son of Margaret Haliburton and Stephen P. Poole.

Chapter 51:
The Rappahannock Johnsons: Little Miss Muffett

The origin of the Johnson family from old Rappahannock County, Virginia (which became Essex County in 1692) is unknown. The first Johnson from this line that is documented is Henry Johnson, born around 1670.

Henry Johnson (1670–1722) and Elizabeth Muffit (1679–?)

Apparently both of Henry's parents died before he was of maturity, and he was listed as an orphan in legal documents. Henry was given one cow in a will, and Tobias Elveret on Henry's behalf secured the assignment from the estate of Robert Henly. When Henry turned twenty-one years of age, he apparently received the cow or equivalent compensation.

Henry and his brother Thomas bought property together in Rappahannock/ Essex County when they were of age. Henry married Elizabeth Muffit (Muffett), daughter of William Muffit and step-daughter of Richard Bond. Thomas and Henry apparently had another brother, Richard, who also participated in some of their transactions.

Elizabeth Muffit's father, William, had two brothers (Elizabeth's uncles). They were all highly educated. William Muffit was a fellow of Cambridge (1567) and later governor of the well-known and still existing Queen Elizabeth School in Chipping Barnet, England. Another brother was a church rector and author of several religious books. The third brother, Thomas Muffett, earned his medical degree in 1582 and focused his studies on insects with further emphasis on arachnids. According to an oft quoted story, one day, Thomas observed his daughter, Patience, eating her cereal when a spider started across the table. He wrote a poem about the incident:

Little Miss Muffett
Sat on her tuffett,
Eating her curds and whey.
Along came a spider,
And sat down beside her,
And frightened Miss Muffett away.

This popular children's nursery rhyme has been repeated for more than four hundred years.

Silvanus (Sill) Johnson (1696–1763) and Henry Johnson (1742–1807)

Sylvanus (Sill) Johnson was the son of Elizabeth and Henry Johnson. He was born about 1696 in Lancaster County, Virginia, and later moved to Amelia County, Virginia. Amelia County was experiencing considerable new development and was formally made a county in 1735. Sill likely moved there to take advantage of land development and appreciation opportunities as well as less expensive land for farming. He registered a livestock trademark in 1743 and was appointed to assist in a land survey for a new road near Snales Creek. Shortly thereafter he purchased 934 acres on Snales Creek, apparently with the knowledge that a new road was to be built in the area.

Between 1750 and 1755, Sill Johnson moved to Johnston County, North Carolina, where land was less expensive and growth accelerating. Sill clearly moved as opportunities arose and was not tied to any location. His first wife was named Elizabeth (last name unknown), and they had four children. He died in 1763.

Henry Johnson, son of Sill and Elizabeth, was born around 1742 in Essex County, Virginia. He married Sealy West, and their daughter Esther was born in Johnston County in 1769. She married Starling Johnson, from the Isle of Wight Johnsons. The marriage united two of the Johnson families living in Johnston County at the time. Their daughter Sarah Sally Johnson married William Poole, uniting the Johnson and Poole/Pettypool families.

Chapter 52:
The Bledsoe Family: Leaders Throughout American History

Pedigree Chart for Elizabeth Bledsoe

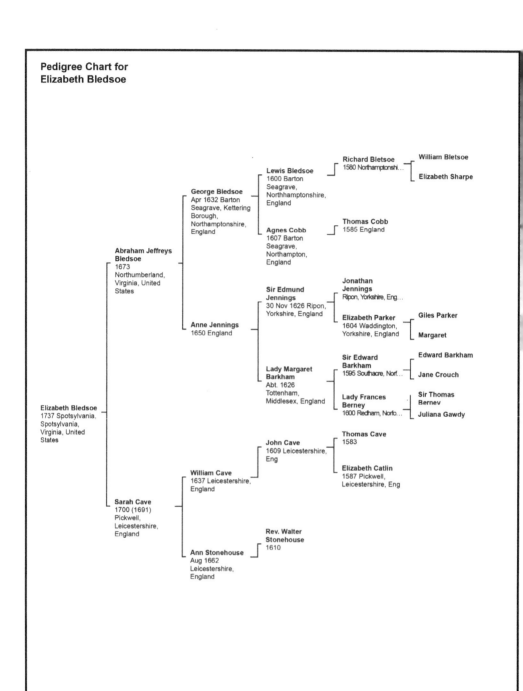

Elizabeth Bledsoe
1737 Spotsylvania, Spotsylvania, Virginia, United States

Abraham Jeffreys Bledsoe
1673 Northumberland, Virginia, United States

George Bledsoe
Apr 1632 Barton Seagrave, Kettering Borough, Northamptonshire, England

Anne Jennings
1650 England

Lewis Bledsoe
1600 Barton Seagrave, Northhamptonshire, England

Agnes Cobb
1607 Barton Seagrave, Northampton, England

Sir Edmund Jennings
30 Nov 1626 Ripon, Yorkshire, England

Lady Margaret Barkham
Abt. 1626 Tottenham, Middlesex, England

Richard Bletsoe
1580 Northamptonshi...

Thomas Cobb
1585 England

Jonathan Jennings
Ripon, Yorkshire, Eng...

Elizabeth Parker
1604 Waddington, Yorkshire, England

Sir Edward Barkham
1595 Southacre, Norf...

Lady Frances Berney
1600 Redham, Norfo...

William Bletsoe

Elizabeth Sharpe

Giles Parker

Margaret

Edward Barkham

Jane Crouch

Sir Thomas Berney

Juliana Gawdy

Sarah Cave
1700 (1691) Pickwell, Leicestershire, England

William Cave
1637 Leicestershire, England

Ann Stonehouse
Aug 1662 Leicestershire, England

John Cave
1609 Leicestershire, Eng

Rev. Walter Stonehouse
1610

Thomas Cave
1583

Elizabeth Catlin
1587 Pickwell, Leicestershire, Eng

Genealogy 38: Elizabeth Bledsoe

The Bledsoe family came from England. The name Bledsoe (or Bletsoe) is thought to be of Italian origin and introduced into England about the time of the Crusades.

In England, at least some of the Bledsoes were members of the aristocracy, and they have a coat of arms. There is also a Bletsoe Castle in Bletsoe, in the English county of Bedfordshire.

The first Bledsoe immigrant to America was George Bledsoe, who immigrated under the sponsorship of Hugh Gwynn, the same man who saved Pocahontas and founded Gwynn's Island. Gwynn was credited for bringing Bledsoe to Virginia and was entitled to a headright as a result. George was a builder and likely worked for Hugh in return for his passage.

The first appearance of George Bledsoe in Virginia is a court proceeding involving a land ownership dispute. Evidently George moved to a site that had been previously registered to someone else but never occupied. That man's son, James Ransom, claimed ownership but the court evidently agreed with Bledsoe.

George Bledsoe lived in Northumberland County, Virginia. He married Anne Jennings, who immigrated from England and was the daughter of Lady Margaret Barkham and Sir Edmund Jennings, a highly regarded, longtime member of Parliament. Anne's brother, Edmund Jennings, was president of the Council of Virginia and later acting governor of Virginia.

George became a community leader and respected citizen in Northumberland. He served for a time as constable and was listed as a member of several grand juries. He was active buying and selling land and crops and acquired considerable means during his lifetime. He was involved in several legal disputes but seems to have been victorious in all.

George and Anne had six children including Abraham, who was born in 1673 in Northumberland, Virginia. He was a planter, generally growing tobacco, and was active buying and selling land for his farm business. He married Katherine Ball, daughter of Thomas Ball, a prominent local resident, and she died around 1718. Abraham then married Sarah Cave, who had immigrated from England, in Spotsylvania, Virginia, in 1723. They had several children who migrated throughout Virginia and North Carolina, primarily in the business of growing and exporting tobacco.

Abraham and Sarah's daughter Elizabeth was born in 1733 and married John Johnson in 1751. They had six children including Starling. Two of Elizabeth's brothers, Isaac and Anthony, moved to Tennessee and established Bledsoe's Station (also known as Bledsoe's Fort) to protect early settlers from Native American attacks.

Anthony died there from a Cherokee attack in 1788. The following year, two of his nephews were killed in an ambush nearby and his brother, Isaac, was killed just outside the fort in 1793. The site is now part of the Bledsoe's Fort Historical Park in Sumner County, Tennessee.

Prior to their deaths and the Revolutionary War, Isaac, Anthony, and their brother Abraham often accompanied Daniel Boone on long hunts into Kentucky before the area became settled.

The Bledsoe descendants had significant roles in colonial American history. Some were military officers and fought in wars with Native Americans and in the Revolutionary War; others were notable clergymen, authors, and lawyers. Samuel Bledsoe later became president of the Atchison, Topeka and Santa Fe Railway, and Jesse Bledsoe was a U.S. Senator representing Kentucky. According to one source, "The history of the Bledsoes in America is that of an active, keen minded, and progressive race." [159]

Chapter 53:
The Fulgham Family: Planter or Pirate?

Pedigree Chart for Susannah Fulgham

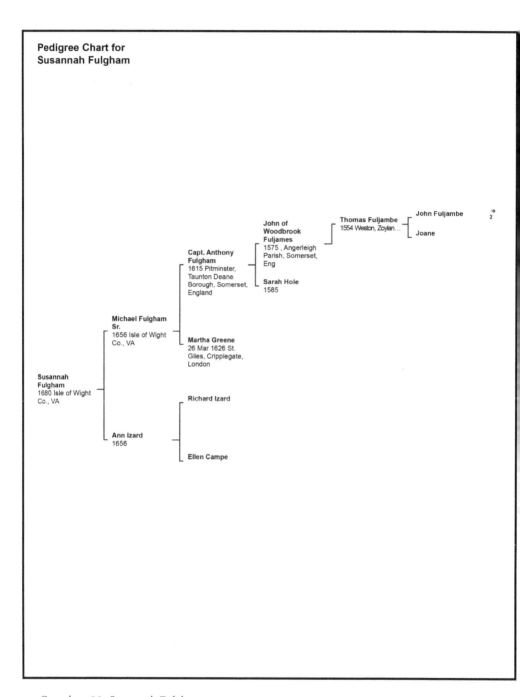

Susannah Fulgham
1680 Isle of Wight
Co., VA

Michael Fulgham Sr.
1656 Isle of Wight
Co., VA

Ann Izard
1656

Capt. Anthony Fulgham
1615 Pitminster,
Taunton Deane
Borough, Somerset,
England

Martha Greene
26 Mar 1626 St.
Giles, Cripplegate,
London

Richard Izard

Ellen Campe

John of Woodbrook Fuljames
1575 , Angerleigh
Parish, Somerset,
Eng

Sarah Hole
1585

Thomas Fuljambe
1554 Weston, Zoylan...

John Fuljambe

Joane

2

Genealogy 39: Susannah Fulgham

The Fulgham and West families were very close and neighbors in Isle of Wight, Virginia. Susannah Fulgham married Henry West before 1725.

The Fulgham lineage goes back to the year 1040 in England. The name has been spelled many different ways including Folechamp, Fuljambe, Fulliame, and Fuljames. The earliest family member known is Godfrey de Foleschampe (born 1040) who came to England with William the Conqueror and is listed in the second roll of the Battle Abbey. Godfrey's great-grandson, Henry Fuljambe, accompanied Richard the Lionheart on the Third Crusade (1189–1192), where the family arms and shield were earned.

Many generations later, Captain Anthony Fulgham was born around 1615 in Pitminster, in the English county of Somerset. He was the third of five surviving children of John Fuljames and Sarah Hole. Anthony married Elizabeth Norris in 1638 in Pitminster, and they had three children born in Pitminster (John, Thomas, and Elizabeth). His wife, Elizabeth, died in 1645, the same year her son John was born so she may have died in childbirth.

The Fulgham family was loyal to the Crown. One of the Fulgham siblings married John Cotton; the Cotton family was one of the most loyal and dedicated families to the Crown. But Anthony liked having options and in 1641, just before the English Civil War began, Anthony left his family in England, travelled to Virginia, and applied for a land patent before returning to England the same year. With the war between Charles I and the Parliamentarians underway in 1643, Anthony returned to Virginia and claimed his land.

Later, Anthony's wife died, and after Cromwell's victory over Charles I, Anthony returned to Virginia and his property and was the first Fulgham to permanently relocate to Virginia.

Anthony made at least two and possibly several trips back and forth between Isle of Wight, Virginia, and England. Over time, he was credited with bringing twenty-two immigrants including his son John and second wife, Martha Green. With each passenger, he received a land grant, and thereby acquired substantial properties.

Anthony was a planter and a lawyer. He served as justice of the county court and a captain in the local militia. He accumulated significant acreage in Isle of Wight, including a parcel of 1,600 acres in 1665.

But Captain Anthony apparently was not just a tobacco planter and lawyer. According to family history, he was also a pirate. Most likely he was actually a privateer when not overseeing his plantation. At the time, the Dutch dominated world trade, including the tobacco trade from Virginia. The English and Dutch were rivals and fought three wars between 1652 and 1674. The English resented that the Dutch controlled shipping and trade from the English colonies, and the English Parliament passed the Navigation Acts, prohibiting the colonies from sending goods anywhere but to Britain on British ships, and mandating that goods imported to the colonies come only from Britain.[160] Because the English Navy was preoccupied with wars in Europe, the Parliament authorized colonial and British ships to seize ships and cargoes from other countries violating the Navigation Acts. Reportedly, Captain Anthony thought privateering was a good way to supplement his income from farming and practicing law. The Navigation Acts caused the price of tobacco to plummet, but the ever planning and strategizing Captain Anthony would have been just fine with proceeds from his privateering adventures.

He died in 1669 in Isle of Wright. He and Martha had three children in Virginia including Michael, who married Ann Izard. They were parents to Susannah Fulgham West.

Chapter 54:

The Norwood and Jordan Families: Colonial Virginia Leaders

Pedigree Chart for
Mary Norwood

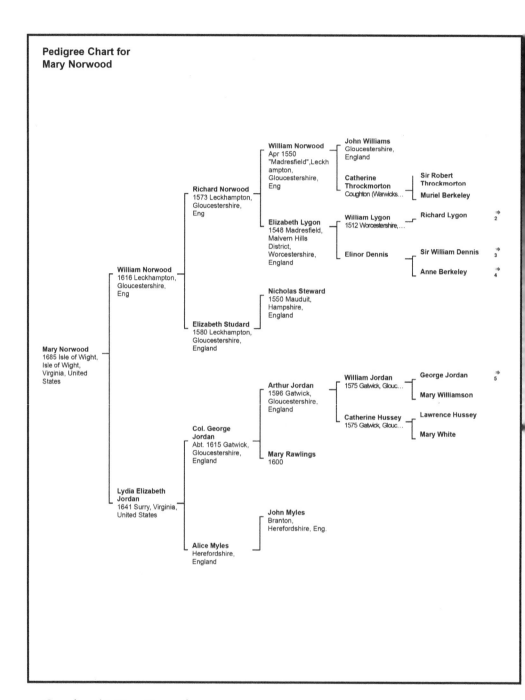

Mary Norwood
1685 Isle of Wight,
Isle of Wight,
Virginia, United
States

William Norwood
1616 Leckhampton,
Gloucestershire,
Eng

Richard Norwood
1573 Leckhampton,
Gloucestershire,
Eng

William Norwood
Apr 1550
"Madresfield",Leckh
ampton,
Gloucestershire,
Eng

John Williams
Gloucestershire,
England

**Catherine
Throckmorton**
Coughton (Warwicks...

Sir Robert
Throckmorton

Muriel Berkeley

Elizabeth Lygon
1548 Madresfield,
Malvern Hills
District,
Worcestershire,
England

William Lygon
1512 Worcestershire,...

Richard Lygon

2

Elinor Dennis

Sir William Dennis

3

Anne Berkeley

4

Elizabeth Studard
1580 Leckhampton,
Gloucestershire,
England

Nicholas Steward
1550 Mauduit,
Hampshire,
England

**Lydia Elizabeth
Jordan**
1641 Surry, Virginia,
United States

**Col. George
Jordan**
Abt. 1615 Gatwick,
Gloucestershire,
England

Arthur Jordan
1596 Gatwick,
Gloucestershire,
England

William Jordan
1575 Gatwick, Glouc...

George Jordan

5

Mary Williamson

Catherine Hussey
1575 Gatwick, Glouc...

Lawrence Hussey

Mary White

Mary Rawlings
1600

Alice Myles
Herefordshire,
England

John Myles
Branton,
Herefordshire, Eng.

Genealogy 40: Mary Norwood

The Norwood family dates back to early England. The name "Norwood" means North Wood in Old English. Many people with this name could be found in southeastern England. Generally the Norwoods were landed gentry and nobility.

The earliest known Norwood family line descends from Jordan Norwood who owned the Manor of Northwood, County Kent, around 1135. If we count Jordan as Generation 1, Henry Norwood would have been Generation 15. He was born around 1525 in Leckhampton, Gloucestershire and married Catherine Throckmorton, daughter of Sir Robert Throckmorton. He died in Leckhampton in 1561. The Throckmortons were nobility, descended from King Edward III. Henry and Catherine had six children including William.

William was already from a noble family but he raised the bar further by marrying Elizabeth Lygon (or Ligon), daughter of William Lygon of Madresfield and a descendent of King Edward I. William and Elizabeth lived their lives in Gloucestershire, England. She died there in 1598, and he died there in 1632.

William and Elizabeth's grandson William was born in 1615 or 1616. Like his ancestors, William had close ties to the royal family and was a supporter of King Charles I. When Cromwell and the Parliamentarians revolted in 1642, William left London and followed his King to the north of England to secure recruits and raise an army to fight Cromwell. After Cromwell's victory, William collected his family and fled his family's generations-old homeland for Virginia in 1648.

Many of William's close relatives fled too, suggesting the entire family was at risk of retribution from Cromwell. Among William's cousins who emigrated around the same time (or somewhat before) were Governor William Berkeley; Henry Norwood, the colony treasurer; Charles Norwood, the colony Clerk; and Colonel Thomas Ligon. William apparently settled in Isle of Wight, Virginia but then moved to nearby Surry County, where he bought a parcel of land in 1653.

William and the Norwood family were evidently very close to the Jordan (or Jurdan) family, who were also from Gloucestershire and supporters of the Crown. William married Lydia Jordan in 1660; he died in Surry County in 1702 at an advanced age (over eighty years).

Lydia's father was Colonel George Jordan, who emigrated from England with his brother and their father, Arthur, arriving in Virginia in 1635. George became a prominent member of Virginia society, serving as justice of Surry County for many years beginning in 1652. He served in the House of Burgesses in 1659, 1674, and 1676 and was attorney general for the Virginia colony from 1670 until his death in 1678. He was also a colonel in the militia.

George Jordan married Alice Myles, daughter of John Myles. Alice was born in Herefordshire, England; she and George are believed to have been married in Herefordshire and immigrated to Surry County, Virginia around 1635. They lived in an area called "Four Mile Tree Plantation" in Surry County. Today the plantation house is a historic landmark. In George's will, he asked to be buried in the Four Mile Tree orchard. Alice was also buried at the plantation Her tombstone is the oldest legible tombstone in Virginia. The inscription reads:

Here lyeth Buried the Body of
Alice Myles daughter of
John Myles of Branton neare
Herreford Gent and late wife
Of Mr. George Jordan in Virginia who
Departed this life the 7th of January 1650.
Reader, her dust is here Inclosed
Who was of witt and grace composed
Her life was Vertuous during breath
But highly Glorious in her death.

Chapter 55:
The Jordan Family (Wiltshire England): Jordan's Journey and a Woman Pursued

Pedigree Chart for
Mary Millicent Jordan

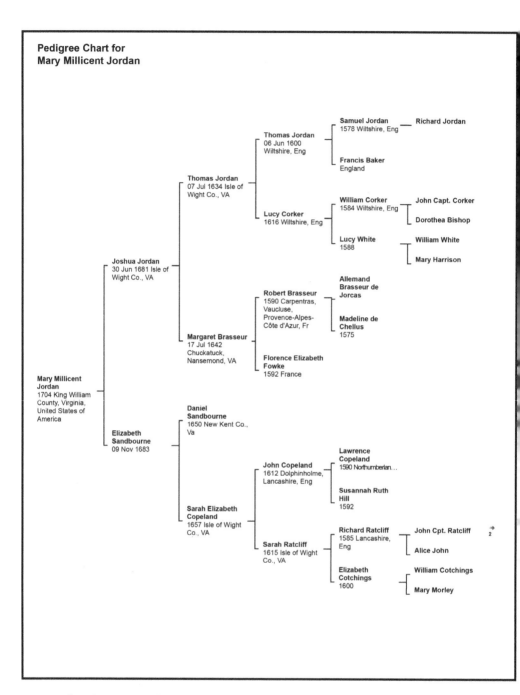

Mary Millicent Jordan
1704 King William County, Virginia, United States of America

Joshua Jordan
30 Jun 1681 Isle of Wight Co., VA

Thomas Jordan
07 Jul 1634 Isle of Wight Co., VA

Thomas Jordan
06 Jun 1600 Wiltshire, Eng

Samuel Jordan
1578 Wiltshire, Eng

Richard Jordan

Francis Baker
England

Lucy Corker
1616 Wiltshire, Eng

William Corker
1584 Wiltshire, Eng

John Capt. Corker

Dorothea Bishop

Lucy White
1588

William White

Mary Harrison

Margaret Brasseur
17 Jul 1642 Chuckatuck, Nansemond, VA

Robert Brasseur
1590 Carpentras, Vaucluse, Provence-Alpes-Côte d'Azur, Fr

Allemand Brasseur de Jorcas

Madeline de Chellus
1575

Florence Elizabeth Fowke
1592 France

Elizabeth Sandbourne
09 Nov 1683

Daniel Sandbourne
1650 New Kent Co., Va

Sarah Elizabeth Copeland
1657 Isle of Wight Co., VA

John Copeland
1612 Dolphinholme, Lancashire, Eng

Lawrence Copeland
1590 Northumberlan...

Susannah Ruth Hill
1592

Sarah Ratcliff
1615 Isle of Wight Co., VA

Richard Ratcliff
1585 Lancashire, Eng

John Cpt. Ratcliff

Alice John

Elizabeth Cotchings
1600

William Cotchings

Mary Morley

→ 2

Genealogy 41: Mary Millicent Jordan

Colonel George Jordan was not the only Jordan to emigrate from England in the early 1600s. There is a state historic marker on Virginia Highway 252 commemorating "Samuel Jordan of Jordan's Journey." Samuel Jordan was from Wiltshire, England, about eighty miles west of London. Samuel is believed to have married Francis Baker in England, and they had a son named Thomas Fletcher Jordan, born in Wiltshire around 1600.

Samuel immigrated to Virginia by 1610. Some reports indicate he was a passenger on the *Sea Venture* with John Rolfe and Stephen Hopkins or he may have been a passenger on one of the other ships that sailed at the same time but were separated in the hurricane. Regardless he was in Jamestown by 1610. He married a woman named Cecily (perhaps Cecily Reynolds), who had arrived in Jamestown around 1611. He soon developed a plantation first known as "Beggar's Bush" and later as "Jordan's Journey." It was about thirty miles upriver from Jamestown, and the buildings were surrounded by a wall in a fortress-style layout. He and his family survived the Powhatan attacks during the Jamestown Massacre there, and Jordan's Journey became a safe haven and place of protection for dozens of nearby settlers who abandoned their homes during the ensuing Anglo-Powhatan War.

Samuel and Cicely and their two daughters remained at Jordan's Journey until his death there in 1623. After Samuel died, things became complicated for his widow. She was apparently quite beautiful, outgoing and friendly. Other women in Jamestown tolerated her but kept a wary eye on their husbands. With Samuel's death, his entire large estate became Cicely's, making this beautiful woman also very rich. Single men immediately began calling on her including the minister who had just conducted Samuel's funeral.

Reverend Grivell Pooley proposed marriage to Cecily just days after Samuel's death. She declined, telling him it was too soon, but he was adamant. In fact, he proposed to her again in front of friends and recited his portion of the wedding vows. When she said nothing, he recited her portion of the wedding vows for her. She went home without talking.

Later Cecily agreed to marry Colonel William Farrer. Reverend Pooley was incensed. He took the matter to court in the first "breach of promise" lawsuit in America and filed further suits with the Council of Virginia and even in London. Women had so few rights at the time that the council refused to rule on the lawsuits even though Reverend Pooley was clearly overreaching. Eventually, Pooley admitted defeat and withdrew his suits. Then the governor and the council proclaimed it illegal in the future for a woman to engage herself to more than one man at a time. In other words, they blamed the woman for the dispute.

Thomas, Samuel's son by his first marriage, did not accompany Samuel to America but emigrated from England in 1623 at the age of twenty-three. Around 1633

Thomas married Lucy Corker, daughter of Captain William Corker and Lucy White. They had five children including Thomas Jr.

Thomas Jordan Jr. was born in 1634 in Isle of Wight County, Virginia. He married Margaret Brasseur, the daughter of Robert Brasseur and Florence Fowke. Robert was a Huguenot immigrant from France who most likely came to Virginia to escape the widespread religious persecution underway then in France (see Chapter 1). Margaret and Thomas became Quakers and suffered attacks and discrimination. Thomas was arrested for attending Quaker meetings and imprisoned several times.

Thomas Jr. and Margaret had twelve children, including Joshua, who was born in 1681 in Isle of Wight. Joshua married another Quaker, Elizabeth Sandbourne, child of Daniel Sandbourne and Sarah Copeland.

Joshua and Elizabeth lived in Isle of Wight County their entire lives and had ten children; he died around 1718. His will contains an unusual provision regarding his devotion to his religion and his mother-in-law. The will says that Joshua "desired that his mother-in-law, Sarah Sandbourne, shall be honorably taken care of by my wife and daughter and shall not want for anything that can be done for her, likewise shall have a horse and saddle to go to Meeting when she sees fit." It is not clear why Joshua felt he needed to remind his wife to take care of her mother; perhaps his wife was not as committed to attending Quaker meetings.

One of Joshua and Elizabeth's daughters, Mary, was born in 1704 and married John George (Sr.) in 1724, uniting the Jordan and George lines. Incidentally, these Jordans pronounced their last name "Jerr-don," unlike other Jordans including those from Essex, England. However, over time, the pronunciation became the more traditional "Jordan."

Chapter 56:

The Washington George Family: A Storied Family History

Pedigree Chart for
Washington LaFayette George

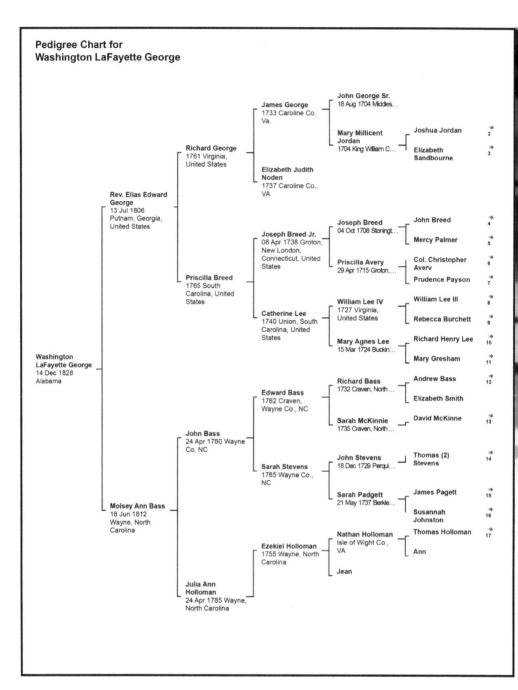

Genealogy 42: Washington Lafayette George

Pedigree Chart for
Robert Fawdon George

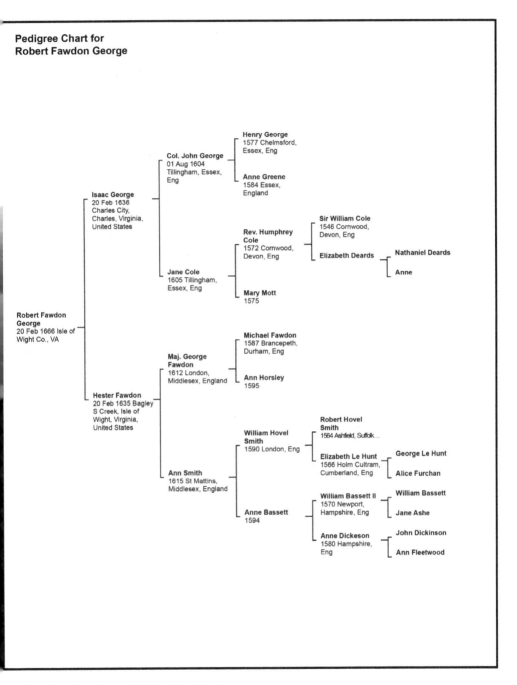

Robert Fawdon George
20 Feb 1666 Isle of Wight Co., VA

Isaac George
20 Feb 1636 Charles City, Charles, Virginia, United States

Col. John George
01 Aug 1604 Tillingham, Essex, Eng

Henry George
1577 Chelmsford, Essex, Eng

Anne Greene
1584 Essex, England

Jane Cole
1605 Tillingham, Essex, Eng

Rev. Humphrey Cole
1572 Cornwood, Devon, Eng

Mary Mott
1575

Sir William Cole
1546 Cornwood, Devon, Eng

Elizabeth Deards

Nathaniel Deards

Anne

Hester Fawdon
20 Feb 1635 Bagley S Creek, Isle of Wight, Virginia, United States

Maj. George Fawdon
1612 London, Middlesex, England

Michael Fawdon
1587 Brancepeth, Durham, Eng

Ann Horsley
1595

Ann Smith
1615 St Mattins, Middlesex, England

William Hovel Smith
1590 London, Eng

Robert Hovel Smith
1564 Ashfield, Suffolk...

Elizabeth Le Hunt
1566 Holm Cultram, Cumberland, Eng

George Le Hunt

Alice Furchan

Anne Bassett
1594

William Bassett II
1570 Newport, Hampshire, Eng

Anne Dickeson
1580 Hampshire, Eng

William Bassett

Jane Ashe

John Dickinson

Ann Fleetwood

Genealogy 43: (General) Robert Fawdon George

This line of the George family was living in Essex, England in the 1500s and possibly long before. The first immigrant from this family was Colonel John George, born in 1604 in Tillingham, Essex. He married Jane Cole, also from Tillingham, in 1623. They apparently had five children in Essex before they immigrated to Isle of Wight, Virginia, in 1632. John George secured land on Bayles Creek in nearby Charles City County in 1634, near what is present day Smithfield.

Colonel John George (1604–1676)

John George quickly established himself as a leading citizen and served twice in the House of Burgesses. He joined the militia and was a major in 1654, rising later to colonel. In addition to being a planter and a burgess, John was a lawyer and served as justice for Charles City County.

In 1676, the General Assembly authorized Colonel George to impress men and horses and build forts on the frontier to defend against Native attacks. The forts were built and garrisoned, but many thought this was insufficient to protect the settlers and wanted a more aggressive campaign. This disagreement led to Bacon's Rebellion (see Chapter 37).

Colonel George sided with Governor Berkeley during Bacon's Rebellion. He was probably a justice in the colonial court during that uprising and would not have been sympathetic to the rebels. Later, at the advanced age of seventy-five, he took the field and commanded militia troops to protect against potential Native American attacks.

John and Jane George's descendants included Isaac George (1635–1685), Robert George (1665–1733), and John George (1704–1784). John George married Mary Jordan and they had several children including James.

James George (1733–1799) and Richard George (1761–1799)

John and Mary's son James was born in 1733 in Caroline County, Virginia. He married Elizabeth Noden, daughter of Hugh Noden and Elizabeth Pender; she was also from Caroline County. Both James and his wife Elizabeth apparently died in 1799, probably of disease. There were several diseases circulating in Virginia at the time including smallpox and diphtheria. In the same year, 1799, also in Virginia, George Washington died. His secretary, Colonel Tobias Lear, wrote about Washington's illness and the attempts to save him.

At daybreak on the 14th [December], Colonel Tobias Lear came in and found the General breathing with difficulty... A mixture of molasses, vinegar, and but-

ter was given, but he (GW) could not swallow a drop… Later he tried to use a gargle of vinegar and sage tea but in attempting to gargle, he almost suffocated… His physicians had ordered that he be bled a number of times in the course of his illness and an incredible amount [of blood] — about 82 ounces or about 5 pints or units of blood were removed from him… He died between ten and eleven p.m. on December 14, 1799.[161]

George Washington probably died of an infection related to his esophagus called epiglottitis. It is unknown what James and Elizabeth died from, but medical care was rather primitive at the time and cures limited.

Richard George was the oldest son of James and Elizabeth and was born in 1761. He evidently married someone in Virginia in 1783 and had children with her. After she died, he moved to Warren, Georgia, around 1798 and married Priscilla Breed there. He would have been thirty-nine years old, and she was eighteen. Richard and Priscilla had six children including Elias George. Prior to 1817, they moved to Perry, Alabama.

Richard fought with the patriots in the Revolutionary War as a member of the South Carolina militia with his father-in-law, Joseph Breed Jr. They fought in a series of battles (see Chapter 31).

Reverend Elias George (1806–1890)

Richard and Priscilla's son Elias George was born in 1806 in Putnam County, Georgia, but moved with his family to Alabama when he was still a child. He became a well-known preacher as well as a plantation owner. In 1828, at the age of twenty-one, he married Molsey Ann Bass. When Elias was about forty years old, he and his family moved to Marion, Louisiana, where he built an impressive new house that remains as a historic landmark that his daughter Louisa described in her memoirs.

A story about Elias and his brother Stewart was appeared in the book *Notable Men of Alabama,* published in 1904:

Elijah Cothran was born at Dunedin, county of Monaghan Ireland. He ran away at the age of eight, was taken by an English sea captain known for his cruelty but escaped again when his ship reached the port of Mobile Alabama. He found shelter in a boat owned by Stewart George and was taken in and hidden by Stewart's brother, Elias. The Georges raised the young boy with their sons and taught him how to make shoes and boots when he grew up. By the age of twenty, he had his own successful business and went on to marry and have several children and become a valued member of the community.[162]

"In the Gloaming," one of the most popular ballads ever written, has its origin in the George household. Reverend Elias George needed a governess and music teacher for his children on his twenty-acre estate in Marion. He placed an ad in a New Orleans newspaper and hired a Mrs. Harrison, who came with her daughter, Annie Fortescue Harrison (also called Ann Porter).[163] Annie composed the Irish ballad in 1877, and it was a hit that year throughout the country. It remained popular and received further attention when released by the American Quartet in 1910.[164] Later, it became the subject of a book and a movie. Elias was active in civic affairs; he was an early pioneer in Louisiana and his obituary, which appeared in the New Orleans *Daily Picayune* on May 15, 1890, reflects his high regard:

> *Last Wednesday night Rev. Elias George, one of the oldest and most highly respected citizens of Union parish, passed peacefully away in the cold embrace of death, at the residence of his son, Mr. Elias George, Jr., ten miles north of Farmerville. The deceased lived to the ripe old age of 85 years. He leaves a number of grown-up children, who are among the best and most worthy citizens of Union parish, to mourn his loss.[165]*

Elias and Ann had eleven children including Washington Lafayette George. In 1926, one of their daughters, Louisa, wrote a memoir about her family and their life; that memoir is presented below.

Washington Lafayette George (1828–1857)

Washington Lafayette George was born in 1828 in Perry County, Alabama. He married Martha Johnson in Perry in 1846; he was seventeen years old and she was sixteen.

They soon moved to Union Parish, Louisiana, where his family lived at that time. Their three children were born in Union Parish, and Washington died there in 1857. His estate was valued about $13,400, less about $5,900 in debts. His plantation of four hundred acres was only valued at $1,250, but his slaves had a value of over $10,000 according to the estimators.

Washington and Martha's daughter Josephine (or "Josia") was born in 1849 in Union County, Louisiana. She married Gaston Percy George in 1868, when she was nineteen years old. They moved to Arkansas, where Gaston's family lived, and had six children including my grandmother, Susan R. George. Josie died in 1898 in Ashley County, Arkansas; her husband Gaston Percy George died later, in 1909.

Memoirs of Louisa George Tompkins

Written in 1926 at the age of 84 years.[166] Abridged and edited.

Part 1: The First Home

I was born on a farm near Hamburg, Perry County, Alabama in 1842. Elias George and mother, Ann Bass George, were the parents of nine children, — four sons and five daughters, of whom I was third from the youngest. All lived to maturity, married and raised families, except one brother, "Jeffy", two years my senior, who at the age of eight years was thrown from a runaway horse.

My parents were missionary Baptists, and we were early taught to reverence the name of Jesus, respect the Sabbath day, be kind and charitable to the poor, to servants, and to animals. There was family worship every night before retiring, and my mother would have the servants come in and to join us at such times. We were a happy family because children and servants were taught obedience to those who ruled them. We loved our servants and they loved us.

My father, being a slaveholder, had a large plantation on which many supplies for home consumption were raised, such as corn, cotton, potatoes, barley, and peas. The home was a large, rambling two-storied building, and each of the various rooms had a fireplace. But the room that charmed me most was the nursery, — a large room with windows facing southward, overlooking the pasture, and in the springtime there was much interest in the horses and the little lambs as they chased each other and gamboled in the field.

Our black mammy Chloe, was installed as guardian and caretaker of the nursery. Its inmates included three children, from one to five years old and two nurse girls, Mariah and Harriet, who were ten and eleven years old. The girls, under the supervision of mammy Chloe, would see to our bathing, dressing, and feeding. When the weather permitted, we were kept out doors in the sunshine and although the girls ran and played with us, our black mammy was ever near and watchful that no harm befell us.

It is difficult to make it understood what love we had for Mammy and the girls. This attachment lasted even to old age.

I would not have one think that our precious mother neglected her little children under these conditions and surroundings. She had duties devolving upon her, which could not be done by others. There were nine children to clothe and feed. While she had servants who cooked, washed, ironed and sewed, she supervised each department. There were no sewing machines nor ready-made clothing. We were strangers to most of the conveniences in common use today. Even soap and candles were made at the plantation. My father raised everything possible at home and a yearly trip to New Orleans resulted in the equivalent of a carload of provisions, dress goods from England or New England and many other things needed for the plantation. Oranges, apples, dried fruits, and candy were bought by the barrel.

How well do I remember the picturesque surroundings of our home. There was a long sloping hill to the rear of the house, at the foot of which was a cold, gushing spring, and directed channels went forth to the house lot, chicken yard, and other needed places. A milk house was built over this spring, the floor of which was laid of large, flat rocks, so arranged that the stream was conducted over a channel two or three inches lower than the floor and wide enough to hold several pans of milk and butter.

Other impressions of this home were the negro quarters which were a half-mile from the house. And there was a summer-house covered with coral and French honeysuckle vines where the mocking birds often built their nests. Also, there were the flowers which grew profusely along the branch and filled the air with their fragrance.

These are the memories of my first home.

Part 2: Migration to Louisiana

It is needless to say that the dear old home where my mother and father had lived since their marriage and which had been the birthplace of their nine children, was doomed. Also, a beautiful new home near Marion, Louisiana was being completed. This was a large, two-story house, quite modern in all its appointments (for that time). The inside work was superior to anything of its kind today; the plastering was very hard and glazed. The parlor and hall were heavily frescoed around the edges of the ceiling, with a large wreath of flowers in the center of each for the chandeliers. My older sisters and brothers were at the age when they needed to be in college, as they had outgrown the country school. To educate them had been the incentive for building in Marion, as it was a residential city of schools and churches.

But to my father, nothing was too great a sacrifice for this "Land of Paradise", — not even the many friends and relatives with their earnest protests, or his popularity as a minister of the gospel. Nothing could outweigh his desire to possess a home in this unexplored wilderness — a venture of toil, self-denial, hardships, and untried experiences. Without taking it to the Lord in prayer, and seeking divine guidance of Him whom he served, he straightway sold his valuable *plantation and lovely new home at a sacrifice, and was soon in readiness for the journey by caravan.*

Early in the spring of 1848, the day for departure arrived. Three or four families decided to cast their lot with us in going west, which at that time was as far distant as is California now. The trip had to be made in private conveyances, drawn by horses and mules, and it would take weeks to reach our destination. Besides this, my father was taking with him 400 Durham cattle which were to be driven by herdsmen.

The caravan included about 50 covered wagons, carriages, carry-all's, and buggies. These and the horseback riders assembled at our home, and many friends came to bid us "un bon voyage". How well do I remember that first day, which to me seemed a gala affair with many more to follow. I was too young (six years) to realize what it meant to those on whom the burden fell, nor what awaited us in the future. The morning was bright and beautiful, and although the sun gladdened the earth, it was unable to penetrate the gloom which hung like a pall of dark foreboding in the hearts of some who reluctantly bade a last farewell to loved ones.

My mother rode in a carriage with four of her young children; a brother older and a sister and brother younger than I. The driver's seat was high in front, and in the style of the period, the nurse's seat was in the rear. This was supplied with a step or foot rest and arms, as with an armchair. The first day being cold and crisp, mother had the driver stop at a store as we passed through Greensborough, and bought us children beautiful wool hoods and each a tin cup, painted red and blue, with "Boy" or "Girl" stamped on it. These were suspended from our necks with ribbons.

The caravan necessarily traveled slowly and when we children were tired of riding, mother would let us get out and walk, always attended by the nurse. Long before night, the captain, (father) always went ahead to find and arrange for a suitable camp ground where wood and water could be obtained, for provisions also to be made for the cattle as well as the teams of mules and horses. Having found such a place, he would wait for the crowd.

The camp ground reached, the overseer of the negroes superintended the location of wagons, tents, and animals. The negroes' tents were grouped by themselves and the white families were in a different location. Each family of negroes had its separate tent; each woman cooking for her own family, while the men got the wood, attended to the feeding and caring for the stock and pitched the tents. There were log fires in front of family tents, and after all were fed and the little children were in bed, the white families would visit each other, — sit around and exchange experiences and jokes till nine or ten o'clock. The negroes would have their social time until the gong sounded for retiring; after which quiet soon reigned, except for the occasional lowing or neighing of an animal. At five o' clock, the gong again sounded and all were up and hustling with preparations to travel. Then at noon, a stop for a couple of hours was made, with rest and lunch for man and beast.

We had to cross the Tombigbee River in Alabama which we found to be a half-mile wide from recent rains. It took two or three days to make the crossing, for the cattle had to be ferried across. Upon taking one load, the cattle became frightened and stampeded, and several leaped from the flat-boat and were carried by the swift current downstream, and two or three of these were never recovered.

Having surmounted this obstacle, we proceeded on our journey with nothing of importance to note except that one night we camped in a lovely grove of oak trees enclosed with a rail or worm fence. A railroad track ran along the outside of this enclosure, and we were warned not to cross the fence; that a train would pass by very soon. We hadn't waited long when a shrill whistle heralded its approach. We all stopped and gazed at the wonderful monster, as it seemed to me, for in those days, railroads were rare to country people.

At last we reached the Mississippi, which we crossed at Vicksburg on a ferry. We finally reached our destination which was a beautiful grove of oak trees, in the midst of which was an eight-roomed cottage. Also, there was a summer-house covered with coral honeysuckle and woodbine and in the yard there was an abundance of flowers. My father had purchased this farm with 600 acres of improved land and under cultivation, to serve as a temporary home until there were further developments.

This home was three miles from Marion, a village in north Louisiana, in Union Parish. It was settled and named for Marion, Alabama by its earliest settlers who had come from that place.

Part 3: The First Years in Louisiana

Father had bought 4,000 acres of timbered land within four miles of Marion, which was to be cleared and converted into a plantation, — with cottages for the negroes, a dwelling for the overseer, and with gardens and outhouses. This kept all hands busy for the first year, with only time enough to cultivate the 600 acres of the home place.

Soon after being installed in our new home, my second brother (Frank, 17) and brother Jefferson, 8 years old, started to school in Marion, riding horseback. Coming home one evening, the horse ran away with them; the saddle girth broke, and my younger brother was dashed against a tree. He lived only a few hours. Brother Frank (cousin Onie's father) after lingering between life and death for several days finally survived. This was mother's second deep sorrow. Indeed, to all the family, it was the darkest day we had ever known.

The next Fall, found that much had been accomplished in clearing and building, and by the time winter had set in, all the negroes were comfortably housed with large fireplaces in their cabins and good beds and plenty of wood. For our family, a temporary dwelling had been built about a mile from the plantation on a high hill with a good spring of water, and to the rear of the house was a branch running in a ravine. In the spring many wild-flowers filled the air with their fragrance.

After moving into this newly built forest home, five miles from town, my two oldest sisters, Lizzie, 15 and Sue, 13 attended school in Marion, boarding at the home of mother's brother, Uncle Dick Bass. The carriage was sent for them Friday afternoons, and took them back early Monday mornings.

The Spring following, father began to build a residence in Marion, having purchased 25 acres of land with a bold spring and a branch of fresh water flowing from it, which soon ran through the horse-lot and orchard, all of which was prearranged when planning the home surroundings. Our parents were bending every effort to hasten the time when we could move to town and get those old enough into school.

But alas! alas! "Man proposes but God disposes." Although our forest home stood on a beautiful hill, with a spring of pure water, — and to all appearances, a most healthful location, we little dreamed that an enemy was lurking in the air, having risen from the low damp marshes and stagnant pools of water which had not been drained; and that the dying vegetation was filling the atmosphere with poisonous germs and these were inoculating almost every member of the family (white and colored) with yellow fever germs.

We were all infected about the same time the physicians advised the family's removal to an old and settled place. My grandmother's home was about four miles distant, — and being unoccupied, we moved into it — carrying four sick children on beds in a carry-all. The children were a sister (Jane), my brother Elias, a colored girl my age, and myself. Two of the house servants (Julia, the cook), and Mary, the house maid, were removed to the plantation. The gardener and the milkmaid escaped. These along with two other women from the farm went with the family as house servants and to help nurse the sick. Every day, mother rode horse-back to visit Julia and Mary to see that they were properly cared for. Physicians attended them daily and every effort was made to save them, — but all in vain. Mother was heart-broken over this sad calamity for they were almost like her own children, and they were devoted to her. The little negro girl my age who was taken to Grandma Bass's place, died a few days later. There were no trained nurses in those days, but the neighbors did everything they could in caring for the sick. In a pioneer country, citizens were dependent upon each other in times of adversity.

Our father and mother were almost overwhelmed with grief. Three good servants were dead and three children were expected to die at any time. But the cup of sorrow was not yet full and once more the death angel appeared, taking our faithful, devoted, and precious mother.

She had been for the last time to see her sick servants. She found the maid dead and the cook in a dying condition. Mother prayed with her and comforted her as best she could. Upon leaving, Julia put her arms around mother's neck and said, "Miss Ann, meet me in heaven".

The next day mother was not feeling well but did not go to bed. That night, she had a congestive chill, and at four a.m., she went to meet Julia in heaven. Her death was so sudden and unexpected, that father was beside himself with grief and for several months the physicians were afraid he would lose his mind. I grieved for mother and Sarah, the Negro girl who was my competitor in knitting

Beginning to walk a little, I decided I wanted to go to Aunt Caroline's, and seeing that I was determined, Mammy Chloe took me up on her shoulder and carried me over. Dear old Mammy Chloe, — how I loved her. Right here, I want to say that she nursed me when my first child (Paul) was born in my father's home where we were living during the Civil War. Mammy died during the War.

Aunt Caroline let me stay as long as I desired (several weeks), and when the last strand of hair disappeared from my head, she knitted me a black silk cap. She also bought some red, green, and white material for a quilt and taught me how to sew the squares together into a double-chained square. This was a very wise thing to do, for I was very irritable and discontented, but upon getting busy with my quilt, I was no longer any trouble.

We were indeed a sad family. My oldest sisters (Lizzie and Sue) had to leave school to be at home with us four younger children, — three of us still invalids, though slowly gaining in health. Sue and Lizzie were children in experience but brave, dear sisters who did what they could. The new house-servants were untrained for domestic work but they were good and willing to learn, and under the supervision of father's sister, Aunt Caroline McAdams, who lived on a high hilltop nearby, they became quite proficient. Aunt Caroline was a widow with one daughter and three sons, and she did all within her power to mother and *care for us. We saw little of father; he was so stricken, yet he saw that we had everything needed. He was so depressed in spirit that he stopped building the house in Marion.*

Father was troubled on all sides. His good overseer, whom he brought with him from Alabama, had also died and he hired another who understood very little of superintending a large plantation of negroes and farm work. However, it was a good thing, even a blessing that father had to supervise till the new manager was fully initiated into the routine of duties dependent on him. The sight of his motherless children was a fresh stab of the dagger to his poor bleeding heart.

The three months' sickness left me no flesh nor strength. I was so emaciated that they carried me around like a baby. Dr. Traylor, the physician said I could have all the sugar and sugar cane I wanted. I kept a bowl of sugar on the bed-table.

Part 4: School Days

A year had passed since dear mother left us and I was stronger, so father decided to send Sue, 15; Jane, 13; and me, 9 to school and board us with Uncle Dick (Bass, mother's brother) in Marion. Sissy, now 17, had to stay at home to look after Bud (Elias), 7; and Melinda, 5.

I can't express the great delight and joy when I was permitted to go to school, and to have a slate, book, and a pencil of my own; and to have a lesson assigned me in Webster's Blue Backed Spelling Book — one of which I have now, and which I treasure as a souvenir of my first school days and which, like myself, remains alone, — a relic of the past.

Marion was then a village of about 20 families, the most of whom were prosperous farmers with plantations a few miles out in the country. These were cultivated by negroes and supervised by competent white overseers. Though a village in size, Marion had the finest school in north Louisiana. The principal was a highly accomplished lady from Virginia, and her sister was the music teacher. Their names were the Misses Harriet and Mary Whiting, and I want to say that they were the best teachers I ever had, — even better than those in the Judson College.

There were only three of us in the primary class, — and the other two were about my age. All of us were ambitious to excel, and each of us was generally perfect in lessons and deportment. While at school I often had chills and fever, but I could not be induced to go home to be doctored, till Miss Harriet promised to give me my credits if I would study and recite my lessons to Sue, who agreed to hear them and make faithful reports. I would often lie in bed and study while I had fever.

Doctor Traylor, father's family physician, finally took me from school and kept me in his home for three weeks while he doctored and finally cured me. He was the father of Kate Traylor, one of my classmates and rivals. He was like a dear father and had Kate and me sleep in a trundle bed in his wife's room. I had every care, with a servant in an adjoining room to be called if needed.

School days in Marion were drawing to a close. Our devoted teachers, Misses Harriet and Mary Whiting, whom we all loved and respected, honored, and obeyed, were leaving. Miss Mary, the music teacher, married a lawyer and located in Omaha. Miss Harriet returned to Virginia and was later married.

The next Fall (1856) father decided to send me back to school in Marion, Alabama where there was a large female college (The Judson) and male college (The Howard) of 300, and each was a Missionary Baptist college.

I remained throughout the whole term which closed with graduating exercises and a concert, — the grandest it has been my pleasure to hear and in which it was my privilege to have part in several instrumental numbers and choruses. The Concert, with all the closing exercises, was held in the city auditorium and about 150 pupils took part.

We wore uniforms at Judson. Our winter uniform was a green suit with a green dolman for a wrap. There was no jewelry, not even a breastpin for the collar, which was of plain white linen pinned neatly at the throat, and there were no low necks or short sleeves. In summer, the uniform was pink and white.

There was no difference shown with richest or poorest; all fared and shared alike. One a month, each girl was permitted to have fifty cents worth of candy, nuts and fruit.

Later, father came to Alabama on business and visited me. I was so happy I cried for joy and became very homesick. And since I was also discouraged with my schoolwork, pleaded with him to take me home. After much persuasion he consented, and what joy! I began that day to pack my trunk as we were to start the next day.

Bidding friends and teachers goodbye, we took the train the following morning for Selma, where on the Alabama River there was a boat for Mobile and thence we crossed the Gulf to New Orleans. After spending several days in that city, we boarded one of the finest and most popular boats at that time, the "Doctor Buffington," which ran from New Orleans to Little Rock. Her patrons were mostly farmers and merchants. There were so few railroads in the country that all transportation was dependent on river navigation. These were fordable in summer but out of service to large steamers, except in the winter.

The boat landed at nine a.m. on the third day of our trip from New Orleans and five of us landed. There was Hattie Bryant, a girl of my age, and two young men from Marion. Father went ahead on horseback to Marion which was ten miles away. Our baggage was sent in a wagon and we had to wait until father sent the carriage for us. But we started walking to meet the carriage and had gone two miles before it approached us.

(1858) I had not been home long when my father began to receive numerous answers to an advertisement which he had placed in the "New Orleans Pic- ayune" calling for a school teacher and a music teacher. He had me help him make a choice. From among the thirty or forty letters, I selected a mother and daughter and this letter also suited father. This he answered and a few weeks later Mrs. Harrison and Anna Porter were added to our family. They were all that could be desired both as teachers and as companions. Both were well-read and quite intellectual. Porter sang and played beautifully. She was a fine enter- tainer, — so full of life and vivacity and with never a loss for a word. The first time I ever heard "Kathleen Mavourneen" was when it was sung by her. She and I became constant companions even though she was two years older than I. And what she was in companionship to me, her mother was to Sissy (Sister Elizabeth). They were both fond of reading and search for knowledge. Sissy often wrote continued stories for the "Boston Olive Branch" and her nom de plume was "Isabelle Gayle". She also wrote for "Godey's Ladies' Magazine".

Part 5: Plantation Life

After the death of my mother, father seemed so disconsolate and broken in spirit, that his friends and older children encouraged him to find a companion for himself and a mother for his children. He finally wrote to Mrs. Ross, — a very excellent lady of character, culture, and refinement, reared and educated in Richmond, Virginia and who was then living on a plantation that adjoined our former home in Alabama. This lady and her sister, Sarah and Mary, were both widows; Mr. Bryant, husband of Mary, had died soon after moving to Alabama, and Mr. Ross, Sarah's husband, died not long after we came to Louisiana.

It was satisfactorily arranged between my father and Mrs. Ross, — and the fol- lowing spring (1852), father went back to Alabama and they were married. It took two or three months to arrange her affairs and get all things in order for the moving to Louisiana. As the sisters would not be separated, transportation for the two families had to be made and each had many slaves and several children.

It was a big responsibility but it effectuality diverted father's mind from his own personal grief.

Finally, the second caravan left the same neighborhood for Louisiana, similar to the first which had gone four years before, — with many vehicles and covered wagons. All arrangements for homes and land had been made previously and were awaiting their arrival.

One afternoon, when Sue, Jane, and I were attending school, a handsome youth, about 18 years old, came into the classroom and asked for the George sisters, — introducing himself as Jim Ross, our stepbrother. On looking out of the window, we were surprised to find the street lined with carriages, buggies, wagons, and horses. The young people had come in advance of the wagons, while my father's wife and her sister were in a carriage to the rear. My father was on horseback.

Our teacher excused us and we went out to meet our new relatives who insisted that we go home with them, which we were only too delighted to do. We didn't even ask permission of our aunt, with whom we were boarding, but sent word where we were.

Father was so busy seeing that the negroes were settled, that he did not know until that night that we had come home with the crowd. When he finally came into the house, three eager girls unexpectedly threw their arms around him. Imagine our amazement when he did not respond, but seemed dismayed at our presence. He said that we must return to school early in the morning, because there was cholera among the negroes, — contracted while passing through the Mississippi swamps. A negro woman had died of it that night just as the wagon in which she rode, stopped at the gate. The next morning before breakfast, a girl 12 years old, came in and said she was sick. Father examined her and gave her the cholera remedy, but at noon she was dead. The place was immediately quarantined. In two weeks 16 negroes had succumbed. After that, there were no new cases, but it was many weeks before we were permitted to go home again.

When, once more, things were running smoothly on the plantation, work began with speed on the new house in Marion which father had stopped building after mother's death. During that period, we resumed our former custom of weekend visits to our country home and this gave us much pleasure. We were always taken back on Monday mornings, for school began at 8 a.m. and closed at 5 p.m., with two hours for recreation. We liked horseback riding, and by request, they would bring horses with side-saddles for us to ride home. Ladies were never seen to ride astride then, but many became fine equestrians, even running through the forest in a deer or fox chase, — the horse leaping over logs or anything that happened to be in his way.

During dear mother's life, we were allowed to romp and play with the children of the house servants. Although we worked and played together, the colored children were obedient and kind, and we were taught to be just and kind to them. My mother, (Miss Ann, as they called her) settled any differences which arose between us. As I see it now, she was impartial in her judgement, but then, I thought she was partial to the colored children. Each child over six had his little chores and appointed tasks, according to his age, which had to be done before he was allowed to play. Our little hands kept the knives, forks, and other silverware shining and bright; scoured the milk-pans, buckets, and dippers, and all the tin and copper vessels. Also, the children kept the yards clean.

May 1st was always looked forward to with great pleasure, for on that day we all, white and colored children alike, were permitted to leave off our shoes and stockings for the first time since the last early autumn, and what joy was ours for this privilege.

As we grew older and started school, the pathway between servant and mistress became more marked, — the servants took their places in deference and respect. At the same time, our love and childhood associations bound us together in life-long affection and friendship.

The new home in Marion, with all the outhouses for the servants, was at last ready for occupancy. The house was commodious with parlor, dining room, six bedrooms, each with a fireplace, and every convenience known at that time. Father had a large hall built over the kitchen and a spacious storeroom. Steps to this hall were built from the outside to a porch above and the hall was furnished with chairs, tables, and beds, and many extra mattresses which were stored away for use during the occasions of summer church revivals, school concerts and exhibitions, and examinations, when people came from far and near. At this time, there was not only a large family of our own, but father, having a cordial, hospitable nature would never turn anyone away even if he'd been consulted, and the public seemed to think "Parson George" has established a wayside inn with a "Welcome to All! without money and without price", because he had a big house and plenty of servants. When we moved in, the furniture which had been purchased in New Orleans was delayed in its delivery, and the family had to make use of whatever furniture that was at hand. The floors were bare and rooms comparatively empty and the echoes that resounded from the plastered walls and the uncarpeted stairways, were fearful to little children, for the negroes, who were very superstitious had taught us to believe in ghosts, — and when going up to our bedrooms at night, we could easily imagine that "spooks" inhabited every corner. It was a long time before I overcame this fear.

Our home was located in a beautiful, level grove of oaks and pines. There were 25 acres. Five-hundred yards in front of us, with no buildings to obstruct, was *the school. To the rear of our dwelling, the land sloped down to a bold spring and a running brook which was about four-hundred yards away.*

Our home was full of merriment and joy with young people often meeting for a social evening. My sisters and step-brothers, with piano, violin, and flute, added by other members of the family, never lacked for entertainment.

It was necessary to keep quite a coterie of servants. Their individual duties were as follows: two cooks, Ann and Emoline; dining room maid and helper, Easter and Rose; seamstress, Harriet; Laundress, Louisa. Mother's maid, Leta, a girl of 15; Linn, Bud's (Elias, Jr.), and my maid, Rose; gardener, Carter; and two 15 year old boys, Sam and Lex to keep fires, attend horses, and do other chores.

In the summer of this year, there was a big Baptist meeting held at Concord Church which was two miles from town, the oldest meeting house (so-called church) in that part of the country. Father and other Baptist ministers were in charge. The greater part of Marion and the surrounding country attended all-day services, with dinner on the grounds. I became very much interested in my soul's salvation at this time. I learned from God's Word that I must repent my sins and "be baptized for the remission of sins". I made up my mind to obey God and was baptized according to Matthew 3:11 — 13.

Chapter 57:
The Breed Family and the Great Awakening

Pedigree Chart for Priscilla Breed

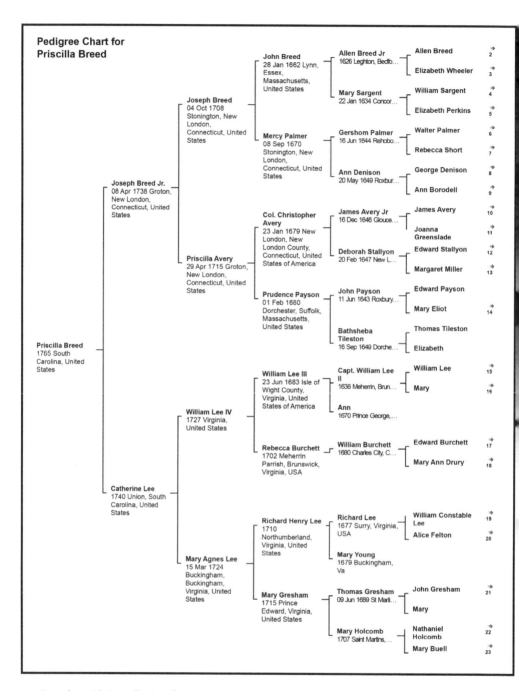

Genealogy 44: Priscilla Breed

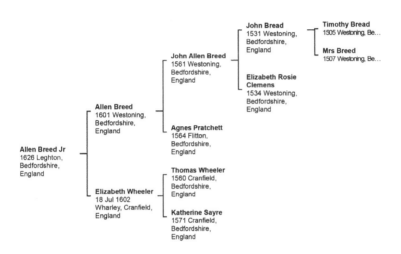

Genealogy 45: Allen Breed Jr.

The Breed surname originated in Holland, where it was initially spelled Brede.[167] A principal thoroughfare in Leiden, Holland, is Brede Street. The town of Brede, in the county of Sussex, England, was founded by people from Holland at the beginning of the twelfth century. Through the years in England various spellings were used including Bred, Bread, Breeds, and Brede; London still has a Bread Street dating back to the earlier era. Allen Breed, the first English immigrant to America from this family, spelled his surname Bread. Later family members in America changed the spelling to Breed.

According to one historian, the Breeds in America have been "positive, determined, persevering, and thrifty."[168] The name is deeply connected to American history: the famous Battle of Bunker Hill in the Revolutionary War was really fought on Breed's Hill, and the national monument marking that battle sits on Breed's Hill today.

Allen Breed (1601–1690)

Allen Breed was the first of the family to immigrate to America. He was born in Westoning, England in 1601 and evidently owned a wholesale grocery business in Liverpool. He was a devout Puritan and emigrated to Massachusetts in 1630, arriving with Governor John Winthrop on the *Arbella* or a sister ship. A fleet of eleven ships departed Cowes — four, including the flagship *Arbella*, on April 8, 1630, and seven the next month. The journey lasted seventy-five days and included gales, storms, cold, fog, and occasional good weather. There was great discomfort with passengers confined to small quarters and with limited food. There was no water for baths or washing of clothes.[169]

After arriving in Salem, most of the seven hundred passengers went to Boston; but Allen and others stopped in Saugus and then founded the town of Lynn. He received two hundred acres in 1638 and settled there in the part of town that came to be known as "Breed's End." In 1640, Allen and several others moved to Long Island and established the town of Southampton, but he moved back to Lynn by 1661. There he was elected to a seat in the pulpit, reflecting his esteemed character.

John Breed (1662–1751)

Allen's grandson, John, was born in 1662 in Lynn, Massachusetts. He married Mary Kirtland in 1686 in Lynn. They had one child, Sarah, who apparently died as an infant, and Mary died not long after. After his wife and daughter died, John must have been devastated; he moved away from Lynn and settled in Stonington, Connecticut, where he was one of the earliest settlers. He bought land from Deacon Gershom Palmer and then married the deacon's daughter Mercy Palmer in 1690. Mercy was born in 1670 in Stonington; her mother was Ann Denison, daughter of Captain George Denison, a distinguished soldier who fought in King Philip's War.

John built an impressive house in Stonington as well as a bark mill for use in his tanning business. The millstone from John's business has been preserved and now serves as the stepping stone into the front door of the house, which was rebuilt after standing 211 years. John and Mercy were active members of the First Congregational Church of Stonington.

John and Mercy had eleven children. He died in Stonington in 1751 and Mercy died there the following year. They are buried at the Wequetequock burial ground. The inscription on their slate tombstone reads:

In memory of a pious pair, this carved stone is erected here, viz., of Mr. John Breed and his wife Mercy, who lived together in ye marriage state, in a most religious manner, about sixty-four years, and then deceased, leaving numerous offspring, he in 1751 about ninety years of age, and she in 1752 about eighty-three years. Erected in ye year 1772 by 6 of their children then Living:

Behold the righteous live long in the earth,
And in old age resign their breath;
They and their offspring here are blest;
When done with life they go to rest.

Joseph Breed (1708–1786)

Joseph Breed, son of John and Mercy, was born October 4, 1708, in Stonington, Connecticut. He was christened the following January at the First Congregational Church in Stonington. Most of the church members were farmers; the member families included Colonel Christopher Avery and his wife Abigail. Joseph likely met their daughter Priscilla Avery at the church, and Joseph and Priscilla were married there June 2, 1737.

Joseph and his family lived in nearby Groton, Connecticut after their marriage and had several children. During the 1740s in Connecticut, a religious "Great Awakening" was happening among congregations of established churches. Members were increasingly falling under the influence of a travelling minister, George Whitefield. His revivals drew hundreds of people, creating considerable excitement among Christians. Many left their traditional Congregational churches to become Baptists and attend revival meetings with participatory sermons characterized by trembling, shouts, and screams.

Those who joined the new movement were called "New Lights" or "Separatists." Joseph and Priscilla Breed were among them. While never formally trained, Joseph became a preacher in the new church.

By 1751, the established churches had enough. They confronted declining memberships and the growth of an alternative form of religions practice by casting out the unwanted members. Others did not wait to be cast out, and left.

About 1752, Joseph and his family joined preachers Shubal Stearns and Daniel Marshall and moved to Onnaquaggy, upstate New York at the head of the Susquehanna River. Their goal was to "convert the heathens." However, the Mohawk "heathens" were not welcoming, and the entire missionary group moved to Frederick County, Virginia, which afforded a safer environment in which to preach. Joseph purchased land in Frederick in 1754 and was listed as a member of Shubal Stearns's "separatist" group.

In Frederick, the Separatists came into conflict with other Christians, which resulted in armed fights. Joseph and eleven other Separatists and families, including Shubal Stearns and Daniel Marshall, left their church in Virginia and moved to the Cape Fear area of North Carolina in 1755. They started the Sandy Creek Baptist Church beginning with fifteen members. Years later, church membership surpassed six hundred. Carolinians had never before experienced the revival style of preaching, and huge crowds came to hear it.

In 1759, the Breeds and a few others moved to Union County, South Carolina, where they continued to build new churches on the frontier. Fairforest Church was their first Baptist church in upper South Carolina, followed by four other congregations in nearby communities. The established churches tried to force the newly arrived Separatists out of South Carolina but without success.

With the approaching Revolutionary War, Joseph initially refused to take sides because of his opposition to war itself. Joseph and his family then moved to Georgia, possibly because of his neighbors' anger at Joseph's passivity. Eventually, Joseph came to support the Revolution, and his wife Priscilla's action feeding Colonial troops merited recognition as a supporter of the Revolution. Their son Joseph Jr. was a Patriot soldier and fought in many battles.

In 1773, the group moved again, this time to Monroe County, Kentucky, where they started the Mill Creek Church. By 1778 the church had 128 members. By 1804 a larger meeting house was erected in what is now Tompkinsville, Kentucky. Today, that site is a state park. It is referred to as the "Old Mulkey Meetinghouse," in honor of Reverend Phillip Mulkey, one of Joseph's colleagues.

Joseph is believed to have died in 1786, possibly in Washington County, Georgia; although this is not certain. It is also possible he died in Kentucky. His wife Priscilla and her second husband, Obediah Howard, are buried in the churchyard of Old Mulkey Meeting House, as are some of Joseph Breed's descendants.

Joseph Breed Jr. (1738–1807)

Priscilla and Joseph's oldest son Joseph (Jr.) was born in 1738 in Stonington, Connecticut, before his parents left to devote their lives to the church. He accompanied them on their journeys.

Joseph Jr. married Catherine Lee around 1762. She and her family were from Union County, South Carolina, where Joseph and his family were living at the time. They had ten children while living in South Carolina. He was a planter and received a land grant there of 150 acres on Fairforest Creek. He sold the land in 1783 when he and his family moved to Wilkes County, Georgia, near where his aging parents and his younger siblings were living at the time. His father died a few years later. Perhaps Joseph moved there to be closer to his family or take advantage of opportunities identified by his family.

With the start of the Revolutionary War, Joseph Jr., his brother Nathan, and his son-in-law, Richard George, joined Colonel Thomas Brandon's regiment of South Carolina militia. They fought in many battles (see Chapter 31).

Joseph Breed, Jr. returned home to a hero's welcome. He died in 1807 in Warren County, Georgia. There is a monument in the courthouse square in Warrenton, Georgia which lists Revolutionary War soldiers buried in Warren County including Joseph Breed and his brother-in-law Richard Lee.

Joseph and Catherine's daughter Priscilla was born in 1780 in Union County, South Carolina. She moved with her family to Georgia when she was three years old and grew up there. In 1798, she married Richard George in Warren County, Georgia. They had six children including Elias George. Sometime between 1801 and 1817, she and the family moved to Perry County in Alabama, where she died in 1825.

Figure 23: The Battle of Bunker Hill

Chapter 58:

The True Story of the
Battle of Bunker Hill[170]

T he last stop on Boston's Freedom Trail is a shrine to the fog of war. The story which follows is from an interview (abridged) with author Nathaniel Philbrick.

"Breed's Hill," a plaque reads. "Site of the Battle of Bunker Hill." Another plaque bears the famous order given American troops as the British charged up not-Bunker Hill. "Don't fire 'til you see the whites of their eyes." Except, park rangers will quickly tell you, these words weren't spoken here. The patriotic obelisk atop the hill also confuses visitors. Most don't realize it's the rare American monument to an American defeat. In short, the nation's memory of Bunker Hill is mostly bunk.

Boston in 1775 was much smaller, hillier and more watery than it appears today. The Back Bay was still a bay and the South End was likewise underwater; hills were later leveled to fill in almost 1,000 acres. Boston was virtually an island, reachable by land only via a narrow neck. And though founded by Puritans, the city wasn't puritanical. One rise near Beacon Hill, known for its prostitutes, was marked on maps as "Mount Whoredom."

Nor was Boston a "cradle of liberty"; one in five families, including those of leading patriots, owned slaves. And the city's inhabitants were viciously divided. At Copp's Hill, in Boston's North End, Philbrick visits the grave of Daniel Malcom, an early agitator against the British identified on his headstone as "a true son of Liberty." British troops used the patriot headstone for target practice. Yet Malcom's brother, John, was a noted loyalist, so hated by rebels that they tarred and feathered him and paraded him in a cart until his skin peeled off in "steaks."

[The Patriot's] cause was also "profoundly conservative." Most sought a return to the Crown's "salutary neglect" of colonists prior to the 1760s, before Britain began imposing taxes and responding to American resistance with coercion and troops. "They wanted the liberties of British subjects, not American independence," Philbrick says.

That began to change once blood was shed, which is why the Bunker Hill battle is pivotal. The chaotic skirmishing at Lexington and Concord in April 1775 left the British holed up in Boston and hostile colonists occupying the city's surrounds. But it remained unclear whether the ill-equipped rebels were willing or able to engage the British Army in pitched battle. Leaders on both sides also thought the conflict might yet be settled without full-scale war.

This tense, two-month stalemate broke on the night of June 16, in a confused manner that marks much of the Revolution's start. Over a thousand colonials marched east from Cambridge with orders to fortify Bunker Hill, a 110-foot rise on the Charlestown peninsula jutting into Boston Harbor. But the Americans bypassed Bunker Hill in the dark and instead began fortifying Breed's Hill, a smaller rise much closer to Boston and almost in the face of the British.

The reasons for this maneuver are murky. But Philbrick believes it was a "purposeful act, a provocation and not the smartest move militarily." Short on cannons, and the know-how to fire those they had with accuracy, the rebels couldn't do much damage from Breed's Hill. But their threatening position, on high ground just across the water from Boston, forced the British to try to dislodge the Americans before they were reinforced or fully entrenched.

On the morning of June 17, as the rebels frantically threw up breastworks of earth, fence posts and stone, the British bombarded the hill. One cannonball decapitated a man as his comrades worked on, "fatigued by our Labour, having no sleep the night before, very little to eat, no drink but rum," a private wrote. "The danger we were in made us think there was treachery, and that we were brought there to be all slain."

Exhausted and exposed, the Americans were also a motley collection of militia from different colonies, with little coordination and no clear chain of command. By contrast, the British, who at midday began disembarking from boats near the American position, were among the best-trained troops in Europe. And they were led by seasoned commanders, one of whom marched confidently at the head of his men accompanied by a servant carrying a bottle of wine. The British also torched Charlestown, at the base of Breed's Hill, turning church steeples into "great pyramids of fire" and adding ferocious heat to what was already a warm June afternoon.

All this was clearly visible to the many spectators crowded on hills, rooftops and steeples in and around Boston, including Abigail Adams and her young son, John Quincy, who cried at the flames and the "thunders" of British cannons. Another observer was British Gen. John Burgoyne, who watched from Copp's Hill. "And now ensued one of the greatest scenes of war that can be conceived," he wrote of the blazing town, the roaring cannons and the sight of red-coated troops ascending Breed's Hill.

However, the seemingly open pasture proved to be an obstacle course. The high, unmown hay obscured rocks, holes and other hazards. Fences and stone walls also slowed the British. The Americans, meanwhile, were ordered to hold their fire until the attackers closed to 50 yards or less. The wave of British "advanced towards us in order to swallow us up," wrote Pvt. Peter Brown, "but they found a Choaky mouthful of us."

When the rebels opened fire, the close-packed British fell in clumps. In some spots, the British lines became jumbled, making them even easier targets. The

Americans added to the chaos by aiming at officers, distinguished by their fine uniforms. The attackers, repulsed at every point, were forced to withdraw. "The dead lay as thick as sheep in a fold," wrote an American officer.

The disciplined British quickly re-formed their ranks and advanced again, with much the same result. One British officer was moved to quote Falstaff: "They make us here but food for gunpowder." But the American powder was running very low. And the British, having failed twice, devised a new plan. They repositioned their artillery and raked the rebel defenses with grapeshot. And when the infantrymen marched forward, a third time, they came in well-spaced columns rather than a broad line.

As the Americans' ammunition expired, their firing sputtered and "went out like an old candle," wrote William Prescott, who commanded the hilltop redoubt. His men resorted to throwing rocks, then swung their muskets at the bayonet-wielding British pouring over the rampart. "Nothing could be more shocking than the carnage that followed the storming [of] this work," wrote a royal marine. "We tumbled over the dead to get at the living," with "soldiers stabbing some and dashing out the brains of others." The surviving defenders fled, bringing the battle to an end.

In just two hours of fighting, 1,054 British soldiers — almost half of all those engaged — had been killed or wounded, including many officers. American losses totaled over 400. The first true battle of the Revolutionary War was to prove the bloodiest of the entire conflict. Though the British had achieved their aim in capturing the hill, it was a truly Pyrrhic victory. "The success is too dearly bought," wrote Gen. William Howe, who lost every member of his staff (as well as the bottle of wine his servant carried into battle).

Badly depleted, the besieged British abandoned plans to seize another high point near the city and ultimately evacuated Boston. The battle also demonstrated American resolve and dispelled hopes that the rebels might relent without a protracted conflict. "Our three generals," a British officer wrote of his commanders in Boston, had "expected rather to punish a mob than fight with troops that would look them in the face."

The intimate ferocity of this face-to-face combat is even more striking today, in an era of drones, tanks and long-range missiles. At the Bunker Hill Museum, Philbrick studies a diorama of the battle alongside Patrick Jennings, a park ranger who served as an infantryman and combat historian for the U.S. Army in Iraq and Afghanistan. "This was almost a pool-table battlefield," Jennings observes of the miniature soldiers crowded on a verdant field. "The British were boxed in by the terrain and the Americans didn't have much maneuverability, either. It's a close-range brawl."

However, there's no evidence that Col. Israel Putnam told his men to hold their fire until they saw "the whites" of the enemies' eyes. The writer Parson Weems invented this incident decades later, along with other fictions such as George Washington chopping down a cherry tree. In reality, the Americans opened fire at about 50 yards, much too distant to see anyone's eyes. One colonel did tell his men to wait until they could see the splash guards — called half-gaiters — that British soldiers wore around their calves. But as Philbrick notes, "Don't fire until you see the whites of their half-gaiters' just doesn't have the same ring." So the Weems version endured, making it into textbooks.

In 1775, when Americans marched past Bunker Hill and fortified Breed's instead, a British map compounded the confusion by mixing up the two hills as well. Over time, the name Breed's melted away and the battle became indelibly linked to Bunker [Hill]. [According to Philbrick], this enduring confusion is emblematic of the Bunker Hill story. "The whole thing's a screw-up," he says. "The Americans fortify the wrong hill, this forces a fight no one planned, the battle itself is an ugly and confused mess. And it ends with a British victory that's also a defeat."

Note: Breed's Hill was named after Ebenezer Breed, who owned the property. His father, John, was the brother of ancestor Allen Breed Jr.

Chapter 59:

The Avery Family: The Avery Hive, Home of the Averys for 240 Years

Pedigree Chart for
Priscilla Avery

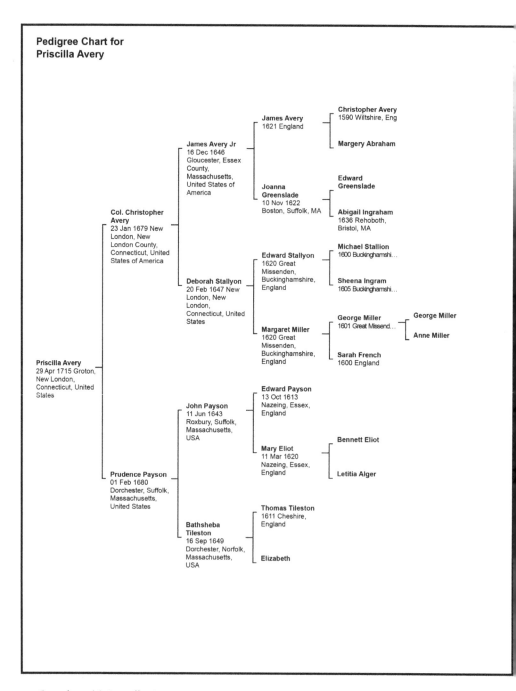

Priscilla Avery
29 Apr 1715 Groton,
New London,
Connecticut, United
States

Col. Christopher Avery
23 Jan 1679 New
London, New
London County,
Connecticut, United
States of America

James Avery Jr
16 Dec 1646
Gloucester, Essex
County,
Massachusetts,
United States of
America

James Avery
1621 England

Christopher Avery
1590 Wiltshire, Eng

Margery Abraham

Joanna Greenslade
10 Nov 1622
Boston, Suffolk, MA

Edward Greenslade

Abigail Ingraham
1636 Rehoboth,
Bristol, MA

Deborah Stallyon
20 Feb 1647 New
London, New
London,
Connecticut, United
States

Edward Stallyon
1620 Great
Missenden,
Buckinghamshire,
England

Michael Stallion
1600 Buckinghamshi…

Sheena Ingram
1605 Buckinghamshi…

Margaret Miller
1620 Great
Missenden,
Buckinghamshire,
England

George Miller
1601 Great Missend…

George Miller

Anne Miller

Sarah French
1600 England

Prudence Payson
01 Feb 1680
Dorchester, Suffolk,
Massachusetts,
United States

John Payson
11 Jun 1643
Roxbury, Suffolk,
Massachusetts,
USA

Edward Payson
13 Oct 1613
Nazeing, Essex,
England

Mary Eliot
11 Mar 1620
Nazeing, Essex,
England

Bennett Eliot

Letitia Alger

Bathsheba Tileston
16 Sep 1649
Dorchester, Norfolk,
Massachusetts,
USA

Thomas Tileston
1611 Cheshire,
England

Elizabeth

Genealogy 46: Priscilla Avery

Christopher Avery (1590–1679)

Christopher Avery is thought to have been born about 1590 in Salisbury, England, but he may have been born in Devonshire. He did live in Devonshire as a young man and was a weaver of high-quality goods including Kersey fabric. He married Margery Abraham in 1616 in Abbotskerswell in the English county of Devon. She was the widow of Thomas Stephens of Ipplepen (also in Devon) and daughter of Robert and Dorothy Abraham. Christopher and Margery had a son, who they named James, in 1620.

Margery died in 1626, and Christopher married Alice Berdon in Devonshire in July of 1630. Not long afterwards, Christopher and his son James departed for Massachusetts, traveling on the *Arbella* with Governor Winthrop in 1630. He never returned to his new wife in England, and he was subsequently fined several times by the Puritan leaders of Massachusetts for "living apart from his wife." Evidently the thought of living with his new wife was worse than paying all the fines.

Christopher apparently never had more children; it would have been a challenge living in Puritan New England and his wife living in England. He purchased a house in Boston in 1659 but sold it four years later and followed his son, James, to Pequot on the Thames, later renamed "New London" Connecticut. He served on a jury and was made a Freeman (i.e. a citizen with voting rights) in Connecticut. He died and was buried in New London in 1679.

Captain James Avery (1620–1700)

James Avery was born in England in 1620 and accompanied his father to Massachusetts at the age of ten. He married Joanna Greenslade in 1643. She was born in Boston, but her father, Edward Greenslade, was also from Devon, England. James and Joanna lived in New London, Connecticut, and had ten children.

From New London, the family and several other followers of Reverend Richard Blinman moved to Groton, east of New London. In 1656 James built a house, later referred to as the "Hive of the Averys." In 1684, he purchased the thirty-year-old Blinman church, the first church of New London, which had been vacated and fallen into disrepair after Reverend Blinman moved away following a dispute with parishioners. Under the condition that he should remove the church within a month, James reused the materials from the church to expand his Hive.

The Hive of the Averys stood for about 240 years and was home to successive Avery generations. There is much written about the Hive, including a poem by Edith Avery Barber in 1929:

The Old Avery Place

Thru' the sunshines of summer and the drear storms of winter,
Thru' the sorrows of age and youth's joy and thrill,
It has stood as a landmark so calm and serene —
A shelter — a home — softly mellowed by tim —
That "Old Avery Place" on the hill.
It has stored in its being the echoes of life,
It has filled each cranny as a miser his fill —
The laughter of children, the patter of feet,
The promise of youth and fulfillment of age —
That "Old Avery Place" on the hill.
For countless long years — a hundred and more
It has sheltered them all — child, youth and man,
And sent them all forth so smiling and strong
For the hardships and duties and blessings of life
(As the "Old Avery Place" t'will be known for long.)
As we travel our way, let's be worthy our name;
Let's be dauntless and fearless and reverent and strong;
Let's uphold its traditions so rugged and true:
Let us cherish it, honor it, and keep it from stain;
Then here's to the "Averys" — clan, family, and name.

The Hive burned down in 1894. The grounds were later graded and a monument erected by descendants of James Avery. The historical monument remains today as do other monuments commemorating the life of James Avery.

James Avery was a leading citizen of New London and Groton. He was an officer of the town for twenty-three years and twelve times deputy of the General Court. He was very active in the church as well.

He was a captain of the New London companies and served throughout King Philip's War, including commanding a company of Pequot warriors. In 1676, he served as captain of one of four companies assigned to protecting the frontier. Captain Avery was later tasked with raising a company to protect the settlers from Native American raids and reprisals, and he continued to lead in this regard.

James Avery Jr. (1646–1728)

James Avery Jr. was born in 1646 in New London, Connecticut. He married Deborah Stallyon in 1669, and they had fourteen children. Deborah's parents, Edward Stallyon and Margaret Miller, were both born in Buckingham, England and immigrated to Connecticut.

James continued the community leadership exhibited by his father. He took the oath of a Freeman in 1669, served as selectman several times, was justice of the peace, and served as deputy of the General Court many times both from New London and Groton.

He was a friend of the Pequot tribe, which his father had led into battle during the King Philip's War (see Chapter 20). In 1720, he was appointed advisor and counsellor to the tribe and was often called upon as an interpreter. In 1723, he was made Guardian of the Tribe and instituted numerous lawsuits to recover land that had been unfairly seized from them. He was often asked to settle boundary disputes because of his intelligence and reputation for fairness.

As captain in the militia, he was often called upon to lead the fight against hostile Native bands. He received a letter of thanks from Connecticut Governor John Winthrop for his help and leadership in the wars with Native tribes. He also received a similar letter from Massachusetts Governor Joseph Dudley.

He acquired land from his father as well as his father-in-law. James and Deborah lived in the family home — the Avery Hive — until he died in 1728. Deborah died the following year. They are buried in the family cemetery.

Colonel Christopher Avery (1679–1753)

Christopher Avery was born in 1679 or 1680 in New London, Connecticut. He married Abigail Parke, daughter of Captain John and Mary Parke from Preston, Connecticut, on December 19, 1704. They had four children between 1705 and 1712. Abigail died in 1713.

Christopher, a widower with four young children, next married Prudence Payson Wheeler, widow of Richard Wheeler and daughter of John Payson and his wife Bathsheba Tileston. Christopher and Prudence had five children between 1715 and 1725. She died in 1726, leaving Christopher a widower with young children for the second time.

He next married Esther Hammond Prentice, widow of Samuel Prentice and daughter of Nathaniel Hammond and his wife, Mary Hyde. They married in 1735. After her death, Christopher married for a fourth time: this time to Susanna Baker Elderkin, widow of John Elderkin. Death and remarriage was common in the colonies, but Christopher's experience of four wives was not typical. He and his four wives were buried on the family estate in Groton, Connecticut.

Christopher was an important man in Groton and New London. He was a longtime member of the militia, joining first at the age of sixteen and rising to the rank of colonel by 1740. He served during King William's War (1688–1697), Queen Anne's War (1702–1713), and King George's War (1744–1748).

Christopher lived his entire life in New London and Groton, Connecticut. He carried on the family tradition of community and military service and leadership. He served as selectman multiple years, as well as a surveyor, and as justice for New London County. He was clerk of the Groton North Society Church and deputy to the General Court. Christopher owned and lived on land in the northwest part of Groton (now called Ledyard) and died there in 1753.

Christopher and Prudence's daughter Priscilla married Joseph Breed in 1737.

Chapter 60:

The Payson and Eliot Families with John Eliot, "Apostle to the Indians"

Colonel Christopher Avery's wife, Prudence, was the daughter of John Payson and Bathsheba Tileston. The first of the Payson immigrants to America was Edward Payson, who was born in 1613 in Nazeing, in the county of Essex in England. He came to Massachusetts in 1633 and was admitted to the First Church of Roxbury in 1634. He was a "husbandman" (farmer) and became a Freeman (with voting rights) in 1640.

He married Ann Parke in 1640; unfortunately she died with the birth of their first child, Mary, the following year. Mary also apparently died as an infant.

Edward then married Mary Eliot in 1642. She was daughter of Bennett Eliot and Letitia Alger. She was also the sister of the Reverend John Eliot, the "Apostle to the Indians." Reverend Eliot became quite famous in colonial Massachusetts history. He represented the Puritan town of Roxbury in proceedings against Anne Hutchinson, who was found guilty and banished from Massachusetts. He founded the Roxbury Latin School in 1645 and co-edited the *Bay Psalm Book,* the first book published in the North American colonies.

John Eliot devoted much of his life to being a missionary to the local Native American tribes, especially the Massachusett and other, related Algonquian tribes. He learned the Massachusett language and translated the Bible and the Ten Commandments into a language that local tribes could understand. His "Indian Bible" was the first complete Bible printed in the Western Hemisphere. He represented tribal claims against Massachusetts settlers, and regularly preached to the local Native communities. Under his leadership, fourteen separate "Praying Indian" communities were established, but these towns were ultimately disrupted during King Philip's War and never recovered.

Reverend John's sister Mary and her husband, Edward Payson, had twelve children. They moved from Roxbury to Dorchester around 1657. Edward acquired considerable land in the Dorchester area, leaving over one thousand acres to his son John and other acreages to other sons and daughters.

John Payson was born in 1642. In 1670, he married Bathsheba Tileston, daughter of Thomas and Elizabeth Tileston. Thomas immigrated from Cheshire, England. John and Bathsheba had six children between 1670 and 1680. Their last child, Prudence, was born in 1680, and Bathsheba died the following year.

John was active in community affairs. One of the big issues in Dorchester during the late 1660s was the use of the common green for sheep grazing. Apparently the green was being overgrazed, and the town's selectmen attributed the problem to non-residents bringing in their sheep. They imposed a system of fines and authorized John Payson to build a large barn; but it is not certain if the barn and the sheep-grazing fines were part of a related solution.

John married a woman named Hannah (last name unknown) after Bathsheba's death, and they had five children. John died in Roxbury in 1719 at the age of seventy-six. John and Bathsheba's youngest child, Prudence, married Richard Wheeler, who died ten years later. Then she married Colonel Christopher Avery.

Chapter 61:
The Palmer Family:
New England Pioneers

Pedigree Chart for Mercy Palmer

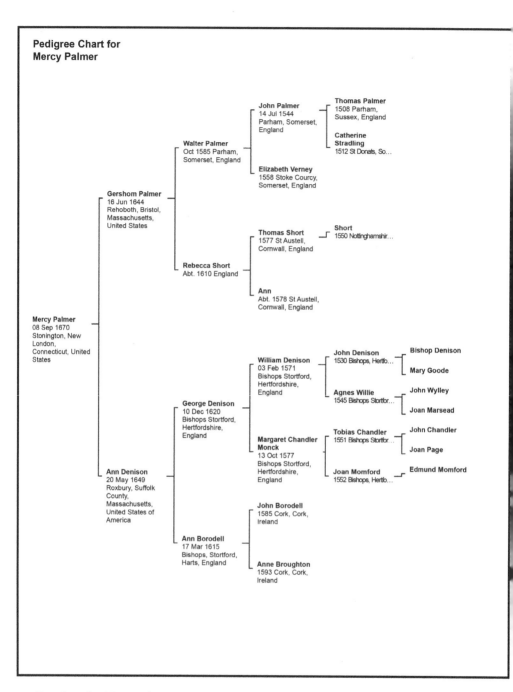

Genealogy 47: Mercy Palmer

Mercy Palmer married John Breed in 1690 in Stonington, Connecticut. Her grandfather, Walter Palmer immigrated from Parham, in Somerset, England and was one of the pioneers in Massachusetts and Connecticut and a founder of Stonington.

The Palmer name dates back to the Crusades. Returning soldiers brought back palm leaves as a token of their pilgrimage and became widely known as "palm bearers." Eventually, they were just referred to as palmers.

The first Palmer from England to emigrate was William, who came on the ship *Fortune* a year after the *Mayflower*. William lived in Salem and produced many descendants.

The second Palmer was Mercy's grandfather, Walter. Walter was born in 1585, probably in the village of Yetminister in Dorset. He was a devout Christian and Puritan and was uncomfortable with the church rules laid down by Queen Elizabeth. He married for the first time (possibly to Ann Elizabeth Horne) in England in 1606, and they had five children. She apparently died around 1628.

Walter and his children set out for America with Governor John Endicott, arriving in Salem in 1629. They sailed from Gravesend, England, on the *Four Sisters*, one of a fleet of six ships filled with Puritans. Upon arriving in Massachusetts, Walter and his brother Abraham joined five others, including the three Sprague brothers, and proceeded twelve miles inland through the woods to find a suitable place to start a new community, which was later called "Charlestown." Walter built the first house in Charlestown. Charleston was later annexed and is now the oldest neighborhood in Boston.

Walter married Rebecca Short in 1633 in Roxbury. She immigrated in 1632 as a maid/servant and was a member of the Roxbury First Church, where they were married. Roxbury Church's members were generally from Essex and Hertfordshire in England and under the religious direction of Reverend John Eliot. Rebecca and Walter had seven children.

Walter was a huge man, weighing over three hundred pounds and measuring about six feet four inches tall. He served as selectman and constable of Charlestown and was well respected. He was a farmer and had livestock.

Eventually Walter and his good friend William Chesebrough felt there would be better farming opportunities elsewhere; Walter was growing English grasses to support his livestock, but he believed the local soil lacked necessary nutrients and desired a larger tract of land. Palmer and Chesebrough moved to the Plymouth Colony with a few others to set up a new town now called Seekonk in 1643. The town grew over time and was renamed Rehoboth. Walter had particularly high standing in the community and was chosen as selectman, deputy of the court, constable, and grand juryman. Later, Walter joined his friend William Chesebrough and moved to southern Connecticut, where they established what was referred to as Southerton, which subsequently became part of Stonington.

Walter's farm was at Wequetequock Cove. It can be visited today and is situated on 232 acres. Walter died there in 1661. The family burying ground is there as are the remnants of Walter's grist mill. There was a Palmer family reunion in Stonington in August 1881, and approximately three thousand of Walter's descendants attended, including President Ulysses Grant. At the time, there were thought to be six to seven thousand direct descendants of Walter Palmer in America, and that was 140 years ago.

One of Walter's and Rebecca's children was Gershom Palmer. He was born in Rehoboth, Massachusetts, in 1644. In 1667, he married Ann Denison, the daughter of Captain George Denison and Ann Borodell; both had emigrated from England although Ann's grandparents may have been from County Cork, Ireland. Ann Borodell was apparently from an aristocratic family and taught her daughter Ann refined manners despite their remote location on the frontier.

Gershom continued the family tradition of church involvement and civic duties. He was a deacon in the First Church of Stonington.

Gershom and Ann had eleven children including Mercy. Ann died in 1694 at the age of forty-five, and Gershom died in 1718 in Stonington, where he lived his entire adult life.

Chapter 62:

The Denison Family:
Indian Fighter, Indian Friend

ershom Palmer's wife, Ann Denison, came from a family with a long
English history. The Denisons or Denysons likely came to England with the
Normans in the eleventh century. They descended from the royal line of the
Stuarts, and there is an oft-repeated proverb in the family: *Kings come of us, not we
of kings.*[171]

John Denyson was born in 1530, probably in Bishop's Stortford, in Hertfordshire
England. He married Agnes Willie in 1561.

One of John and Agnes's sons, William, was born in 1571 in Stortford. He was a
merchant and well situated in Stortford with a good estate; he married Margaret
Chandler Monck, widow of Henry Monck and daughter of John and Joan Chandler.

William was a Puritan and decided to move to America despite his comfort and
status in Stortford. He recalled his nineteen-year-old son, Daniel, who was studying
at Cambridge, and emigrated to America in 1631 with Margaret, Daniel, and two
younger sons, Edward and George.

The family sailed on the ship *Lyon,* with John Eliot, who became the "Apostle to the
Indians" (see Chapter 60). At the time of sailing, however, Eliot probably served as
tutor to William's sons. The Denison family did not lack money and valued education very highly.

The family settled in Roxbury, Massachusetts (now part of Boston). He brought
with him "a very good estate."[172] He started a malt brewing business which was
well received and highly popular. William was active in the community, was made a
Freeman in 1632, selected as constable in 1633, and served as deputy to the Massa-

chusetts General Court. Margaret, referred to as "Old Mother Dennison," died in 1645. William died in 1653.

William's and Margaret's fourth son, George, was born in in Stortford in 1618 or 1620 and emigrated with his parents. He returned to England later and fought with Cromwell's army. While in England, he married Ann Borodell, and they emigrated to Connecticut — probably motivated by Cromwell's defeat and the restoration of the King. The couple settled in Stonington.

In Stonington, he spent much time in public service including serving as deputy to the Connecticut General Court for many years. He also had a long military service and served on the war committee for New London when the area was threatened by the Dutch. He was captain in King Phillip's War and was later appointed provost marshal. In 1689, at age sixty-nine, he was appointed captain of the volunteer troops to lead the fight against Native American attacks.

When not fighting warring Native bands, he befriended peaceful ones, treating them with respect. He was given land by Mohegan sachems Uncas and Oneco for his assistance.

Captain George was highly regarded. He and his wife Ann were remarkably handsome, and he served with great distinction in the Indian wars.[173] According to historian Francis Caulkins, "Our early history presents no character of bolder and more active spirit than Captain George Denison… In emergencies he was always in demand and almost constantly placed in important public positions." [174]

George and Ann had seven children including Ann, who married Gershom Palmer. When Ann was young and before she married Gershom, her father brought charges in court against a young man named John Carr, accusing him of engaging Ann's affection without leave, of encouraging her to leave her father's house and marry him, of taking various things from the family house, and of defaming his daughter. The court found Carr guilty and fined him.

Chapter 63:

The Lee Families: The Declaration of Independence and the Commanding General of the Confederate Army

Pedigree Chart for Catherine Lee

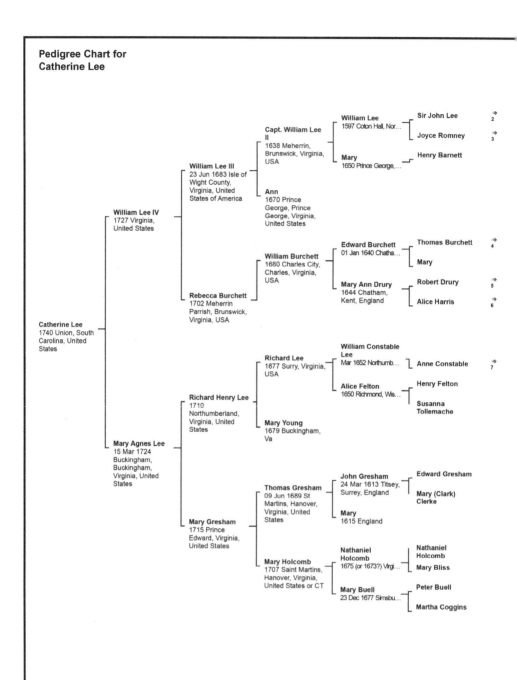

Catherine Lee
1740 Union, South Carolina, United States

William Lee IV
1727 Virginia, United States

William Lee III
23 Jun 1683 Isle of Wight County, Virginia, United States of America

Capt. William Lee II
1638 Meherrin, Brunswick, Virginia, USA

William Lee
1597 Coton Hall, Nor...

Sir John Lee
2

Joyce Romney
3

Mary
1650 Prince George,...

Henry Barnett

Ann
1670 Prince George, Prince George, Virginia, United States

Rebecca Burchett
1702 Meherrin Parrish, Brunswick, Virginia, USA

William Burchett
1680 Charles City, Charles, Virginia, USA

Edward Burchett
01 Jan 1640 Chatha...

Thomas Burchett
4

Mary

Mary Ann Drury
1644 Chatham, Kent, England

Robert Drury
5

Alice Harris
6

Mary Agnes Lee
15 Mar 1724 Buckingham, Buckingham, Virginia, United States

Richard Henry Lee
1710 Northumberland, Virginia, United States

Richard Lee
1677 Surry, Virginia, USA

William Constable Lee
Mar 1652 Northumb...

Anne Constable
7

Alice Felton
1650 Richmond, Wis...

Henry Felton

Susanna Tollemache

Mary Young
1679 Buckingham, Va

Mary Gresham
1715 Prince Edward, Virginia, United States

Thomas Gresham
09 Jun 1689 St Martins, Hanover, Virginia, United States

John Gresham
24 Mar 1613 Titsey, Surrey, England

Edward Gresham

Mary (Clark) Clerke

Mary
1615 England

Mary Holcomb
1707 Saint Martins, Hanover, Virginia, United States or CT

Nathaniel Holcomb
1675 (or 1673?) Virgi...

Nathaniel Holcomb

Mary Bliss

Mary Buell
23 Dec 1677 Simsbu...

Peter Buell

Martha Coggins

Genealogy 48: Catherine Lee

**Pedigree Chart for
Sir John Lee**

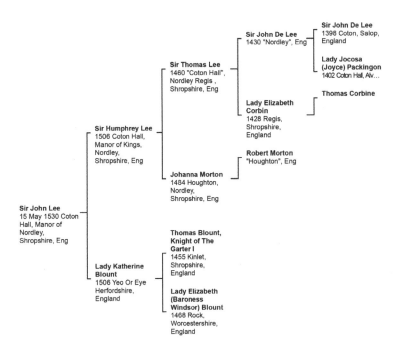

Sir John Lee
15 May 1530 Coton
Hall, Manor of
Nordley,
Shropshire, Eng

Sir Humphrey Lee
1506 Coton Hall,
Manor of Kings,
Nordley,
Shropshire, Eng

Lady Katherine
Blount
1506 Yeo Or Eye
Herfordshire,
England

Sir Thomas Lee
1460 "Coton Hall",
Nordley Regis ,
Shropshire, Eng

Johanna Morton
1484 Houghton,
Nordley,
Shropshire, Eng

Thomas Blount,
Knight of The
Garter I
1455 Kinlet,
Shropshire,
England

Lady Elizabeth
(Baroness
Windsor) Blount
1468 Rock,
Worcestershire,
England

Sir John De Lee
1430 "Nordley", Eng

Lady Elizabeth
Corbin
1428 Regis,
Shropshire,
England

Robert Morton
"Houghton", Eng

Sir John De Lee
1398 Coton, Salop,
England

Lady Jocosa
(Joyce) Packingon
1402 Coton Hall, Alv…

Thomas Corbine

Thomas Corbine

Genealogy 49: Sir John Lee

The Lee family in England dates back to King William the Conqueror and the Norman invasion in the eleventh century. Hugh De Lega fought at William's side and as a reward was given a large land grant in Shropshire, which lies in west central England between Wales and Birmingham. Hugo de Lee apparently was among the first Lees to live in Shropshire, where he appears in the record around 1100. Reginaldus de Lee, the (Norman) sheriff of Shropshire, dates back to 1201. Over the centuries, several Lee family members served as high sheriff of Shropshire.

Sir John Lee (1530–1605) married Joyce Romney (1530–1605) in 1553, and they had eight sons. They lived in Coton Hall, which was the ancestral home of the Lee family for five hundred years.

It was from Coton Hall that Lee family members departed for America. Some went for the purposes of trade and returned to England; at least two remained in Virginia and from them the Lee family in America evolved as leaders of the Virginia colony.

William Lee

William Lee (I) was believed to be the second son of Sir John Lee and Joyce Romney and as a result did not inherit much of his father's extensive estate. His father and mother seem too old to have birthed William, and there may be a missing, undocumented generation. Regardless, William was anxious to build a home and reputation for himself and emigrated to Virginia on the ship *Assurace de Lo* arriving in Charles City County in 1635 at the age of thirty-eight. Around 1637, he married a woman named Mary and acquired considerable land. The land titles list him as a "gentleman." He and Mary had a son William Lee (II) born about 1638. William (I) died March 22, 1653, leaving his entire estate to William (II).

William (II), or Captain William Lee as he was also known, married a woman named Ann around 1681. They had two sons, William (III) and John, and lived in Virginia.

William (III) was born in 1683 in Isle of Wight, Virginia. He married Rebecca Burchett, whose family came from Chatham, England. They had a son, William (IV), and four daughters.

William (IV) was born about 1727 and married in 1745 to Mary Agnes Lee, a cousin. They had ten children in Virginia but moved to Union County, South Carolina around 1770. He bought and developed a plantation between the Tyger and Saluda rivers and died there in 1773. William and Mary's daughter Catherine married Joseph Breed Jr.

Richard Henry Lee

Richard, William's younger brother, followed William to Virginia around 1640. Richard's grandson, Richard Henry Lee, formed the Association of Westmoreland to protest the Stamp Act. A year earlier, the Virginia House of Burgesses approved the Virginia Resolves encouraging disobedience to the Stamp Act.

Years later, Richard Henry Lee was selected to represent Virginia in the Continental Congress. On June 7, 1776, Richard formally proposed a resolution to declare independence from Great Britain, and John Adams seconded the motion. The "Lee Resolution" was passed on July 2, 1776, and the formal Declaration of Independence, drafted by Thomas Jefferson, was adopted on July 4, 1776. The Revolutionary War got under way in earnest.

Richard Henry Lee's daughter Mary Agnes married her cousin William Lee (IV). Their descendants include General Robert E. Lee, born 1807, who led the Confederate States Army from 1862 to its surrender in 1865.

Chapter 64:
The Nansemond Tribe and the Basse (or Bass) Family

Pedigree Chart for
Molsey Ann Bass

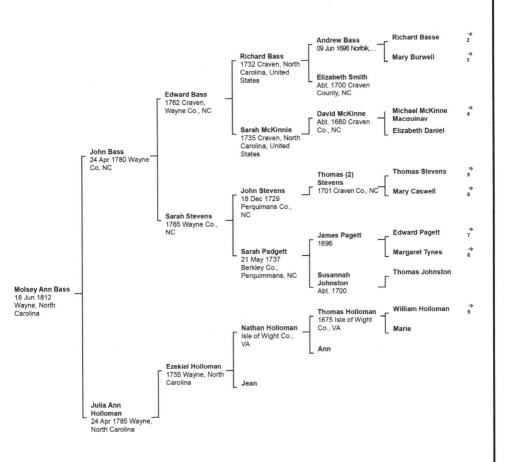

Molsey Ann Bass
18 Jun 1812
Wayne, North
Carolina

John Bass
24 Apr 1780 Wayne
Co, NC

**Julia Ann
Holloman**
24 Apr 1785 Wayne,
North Carolina

Edward Bass
1762 Craven,
Wayne Co., NC

Sarah Stevens
1765 Wayne Co.,
NC

Ezekiel Holloman
1755 Wayne, North
Carolina

Richard Bass
1732 Craven, North
Carolina, United
States

Sarah McKinnie
1735 Craven, North
Carolina, United
States

John Stevens
18 Dec 1729
Perquimans Co.,
NC

Sarah Padgett
21 May 1737
Berkley Co.,
Perquimmans, NC

Nathan Holloman
Isle of Wight Co.,
VA

Jean

Andrew Bass
09 Jun 1698 Norfolk,...

Elizabeth Smith
Abt. 1700 Craven
County, NC

David McKinne
Abt. 1680 Craven
Co., NC

**Thomas (2)
Stevens**
1701 Craven Co., NC

James Pagett
1696

**Susannah
Johnston**
Abt. 1700

Thomas Holloman
1675 Isle of Wight
Co., VA

Ann

Richard Basse

Mary Burwell

**Michael McKinne
Macauinav**

Elizabeth Daniel

Thomas Stevens

Mary Caswell

Edward Pagett

Margaret Tynes

Thomas Johnston

William Holloman

Marie

2

3

4

5

6

7

8

9

Genealogy 50: Molsey Ann Bass

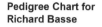

**Pedigree Chart for
Richard Basse**

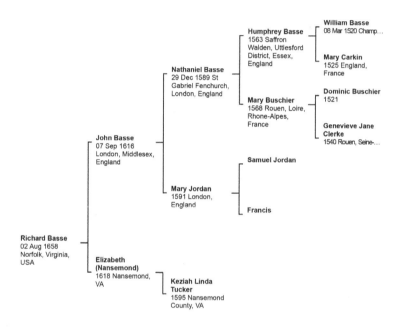

William Basse
08 Mar 1520 Champ...

Humphrey Basse
1563 Saffron
Walden, Uttlesford
District, Essex,
England

Mary Carkin
1525 England,
France

Nathaniel Basse
29 Dec 1589 St
Gabriel Fenchurch,
London, England

Dominic Buschier
1521

Mary Buschier
1568 Rouen, Loire,
Rhone-Alpes,
France

Genevieve Jane
Clerke
1540 Rouen, Seine-...

John Basse
07 Sep 1616
London, Middlesex,
England

Samuel Jordan

Mary Jordan
1591 London,
England

Francis

Richard Basse
02 Aug 1658
Norfolk, Virginia,
USA

Elizabeth
(Nansemond)
1618 Nansemond,
VA

Keziah Linda
Tucker
1595 Nansemond
County, VA

Genealogy 51: Richard Basse

The treaty between the Jamestown colonists and the Powhatan Confederacy was agreed in 1632 and set aside land for the tribes including the Nansemond on the northwest and south branches of the Nansemond River. Many Nansemond converted to Christianity and sought to integrate into the colonists' way of life. Settlers and Nansemond also began to intermarry, beginning with the 1638 marriage of a Nansemond woman, Elizabeth, who was the daughter of the Nansemond chief, and Englishman and ancestor John Basse. The Nansemond who rejected Christianity, sometimes called "the Pochick," unsuccessfully fought the English again in 1644 in the third Anglo-Powhatan war while the Christian Nansemond, including Elizabeth and her family, remained peaceful. The Nansemond and the Basse and Wheeler families subsequently intermarried and grew up together. However, because of increased pressure from colonists, who typically distrusted all Native Americans and coveted the tribal lands, the Nansemond moved further distant from existing settlements and closer to the Great Dismal Swamp, which afforded more protection from attacks and was considered less desirable farmland.

John Basse's known ancestry dates back to his great-grandparents, William Basse and his wife Mary Carkin. William was born in northern France in 1520 and was a member of the Huguenots (see Chapter 1). Mary's family was also Huguenot; they had several children in England including Humphrey.

Humphrey Basse (1563–1616)

William's and Mary's son Humphrey was born in London in 1563. He married Mary Buschier in 1588. He had a prosperous business and owned an expensive clothing shop on High Street. He was also an investor in the Virginia Company, which sponsored English settlers to move to Virginia and seek their fortune. Humphrey and Mary had eighteen children between 1589 and 1615. They attended Saint Helen's Church in Bishopsgate at the same time William Shakespeare was a member and likely were friendly with Shakespeare. William Shakespeare, Humphrey Basse, and Mary Basse all died in 1616. It is likely they all died of disease, probably typhus, which was prevalent in the area at the time. Humphrey left an extensive will distributing his considerable assets among his large family including young children.

Nathaniel Basse (1589–1654)

Humphrey and Mary's second child and oldest surviving son, Nathaniel, was born in 1589 and inherited considerable assets including his father's investment in the Virginia Company. Nathaniel was one of the few Company investors to go to Virginia, arriving with his wife Mary Jordan and their children on April 27, 1619. Nathaniel was twenty-nine years old.

Rather than settle in the struggling town of Jamestown, Nathaniel and a group of early settlers headed south of Jamestown to an area known as Lawne's Creek, which later became part of Isle of Wight County. Three leaders of the new Lawne's Plantation included Sir Richard Worsley, Captain Christopher Lawne, and Nathaniel Basse. Soon Worsley and Lawne died, leaving young Nathaniel in charge. In 1621, Nathaniel Basse and others established another plantation, Basse's Choice, on Pagan Bay and the James River. Today, Basse's Choice is a brand name of Smithfield Ham; Smithfield is a major employer in the area and offers historical tours.

In 1622, Nathaniel traveled back to England to recruit more settlers and possibly to raise money for the settlement. During his trip, the Jamestown area was devastated by the Jamestown Massacre, when the Powhatan killed about one-third of the settlers including one of Nathaniel's children. Reports soon after the massacre indicated all at Captain Basse's house and twenty-six of the seventy-nine residents of Basse's Choice were killed. It is not known why only one of Nathaniel's children apparently died, perhaps some were with him on a ship and others were visiting elsewhere.[175]

In spite of the massacre, an influx of new settlers arrived, attracted by the success of tobacco as a cash crop, and the area began to grow. Nathaniel was a leading citizen, representing his area in the Virginia House of Burgesses and taking on public responsibilities. His wife Mary returned to England and died there at age thirty-nine. She is thought to have returned after suffering from acute depression, having birthed eleven children in thirteen years including three sets of twins. Mental health facilities in England which essentially housed the mentally ill were well established including Saint Mary of Bethlehem asylum while none existed in Virginia at that time.

Mary's parents were Samuel Jordan and Francis Reynolds. Samuel Jordan emigrated from Wiltshire, England in 1609, either on the *Sea Venture* or a sister ship. Samuel Jordan later established a plantation near Jamestown called Jordan's Journey, and he became a man of great importance in the early days of the Jamestown colony (see Chapter 55).

Nathaniel Basse focused his energies on supervising and managing farming activity at Basse's Choice, growing tobacco, corn, and flax. He likely had sheep for wool. Nathaniel would have had indentured servants from Europe and Africa to do the physical work. In those early years, both black and white indentured servants generally served seven years in return for the master paying their passage to Virginia. Slavery came later in Virginia's history.

Nathaniel returned to England; it is not known if he was on a business trip or intended to stay, but he died in England in 1654 at the age of sixty-four.

John Basse (1616–1699) and Elizabeth Keziah (1618–1676)

John Basse was Nathaniel and Mary's oldest surviving son, born in 1616 in England and emigrating with his parents. John married Elizabeth, daughter of the chief of the Nansemond tribe in 1638. Her Christian last name was likely Keziah. She changed her name and accepted Christianity as part of the marriage agreement. It is very possible that the marriage was arranged to help assure peace between the Nansemond, the Powhatan and the colonists, who had recently been at war.

John Basse's brother Edward also married a Nansemond, identified as Mary Tucker. The marriages between the Basse family and the Nansemond led to many generations of future Americans.

Richard Basse (1658–1722)

John and Elizabeth's son Richard Basse was born in 1658. He married Jane Bryant and they had five children. Jane died in 1689. Richard then married Mary Burwell, and they had seven children.

During Richard's life, he would have experienced continued challenges from ongoing white settlers' attacks on Native Americans. Typically, when settlers responded to a Native raid or attack, they often killed whatever Native people they could find, not differentiating between friendly and hostile tribes.

Intermarriage with the Nansemond continued as settler men found local Native American women more hospitable, supportive, and locally knowledgeable than the "pure Anglo-Saxon female riff-raff who were shipped to Virginia from the streets and gaols of London." [176] Intermarriage between Native Americans and white settlers became so common, Virginia banned such marriages in the late 1690s. In response, many settlers moved to nearby North Carolina, where mixed marriages were not banned until 1749.

Local tribes including the Nansemond were constantly harassed and persecuted. The Treaty of 1677 between King Charles II and the Virginia Native Nations offered protection to the tribes from encroachment, slavery, and forced servitude, but enforcement was often lax.

Andrew Bass (1698–1770)

Richard and Mary's firstborn was Andrew, who was born in 1698 in Norfolk County, Virginia, where many of the Nansemond lived. He grew up to marry Elizabeth Smith, and they moved to Craven County, North Carolina; their son Richard was likely born there in 1732.

In North Carolina, the family's connection with the Nansemond tribe was greatly diminished. At some point around this time, they began spelling their name "Bass" instead of "Basse."

Andrew purchased considerable land in Craven County and in nearby Dobbs County (part of which later became Wayne County). He became a wealthy landowner with a large estate. His descendants include ancestors Richard Bass (1732–1793), Edward Bass (1762–1802), and John Bass.

John Bass (1780–1822)

John was born around 1780 in Wayne County, North Carolina, where he married Julia Ann Holliman in 1805. Her family ancestry beginning with Christopher Holloman (or Hollyman) emigrated from England to Isle of Wight County, Virginia. He built a house that remains as a historic building on his Virginia plantation. Subsequently, the descendants moved to Craven County, North Carolina, where Julia was born.

They lived in Wayne County until about 1813, when they moved to Perry County in Alabama. John and Julia were early pioneers and likely took advantage of the Native people's removal by accumulating land and slaves to grow cotton and other crops.

John Bass died in 1822 at the age of forty-two. He left nine children, all minors. His wife, Julia, later married Jetson Green; and they moved to Union County, Louisiana, probably with Julia's daughter Molsey Ann Bass and Molsey's family.

John's and Julia's daughter Molsey Ann Bass was born in 1812 in Wayne County, North Carolina and moved to Perry, Alabama with her parents. There she married Rev. Elias George in 1828, after turning fifteen years old. The couple moved to Union County, Louisiana where Molsey died in 1850 at the age of thirty-eight. One of Molsey's and Elias's daughters, Louisa, wrote a memoir on their life and journey to Louisiana which appears earlier in this book (see Chapter 56). One of their sons, Washington George, was my great great-grandfather.

Chapter 65:

The Burwell Family:
The Fairfield Plantation and
Virginia Aristocrats

Pedigree Chart for
Mary Burwell

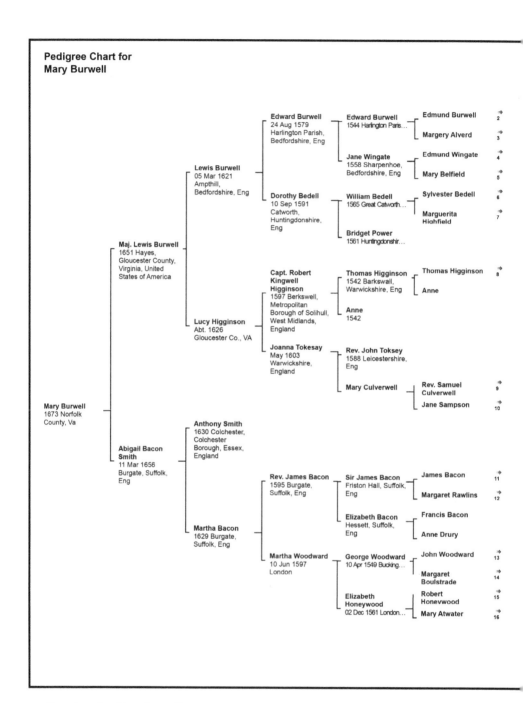

Mary Burwell
1673 Norfolk
County, Va

Maj. Lewis Burwell
1651 Hayes,
Gloucester County,
Virginia, United
States of America

**Abigail Bacon
Smith**
11 Mar 1656
Burgate, Suffolk,
Eng

Lewis Burwell
05 Mar 1621
Ampthill,
Bedfordshire, Eng

Lucy Higginson
Abt. 1626
Gloucester Co., VA

Anthony Smith
1630 Colchester,
Colchester
Borough, Essex,
England

Martha Bacon
1629 Burgate,
Suffolk, Eng

Edward Burwell
24 Aug 1579
Harlington Parish,
Bedfordshire, Eng

Dorothy Bedell
10 Sep 1591
Catworth,
Huntingdonshire,
Eng

**Capt. Robert
Kingwell
Higginson**
1597 Berkswell,
Metropolitan
Borough of Solihull,
West Midlands,
England

Joanna Tokesay
May 1603
Warwickshire,
England

Rev. James Bacon
1595 Burgate,
Suffolk, Eng

Martha Woodward
10 Jun 1597
London

Edward Burwell
1544 Harlington Paris...

Jane Wingate
1558 Sharpenhoe,
Bedfordshire, Eng

William Bedell
1565 Great Catworth...

Bridget Power
1561 Huntingdonshir...

Thomas Higginson
1542 Barkswall,
Warwickshire, Eng

Anne
1542

Rev. John Toksey
1588 Leicestershire,
Eng

Mary Culverwell

Sir James Bacon
Friston Hall, Suffolk,
Eng

Elizabeth Bacon
Hessett, Suffolk,
Eng

George Woodward
10 Apr 1549 Bucking...

**Elizabeth
Honeywood**
02 Dec 1561 London...

Edmund Burwell 2

Margery Alverd 3

Edmund Wingate 4

Mary Belfield 5

Sylvester Bedell 6

**Marguerita
Highfield** 7

Thomas Higginson 8

**Rev. Samuel
Culverwell** 9

Jane Sampson 10

James Bacon 11

Margaret Rawlins 12

Francis Bacon

Anne Drury

John Woodward 13

**Margaret
Boulstrade** 14

**Robert
Honevwood** 15

Mary Atwater 16

Genealogy 52: Mary Burwell

344

Mary Burwell married Richard Basse in Nansemond (now Norfolk) Virginia. The Burwell family has a long and distinguished history in England. The name apparently comes from Old English and refers to a fort (*burh*) located next to a spring (*well*). There has been a village of Burwell in Cambridgeshire, England, since at least 1060. The village is located next to a spring and near the twelfth-century Burwell castle. Someone named Burwell would have been a person who came from the village of Burwell.

Lewis Fairfield Burwell was born in 1621 in the ancestral family home in Bedfordshire, not far from Burwell. He left England and arrived in Virginia around 1640. He came with his mother and his stepfather, Roger Wingate. The Burwells, and Roger Wingate specifically, apparently sought adventure and the prospect of accumulating greater wealth in Virginia.

In 1651, Lewis married Lucy Higginson, daughter of Captain Robert Higginson and Joanna Toksey. Robert Higginson had emigrated to Gloucester, Virginia from Warwickshire, England with his wife before 1628. He was a painter–stainer in England, meaning he was either an artist or one who dyed fabrics for sale. He was also captain and commander of the Middle Plantation, which was the predecessor to Williamsburg, Virginia, and was sent with eighty men to respond to the 1644 Jamestown Massacre.

Lewis began the family involvement with early Virginia history. The Burwells are considered one of the First Families of Virginia.[177] According to John Quincy Adams, the Burwells were typical Virginia aristocrats of their period: forthright, bland, somewhat imperious and politically simplistic.[178] In 1713, so many Burwells had intermarried with Virginia political elite that Governor Spotswood complained that most of the Council were related to the Burwell families.[179]

Lewis Burwell accumulated considerable acreage in Virginia by earning headrights from importing others (including servants and slaves) and purchasing property. He also inherited his mother's considerable holdings when she died.

Lewis quickly became active in his adopted Virginia colony. In 1646, he was a major in the militia and was a member of the Virginia delegation sent to England to invite King Charles II to come to Virginia for a visit.

He developed the Fairfield Plantation in Gloucester County, which became a center of cultural and political activity and the ancestral home of the Burwell family in America. Before it was called Fairfield, the site was referred to as Carter's Creek. Six generations of Burwells lived at Fairfield from 1642 to 1787, when it was sold to Colonel Robert Thruston. The site is currently an archeological dig documenting the lifestyle of a major southern plantation.

Lewis and Lucy had a son, Lewis (II), born in 1651. His first marriage was to Abigail Smith, niece and heiress to Nathaniel Bacon and daughter of Anthony Smith and Martha Bacon, both from prominent Virginia families. They had ten children. Abigail died in 1692 at the age of thirty-six. Lewis then married Martha Lear, daughter of Colonel John Lear, and they had six children.

Lewis (II) was well-known in the area as a major planter and active in community affairs. He served as governor of the College of William and Mary in 1702 and was on the Governor's Council from 1702 until he died around 1710 or 1711. Burwell's Bay in Isle of Wight County was named after him.

Mary was the first child born to Abigail and Lewis, born in 1673. She married Richard Bass in 1695, uniting one family descended from English aristocracy with another with Native American roots.

Chapter 66:

The Stevens Family:
A Leader in Cromwell's Rebellion
Escapes to America

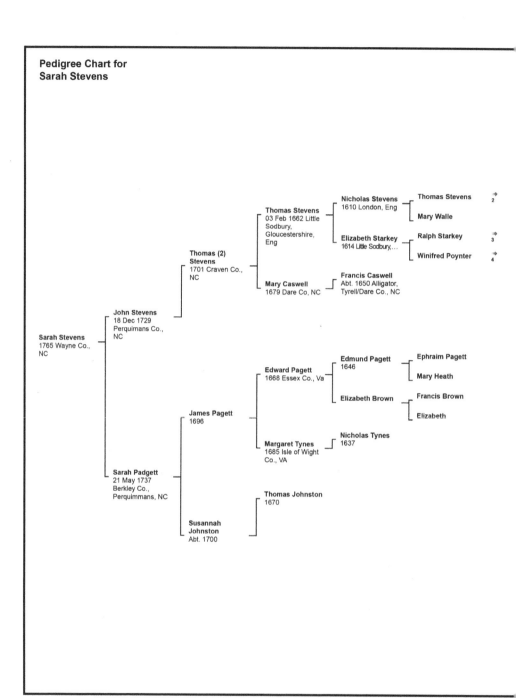

Pedigree Chart for
Sarah Stevens

Sarah Stevens
1765 Wayne Co.,
NC

John Stevens
18 Dec 1729
Perquimans Co.,
NC

Sarah Padgett
21 May 1737
Berkley Co.,
Perquimmans, NC

**Thomas (2)
Stevens**
1701 Craven Co.,
NC

James Pagett
1696

**Susannah
Johnston**
Abt. 1700

Thomas Stevens
03 Feb 1662 Little
Sodbury,
Gloucestershire,
Eng

Mary Caswell
1679 Dare Co, NC

Edward Pagett
1668 Essex Co., Va

Margaret Tynes
1685 Isle of Wight
Co., VA

Thomas Johnston
1670

Nicholas Stevens
1610 London, Eng

Elizabeth Starkey
1614 Little Sodbury,...

Francis Caswell
Abt. 1650 Alligator,
Tyrell/Dare Co., NC

Edmund Pagett
1646

Elizabeth Brown

Nicholas Tynes
1637

Thomas Stevens →2

Mary Walle

Ralph Starkey →3

Winifred Poynter →4

Ephraim Pagett

Mary Heath

Francis Brown

Elizabeth

Genealogy 53: Sarah Stevens

Sarah Stevens married Edward Bass around 1779 in North Carolina. The first Stevens to immigrate to America was Nicholas Stevens. He was born about 1610 in London; his parents were Thomas Stevens and Mary Walle. In 1641, Nicholas married Elizabeth Starkey in London. It is not certain exactly when he emigrated from England because he travelled under an assumed name, seeking to avoid capture from Royal authorities because of his leadership in Cromwell 's army during the English Civil War (see Chapter 1). He likely arrived around 1660.

Nicholas, his family, and his brother Anthony initially settled in Taunton, Massachusetts. Not long after arriving in Massachusetts, Anthony moved to Jamestown, Virginia, and Nicholas soon followed. The English government sent agents to New England searching for Cromwell refugees, and the Stevenses likely elected to disappear into southern Virginia.

They initially lived in Westmoreland County, Virginia, but Nicholas and his family moved to Albemarle, North Carolina. The Albemarle area was opened for settlement beginning in 1663, and immigrants were encouraged and rewarded with free land. Most of the new residents came from the nearby Jamestown area.

Nicholas and Elizabeth had three sons including Thomas, who married Mary Caswell. Their son Thomas (II) was born in 1701 in Craven County. Thomas (II)'s son John was born in 1729.

John married Sarah Padgett, daughter of James Pagett and Susannah Johnson. John and Sarah had a daughter named Sarah, who married Edward Bass, uniting the Stevens family, which came from the rebellion against royalty in England, with the Bass family, which came from the Huguenots, and their rebellion against religious doctrine and authority in France.

Chapter 67:

The Pugh Family:
From Wales to North Carolina

**Pedigree Chart for
Julie Ann Pugh**

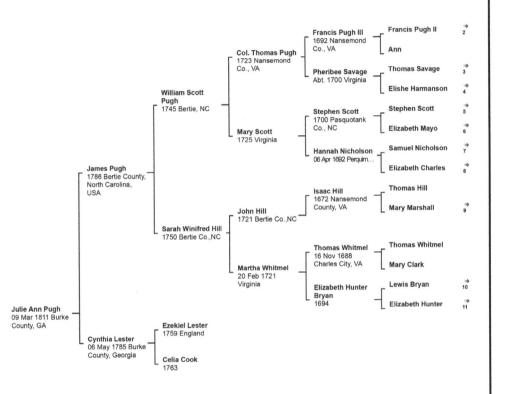

Julie Ann Pugh
09 Mar 1811 Burke
County, GA

James Pugh
1786 Bertie County,
North Carolina,
USA

Cynthia Lester
06 May 1785 Burke
County, Georgia

William Scott
Pugh
1745 Bertie, NC

Sarah Winifred Hill
1750 Bertie Co.,NC

Ezekiel Lester
1759 England

Celia Cook
1763

Col. Thomas Pugh
1723 Nansemond
Co., VA

Mary Scott
1725 Virginia

John Hill
1721 Bertie Co.,NC

Martha Whitmel
20 Feb 1721
Virginia

Francis Pugh III
1692 Nansemond
Co., VA

Pheribee Savage
Abt. 1700 Virginia

Stephen Scott
1700 Pasquotank
Co., NC

Hannah Nicholson
06 Apr 1692 Perquim…

Isaac Hill
1672 Nansemond
County, VA

Thomas Whitmel
16 Nov 1688
Charles City, VA

Elizabeth Hunter
Bryan
1694

Francis Pugh II   →2

Ann

Thomas Savage   →3

Elishe Harmanson   →4

Stephen Scott   →5

Elizabeth Mayo   →6

Samuel Nicholson   →7

Elizabeth Charles   →8

Thomas Hill

Mary Marshall   →9

Thomas Whitmel

Mary Clark

Lewis Bryan   →10

Elizabeth Hunter   →11

Genealogy 54: Julie Ann Pugh

Julie Ann Pugh married Albertis Johnson in 1827 in Perry, Alabama. The history of the Pugh family and how they arrived in Alabama is an interesting story. The Pugh ancestry comes from Wales. It is believed that the Pugh family descended from Sir Owen Glendower through his son Hugh Glendower. The name Pugh is thought to originate from the Welch expression "ap Hugh" or son of Hugh. The name was later anglicized to simply "Pugh."

Francis Pugh was born about 1630 in Wales. He was the son of a Welsh squire who lived at Glendower Hall, Glendower, Caernarfonshire Wales. In 1666, Francis and his brothers Daniel and Thomas emigrated to Jamestown. They were all men of means.

Emigrants from Wales were typically seeking escape from poverty, greater economic opportunities, or religious freedom. In 1660, King Charles II was restored to the throne and instigated a series of acts of religious intolerance including loyalty pledges and strict worship protocols which were unacceptable to many. At the time, residents of Wales, and sometimes whole communities, fled to America. It is unknown why the three sons from a well-to-do family departed Wales when they did, but it could have been related to religious differences and conflict.

Francis settled near Suffolk, Virginia, in Nansemond County. He imported considerable brick from England and built a large residence he called "Jericho." He married Anne Howe, and they had a son, Francis (II), who also married a woman named Ann.

Francis (III), son of Francis (II) and Ann, married Pheribee (various spellings) Savage in 1722. They lived in Nansemond County and then moved across the state line to Bertie County, North Carolina, which was part of the Chowan Precinct of Albemarle County. He served as justice of the peace in the Chowan Precinct and was a wealthy landowner and planter. He owned considerable land in Bertie. He also owned ships and transported tobacco and walnuts and other products to England.

One of Francis and Pheribee's sons, Thomas, was born in 1723. During the Revolutionary War, Thomas was a lieutenant colonel with the North Carolina militia. In 1776, he was a delegate from Bertie County to the North Carolina Provincial Congress, which approved the first state constitution and a declaration of rights, elected a governor, and authorized raising a permanent militia.

Colonel Thomas Pugh was described as "a man of prominence, and with his brother, John, was among the first patriots identified with the struggle for freedom from the British Government. He was also a man of intellect and shrewdness and was one of the wealthiest men of his section." [180]

William Scott Pugh, son of Colonel Thomas and his wife, Mary Scott, was born in 1745 in Bertie, North Carolina. He and his brother Thomas fought the British in the Revolutionary War; and both were wounded in the Battle of Guilford Courthouse in North Carolina.

William recovered from his wounds; and he and his wife, Sarah Winifred Hill, had ten children including James, who was born in 1786. James married Cynthia Lester in 1804, and they moved to Burke County, Georgia. They had five children including a daughter named Julie Ann.

The Pugh Women's Ancestry: English Witches and a Teenager in Jamestown

Some wives of the Pughs had even more interesting backgrounds. History has often focused on the male descendants, but the history of the Pugh family in America shows the importance of documenting the women.

Elizabeth Simpson (1616–1673)

Mary Scott was the wife of Colonel Thomas Pugh and mother of William Scott Pugh. Her parents were Stephen Scott and Hannah Nicholson. Hannah's great-great-grandparents, Edmund and Elizabeth Simpson, were the first Nicholsons to emigrate from England. They moved to Massachusetts in 1644 and were among the original Puritan families in the town of Marblehead, Massachusetts.

By 1655, Edmund and Elizabeth had six children, but life in the colony was increasingly dominated by intolerant Puritans. Anyone who worshiped outside of the official Puritan Congregational Church was labeled a heretic and subjected to severe discipline including death. Even though there were various religious groups arriving each week, the Catholics and the Quakers were the most adamant in refusing to adhere to Puritan rule.

Although the Catholics in Massachusetts were frowned upon, they tended to keep to themselves. However, the Quakers wreaked havoc on the Puritans every chance they got including disrupting church services, banging pots and pans, and yelling from behind the bars of the overcrowded jails to express their independence from the Puritan version of the "purified" Anglican church. Supported by the Puritan governor, the Puritans believed that Quakers should either join the official church or leave the colony on the next available ship. The catch in that rule was the fact that any ship's captain who would take them was fined five hundred pounds. So the Quakers were stuck there with no way to leave, and their torment continued.

Edmund Nicholson (b. 1612) was a fisherman by trade and at sea most of the time. Meanwhile, his wife Elizabeth became outspoken about the harsh treatment of other worshipers, especially the Quakers. This drew attention from the Puritan preachers who thought she was becoming too influenced by the Quakers and needed to be disciplined.

In 1660, the church officials found the excuse they needed to bring Elizabeth under control. Edmund Nicholson's body was found floating in the water, and Elizabeth and her two oldest sons, Christopher and Joseph, were immediately apprehended and thrown in jail, accused (despite the lack of evidence) of murdering the drowned Edmund. She was also accused of being a witch. At the same time in England, King Charles II passed his Act of Toleration and sent word to Salem to cease the hangings of Quakers and others. The church officials in Massachusetts knew that they could not hang Elizabeth and her two sons, but they could still make their lives miserable. Trials were held even though there was no proof of any wrongdoing. All of Elizabeth's land and possessions were confiscated, and her sons were subjected to public whippings in both Boston and Salem and were forced to stand on gallows with hangman's nooses about their necks on a daily basis.

By 1664, the brothers Christopher and Joseph had simply had enough of the Puritan colony. Christopher and his wife Hannah Rednap moved to Perquimans County, North Carolina, and brother Joseph with wife Jane settled in Rhode Island. Elizabeth Nicholson remarried to a Mr. Browne and died nine years later in 1673. In 1688, Christopher and Hannah's son Samuel married Elizabeth Charles (daughter of William Charles) in Perquimans County.

Samuel's and Elizabeth's daughter Hannah Nicholson married Stephen Scott, and their daughter Mary Scott became the wife of Colonel Thomas Pugh.

Pheribee Savage Pugh (1700–1754)

Pheribee Savage was the wife of Francis Pugh (III) and mother of Colonel Thomas Pugh. Her immigrant ancestor was Thomas Savage, who arrived in Jamestown on the first supply ship in 1608, when he was only thirteen years old. More than eighty percent of the early Jamestown colonists died, but Thomas survived. Captain Christopher Newport took him under his wing. John Smith and Captain Newport negotiated with the Powhatan chief Wahunsonacock after the settlers at Jamestown arrived in the hopes of securing food and cooperation. As a result of their discussions, they agreed to have young Thomas Savage live with the Powhatan tribe to learn their language and customs. Thomas lived with the tribe for three years.

When Wahunsonacock's brother grew jealous of Thomas and demanded his removal, Wahunsonacock sent Thomas to live with Debedeavon, chief of the Accawmack tribe, a peaceful and friendly tribe on the Eastern Shore of Maryland. Debedeavon and the Accawmack tribe became fond of young Thomas and gave him nine thousand acres of land to be later called "Savage's Neck." Later, during or shortly after the 1622 massacre at Jamestown, Thomas engaged in fighting the Powhatan warriors and had an arrow that apparently went through his body. He lived and was given the title Ensign Thomas Savage by the surviving settlers.

Thomas Savage later became a much sought-after interpreter connecting settlers and Native Americans. He was apparently trusted by both sides. In the famous painting, "The Marriage of Pocahontas," by Henry Brueckner, a young man in the painting is believed to be Thomas Savage. That painting was donated by Nelson Rockefeller and is in the Library of Congress.

Thomas Savage married Hannah Ann Tyng and had a son, Captain John Savage. John married Mary Robbins, and their son Thomas Savage was Pheribee's father.

Figure 24: The Burning of Washington

Chapter 68:

The War of 1812

Many ancestors, including Sarah Stevens and Edward Bass, lived through the War of 1812 as did James and Cynthia Pugh; their relatives, including John Bass and another James Pugh, served in the war. This was an odd war. It was as if the mouse declared war on the lion, and after five long years both parties went back to where they started. There was no change in boundaries, neither country made any significant concessions, and conditions remained unchanged. Many battles were fought, many died, a capital was burned, and both sides could relish the memory of an occasional heroic action or victory. The largest and perhaps most consequential battle was fought after the peace treaty was signed but before participants had been notified.

Americans were angry at the British during the times leading up to the declaration of war. The British were at war with Napoleon and in need of crews for their large navy. One source of manpower was to detain American vessels and forcibly impress American sailors into British naval service. The British navy impressed thousands of Americans in this manner. They also occasionally seized American ships to help in the fight against the French, and the French began to seize American vessels to fight the British.

Americans in the Northeast longed to capture Canada and expand the new nation. There were probably 7.5 million Americans in 1812 and only five hundred thousand residents of the Canadian territory, which was lightly defended. The Americans thought most of the Canadian residents would help defeat the British and welcome joining the United States, but no one evidently asked the Canadians. And Americans in the west thought British traders were conspiring with Native Americans to cause problems on the frontier and block future westward expansion.

In light of the many grievances, the United States declared war on Great Britain in June of 1812. Britain did not react quickly because they were preoccupied with the bigger war against Napoleon in Europe and were probably dismissive of the Americans with their small navy that was certainly no match for the British navy.

The Americans, led by militia companies from the northeast, likely including ancestors Johannes Bloom, John Case, John Egbert, and others, fought a series of indecisive battles against British troops along the Canadian border, wining some and losing more. The Canadian forays were largely failures.

British warships attacked American coastal cities. The largest attack was the Battle of Craney Island near Norfolk, which was contested by the Virginia militia including ancestors Jared McDonald Jr. (see Chapter 5), Stephen Pool, and others.

The most famous confrontations included the attack on Washington D.C., and then Baltimore in August 1814. The British ships entered the Chesapeake Bay and disembarked about five thousand troops including seasoned solders from the recent European conflict. Washington was lightly defended because the Secretary of War, John Armstrong, did not believe the British would attack Washington because the city "lacked strategic value." [181] The Maryland militia, led by General William Winder, a lawyer with limited military experience but with good political connections, had about four hundred soldiers and 1,500 poorly trained and under-equipped militiamen.

Ancestor Colonel George Minor and his seven-hundred-man Sixtieth Regiment of the Virginia militia, were summoned from Falls Church, Virginia, to help defend Washington. However, because of confusion and bureaucratic bungling at the War Department, they were never dispatched to Bladensburg, Maryland, where the British and American forces were converging. The British troops overwhelmed and routed the Americans at the Battle of Bladensburg and marched on to Washington virtually uncontested. Colonel Minor removed back to Virginia and took supplies of gunpowder and arms from the Washington Naval Yard to prevent their being seized by the British. The British sacked and burned the capital including the president's house (later named the White House) before marching back to their ships on the Chesapeake.

Along the way back, the British arrested some Americans they accused of being traitors, including a sixty-five-year-old doctor, William Beanes, whose family orig-inally emigrated from Scotland. One of Beanes's patients was the brother-in-law of a Georgetown-based lawyer and the patient asked the lawyer to engage with the British and plead for the doctor's release. This lawyer and a government lawyer from Baltimore were able to obtain a meeting with British Commanding General Ross and British Admiral Cochrane on Cochrane's flagship, *HMS Tonnant.* After a long and spirited discussion and persuasive presentation, the general and admiral agreed to release the doctor, and the two lawyers departed with their client to another nearby ship, *HMS Minden.*

It was already night when they returned, and the British attack and bombardment of Baltimore and Fort McHenry had commenced. From the deck of the *Minden,* the two lawyers and the doctor watched the bombardment. They watched the red con-trails of the Congreve rockets and the British mortars that were set to explode above the fort raining shrapnel on those below. Above Fort McHenry flew an oversized American flag, thirty feet by forty-two feet. The flag had been sewn by Mrs. Mary Pickersgill and her daughter Caroline, working by candlelight in a nearby brewery so they could spread out the cloth.

As the night progressed, Doctor Beanes kept asking, "Is the flag still there?" Finally, daylight appeared, and the flag was still flying. The Georgetown lawyer, Francis Scott Key, took out an envelope and scribbled a few lines. Two days later, Key elaborated on his verse,

O say can you see, by the dawn's early light,
What so proudly we hail'd at the twilight's last gleaming?
Whose broad stripes and bright stars, through the perilous fight,
O'er the ramparts we watch'd, were so gallantly streaming?
And the rocket's red glare, the bombs bursting in air,
Gave proof through the night that our flag was still there.[182]

That verse and the verses that followed became known as "The Star-Spangled Banner" and was adopted officially as America's national anthem in 1931.

The Americans held at Baltimore and the British withdrew from the Chesapeake region as a result.

The Treaty of Ghent ending the War of 1812 was signed on December 24, 1814, in Ghent, Belgium, but news of its execution did not reach America until February 1815. In the interim, the last battle of the war was fought—an American victory in New Orleans. Although outnumbered, Americans led by General Andrew Jackson defeated British troops led by Major General Sir Edward Pakenham; the British suffered about two thousand casualties compared to only sixty American casualties. Much later, Jimmy Driftwood wrote the song, "The Battle of New Orleans," which became the top-selling country and western song and one of the top one hundred country and western songs of all time.[183]

Chapter 69:
Conclusions

My ancestors came from England, Scotland, Ireland, Wales, Germany, and the Netherlands with a few from other places like France and Switzerland. Some were Native Americans. Those who arrived from Europe came in the 1600s and 1700s and were here for the founding of what became the United States of America.

Some came to New England as Puritans seeking freedom of religion. They settled in and established towns in Massachusetts and Connecticut and nearby states. They contributed to and created what we now know as New England. Land lots were relatively small, winters were harsh, and conflict with local Native American tribes frequent. But the ancestors survived and multiplied.

Another stream of immigrants came from Scotland, Ireland, Ulster, Germany, and England and settled in Pennsylvania also seeking religious freedom but not necessarily Puritans. They typically sought a better life for their families. After settling in Pennsylvania and nearby New Jersey and New York, descendants moved to the Midwest including Ohio and nearby states, seeking more affordable and available land and a better future and economic opportunity for their children.

Still another stream of immigrants left England, Scotland, and Wales for Jamestown and southern Virginia. Some were attracted by adventure and the possibilities of owning land and making money; others were sons and daughters of wealthy Englishmen but not the firstborn sons who would inherit most of the wealth. Many left when Cromwell defeated King Charles I; a few of Cromwell's supporters left when Charles II was restored. They wanted to achieve their own success and create wealth for themselves and their families. Some brought money and a life accustomed to wealthy living and community service, which led to leadership positions in the colony, accumulation of large plantations, and importation of slaves to operate the plantations. Others came as indentured servants with no hope of ever owning land or a business in England.

After living in southern Virginia, many moved on to nearby North Carolina and then to more distant southern states as Native Americans were forced out and land for settlers became available. They moved on to South Carolina, Alabama, Georgia, Louisiana, and Arkansas.

The ancestors generally followed major immigration trends; there were few outliers to popular immigration flows. And they were survivors. These were the men and women who founded what we call America.

Despite the many backgrounds, nationalities, and, in some cases, historic family ties to the English royalty, the ancestors were quick to take up arms in support of the American Revolution. They joined the militia and fought the Native tribes during the many conflicts during early settlement; they fought the British in 1812, and they choose sides and fought in the Civil War, sometimes against each other.

It is important to acknowledge the challenges and hardships endured by the ancestors, particularly those who came early. Virtually everyone lost at least one spouse and children. Living on the frontier meant living in constant fear of attack by hostile Native tribes, in which the men could be brutally killed and the women and children either killed or taken as slaves. Food could be scarce at times, and work was hard and never ending. Lives were short, especially for the women, and medical care rudimentary. Life was a struggle.

it is also important to recognize the suffering of the Native Americans, most of whom died of disease and others who were forced to vacate traditional lands to make way for new settlers. Even if the settlers had not arrived when they did, eventually Europeans would have discovered America and brought disease and war; it was inevitable. The lives of Native Americans, isolated from the rest of the world, would never be sustained. But they suffered setbacks for more than two centuries culminating in the Indian Removal Act of 1830 and the subsequent Trail of Tears.

And we should not forget the African slaves whose suffering made possible the large southern plantations and economic prosperity enjoyed by planters and their families. The importation of African slaves was caused solely by the pursuit of profit and greed. The planters needed cheap labor to sustain their lifestyles, and slaves filled that need. There does not appear to have been any serious or widespread discussion of the morality of slavery in those times and places.

If the early ancestors could see what has happened over the past four hundred years to the wilderness they called America, they would be amazed. And we can thank them for taking the chance, surviving against the odds, and starting us all on this journey. We owe it to them as well as the natives and slaves whose sacrifices contributed to this transformation, to leave this land to our descendants in good shape and able to sustain our children and future ancestors for next four hundred years.

Acknowledgments

Susan Zoby-Wilkinson of Norfolk, Virginia was the principal researcher for this book. Her ancestry research has been on-going for several years and her guidance and problem solving invaluable.

Other researchers who helped me along the way and focused on specific issues included the following.

- Beth Wallis
- Carolyn Burns
- Crystal Hall
- Harlan Jessup
- Kelly Davis
- Kimberley Bosely
- Nancy Bean
- Nancy Coleman
- Susan Michael
- Suzannah Beasley
- Terry Ann Nicholson

Index of Illustrations

Illustrations provided by and licensed from North Wind Pictures Archive
Northwindpictures.com

Index of Genealogies

Appendix A:
Known, Direct Ancestors in the Revolutionary War

- Edward Bass
- Richard Bass
- Stephen Bingham
- Peter Bloom
- Cornelius Bowman
- Joseph Breed
- John Case
- Jonathan Earp
- John Egbert
- John Ford
- Thomas Ford
- John George
- Nathan Holloman
- Daniel Hovey
- Henry Johnson
- John Johnson
- Smith Johnson
- Ambrose Jones
- William Lee

- Lewis Lyles
- Comfort Ludington
- Elisha Ludington
- Thomas Marshall
- Jared McDonald
- Seth Nickerson
- William Powell
- William Powell
- Thomas Pugh
- William Smith
- John Stevens
- David Wakeman
- Robert West
- Minor Winn Jr
- Samuel Wilder
- William Wilder
- Daniel Wood
- Nehemiah Wood
- Elisha Woodward

Appendix B:
Known, Direct Ancestors in the Civil War

The following ancestors met on the battlefields as enemies (those in your Direct Line are in Bold type):

7 Days Battle *June 25–July 1, 1862*
Carter Burwell 32nd VA Infantry, Confederacy
vs. **John Ehret** 72nd PA Infantry, Union

Antietam *Sept 1862*
Samuel W. Lomax, 3rd Batt SC, Confederacy
vs. **John Ehret** 72nd Infantry PA, Union

Fredericksburg *Dec 1862*
Carter Burwell 32nd VA Infantry
vs. No known Union relatives

Louisiana *1863–1865*
Col. Thomas Poole 28th LA Volunteers, Confederacy
vs. Louisiana Union Troops—No known relatives

Chancellorsville *May 1863*
Thomas Pugh 16th NC Regiment, Confederacy
Samuel W. Lomax 3rd Batt SC, Confederacy
vs. No known Union relatives

Gettysburg *July 1863*
Carter Burwell 32 VA Infantry, Confederacy
Starling Johnson 53rd NC Infantry, Confederacy
Thomas Pugh 16th NC Infantry, Confederacy
Samuel W. Lomax 3rd Batt SC, Confederacy
vs. **John Ehret** 72nd PA Infantry, Union

Wilderness *May 1864*
Starling Johnson 53rd NC Infantry, Confederacy
Samuel W. Lomax 3rd Batt SC, Confederacy
vs. No known Union relatives

Cold Harbor *May 31–June 12, 1864*
Starling Johnson 53rd NC Infantry, Confederacy
Carter Burwell 32nd VA Infantry, Confederacy
Thomas Pugh 16th NC Infantry, Confederacy
Uriah Bass 51st NC Infantry, Confederacy
vs. **Thomas MacDonald** 13th OH Cavalry Volunteers, Union

Petersburg 10 months *1864–1865*
William R. Holmes 56th NC Infantry, Confederacy
Uriah Bass 51st NC Infantry, Confederacy
Samuel W. Lomax 3rd Batt SC Infantry, Confederacy
Thomas Pugh 16th NC Infantry, Confederacy
vs. **Thomas MacDonald** 13th OH Cavalry Volunteers., Union
John Ehret 72nd PA Infantry, Union

Hatcher's Run & Fort Stedman *1865*
Thomas MacDonald 13th Oh Cavalry Volunteers, Union
vs. No known Confederate relatives

Appomattox Apr *1865*
Carter Burwell 32nd VA Infantry, Confederacy
Starling Johnson 53rd NC Infantry, Confederacy
Thomas Pugh 16th NC Infantry, Confederacy
William R. Holmes 56th NC Infantry, Confederacy
vs. **Thomas MacDonald** 13th OH Cavalry Volunteers, Union

Endnotes

1.   James Evans, Emigrants, *Why the English Sailed to the New World* (London: Weidenfeld & Nicolson, 2017), 12.

2.   James J. Leyburn, *The Scotch-Irish, A Social History* (Chapel Hill: University of North Carolina Press, 1962).

3.   James M. Volo and Dorothy Denneen Volo, *Family Life in 17th and 18th Century America* (Westport, CT: Greenwood Press, 2006), 24.

4.   Wikipedia, "German Americans," accessed March 17, 2020, https://en.wikipedia.org/wiki/German_Americans.

5.   Wikipedia, "Scottish Americans," accessed March 17, 2020, https://en.wikipedia.org/wiki/Scottish_Americans.

6.   Wikipedia, "Welsh Americans," accessed August 7, 2020, https://en.wikipedia.org/wiki/Welsh_Americans.

7.   Wikipedia, "Irish Americans," accessed March 17, 2020, https://en.wikipedia.org/wiki/Irish_Americans.

8.   Wikipedia, "Italian Americans," accessed March 17, 2020, https://en.wikipedia.org/wiki/Italian_Americans.

9.   Wikipedia, "Vietnamese Americans," accessed March 17, 2020, https://en.wikipedia.org/wiki/Vietnamese_Americans.

10.   Wikipedia, "Cuban Americans," accessed March 17, 2020, https://en.wikipedia.org/wiki/Cuban_Americans.

11.   Wikipedia, "Mexican Americans," accessed March 17, 2020, https://en.wikipedia.org/wiki/Mexican_Americans.

12.   Joellyn Zollman, "Jewish Immigration to America: Three Waves," Myjewishlearning.com, accessed August 21, 2020, https://www.myjewishlearning.com/article/jewish-immigration-to-america-three-waves/.

13.   Emily Guskin, "How many Jews live in the U.S.? That depends on how you define 'Jewish,'" Washington Post, February 23, 2018, https://www.washingtonpost.com/news/post-nation/wp/2018/02/23/measuring-the-size-of-the-u-s-jewish-population-comes-down-to-identity/.

14.   James Pethokoukis, "Are we really not sure if immigrant CEOs in Silicon Valley is a good thing or not? (It is.)" AEIdeas (blog), November 16, 2016, https://www.aei.org/economics/are-we-really-not-sure-if-immigrant-ceos-in-silicon-valley-are-a-good-thing-or-not-it-is/.

15.   Stuart Anderson, "55% of America's Billion Dollar Startups Have An Immigrant Founder," Forbes, October 25, 2018, https://www.forbes.com/sites/stuartanderson/2018/10/25/55-of-americas-billion-dollar-startups-have-immigrant-founder/#-6808c41748ee.

16.   Maya Kosoff, "12 Immigrants behind some of Silicon Valley's Biggest Companies," Vanity Fair, February 3, 2017, https://www.vanityfair.com/news/photos/2017/02/12-immigrants-behind-some-of-silicon-valleys-biggest-companies.

17.   "Indentured Servants in the U.S.," *PBS History Detectives*, Oregon Public Broadcasting, accessed October 7, 2020, https://www.pbs.org/opb/historydetectives/feature/indentured-servants-in-the-us/.

18.   "Poors in Tutor England," Tudorplace.com, accessed October 7, 2020, http://www.tudorplace.com.ar/Documents/poors.htm.

19.   Marjie Bloy, "The 1601 Elizabethian Poor Law," The Victorian Web, accessed November 10, 2020, http://www.victorianweb.org/history/poorlaw/elizpl.html.

20.   *Historical Southern Families, Volume XXIII*, (Baltimore, MD Genealogical Publishing Company, 1980) pp 1-3.

21.   Dana Huntley, "The Cavalier flight to Virginia," British Heritage Travel (website), accessed October 7, 2020, https://britishheritage.com/cavalier-flight-virginia.

22.   Huntley, "Cavalier flight to Virginia."

23.   Wikipedia, "Puritans," accessed July 15, 2020, https://en.wikipedia.org/wiki/Puritans#Puritans_and_Separatists.

24.   Wikipedia, "Thirty Years War," accessed March 17, 2020, https://en.wikipedia.org/wiki/Thirty_Years%27_War.

25.   Wikipedia, "Nine Years' War," accessed March 17, 2020, https://en.wikipedia.org/wiki/Nine_Years%27_War.

26.   Wikipedia, "War of the Spanish Succession" accessed March 17, 2020, https://en.wikipedia.org/wiki/War_of_the_Spanish_Succession.

27.   Wikipedia, "Ludwigsburg Palace," accessed March 21, 2020, https://en.wikipedia.org/wiki/Ludwigsburg_Palace.

28.   Ralph Beaver Strassburger, *The Strassburger Family and Allied Families of Pennsylvania* (Gwynedd Valley, PA: 1922), 23.

29.   Strassburger, *The Strassburger Family*, 28.

30.   Cynthia J. Van Zant, *Brothers Among Nations*, (Oxford: Oxford University Press, 2008), 59.

31.   Wikipedia, "Huguenots," accessed November 2, 2020, https://en.wikipedia.org/wiki/Huguenots.

32.   Wikipedia, "Huguenots," https://en.wikipedia.org/wiki/Huguenots.

33.   Wikipedia, "Huguenots," https://en.wikipedia.org/wiki/Huguenots.

34.   Evans, *Emigrants*, 4.

35.   Evans, *Emigrants*, 5–6.

36.   Evans, *Emigrants*, 9.

37.   "Coming to America," National Humanities Center Toolbox Library: Primary Resources in U.S. History and Literature, accessed July 27, 2020, http://nationalhumanitiescenter.org/pds/becomingamer/growth/text3/text3read.htm.

38.   Burton N. Derick, *The Nickerson Family and the History of William Nickerson, the Immigrant, Founder of Chatham, Mass*, (Chatham, MA: The Nickerson Family Association, 1998), 13.

39.   "Passage to America, 1750," Eyewitness to History, accessed July 27, 2020, http://www.eyewitnesstohistory.com/passage.htm.

40.   Wikipedia, "Immigration to the United States," accessed August 21, 2020, https://en.wikipedia.org/wiki/Immigration_to_the_United_States.

41.   Wikipedia, "Settlement of the Americas," accessed July 28, 2020, https://en.wikipedia.org/wiki/Settlement_of_the_Americas.

42.   Charles C. Mann, *1491* (New York: Random House, 2005); Alexander Koch et al., "European colonization of the Americas killed 10 percent of world population and caused global cooling," accessed July 31, 2020, https://www.pri.org/stories/2019–01–31/european-colonization-americas-killed-10-percent-world-population-and-caused.

43. Lewis Lord, "How Many People were here before Columbus?" *U.S. News and World Report,* August 18–25, 1997, 68–70, https://www.bxscience.edu/ourpages/auto/2009/4/5/34767803/Pre-Columbian%20population.pdf.

44. Wikipedia, "Captives in American Indian Wars," accessed July 28, 2020, https://en.wikipedia.org/wiki/Captives_in_American_Indian_Wars.

45. Mann, 1491; Koch et al., "European colonization."

46. John Ferling, *Almost a Miracle* (New York: Oxford University Press, 2007), 15.

47. Ferling, *Almost a Miracle.*

48. John Koster, *"Smallpox in the Blankets,"* Historynet, accessed August 1, 2020, https://www.historynet.com/smallpox-in-the-blankets.htm.

49. M. R. Harrington, *The Indians of New Jersey: Dickon Among the Lenapes* (New Brunswick, NJ: Rutgers University Press, 1966).

50. Wikipedia, "Trail of Tears," accessed September 16, 2020, https://en.wikipedia.org/wiki/Trail_of_Tears.

51. "Frontier Women," Ohio History Central, accessed May 7, 2021, https://ohiohistorycentral.org/w/Frontier_Women.

52. John Hill Wheeler, *Historical Sketches of North Carolina, From 1584 to 1851,* Volume II (Baltimore: Regional Publishing Company, 1974), 186--\187.

53. "History & Archaeology Revolution & Early Republic, 1777--\1800," New Georgia Encyclopedia, accessed September 1, 2020, https://www.georgiaencyclopedia.org/articles/history-archaeology/nancy-hart-ca-1735-1830.

54. Debra Michals, *"Margaret Cochran Corbin,"* National Women's History Museum, accessed May 7, 2021, https://www.womenshistory.org/education-resources/biographies/margaret-cochran-corbin.

55. Kerry Lee Alexander, *"Mary Ludwig Hays",* National Women's History Museum, accessed May 7, 2021, https://www.womenshistory.org/education-resources/biographies/mary-ludwig-hays.

56. Sources for this section include Joseph Thomas McDonald, *The McDonalds and Their Descendants* (Winchester, VA: Piccadilly Printing Company, 1986).

57. Joseph Thomas McDonald, *The McDonalds and Their Descendants* (Winchester, VA: Piccadilly Printing Company, 1986).

58. Alistair Moffat, *The Highland Clans* (New York: Thames & Hudson, 2010), 13.

59. Leyburn, *The Scotch-Irish.*

60. Jewel Spangler, "Baptists in Colonial Virginia," Encyclopedia Virginia, accessed March 18, 2020, https://www.encyclopediavirginia.org/Baptists_in_Colonial_Virginia#start_entry.

61. Stuart Butler, *A Guide to Virginia Militia Units in the War of 1812* (Athens, GA: New Papyrus Publishing, 2011).

62. "Proclamation of 1763," *Encyclopedia Britannica Online,* accessed March 18, 2020, https://www.britannica.com/event/Proclamation-of-1763.

63. Wikipedia, "Ohio and Erie Canal," accessed March 18, 2020, https://en.wikipedia.org/wiki/Ohio_and_Erie_Canal.

64. Wikipedia, "Virginia Military District," accessed March 18, 2020, https://en.wikipedia.org/wiki/Virginia_Military_District.

65. Wikipedia, "Clinton County, Ohio," accessed March 18, 2020, https://en.wikipedia.org/wiki/Clinton_County,_Ohio.

66. "Battle of Shiloh," History.com, accessed March 18, 2020, https://www.history.com/topics/american-civil-war/battle-of-shiloh.

67.   "Battles of Cold Harbor," History.com, accessed March 18, 2020, https://www.history.com/topics/american-civil-war/battles-of-cold-harbor.

68.   "On This Day in History: The Battle of Hatchers Run Was Fought (1864)," The History Collection (website), October 27, 2016, accessed March 18, 2020, https://historycollection.co/day-history-batte-hatchers-run-fought-1864/.

69.   Wikipedia, "Battle of Fort Stedman," accessed March 16, 2020, https://en.wikipedia.org/wiki/Battle_of_Fort_Stedman.

70.   Wikipedia, "13th Ohio Cavalry," accessed March 18, 2020, https://en.wikipedia.org/wiki/13th_Ohio_Cavalry_Regiment.

71.   Wikipedia, "Grand Central Station (Chicago)," accessed March 17, 2020, https://en.wikipedia.org/wiki/Grand_Central_Station_(Chicago).

72.   Library of Congress, *Immigration*, accessed March 18, 2020, https://www.loc.gov/classroom-materials/immigration/irish/irish-catholic-immigration-to-america/.

73.   "History of Optometry," American Optometric Association, accessed March 17, 2020, http://fs.aoa.org/optometry-archives/optometry-timeline.html.

74.   W. M. Paxton, *The Marshall Family* (Cincinnati: Robert Clark & Co, 1885), 15.

75.   Paxton, *The Marshall Family*, 16.

76.   Mark Bridge, "The Wagon," Lone Hand Western/Journal of the Old West (website), accessed March 19, 2020, http://www.lonehand.com/wagon.htm.

77.   Jean Edward Smith, *John Marshall, Definer of a Nation* (New York: Henry Holt and Company, 1996), 24.

78.   Tess Taylor, "Remembering the Randolphs: A Genealogy in Thirteen Meditations," accessed March 18, 2020, https://www.vqronline.org/articles/remembering-randolphs.

79.   Krusen, Jessie Thompson, "Tuckahoe Plantation", Winterthur Portfolio, (Chicago, University of Chicago Press, 1976) p 103, 105

80.   William A. and Wallace B. Fleming, *A Fleming Family with Colonial Ancestors in Virginia, Maryland, and Pennsylvania* (Charleston, WV: Charleston Printing Company, 1947), 1.

81.   "Fleming Family History," The Fleming Family accessed April 15, 2022 http://www.flemmingfamily.org/the-early-flemmings.html

82.   Wikipedia, "Treaty of Paris (1783)," accessed March 18, 2020, https://en.wikipedia.org/wiki/Treaty_of_Paris_(1783).

83.   Wikipedia, "Land Ordinance of 1785," accessed March 18, 2020, https://en.wikipedia.org/wiki/Land_Ordinance_of_1785.

84.   "Northwest Ordinance," July 13, 1787, National Archives, accessed March 18, 2020, https://www.ourdocuments.gov/doc.php?flash=true&doc=8.

85.   R. Douglas Hunt, *The Ohio Frontier, Crucible of the Old Northwest 1720–1830* (Bloomington, IN: Indiana University Press, 1996), 118.

86.   Hunt, *The Ohio Frontier*, 139.

87.   Philip D. Jordan, *The National Road* (Indianapolis: Bobbs-Merrill Company, 1948).

88.   Mark Bridge, "The Wagon," Lone Hand Western/Journal of the Old West, http://www.lonehand.com/wagon.htm.

89.   "The Case Family: Pioneer Settlers of Flemington (1)," Hunterdon Land Trust, accessed July 22, 2020, https://www.hunterdonlandtrust.org/2019/11/20/the-case-family-pioneer-settlers-of-flemington-1/.

90.   David Levine, "The Esopus Wars: A History of the Battle Between the Dutch and Local American Indians in the 1660s," *Hudson Valley Magazine* (website), accessed March 22, 2020, https://hvmag.com/life-style/history/the-esopus-wars-a-history-of-the-battle-between-the-dutch-and-local-american-indians-in-the-1660s/.

91.   Eve LaPlante, *American Jezebel, the Uncommon Life of Anne Hutchinson, the Woman who Defied the Puritans,* (San Francisco: Harper Collins 2004) p 237.

92.   "1687 — The Charter Oak," The Society of Colonial Wars in the State of Connecticut (website), accessed March 17, 2020, https://www.colonialwarsct.org/1687.htm.

93.   William Richard Cutter, *New England Families, Genealogical and Memorial* (New York: Lewis Historical Publishing Company, 1914), 1103.

94.   Anthony Musso, "George Washington a Frequent Guest at Brinckerhoff home" Poughkeepsie Journal, November 15, 2016, https://www.poughkeepsiejournal.com/story/news/local/2016/11/15/dateline-local-history-john-brinckerhoff-house/93912486/.

95.   John Richard Burton, *A History of Bewdley: With Consise Accounts of Some Neighbouring Parishes* (London: William Reeves, 1883), 13.

96.   Robert P. Wakeman, *Being a History of the Descendants of SAMUEL WAKEMAN of Hartford, Conn., and of JOHN WAKEMAN, Treasurer of New Haven Colony, with a Few Collaterals Included* (Meriden, CT: Journal Publishing Company, 1900), 181, 124.

97.   Wakeman, *History of the Descendants,* 164.

98.   Henry B. Meigs, *Record of the Descendants of Vincent Meigs: Who came from Dorsetshire, England to America about 1635* (published 1901), 8–9.

99.   Anna C. Kingsbury, *A Historical Sketch of Nicholas Busby* (Chatham, MA: Nickerson Family Association, 1998), 6.

100.   Kenneth Lockwood, *A New England Town* (New York: W.W. Norton & Company, 1985), 57. (Referenced in Wikipedia: https://en.wikipedia.org/wiki/Michael_Metcalf_(puritan)#CITEREFLockridge1985.)

101.   Wikipedia, "King Philip's War," accessed March 19, 2020, https://en.wikipedia.org/wiki/King_Philip%27s_War.

102.   Wikipedia, "King Philip's War," https://en.wikipedia.org/wiki/King_Philip%27s_War.

103.   Elroy McKendree Avery and Catharine Hitchcock (Tilden), *The Groton Avery Clan,* (Cleveland: 1912), 58–59.

104.   "King Philip's War," History.com, November 13, 2019, accessed October 9, 2020, https://www.history.com/topics/native-american-history/king-philips-war.

105.   Mary Ellen Snodgrass, *American Colonial Women and Their Art: A Chronological Encyclopedia,* (Lanham, MD: Roman and Littlefield, 2017), 37.

106.   Wikipedia, "Henry Adams (farmer)," accessed March 19, 2020, https://en.wikipedia.org/wiki/Henry_Adams_(farmer).

107.   Donald Lines Jacobus, *History and Genealogy of the Families of Old Fairfield* (1930–1932; reproduced., Baltimore: Genealogical Publishing company, 2007), 7.

108.   Wikipedia, "West Point, Virginia," accessed March 14, 2020, https://en.wikipedia.org/wiki/West_Point,_Virginia.

109.   "Biography," The Occom Circle at Dartmouth College (website), accessed March 19, 2020, http://www.dartmouth.edu/occom/occoms-biography/.

110.   "Bingham and Dodd portrait of Lincoln," Library of Congress Public Domain Archive, accessed March 19, 2020,https://loc.getarchive.net/media/bingham-and-dodd-portrait-of-lincoln.

111.   Wikipedia, "World's Columbian Exposition" accessed March 19, 2020, https://en.wikipedia.org/wiki/World%27s_Columbian_Exposition.

112.   Sue N. Haschemeyer (compiler), "Dunn*ck Family Genealogy", accessed March 19, 2020, http://www.dunnuck.com/Ehret.html#Pennsylvania.

113.   Wikipedia, "Panic of 1837," accessed August 24, 2020, https://en.wikipedia.org/wiki/Panic_of_1837.

114.	Wikipedia, "Seven Days Battles," accessed March 19,2020, https://en.wikipedia.org/wiki/Seven_Days_Battles.

115.	Wikipedia, "Battle of Gaines Mill," accessed March 19, 2020, https://en.wikipedia.org/wiki/Battle_of_Gaines%27s_Mill.

116.	Wikipedia, "Treaty of Doak's Stand," accessed April 18, 2020, https://en.wikipedia.org/wiki/Treaty_of_Doak%27s_Stand.

117.	Wikipedia, "Treaty of Doak's Stand," https://en.wikipedia.org/wiki/Treaty_of_Doak%27s_Stand.

118.	In the George line, John George Sr. (b. 1704) married Mary Millicent Jordan, the daughter of Josha Jordan (1681–1717) and Elizabeth Sandbourne (1683–1733). Elizabeth was the daughter of Daniel Sandbourne (1650–1711) who married Sarah Copeland (1657–1722). Sarah was the daughter of John Copeland (1612–1682) and Sarah Ratcliffe (1615–1687). This Sarah as the daughter of Richard Ratcliffe (1585–1630), and Richard was the son of Captain John Ratcliffe (1549–1609), captain of the *Discovery.*

119.	Tony Williams, *The Jamestown Experiment* (Naperville, IL: Sourcebooks, 2011), 191.

120.	Williams, *Jamestown Experiment,* 241.

121.	Philip L. Barbour, ed., *The Complete Works of Captain John Smith, 1580–1631* (Chapel Hill: University of North Carolina Press, 1986), 2:308.

122.	Isle of Wight County Records, *William and Mary College Quarterly Historical Magazine* 7:4 (April 1899), 207–208; accessed April 1, 2020, https://archive.org/stream/jstor-1919740/1919740 djvu.txt.

123.	William Byrd II, *Histories of the Dividing Line Betwixt Virginia and North Carolina,* (New York: Dover Publications , 1967). P 92.

124.	Wikipedia, "Edenton Tea Party," accessed August 7, 2020, https://en.wikipedia.org/wiki/Edenton_Tea_Party.

125.	Robert O. Mellown, "Steamboats in Alabama," *Encyclopedia of Alabama,* accessed July 22, 2021, http://encyclopediaofalabama.org/article/h-1803.

126.	Bolton, S. Charles, "Inequality on the Southern Frontier: Arkansas County in the Arkansas Territory," *Arkansas Historical Quarterly,* 41:53 (Spring 1982). Quoted in "History of Arkansas," accessed September 4, 2020, https://en.wikipedia.org/wiki/History_of_Arkansas#cite_note-59.

127.	Henry Lewis Gates Jr., "How many slaves landed in the U.S.?" The African Americans: Many Rivers to Cross, PBS.org, accessed August 22, 2020, https://www.pbs.org/wnet/african-americans-many-rivers-to-cross/history/how-many-slaves-landed-in-the-us/.

128.	Wikipedia, "1860 United States Census," accessed August 22, 2020, https://en.wikipedia.org/wiki/1860_United_States_Census.

129.	Sarah Pruitt, "5 Myths About Slavery," History.com, June 23, 2020, accessed November 23, 2020, https://www.history.com/news/5-myths-about-slavery.

130.	Archibald Bennett, *Finding Your Forefathers in America,* (Bookcraft 1957) as reported by Fleming Family Traditions Tested: https://chelledge.wordpress.com/elledge-conaway-genealogy/conaway-fleming-gould-family/fleming-traditions/, accessed March 21, 2020.

131.	Ferling, *Almost a Miracle,* 248–249.

132.	Paxton, *The Marshall Family,* 21.

133.	Ferling, *Almost a Miracle,* 356–357.

134.	American Battlefield Trust, "Charleston: Siege of Charleston," accessed September 5, 2020, https://www.battlefields.org/learn/revolutionary-war/battles/charleston.

135.	John Buchanan, *The Road to Guilford Courthouse: The American Revolution in the Carolinas* (New York: John Wiley & Sons, 1997), 218.

136. Wikipedia, "Bloody Bill Cunningham," accessed July 23, 2020, https://en.wikipedia.org/wiki/Bloody_Bill_Cunningham.

137. Wikipedia, "Battle of Cowan's Ford," accessed September 5, 2020, https://en.wikipedia.org/wiki/Battle_of_Cowan%27s_Ford.

138. J. D. Lewis, "The American Revolution in North Carolina," accessed March 28, 2020, https://www.carolana.com/NC/Revolution/revolution_nc_second_regiment.html.

139. J. D. Lewis, "The American Revolution in South Carolina," accessed March 28, 2020, https://www.carolana.com/SC/Revolution/revolution_battle_of_eutaw_springs.html.

140. Wakeman, *History of the Descendants,* 181.

141. Wake County North Carolina Heritage Book, accessed March 28, 2020, https://www.ancestry.com/mediaui-viewer/tree/152131825/person/252017157188/media/6941063f-b061-4f54-a8ed-2496b05d3e4f?_phsrc=UIT2&_phstart=successSource

142. "Death of Micajah Liles," *Alabama Reporter* (Talladega, AL), July 8, 1868, 3.

143. William S. Price Jr., "Cary Rebellion," *Encyclopedia of North Carolina* (2006), accessed August 4, 2020, https://www.ncpedia.org/cary-rebellion.

144. William S. Powell, "Bare Boxing Incident," *Encyclopedia of North Carolina* (2006), accessed March 30, 2020, https://www.ncpedia.org/bare-boxing-incident.

145. David A. Norris, "Bath," *Encyclopedia of North Carolina* (2006), accessed March 30, 2020, https://www.ncpedia.org/bath.

146. Nicholas Graham, "Lumbee Indians Face the Ku Klux Klan, 1958," *Encyclopedia of North Carolina* (2006), accessed December 9, 2017, https://www.ncpedia.org/history/20th-Century/lumbee-face-klan.

147. Wikipedia, "Halifax Resolves," accessed April 19, 2020, https://en.wikipedia.org/wiki/Halifax_Resolves.

148. Warren L. Bingham, "George Washington's 1791 Southern Tour," interview with Mount Vernon Association, accessed October 21, 2020, https://www.mountvernon.org/george-washington/the-first-president/george-washingtons-1791-southern-tour/.

149. Margaret Williamson Huber, "Huskanaw," Encyclopedia Virginia, accessed July 23, 2020, https://www.encyclopediavirginia.org/Huskanaw#start_entry.

150. "Pocahontas," History.com, updated August 21, 2018, accessed July 23, 2020, https://www.history.com/topics/native-american-history/pocahontas.

151. Richard R. Wilt, "Lewis J. Green Sr.," Harrison County Genealogical Society (website), accessed April 29, 2020, http://www.wvhcgs.com/lewisgreen.htm.

152. "Union County," Encyclopedia of Arkansas, accessed April 29, 2020, https://encyclopediaofarkansas.net/entries/union-county-812/.

153. "Union County," Encyclopedia of Arkansas, https://encyclopediaofarkansas.net/entries/union-county-812/.

154. Ford of Virginia and Kentucky, *Historical Southern Families* https://www.genealogy.com/ftm/f/o/r/Charles-W-Ford-CA/GENE1-0001.html, accessed July 22, 2021.

155. "Rule of Law," *Savannah Magazine,* March 15, 2017, accessed September 8, 2020, https://www.savannahmagazine.com/rule-of-law/.

156. "Cotton Gin and Eli Whitney," History.com, updated October 10, 2019, accessed September 2, 2020, https://www.history.com/topics/inventions/cotton-gin-and-eli-whitney.

157. Wikipedia, "Fort Mims Massacre," accessed September 3, 2020, https://en.wikipedia.org/wiki/Fort_Mims_massacre.

158. Robert O. Mellown, "Steamboats in Alabama," Encyclopedia Alabama, September 30, 2008, accessed March 25, 2021, http://encyclopediaofalabama.org/article/h-1803.

159.   Banks NcLaurin, *The Bledsoe Family in America Volume 3,* (Dallas, B McLaurin Jr 1993).

160.   Carmen Minor Smith, "Navigation Acts (1651, 1660)," Encyclopedia of North Carolina (2006), accessed August 14, 2020, https://www.ncpedia.org/navigation-acts-1651–1660.

161.   White McKenzie Wallenborn, "George Washington's Terminal Illness: A Modern Medical Analysis of the Last Illness and Death of George Washington," The Washington Papers (website), accessed August 8, 2020, https://washingtonpapers.org/resources/articles/illness/.

162.   Joel Campbell DuBose, *Notable Men of Alabama: Personal and Genealogical, Volume 1,* (Alabama Southern Historical Association, 1904), 145–146.

163.   *Times-Picayune* (New Orleans), September 8, 1941.

164.   Wikipedia, "In the Gloaming (song)," accessed May 29, 2020, https://en.wikipedia.org/wiki/In_the_Gloaming_(song).

165.   *Daily Picayune* (New Orleans), May 15, 1890, accessed May 29, 2020, http://files.usgwarchives.net/la/union/obits/1890george.txt.

166.   *The Memoirs of Louisa George Tompkins, Union Parish Louisiana,* USGenWeb Archives, accessed May 29, 2020, http://files.usgwarchives.net/la/union/history/tompkins.txt.

167.   William Richard Cutter, *Genealogical and Family History of Northern New York,* (New York: Lewis Historical Publishing Company, 1910) 11–12.

168.   Cutter, *Genealogical and Family History.* P. 11

169.   "Great Migration: Passengers of the Arbella, 1630," Geni.com, accessed July 24, 2020, https://www.geni.com/projects/Great-Migration-Passengers-of-the-Arbella-1630/5754.

170.   Tony Horwitz, "The True Story of the Battle of Bunker Hill," *Smithsonian Magazine,* May 2013, https://www.smithsonianmag.com/history/the-true-story-of-the-battle-of-bunker-hill-36721984/.

171.   The Scottish Nation: Dennistoun," Electricscotland.com, accessed September 8, 2020, https://www.electricscotland.com/history/nation/dennistoun.htm.

172.   *Representative Men and Old Families of Rhode Island, Volume 1* (Chicago: J. H. Beers & Company, 1908), 217.

173.   John Denison Baldwin and William Clift, *A Record of the Descendants of Capt. George Denison of Stonington Conn.* (Worcester, MA: Tyler and Seagrave, 1881) 6–7.

174.   Baldwin and Clift, *A Record of the Descendants.* 7

175.   Albert Dehner Bell, *Bass families of the South, a collection of historical and genealogical source materials from public and private records,* (Rocky Mount, NC: 1911), 47.

176.   Bell, *Bass families of the South,* 104.

177.   Wikipedia, "Burwell family of Virginia," accessed June 17, 2021, https://en.wikipedia.org/wiki/Burwell_family_of_Virginia.

178.   Wikipedia, "Burwell family of Virginia."

179.   Wikipedia, "Burwell family of Virginia."

180.   William Richard Cutter, *Genealogical and Personal Memoirs Relating to the Families of Boston and Eastern Massachusetts Volume 1* (New York, Lewis Historical Publishing Company, 1908) p 207

181.   Walter R. Borneman, *1812: The War that Forged a Nation* (New York: Harper Collins 2004), 222.

182.   Borneman, *1812: The War that Forged a Nation,* 245–246.

183.   Wikipedia, "The Battle of New Orleans," accessed November 16, 2020, https://en.wikipedia.org/wiki/The_Battle_of_New_Orleans.

CPSIA information can be obtained
at www.ICGtesting.com
Printed in the USA
LVHW072331110722
723216LV00006B/154